Alfred Jarry

Alfred Jarry

A Pataphysical Life ALASTAIR BROTCHIE

THE MIT PRESS
CAMBRIDGE, MASSACHUSETTS
LONDON, ENGLAND

For information about special quantity discounts,
please email special_sales@mitpress.mit.edu.
This book was set in Helvetica Neue Pro and Minion Pro
by The MIT Press. Printed and bound in Canada.

Library of Congress Cataloging-in-Publication Data
Brotchie, Alastair.
 Alfred Jarry : a pataphysical life / Alastair Brotchie.
      p. cm.
Includes bibliographical references and index.
ISBN 978-0-262-01619-3 (alk. paper)
1. Jarry, Alfred, 1873–1907. 2. Authors, French—19th
century—Biography. I. Title.
PQ2619.A65Z626 2011
842'.8—dc22
[B]
                         2010047652
10   9   8   7   6   5   4   3   2

Contents

Preface

It is hardly an original observation that the transition between the nineteenth and twentieth centuries was marked by enormous political, scientific, and intellectual upheavals, and that their counterpart in the arts was the emergence of the various movements that would later come to be called "modernism." This artistic revolution was centered in Paris; although the avant-gardes would spread rapidly across much of the globe, it was from there that their message was most often carried. So, for example, at the century's turn both Marinetti and Rubén Darío, soon to be the principal figures of the modern movement in Italy and Argentina, were often among those to be found at the same Parisian salon. Every Tuesday afternoon, in the offices of the *Mercure de France*, then the most advanced literary journal in France, these gatherings were hosted by the novelist Rachilde, wife to the magazine's editor, Alfred Vallette.

Rachilde and Vallette, at the center of Parisian literary circles, would play an important part in the life of Alfred Jarry and were among his most loyal friends. Yet when Jarry died, aged thirty-four, just over one hundred years ago, they undoubtedly shared the opinion common to his contemporaries: that he was an impossibly obscure and oddly inconsistent author whose works were unlikely to survive. This opinion was not entirely unreasonable; Jarry was "writing ahead of his time," which means only that his work became easier to appreciate once read in the context of those he had influenced.

It would take several decades before Jarry began to be recognized as a pivotal figure during this transitional period. Nowadays any cultural history of the last century must assign Jarry a formative role. His impact on modern theater was notably profound, and most accounts of twentieth-century drama begin with a description of his most famous play, *Ubu Roi*. A preliminary list of his literary admirers would include Guillaume Apollinaire, Antonin Artaud, André Breton, Italo Calvino, Julio Cortázar, Guy Debord, Witold Gombrowicz, Eugène Ionesco, Stéphane Mallarmé, Alan Moore, Georges Perec, Jacques Prévert, Raymond Queneau, Tristan Tzara. Wole Soyinka is only one of many to have written versions of *Ubu Roi*, while the best website for the international avant-gardes is called: UbuWeb. An equally extensive roster of artists, commencing with Pablo Picasso and Marcel Duchamp, could as easily be assembled; and philosophers such as Gilles Deleuze and Jean Baudrillard have cited his "philosophy" of Pataphysics as prescient. And yet … when one encounters one of those brief notices of Jarry that appear in biographies of his contemporaries, or in various contexts on the Internet, they are more likely to dwell upon his mode of living than on his works. It is Jarry's life that has been declared exemplary, for personifying the idea of revolt in its purest sense. It is the *attitude* of Jarry that has become a rallying point. He has the reputation of someone whose refusal to accommodate to the norms of everyday existence resulted in a life of intransigent nonconformity.

This book is not much concerned with Jarry's influence. Even so, it is worth noting that this influence began to be felt only once the first flush of modernism was over. Its early manifestations, notably Cubism and Futurism, were effectively replays of realism, concerned with reinterpreting immediate experience. Only when more metaphysical—and, as we shall see, pataphysical—concerns came to the fore would Jarry's example be recalled. It was thus almost inevitable that the Dada movement should proclaim its admiration, and in this context it is easy to appreciate, for instance, why Jarry influenced Duchamp more than he did Picasso.

As for Jarry himself, he appears never to have doubted the value of his own works, nor their eventual reception. When asked his opinion, he typically replied "posterity will decide," in a tone that left little doubt as to the expected verdict. Jarry's self-assessment appears vindicated, and he has now found his place among the authors of unclassifiable classics, in the company of French authors such as Lautréamont, Rimbaud, Artaud, Roussel, Bousquet, Bataille. In the Anglophone world his role has been noted in works such as Cyril Connolly's *100 Key Books of the Modern Movement* (1965) and Harold Bloom's *The Western Canon* (1994). *Ubu Roi* is now one of the most performed plays worldwide, after those of Shakespeare, and usually in youthful productions.[1]

The reassessment of Jarry's writing only really gathered pace after the founding of the Collège de 'Pataphysique in Paris in 1948, whose researches brought forth a mass of new material relating both to Jarry's work and to his life. These early enthusiasts of Jarry the writer tended to downplay the more eccentric aspects of his life; they generally felt that Jarry's works had been obscured by his "myth." They also sought to minimize the importance of Ubu within his work, or stressed that it comprised only a small part (some 10 percent) of Jarry's writings. Yet without Ubu, Jarry's works would look very different—impossible even—and Ubu likewise became an essential part of his daily existence. Jarry's life and character unfold as a succession of paradoxes or, less dramatically, as simple contrariness. Perfectly correlated, his works reflected these contradictions in the broad outlines of an *œuvre* that could encompass both the buffoonery of Ubu, and the subtleties of Jarry's "science" of Pataphysics.

These conflicts in his life, represented by the extremes of Jarry's writing, are open to various interpretations, which are explored briefly in chapter 13 below. The intervening narrative may allow the reader to decide to what extent Jarry fabricated both his life and his myth, or to what extent they were imposed upon him. Jarry's life inevitably influenced how his works were written—one concern of any biography—but biography is a fiction too, just as a life *as lived* is a work in progress. How then was Jarry's life written, and "read," not least by himself?

This book turned out longer than I had anticipated, and I heartily thank my editor, Roger Conover, for permitting this Ubuesque distension. However, I do not feel that there is much here in the way of "padding," and so it is perhaps surprising that it mainly covers a period of only fifteen years, from Jarry's arrival in Paris in 1893 to his premature death in 1907. The mass of available source material is a measure of the fascination Jarry exerted on the literary circles of 1890s Paris, a social scene which did not exactly lack for vivid personalities. Impossible to ignore, he was written about by almost everyone who encountered him during his brief passage through this society; and although this documentation is extensive, it does rather concentrate on his personality, and upon tales of his *outré* behavior.

How should one deal with this wealth of anecdotes? "Serious" authors have tended to adopt a rather censorious policy of ignoring them, or have made casual mention of them with what often seems feigned displeasure. In this biography, however, such episodes are recounted simply because they actually occurred. Yet just as there are extremes in both Jarry's works and his character, so too these anecdotes reflect similar oppositions. There were occasions when Jarry was essentially playing the fool—and such incidents may be as entertaining as their author intended—but he also adhered to other nonconformities, more deeply ingrained, which he practiced with an absolute and stubborn consistency, and the consequences of these convictions were undoubtedly more significant. The distinction is far from clear-cut, and because Jarry frequently overstepped the mark, the one tended to blend imperceptibly into the other, at which point the joke might assume a more disquieting cast. Absurdity and tragedy were as closely entwined in his life as in his work.

Noël Arnaud, certainly among the most sympathetic and knowledgeable of Jarry's biographers, admitted with obvious reluctance: "We must resign ourselves: Jarry was not innocent of his myth." Why this resignation, and in what sense was Jarry guilty? Answering this question—and disentangling Jarry's life from his myth—initially appeared to be one of my principal tasks; but the acknowledgment that Jarry played a role in its creation presented rather more interesting problems. It seemed to me that Jarry the man and Jarry the writer were truly indivisible, that they were connected at a particularly deep and intrinsic level, and that exploring the connection between the one and the other must be an essential part of this biography, more so than is commonly the case. Jarry once wrote an article on "monsters" in which he discussed the definition of this word in the context of mythological beasts. "Usually," he wrote, "the word 'monster' signifies some sort of unaccustomed harmonizing of dissonant elements […] I call 'monster' every original inexhaustible beauty." In the terms of these definitions, Jarry's works have many inexhaustible beauties, yet he personally retains a monstrous aspect exactly because his character resisted being reduced to anything except a combination of "dissonant elements." Thus, without consideration of his works, or more importantly, of what they represent—their underlying concerns and assumptions—Jarry's character and motivations must remain hidden.[2]

Jarry appeared intent on making his own universe; he formulated its interior logic and defined its external laws. Both his life and his works proceeded from a combination of the same interior impulses, and the same exterior influences; and while these were undoubtedly responsible for the difficulties he experienced in his life, they were also what animated his writing. It is this inseparable conjunction that imparts to his life a heroic aspect. He did not avoid the risks and difficulties entailed; and the consequence was that his best work possesses an authenticity which even on first reading is palpable, but is also difficult to account for. Its source may be found where Jarry's life and works mesh together, and he could never have been "innocent of his myth," since his myth is no more than the *play* in this "machinery with more or less fixed gears." Problems arise only when the attempt is made to sift one from the other, fictional from real. The pataphysician would see no virtue in such a distinction, but the biographer cannot avoid it.[3]

No surprise, then, that one of Jarry's favorite images was the mirror, or the double, and the structure of this biography is intended to reflect this—not too laboriously, I trust. The main part, the evenly numbered chapters, consists of a conventional chronological biography. This is broken up by the intercalary, odd-numbered chapters which are intended to offer a glimpse of undercurrents which connect the most apparently disparate aspects of Jarry's thought and personality. Of necessity, these shorter chapters must range outside the chronology of the remainder of the book, and it is for the reader to decide whether this combination adds up to the harmony of Jarry's definition. I hoped to make of Jarry a believable person, despite the fact that he seemed to devote much of his life to making such a task as difficult as possible. The Jarry who emerges here appears to me more "human" than monstrous, but I do not think that this diminishes him. As befits the inventor of Pataphysics he remains an entirely exceptional being, equally original in both his existence and his writing.

This is the first full-length biography of Jarry in English. The only previous work of substance, the critical biography by Keith Beaumont, is now twenty-five years old. (Subsequent works in English have not improved upon it.) Beaumont considered Jarry's life primarily in relation to his writing, which meant that the biographical portion of his study was somewhat abbreviated. It is also now unavoidably out of date, but as a critical reading in English of Jarry's works, Beaumont's book remains unsurpassed. The present work takes the opposite position so as to give a more detailed biographical account. It incorporates a great deal of material that will be new to English readers, and a more modest portion that will be new to French ones. Various new sources were unearthed during the writing of it, most notably more than thirty previously unknown letters, including his last, written on his deathbed.[4]

A FEW CONVENTIONS IN THE TEXT

The Mercure de France was both a publishing house and a literary magazine; it is italicized here when the magazine alone is referred to. The same applies to other periodicals that also had a book publishing arm. The titles of Jarry's works are given in English when there is a generally accepted translation (and one with which I happen to agree), and self-evident abbreviations are used, thus *Exploits and Opinions of Doctor Faustroll, Pataphysician* is usually referred to simply as *Faustroll*. Otherwise titles appear in the original French. The apostrophe to the word "Pataphysics" is not used (except in reference to the Collège de 'Pataphysique). Jarry signaled its desirability, but never employed it himself. The endnotes indicate the sources used and can be ignored by the general reader. My intention has been to write a readable narrative that conformed to academic standards by being fully sourced, while avoiding academic jargon and discursive footnoting.

PHYNANCE

This was something that played an important role in Jarry's life. The exchange rate between the franc, sterling, and the dollar remained fairly constant between 1896 and 1910, when 5 francs was worth 4 shillings in sterling and one American dollar. There are various methods of calculating what this is worth in today's money, but a rough guide would be that 1 franc in 1896 approximates to around 4 pounds, 5 dollars, or 5 euros at 2009 prices. By the time of Jarry's death in 1907 the franc had lost around 10 percent of its value over the previous decade.[5]

ACKNOWLEDGMENTS

I owe a great deal to those who have helped me over the years with this project, and who have put up with hearing the words "Alfred Jarry" more often than they wished. Certain among them were indispensable. For their assistance with translations I thank Iain White and especially Antony Melville, who checked my own translations and prevented me making an idiot of myself more than once; Eric Walbecq and Paul Edwards in Paris have helped me constantly by alerting me to material I might not have found otherwise, and through their formidable knowledge of 1890s French literature; my thanks to Chris Allen and Gillian Beaumont for their careful copy-editing, and to Thieri Foulc for reading the manuscript and suggesting many improvements; and, especially, to Tanya Peixoto for … so much. I particularly regret that our friend the late Stanley Chapman will not see a copy of this book; his help and encouragement were invaluable.

I would also like to thank the following, and apologize to those I may have omitted: Matthew Abbate (production editor), Dawn Ades, Sally Alatalo, Timothy d'Arch-Smith, Noël Arnaud, Michel Arrivé, Gillian Beaumont (manuscript editor), Rémy Bellenger, Patrick Besnier, Johan Birgander, Christian Bodros, Romana Brunori-Severini (for permission to use photographs from the "album" of Gabrielle Vallette), Philippe Cathé (Pantagruelist), Christophe Champion (who graciously allowed me to photograph his collection of Jarry first editions), Roger Conover, Christiane Cormerais, Adam Dant, Dennis Duncan, Margarita Encomienda (the book's designer), Patrick Frechet, Laurent de Freitas (for permission to quote from the works of Léon-Paul Fargue), Elizabeth Garver (of the Harry Ransom Humanities Research Center, whose help was unstinting), Paul Gayot, Fraser Gillespie (bicycle mechanics), Harry Gilonis, Malcolm Green, Paul Hammond, Julia Hines (medical), Magnus Irvin (halieutics), Simon James and David Smith (Wellsians), Kevin Jackson (decimation of hanging signifiers), Mary Markey (of the Smithsonian Institution), Harry Mathews, Olivier Michaud and Dominique Remande (of the Bibliothèque municipale de Laval), Jean-Paul Morel, Barbara Pascarel, Brian Parshall, Martin Stone (bibliosleuth), Joël Surcouf (of the Archives départementales de la Mayenne), and Léna Weber (for permission to use photographs by Jean Weber).

Translations in the text are my own, with the help of Antony Melville, unless another is indicated in the notes.

Alastair Brotchie
Regent of the Collège de 'Pataphysique

1

FÉLIX-FRÉDÉRIC HÉBERT

Félix-Frédéric Hébert was born in Cherbourg on January 14, 1832. Nothing is known of his child-hood apart from his scholastic career: a steady progress through local schools which culminated, at the age of twenty-one, with his entering the prestigious École normale supérieure in Paris. After three years' study there he graduated as a teacher in the "Natural and Physical Sciences," and returned to Brittany to take up the post of assistant physics teacher at the *lycée* in Rennes. After only a few months, however, he left the school due to some sort of incident involving "a woman of bad reputation," and the following year he was teaching in Angoulême, in 1859 in Le Puy, then in Évreux (1862), Rouen (1864), and Limoges (1868).[1]

1.1, 1.2
F.-F. Hébert, teacher of physics.

His principals' reports from these various establishments were unanimously discouraging. Angoulême: "Well enough liked but little respected by his pupils. His teaching lacks discipline, liveliness, and interest, owing to his inability to prepare his lessons properly." Rouen: "Unable to impose authority on his pupils whom he has frequently to reprimand or punish so as to avoid disorder in the classroom." Limoges: "An extremely slow teacher, who wastes an enormous amount of time and is unable to complete the syllabus. … His results are extremely feeble … his lessons are ill-prepared, particularly the practical experiments, which are marred by repeated accidents."

The few surviving photographs of Hébert show him with a distinctly apprehensive air, which is perhaps not surprising given these dismal assessments of his abilities. Hébert sought the approval and respect of his superiors above everything else, and seemingly imagined that an unassuming and submissive manner might offset his professional failings. His cowed demeanor, carried into the classroom, simply made him an easy target for the mob of schoolboys, whose favorite sport was uncovering the weaknesses of their teachers. And after all these years of teaching, his only defense was utterly ineffective: a pose of bluff pomposity. Here he is concluding a typically maladroit eulogy to the physical sciences at a school prize-giving:

> Therefore, you should love Science, which has made us so great, which has brought to our country an illustration even more imperishable than that of military glory and its bloody trophies; which has furnished the craftsman with a lightening of the heavy burdens of his labor, and provides a vast improvement to all of our lives, and yet can still elevate our souls and direct our thoughts toward Heaven, by every day revealing to us the admirable order established by the divine Creator of the Universe.

The combination of ostentation and bluster was easily sufficient to arouse the contempt of his pupils, but Hébert had the extra misfortune of looking absurd. His corpulence and his too-short legs slowed his movements to a laborious shuffle or a swaying waddle and—even better—he had a slight speech impediment. "He always spoke as if he had a mouthful of porridge." Eventually he realized he was forever to be the butt of his pupils' derision, and in 1877 he appealed to the authorities for a post as an inspector of schools.

His application was rejected. The board of inspectors noted that while his obsequious manner was useful for ingratiating himself with his superiors, it hardly suited him to a position of judgment over them, and that he lacked strength of character and "*sang-froid*." Nevertheless, he was briefly favored by a change in the political situation when a right-wing administration was installed in Limoges. Hébert, having devoted years of oratory to the praise of Family, Church, and Motherland, had his wish granted by the new council. Three months later, however, he was dismissed, when local elections returned a republican. His grievances filled long letters to the educational authorities, but he had no alternative except to return to teaching.[2]

So, in 1881, after an interval of twenty-three years, he returned to Rennes, to the very school in which his teaching career had begun, and his classes then descended into complete disorder. In June 1882 the inspector noted: "M. Hébert's speech is ponderous and muffled. His lessons lack both clarity and organization. His influence on his pupils is almost nil. He does not know how to impose his authority, nor how to get the slightest attention from his pupils." Soon the class was taken over by the vice-principal and Hébert was assigned to teach elementary mathematics, to a class of only fourteen. It made no difference; the uproar from his classroom became impossible to ignore. The inspectors refrained from enforcing his retirement only because of his advancing age and the financial responsibilities incurred by his large family (five children). Finally, in 1892 and after eleven years at Rennes, he was persuaded to retire, on reaching the age of sixty.

A few years later the events of the Dreyfus Affair obliged his return to public service. Alfred Dreyfus had been the highest-ranking Jewish officer ever to serve in the French Army until, in 1894, a court martial found him guilty of passing military secrets to the Germans. After a ceremony of public denigration he was imprisoned on Devil's Island under particularly arduous conditions. It soon became obvious that he was the victim of an anti-Semitic plot, and the "Affair" became the greatest political controversy of its day. Dreyfus's second court martial, in 1899, happened to take place in Rennes; the courtroom was within the *lycée* building itself. He was again found guilty, and sentenced to an additional ten years in prison, even though the evidence brought against him at his first trial had been shown in the interim to have been forged. The verdict was so obviously unjust that the French President pardoned him anyway. Hébert was so outraged by this attempt, in his words, "to rehabilitate a justly condemned traitor" that he entered local politics and was elected a town councilor in 1900. Later the same year a local paper carried this report of a council meeting:

> M. Hébert, by virtue of the seniority granted by his age, was called upon to preside over the meeting for just a few minutes; he took advantage of this to read to the new council the sort of address in which everything is a matter of "city-slickers, gangs of Jewish Freemasons, bribed government officials, the Flag, France, etc." The council did not appear to be particularly gripped by this stale old claptrap, which was clumsily delivered by King Ubu.

It is the reference to King Ubu that explains why anything at all is known of the career of F.-F. Hébert. The young Alfred Jarry had entered his class in 1888, and would soon transform Hébert into the aberrant antihero of *Ubu Roi*. Another future author, Henri Hertz, was a fellow pupil, a couple of years younger than Jarry, and he described their relations:

> Hébert was celebrated for the violent barracking he suffered and for the portentous manner with which he strove to placate his tormentors. He was not one to allow himself to be overcome straightaway, to be too quickly reduced to trembling abasement, not before attempting to defend himself with great blusterings of rage. Hardly ever, anyway. What we loved in him, what made him unique, and inspired a plethora of ingenious inventions aimed at stirring him up, was that we could look forward to beautiful tears, noble sobs, and ceremonious supplications.

Hébert's torture passed through three phases, accompanied on his part by three physiognomies:

Entrance: wary, Hébert paused at the threshold of the classroom. His legs were so short and his stomach so large that he looked as if he was sitting on his backside. His appearance in the doorway provoked gales of laughter. He tried to exorcize this demon by directing angelic looks from tiny eyes, lost in a mass of pallid flab, at the mob which he knew full well would be in uproar in a matter of minutes.

The second phase began when Hébert, his back to the class, took on the appearance of a giant insect heaving itself up the blackboard and depositing trails of chalk behind it. Those of us with ammunition bombarded the shabby elytra of his old jacket. Hébert turned round. Not straight away, because he was deaf, although we were never sure if this deafness was due to a deficiency of hearing or of courage. The fact was that he left it till the last possible moment before taking on the miscreants, and when he decided to act, it was plain to see that he did so reluctantly.

He turned round suddenly. The third phase was then initiated, in which he exhibited his truly royal character, itself contradicted by his uncertain gaze and the despairing grin beneath his great moustache, once red, now stained with tobacco.

First of all, he drew a small silver case from his jacket pocket, took an enormous pinch of snuff and then commenced his harangue: beautifully phrased, carefully formulated, full of solemnity, but completely inappropriate. This was his great talent. His words conformed neither to his features, nor to the circumstances of his predicament. He threatened the innocent, avoided the guilty. His pupils were so insulted by the obvious injustice as to become lovers of justice themselves.

It was during these feats of oratory enunciated through glittering tears that Jarry came forward. He joined the fray at the end, like a matador entering the arena for the *coup de grâce*. Complete silence reigned. Coldly, cuttingly, he put insidious and bizarre questions to Père Heb, who faltered in mid-sentence, his self-righteous manner shattered. Jarry encircled him, stunning him with aphorisms. He demolished him, Père Heb became disconcerted, batted his eyelids, stammered, pretended not to hear, lost his footing. Finally he gave way, collapsing on the table amidst the retorts and apparatus, scrambling for his spectacles, and with a trembling hand he would scribble a note to the headmaster. The class regarded Jarry the victor with a sense of wonder.

And also with trepidation and disquiet, because we felt that Jarry's sarcasm went far beyond the general unruliness, that something within him, some powerful impulse, lay behind the ferocity of his attack. Already it seemed as if Père Ubu was coming into being, modeled on Jarry's victim.[3]

Jarry's ferocity may be attributed simply to fear and loathing. Hébert, the tragic incompetent, with his earnest appeals for order, respect, and tradition, personified something extremely ominous. Subservient, unquestioning, his eagerness to please his superiors had cost him both his dignity and self-respect. As a teacher he was inadvertently effective nevertheless; he offered his pupils a ghastly example, and it was a lesson that some of them learned very well. Hébert was the anti-Narcissus of impending adulthood—what one most dreaded one day recognizing in the mirror. Yet Jarry came to see in him something more than a simple warning against petit bourgeois conformities. Here was an archetype that he could at once embrace and ward off, by forming it into a symbolic representation of "everything in the world that is grotesque": Père Ubu.[4]

2

1873–1891

Hertz's account of Hébert's demolition is the first of several descriptions of Jarry's often uncontrollable nature. He would appear to many of his contemporaries as a prodigious performer, but someone verging on possession and barely able to restrain either his conduct or his imagination. At fifteen, when Jarry entered the *lycée* at Rennes and Hébert's classes, his defiance and his determination to exceed the bounds of normal behavior were already so marked that one suspects they masked something else … but what precisely? Shyness, insecurity, or some deeper resolve? Even as a schoolboy Jarry tended toward a sort of creative self-immolation; he soon acquired something of a "reputation."

2.1
Alfred Jarry, portrait of P. H., 3½ × 2 inches,
Rennes period.

2.2
Alfred Jarry, drawing of P. H. torn from a school
exercise book, Rennes period.

The *lycée* was huge, its buildings arranged around four courtyards, with interminable corridors, enormous cellars and attics, even its own church. In Jarry's day it was also somewhat decrepit, particularly the old part in which Hébert's classes took place. The physics laboratory in which he taught now houses the school museum, which has been named in Hébert's honor, or rather, in honor of what he inspired. The first-floor classroom resembles a medieval operating theater: near the center is a large square work table for experiments, and before it rise tiers of long fixed desks and bench seats. This was the arena in which Jarry encountered Hébert.

...

In 1888, Caroline Jarry had returned to Rennes, where she had been born, with her two children, Alfred and his elder sister Charlotte, having separated from her husband nine years previously. Alfred had left his primary school laden with prizes, and his mother decided he needed the best secondary education to be had, at the *lycée* in the regional capital. He registered as a non-boarding pupil on October 1, a few weeks after his fifteenth birthday, and the family settled into the first of the three different addresses they would occupy over the next two years.

RENNES. — Le Lycée

2.3
Rennes. The *lycée*.

Here Alfred practiced a cult of rebellious unconventionality that was conventional enough in a youth of his age. In later life Charlotte left a brief "poetic" record of her brother, and the lack of any family papers means that these *Notes on Alfred Jarry* are the only firsthand account of his early home life. She recalls his bedroom, with its black walls decorated with skeletons, where he would read till the small hours surrounded by dictionaries, bicycle, guitar, and air rifle; his bombarding of passersby with a peashooter from the windows of the house, or in the street disguised in monk's robes, peashooter concealed beneath the hood; and his chemical experiments, which burnt the house's gutters with acid.[1]

It was at school that Jarry really felt the need to make a mark. The French employ the word *potache* to evoke the adolescent schoolboy and his universe, a turmoil of scatology, insubordination, sexual and other confusion, and frequently of creativity. Jarry played the role with particular verve and conviction, and was loath to renounce it, even in adulthood. Early adolescence proved especially formative for Jarry, who discovered literary and artistic enthusiasms to which he returned throughout his life. He had also found a mode of living, a manner of uncompromising behavior that somehow conformed with his inner drives, and which he rarely dropped, at least in public.

Various of Jarry's ex-school friends were interviewed by his early biographers. They remembered him as pugnacious, precocious, and intelligent. Many recalled his disquieting gaze, his quick wit, his need always to go a little too far: he gave the impression of being both fearless of authority and indifferent to the opinion of his peers. They nicknamed him Quasimodo, because of his short stature, thick-set physique, and arching gait, and remained wary of his sardonic humor and cutting tongue: it seems Jarry was already acquiring his distinctive mode of speaking, precisely accentuating every syllable. His intimates found him a loyal and entertaining friend; mocking, but never spiteful, nor envious. He was also advanced for his age, not only as regards his already vast and obscure reading, but in his "morals" and his fascination with sexual matters. When he arrived at school, breathless, pale with insomnia, shoes filthy and collar askew, he explained that he had been "to the bro-thels" (the school was indeed surrounded by these establishments, due to the proximity of the local barracks). The roots of such swagger may, of course, be associated with his shortness of stature, and with hidden uncertainties concerning his sexuality and its orientation. It all proved too much for some of his classmates:[2]

> I'm no prude, I was always a good Rabelaisian. Among ourselves we *potaches* used a language that was a cross between that of Rabelais and the barracks; but it was the superficial and purely verbal bravado of young schoolboys with no practical experience. Jarry distinguished himself by a vivid and realistic obscenity. He described his visits to brothels (at 15, what's more!), or shocked us with stories of the black masses he read about, where, I don't know, perhaps in some book by Haraucourt. [...] I still recall quite distinctly one of these alarming tales, of a mass presided over by the Devil, which finished with him sprinkling the assembly with sp...k from his own personal and gigantic censer. [...] His father's death, his mother's indulgence, the total lack of parental supervision, all of this contributed toward Jarry becoming a depraved *potache*.[3]

This recollection some forty years after the event should not be taken entirely at face value. For one thing, Jarry's father was not dead at the time, merely estranged from the family. Another ex-pupil recalled: "He had little to learn so far as sexual matters were concerned. […] He tackled these topics with great relish and discussed them with medical precision and extreme coarseness. Respect for women was a sentiment with which he was entirely unfamiliar from the age of 16 onward. I have even asked myself how, given his habitually crude language, he was able to maintain decency before his mother and sister." Jarry made even adults uneasy. Fellow pupils later recalled that in the town as well as the school he occasioned hushed tones among parents and teachers. He was clever, but not malleable, they said. And precocious, quite capable of carrying off all the school prizes, if only he made the effort. A brilliant pupil in fact, but also the worst kind of troublemaker.[4]

…

The ritualistic nature of the humiliations inflicted on Hébert already exceeded the usual formalities of teacher/pupil warfare. The entire *lycée*, including the staff, was well aware of this, and younger pupils keenly anticipated the entertainment. They awaited with impatience their promotion to "the legendary classes of Monsieur Hébert."[5]

Soon after Hébert's return to teaching in 1881, dramatic accounts of the various exploits attributed to him, under the names P. H. (for Père Hébert), Heb, Éb, Ébé, etc., began circulating in the school. Each new generation of his pupils contributed to this epic literature in which Hébert's torments were extended beyond the classroom. At first this was a purely oral tradition. Presently, however, written texts were produced and were passed down from year to year until the Hébert cycle approached Homeric dimensions.

We know about this lost literature from a book published originally in 1921, fourteen years after Jarry's death, by Charles Chassé. Although it was written for rather disreputable reasons (which will be discussed later, in chapter 9), Chassé's book is valuable because it collected a number of personal descriptions of Jarry by his contemporaries. The Hébertian literature comprised dozens of poems, some more than 150 verses long, as well as plays and, for a brief period, weekly newspapers and bulletins. Initially, they were a fairly realistic depiction of Hébert's classroom martyrdom, but the competitive imaginations of dozens of schoolboys soon freed P. H. from everyday reality. Episodes inspired by the works of Rabelais, Lesage, Byron, Shakespeare, *The Lives of the Saints*, *The Count of Monte Cristo* and from schoolbooks, not excluding even Euclid, gradually transformed P. H. into something entirely original. Chassé's book includes a few fragments of the lost poems, along with a summary of the "oral tradition," a text worth citing in full:[6]

> Still visible today in the deserts of Turkestan are the ruins of an immense city which, several thousands of years before the Christian era, was the capital of a great empire whose last sovereigns were Dromberg I, Dromberg II, and Dromberg III. The population of this empire were known as Ginormants. During the reign of Dromberg III, on the banks of the Oxus, P. H. was born,

the offspring of a Ginormant and a Tartar or Mongolian witch who lived in the rushes and reeds bordering the Aral Sea.

Appearance of P. H.—He was born complete with bowler hat, woolen cloak, and check trousers. On top of his head is a single, extendible ear, usually covered by his hat; both his arms are on the same side (likewise his eyes) and, unlike humans, whose feet are situated next to each other, he has one behind the other, so that when he falls over he is unable to pick himself up without assistance and remains prostrated, shouting until someone helps him up. He has only three teeth—of stone, iron, and wood. When the teeth of the upper jaw attempt to break through, he forces them back with blows from his front foot.

N.B. An umbilical point is one of the points on a surface at which that surface is cut by a plane tangential to a circle.

It is possible to demonstrate that:

1. All points on the surface of P. H. are umbilical points.
2. Any body whose surface is entirely composed of umbilical points is a P. H.

P. H. was baptized with essence of pataphysics by an old Ginormant who dwelt in a hovel at the foot of the mountains bordering China. He hired P. H. to watch over his polochons (polochons are animals resembling large pigs; they have no head, but compensate for this lack by having two backsides, one at each end).

For several years, when the snows melted, P. H. led his flock of 3,333 million 333 thousand and 333 polochons down to graze on the steppes between the Caspian and Aral Seas and on the shores of Lake Balkhash. He carried his food in an enormous pocket which he dragged behind him by means of a shoulder strap. On his return, as the first snows fell, his master carefully counted his polochons, a task which took the whole winter to complete.

But his master is exceedingly miserly when it comes to food and one year, toward summer's end, P. H. found himself short of nourishment and devoured a polochon. He had intended telling his boss that it had been carried off by a panther, but he was unfortunately betrayed by one of the polochon's tails which remained caught between his teeth. P. H.'s master immediately dispatched his extra-fast messenger-polochon to Dromberg III with the request that he send the Ginormants to arrest P. H. The latter had slunk off into the night and crossed the mountains into China, where he hoped to find refuge.

But the very next day he saw the pursuing Ginormants silhouetted against the skyline. At once he took to his heels with such haste that he passed through a too-narrow gorge in the Alatau mountains and there left behind two pieces of his woolen cloak. What is more, his *gidouille* [approximately: his gutbag] became so compressed by the sides of the gorge as to gouge out two flat ledges that were still visible at the end of the nineteenth century. However, he got through!

The great mass of Ginormants arrived at the same narrow defile, and in horrendous confusion trampled one another underfoot, those at the back pushing forward without realizing their progress was blocked. If we are to believe the testimony of Herodotus (Bk. III, Ch. xii), the din was heard as far away as Ceylon.

P. H. made good his escape and continued across Mongolia, Manchuria, and Siberia, but the surviving Ginormants took a short cut and were easily able to pick up his tracks, which were unique owing to his feet being situated on the same axis. Reaching the source of the Anadir, he met the Devil to whom he agreed to sell his soul if he would save him. The bargain was struck and at the moment the Ginormants were about to pounce, he dived into the frightful abyss at the bottom of which lies the source of the Anadir, and was immediately transformed into a little copper-colored fish. He descended the river, passed into the sea, and swam through the Bering Strait into the Arctic Ocean. An ice floe swept him to the north of Siberia. Here he remained for a thousand years, preserved in the ice. Following an exceptionally mild winter, he managed to free himself and continued traveling westward and, near the North Cape, he felt the first warm currents of the Gulf Stream. Attracted by the warmth, he passed down the coast of Norway, then into the English Channel and hence to the mouth of the Seine.

There, unfortunately for humanity, he decided to swim upriver and was finally snared by a fisherman near the Pont du Louvre. As soon as he was extracted from the water, P. H. assumed his previous form and the fisherman—seeing the ignoble hat, the porcine snout, and the enormous gutbag looming into view—fled in terror. P. H. removed the entangled fishhook, a painful exercise, and set forth immediately on his criminal exploits. He occupied himself in this manner throughout the fourteenth century during the reign of King Charles V.

A little later, P. H. received his baccalaureate, with poor marks, by dint of terrorizing his examiners. His only scientific apparatus consisted of two or three cuneiform characters which he attempted to reproduce more or less badly.

Soon after, at the head of a gang of bandits commanded by Captain Rolando, he seized the castle of Mondragon, which became his lair.

Then there was the journey to Spain, the usurpation of the throne of Aragon, the departure for Poland as captain of dragoons, etc., etc.

...

Between 1885 and 1886, according to Chassé, two brothers, Charles and Henri Morin, committed the more recent exploits of P. H. to paper. Presumably with the help of other pupils, they wrote and illustrated a series of short plays that detailed the misfortunes of P. H. as summarized by Chassé in the last two paragraphs of his account above. These plays bore the titles *Les Héritiers*, *Le Bastringue*, *La Prise de Ismaïl* (inspired by Byron's *Don Juan*), *Le Voyage en Espagne*, *Don Fernand d'Aragon* (inspired by *Gil Blas*), and all are lost. Finally, the Morins wrote *Les Polonais*

(*The Poles*). The adventures of Heb were most often scribbled out on scraps of paper in Hébert's class, or in those of his fellow teachers. On these occasions, Charles Morin tells us, pupils would sometimes contrive to have them confiscated on purpose, in the expectation that they would amuse Hébert's colleagues as much as their young authors.[7]

Charles Morin, the elder brother, left the *lycée* at the end of the school year of 1888 to pursue his studies in Paris. He put childish things behind him because, as he later told Charles Chassé, he had "better things to do than concern myself with such stupidities." He gave the manuscript of *Les Polonais* to his brother. Nevertheless, in Paris he continued to entertain his new friends at the Polytechnique with the exploits of Heb, so he cannot have been quite as dismissive as he later made out.[8]

Henri Morin was only a month older than Jarry, and for the first year they were in the same class. They were soon close friends, and it was not long before Jarry read the manuscript of *Les Polonais*. His enthusiasm was immediate—in part because *Les Polonais* bears striking resemblances to some of the plays Jarry himself had written at primary school, not least in the schoolboy fascination with the bowels and their products.

Although many of the descriptions of Hébert's misadventures had been written as plays, it seems not to have occurred to any of their authors actually to stage them. It was Jarry who first suggested they should, and in December 1888, or perhaps in early January of the following year, the "Théâtre des Phynances" came into being. It was named in honor of Heb's abiding lust for "phynance," money, extracted with maximum violence from persons weaker than himself, with the aid of his henchmen, the "salopins." Henri and Alfred commandeered the extensive attics of the Morin household and mounted the first of several productions of *Les Polonais*, "to the detriment of our Latin and Greek studies," as Morin later ruefully remarked.[9]

Information about these productions is sparse. Henri assumed the starring role, costumed in a greatcoat stuffed with pillows, and Jarry painted the scenery. Their classmates played the remaining parts, and also made up the audience. All the surviving texts of these plays revel in scatological humor, and later on, in sexual innuendo. It is a fair assumption, then, that these gatherings in the Morin attic were secretive affairs, ceremonials of the Hébert cult to which adults were not invited.[10]

In the summer of 1889, the Morins moved house and the Théâtre des Phynances transferred to Jarry's. Here they lacked a room large enough, or private enough, for live performances, and subsequent productions were adapted for the puppet theater, and later still performed as shadow plays. Most of the puppets were made by Jarry's sister, a competent sculptor. Charles Morin recalled her making "a magnificent bust" of P. H., adding that since Hébert was a neighbor of the Jarrys, he passed their window every day on his way to school, and Charlotte was able to perfect her representation of him.[11]

The Théâtre des Phynances had perhaps two further seasons, but it is uncertain which plays were presented in the school years 1889–1890 and 1890–1891. *Les Polonais*, no doubt, but also new plays written by Jarry and by Henri Morin. Two of these have survived in fragmentary form: *Onésime, ou les tribulations de Priou*, by Jarry, and *La Chasse aux polyèdres* by Morin.

Onésime introduces for the first time more "adult" themes into the Hébert cycle, including alcohol and sex: the play describes the cuckolding of Hébert by Barbapoux, a character based upon one of Jarry's class supervisors. Jarry would endlessly rewrite this piece over the next fifteen years, as the various versions of *Ubu cocu*, and it was eventually published in 1944.[12]

Onésime is very different from Morin's effort. Jarry's play has moments of genuine wit and wordplay amid its schoolboy humor, as well as a structure of sorts. Morin's, on the other hand, is much more amateurish—the plot is a mishmash of repetitions and blind alleys, and smothers its audience in Hébertian oaths and ejaculations which would quickly prove wearisome to any but partisan schoolfellows in on the joke. These plays were probably both written with puppets in mind (one stage direction in *Onésime*, for example, calls for the character's head to be set alight).[13]

We can assume that *Les Polonais* was still in the repertoire around the winter of 1890, because Henri Morin recalled giving Jarry the manuscript so he could adapt it for a shadow-theater production, and these were among the last performances of the Théâtre des Phynances. Jarry, he tells us, resorted to the shadow play only after finding the puppets too difficult to manipulate.[14]

This description of the Théâtre des Phynances is, however, no more than a best guess. Henri Morin's is the only direct account, and he contradicts himself on a number of occasions. In a letter from 1934 published in the introduction to *Ubu intime*, Morin wrote that a shadow-play version preceded the live performances. He says too that he gave Jarry the manuscript of *Les Polonais* both in 1888 and in 1889, also that he sent it to his brother in Paris, or even that he entrusted it to a certain "Boris": the mystery of the original manuscript of *Les Polonais* is indeed labyrinthine. Finally, it remains unclear whether Jarry and Morin used the name "Théâtre des Phynances" for all the various productions at Rennes, or only for the puppet plays. If the live-actor version was indeed preceded by a shadow-play version, it would explain why the published version of *Ubu Roi* bears the subtitle "as performed by the marionettes of the Théâtre des Phynances in 1888," since shadow plays also use marionettes.[15]

More to the point, after all these performances, was *Les Polonais* still the same play as the one written by Charles Morin with his brother? Given the nature of the play, and its origins in the commonality of the Hébert myth, it appears unlikely that Jarry and Henri Morin would have stuck rigidly to the original text as committed to paper, as though it were an established script. Moreover, since Alfred and Henri had been mounting these productions without the elder brother's collaboration, surely the play would have evolved in performance? These matters would assume importance only after the first performance of *Ubu Roi*.[16]

Jarry wrote a couple of other pieces while at Rennes, including *Le Futur malgré lui*, a play which could pass as a conventional satire on the marital customs of the bourgeoisie. Quantitatively his output was considerably reduced compared to his last years at primary school; the productions of the Théâtre des Phynances must have been taking up his time, or he may even have applied himself to his schoolwork.

At the end of the school year 1891, Jarry and his mother left Rennes for Paris. Once again she uprooted herself in order to benefit his education, and the uncomplaining Charlotte tagged along. Among the possessions he took with him were various bits of Hébertian paraphernalia, a number of puppets, and a green exercise book of some thirty pages. Bearing the trademark of Lafond, a stationer's in Rennes where it had been purchased, it was well thumbed, since it contained two separate texts. The Morins had first used it to list a collection of fossils. Then, after the entries of this catalog had been scored through, the text of their original version of *Les Polonais* was snaked around the deletions. It was illustrated, too.[17]

But before Paris, Jarry's early childhood.

...

Alfred-Henri Jarry was born on September 8, 1873, the feast of the Nativity of the Holy Virgin, in Laval, a small town of 25,000 inhabitants on the Mayenne. Laval lies just outside the borders of Brittany, but Jarry would later always claim to have Breton origins. He was born at home, 8, quai de la Mayenne, in the family residence in the center of town. Despite its modest proportions the house was well appointed, and situated in a most prestigious neighborhood: on the river's edge beneath the Palais de Justice. It boasted an aviary stocked with birds, and an ornamental garden with a fountain and rockeries, according to Charlotte, who was then eight years old. She furnishes other details, both fanciful and banal. Her brother entered the world laughing, she says. He was weaned on a soup of rice biscuit flour and vaccinated by the local doctor, who declared him "the strongest and most attractive baby in the whole region"—apart from that of the Comtesse de Monbron. Alfred was baptized on June 8, 1874, and Charlotte was to be his godmother, but since her parents had neglected her own baptism, she was received into the church the same day. The family was not particularly pious.[18]

In later life (by which time he had adopted the regal "we" of Ubu-speak), and preferably in inappropriate circumstances, Jarry had a few things to say on the subject of his parents: "Our father was a fellow of no importance, what is known as a thoroughly good chap. Our mother and he passed away within eight days of one another, right on schedule, so as to leave us their money." On this occasion Jarry was replying to a genteel inquiry at dinner with the actress Marguerite Moreno, wife of the author Marcel Schwob, and her mother. Moreno recalled that her mother was so shocked that Jarry never graced the family table again. Jarry's parents in fact died two years apart, but facts could not be allowed to spoil such provocations. When his close friend Rachilde later inquired after his parents, he used the same opening:[19]

> Our father was a fellow of no importance, what is known as a thoroughly good chap. No doubt he made our sister, a girl in the style of the 1830s and enamored of putting ribbons in her hair, but he cannot have had much to do with the confection of our own precious person! Our mother was a young lady of Coutouly descent, small and sturdy, willful and capricious, whom we were obliged to approve of before we had any say in the matter. She had a fondness for fancy dress. We possess a photograph of her got up as a torero, in short breeches and a small gold-embroidered jacket hung with little bells, with a velvet cap perched on her brow. Like all women she drove her husband to despair, which was perhaps his own fault, owing to his restraint with the bludgeon.[20]

2.4
Laval. The quai de la Mayenne in the 1890s. Jarry's
birthplace is presumed to be the house with three dormer
windows behind the sign reading "Bordeau-Duchemin."
The building second from the left on the riverfront, also
with three dormer windows, would be the future premises
of Monsieur Trochon, purveyor of bicycles.

Rue du Val de Mayenne

Cliché Hamel, Jallier et Cie, Laval

2.5
Laval. The rue du Val de Mayenne in the 1890s.
The building on the right is the shop of Bordeau-
Duchemin, and thus once that of Anselme Jarry.
This photograph dates from a few years later, when
he had been forced to sell his share of the business.
The path up to Jarry's primary school runs off the
road to the left.

If these pronouncements show little in the way of filial respect, they do give us some insight into Jarry's feelings toward each of his parents. He maintained an attitude of indifference to his father, who played only a small part in his life after his early childhood. For his mother, though, he felt genuine affection. Her whimsical, not to say erratic, nature must surely have appealed to her son. No likenesses of his parents have survived, nor indeed have any of the family photographs (hence there are no photographs of Jarry before the age of nineteen).

Anselme, Jarry's father, was born in 1837, a native of Laval. For the previous two centuries the male members of the family had been masons, weavers, and carpenters, but through the thrift and determination of several generations of fiercely resolute womenfolk, they gradually transformed themselves from artisans into property owners and landlords. They were *rentiers*, in fact, the very class of individual from whom P. H. or Ubu extorted "phynance." Most of their property was situated in one particular street, the rue de Bootz in Laval. The family was singularly attached to this thoroughfare. Jarry's great-grandmother acquired the family home, numbers 13 and 15, in 1830, and his grandparents bought numbers 21 and 23 in 1842. A little later, Anselme and his brother acquired numbers 10 and 12. These property transactions make it plain that the Jarry family had become at least moderately wealthy, and family money allowed Anselme, at the age of twenty-six, to set up a textile manufacturing business with a partner. The business was prosperous for a while and they leased further properties in Laval, including the house where Alfred was born, and beneath it, or nearby, a shop for selling their products. The house, due to its prominent position, is visible in many photographs and postcards of Laval.[21]

Caroline, Jarry's mother, *née* Quernest, was five years younger than Anselme, and was a Breton from a more elevated background. Her father, Charles Jean-Baptiste Quernest, was a magistrate in the town of Hédé, some twenty miles north of Rennes. She was cultured and determined, but also, as Alfred remarked, capricious. She was unconventional in her dress, apparently, or so thought the conservative citizens of Laval. Her ancestry was noble, but not as noble as she liked to think. It was a family tradition on her side that they were descended from Erbrand Sacqueville, one of William's fellow conquerors of England, and thus from the Sackville family, the Dukes of Dorset. Painstaking genealogical researches by Arnaud, Bordillon, and Lassalle have failed to verify the matter one way or another, although the probability seems remote.[22]

Even so, Caroline's family was aristocratic enough to harbor the traditional complement of black sheep. Her sister was an alcoholic and took to wandering the streets dressed like a tramp, and her brother Charles likewise nursed a fondness for the bottle. More seriously, her mother suffered bouts of mental illness sufficiently serious to prevent her giving her legal consent to Caroline's marriage; she died in the mental asylum at Rennes early in 1883.[23]

Alfred's parents were married on July 16, 1863, and moved into 13, rue de Bootz. The details of their marriage contract were stricter than was common; it resembled a modern prenuptial agreement. Their first child, Charlotte, was born in 1865; she was followed in 1870 by a son, who died after two weeks. Alfred-Henri was born three years later, by which time the family had moved to the quai de la Mayenne. The house backed onto another building on the street behind, the rue du Val de Mayenne, where Jarry's father's shop was situated.[24]

34 St-BRIEUC— Boulevard Charner

3124. - St-BRIEUC. - Pêcheurs à la Ligne aux Ecluses du Bassin à Flot

Coll. E. H., St-Brieuc

2.6
Saint-Brieuc. The boulevard Charner; Jarry's childhood home is situated halfway down the street on the left, in the house with a sign painted on its side. The path beneath the trees on the right, which is some 15 feet above street level at the far end, is today the Esplanade Alfred Jarry.

2.7
Saint-Brieuc. The harbor where Jarry fished as a child.

Charlotte's *Notes* recall a happy few years for Alfred in this house by the river, but her memory was probably at fault because this is not borne out by evidence from the Laval censuses. The 1872 census identifies the Jarrys as residents of 8, quai de la Mayenne, and shows that this was a different, although adjoining, building to that containing the shop. This was also the residence of a Monsieur Bordeau and his wife (née Duchemin), whose sign is visible in both postcards (figures 2.4, 2.5). By the time Jarry was three, however, number 8 had vanished from the 1876 census, and the Jarrys were living back in the rue de Bootz. They must subsequently have returned to the quai, perhaps then living above the shop (since Duchemin was identified by Charlotte as Anselme's business partner), because Jarry, in his novel *Absolute Love*, recalled his walk to school from there. Each morning he and his mother ascended the narrow alley beside the castle and then up through the precipitous streets of the medieval part of the town. He started at the primary school in May 1878, and it was still then the custom in the provinces for schoolboys to be dressed as girls at this age. At home Charlotte recalls "Fredo" making a little theater out of pages cut from the *Magasin pittoresque*, with skittles dressed up as actors braving a snowstorm of shredded paper.[25]

Anselme's business had been in trouble for some time, and was eventually wound up in June 1879. Bankrupt, he was obliged to take a position as a commercial salesman for various textile mills outside the town. All his properties were mortgaged, the lease on the house on the Mayenne had to be surrendered, and the family faced moving back once more to the rue de Bootz, to a new house recently built by Anselme. Caroline refused; she protested that the plaster hadn't dried out and it made them cough. According to Jarry's first biographer, Paul Chauveau, she had other complaints as well—her husband was traveling all the time, she felt neglected, and so forth. Caroline took the children and left him. The hapless Anselme remained a salesman for the mills thereafter, and gained a probably undeserved reputation in the family as one for whom "the hour of apéritifs was sacred." His prospects revived a little in 1888, when he inherited a share of the family properties on the death of his mother. Precious little remained after he had settled his debts, although he continued to support Caroline and his children.[26]

...

Caroline went to live with her children in Saint-Brieuc, some hundred miles from Laval, on the north coast of Brittany, where her father Charles Quernest had recently retired.

Laval and Mayenne had been quiet and prosaic, but Brittany was altogether different—another world, with its own language, traditions, mythology, and local costume, although Saint-Brieuc itself was not Breton-speaking. Caroline's family was scattered around the nearby towns and villages, with aunts, cousins, and two uncles in Lamballe six miles away. Jarry would remember his years in Brittany as idyllic. At home there was no male competition for the affection of his mother, and outside, especially when staying with relatives, there was the Breton landscape. He was free to roam the ancient forests around Lamballe, famously celebrated in Arthurian legend, and along the coastline of the Côtes-d'Armor around Saint-Brieuc and nearby Erquy. This part of France was essentially unchanged since medieval times: there was virtually no traffic, few modern buildings outside the larger towns, and tourism was yet to be invented. Its scenery would be recalled in Jarry's later fiction, especially in *Absolute Love*, which is set around Lamballe ("Lampaul" in the novel). The novel contains many intense evocations of the countryside, in particular memories of a coastguard's lookout hut up on a cliff top, which became the young Alfred's favorite refuge. Memories of the happiness of these years, a happiness that was perhaps somewhat solitary, would color Jarry's future.

By the time he started at the local school in the autumn of 1879, the family was living at 12, boulevard Charner, a nondescript, overcast street leading up to the railway station. The opposite side of the road is still dominated by a large, walled embankment, which presumably supported a shunting yard. Nowadays it bears the name "Esplanade Alfred Jarry." The family would remain there for nine years.

We know little of Jarry's life here or of his relations with his mother's family, although it is reasonable to assume he saw a fair amount of his grandfather. Charles Quernest had inherited a large and eclectic library from his parents, and it was in his study, surrounded by books, that he devoted himself to exploring the nobler branches of the family tree, an obsession he passed on to his daughter and both grandchildren. Once again, however, Charlotte's *Notes* are our principal source. Apart from reading, she tells us, Jarry had two other passions: entomology and fishing. In 1908 she sent Rachilde a postcard (figure 2.7) which depicted Jarry's favorite spot for fishing as a child. She recalls his hunting for butterflies, "serious as a naturalist," and shrimping in the coastal rock pools on the beach at Val-André, a big straw hat pulled down on his head.[27]

Despite his enduring love for the landscape of Brittany, its mythology and traditions, Jarry found nothing to admire in the inhabitants or town of Saint-Brieuc, which was a commercial center based around its port. "Everything in Saint-Brieuc is more or less stupid," begins an early poem, written when he was thirteen, "and the townsfolk are off their heads." The present-day inhabitants of Saint-Brieuc are still indignantly familiar with this ditty (as I discovered when inquiring after Jarry at the local tourist office).[28]

•••

In 1947, Maurice Saillet came across a file in the offices of the Mercure de France, Jarry's first important publisher. Its title, in Jarry's adult hand, read "*Ontogenesis. Texts predating* Minutes *and some dating after* Ubu Roi, *and which it is more honorable not to publish.*" The folder contained around 260 pages, including all of his now-known juvenilia, some recopied at a later date, and from this material we know that Jarry began writing at least as early as 1885, when he was twelve. Most of it consists of poems or plays in verse, and their influences are obvious: Victor Hugo, Théophile Gautier, Coleridge, and the Romantics in general, all the paraphernalia of whose style is present, whether ruined castles, tempests, specters, gibbets, or dancing skeletons (like those depicted in an undated painting by Jarry which has somehow survived). This was an iconography Jarry returned to frequently, although in later years more often with ironic intentions.

2.8
Alfred Jarry, manuscript of a poem attached to the
"Antlium" cycle of plays, dated August 1, 1886.

A second group of youthful poems is noticeably darker, particularly those written in Jarry's last months at Saint-Brieuc in 1888, such as *Misère de l'homme* (the title says it all) and *La Seconde Vie ou Macaber*. This last sets its scene with the familiar skeletons and gibbets only to move into uncharted domains, the hero's suicide and progress through the realms of the dead. Adolescent angst, perhaps. Charlotte's *Notes* are interesting here for what they don't say: there is no mention of Jarry having any close friends at Saint-Brieuc. His meeting Henri Morin at Rennes in October the same year acquires new significance in this light. It would seem to have been Jarry's first close friendship, and was a meeting that would have literary consequences. When Jarry arrived at Rennes, Henri Morin was quick to show him the manuscript of *Les Polonais*. Presumably Jarry reciprocated and showed Henri some of these youthful productions—in particular a third category of his writings, a sequence of plays and poems caricaturing the citizens of Saint-Brieuc busily engaged in the War of the Shit Pump. Although it lacks an archetypal character of the status of Hébert, this group has much in common with *Les Polonais*, in particular its interest in "base matter."

Originally inspired by the newly purchased sewage pump that trundled through the streets of Saint-Brieuc noisily sucking sludge from the cesspits, these verse dramas were composed between 1886 and January 1888. In a mock-heroic style reminiscent of classical or Shakespearian drama, they relate the struggle between the Antliatores, the servants of the shit pump or Antlium (a neologism derived from a Latinization of the Greek word for a pump), and the Antliaclasts, intent on its destruction. As in the Hébert plays, the characters are based on fellow pupils and teachers at the *lycée*, and the manuscripts are illustrated with scenes from the action. They become increasingly apocalyptic as the pump becomes associated with Taurobolium, the Mithraic ceremony that culminates with the sacrifice of a bull. The plays of the Antlium cycle already employ a technique that would be characteristic of much of Jarry's adult writing, including *Ubu*: the collision of contradictory stylistic devices, erudition with idiocy, the heroic with the craven, the mythological with the everyday. The struggles for the Antlium, as heroic as the Punic Wars, culminate in a disastrous explosion of the shit pump, and with the combatants being "covered in esteem."[29]

...

At Saint-Brieuc at least, Jarry's literary activities did not interfere with his education, and as he progressed up the school, his academic abilities became increasingly evident. At the end of the school year 1886, Jarry won five prizes, four being firsts; in 1887, six, including three firsts; and when the prizes for his final year, 1888, were announced, he was awarded eleven, of which six were firsts. His mother could see a promising future for her son, and the family was sorely in need of one, thus the move to Rennes. Here, too, Jarry was able to distinguish himself academically, and although he received no commendations, he did … enough.

He was also not quite the errant son implied by his later comments about his parents. Soon after the family moved to Rennes in October 1888, Jarry acquired his first bicycle, purchased in Laval from a Monsieur Trochon. Laval, rather than Rennes, appears to have been the center of

Jarry's sporting activities, namely fishing, cycling, and fencing, and these involved frequent or prolonged stays with his father. Jarry joined the Lavallois "Vélocipède Club" at the age of fifteen, and took part in its annual rally in March 1889. These were the very earliest days of cycling. The first modern bicycle, with a diamond frame and a chain-driven back wheel, was John Starley's "Rover," manufactured in 1885 in Coventry, England, and it took a couple of years for such models to catch on in France. Jarry's first bicycle must have been very similar to this machine.[30]

Cycling was thus brought within the financial reach of the whole populace for the first time, and had a dramatic impact on the mobility of the less well-off. However, it was still such a novelty as to be prone to all sorts of misadventures. Many roads were unsurfaced; and attacks by dogs, as yet unaccustomed to these strange beasts, were so common that Jarry considered a riding crop an essential accessory. It was useful too against affronted pedestrians determined to unseat the rider, since such assaults were also common in those days.[31]

Charlotte recalls her brother cycling from Rennes to Mont-Saint-Michel and back, a distance of some forty miles each way, so the trip to Laval, half the distance, was a simple matter. Here he pursued his fencing, at the *salle d'armes* of Maître Blaviel. The only memento of this youthful passion is a report of a tournament from a local newspaper, *L'Avenir de la Mayenne*, for February 10, 1889:[32]

2.9
John Starley's "Rover," 1885.

Monsieur A. Jarry and Monsieur Kavanagh *fils*: a bout which was much commented on and
enthusiastically applauded. These two young men already know how to hold the floor and have
been nicely trained according to the book. Monsieur Jarry recently won the first prize in
the open contest at the Regional Championships in Angers. On Sunday he performed some
fine parries and lightning ripostes.[33]

Jarry distinguished himself in the classroom too, and his reputation for ill-discipline at Rennes
may well have been exaggerated. Charles Chassé's book on Jarry remains the principal source for
his time there, and, for reasons of his own, he encouraged testimonies from former pupils that
would cast Jarry in a bad light. Although colorful, they paint a deliberately skewed portrait.
Despite his seditious proclivities, Jarry must have realized by now that academic success was his
only escape from a provincial and "Hébertian" existence. His literary output at Saint-Brieuc had
been substantial, and toward the end of his time there could be regarded as "serious." If he already
had literary ambitions then he must get himself to Paris, which in turn depended on scholastic
achievement.

Jarry and Henri Morin took the first part of their baccalaureate in 1889: the written section
on July 19 (Latin translation, French composition, foreign language composition), the oral on
August 5. For the latter Jarry was required to translate and comment upon *The Iliad* (Book XVIII),
Virgil's *Georgics* (Book II), Goethe's poem *Hermann und Dorothea*, and to discuss the works of
La Bruyère (*The Characters*) and Rabelais (which he would have relished); in history, his subject
was the Guise family (powerful nobles of the sixteenth century), and in geography, the Vosges/
Ardennes region of France. The second part took place the following year: the written section
on July 17 (philosophy, natural sciences), the oral on the 19th. This time his topics were the Philosophical Hypothesis, Leibniz's Monadology and the works of Aristotle, the division of fractions,
Mariotte's Law of Gases, and Napoleon's Campaign of 1799. Jarry was awarded his *bac* with the
commendation "good," and Morin received the same.[34]

Nothing is known of Jarry's activities between July 1890 and June 1891, except that he stayed
on at the *lycée* in the advanced class of "veterans" preparing for higher education. But in what,
the physical sciences or the humanities? Morin plumped for practicality and the École Polytechnique, but Jarry was equally competent in both the arts and the sciences. According to Henri
Morin he hesitated, although his family urged the Polytechnique. Jarry demurred, then made
his choice: the arts and literature, although his "science of Pataphysics" would underpin both his
literary works and his life with a scientific method that was all his own.[35]

3

OUR SCIENCE OF PATAPHYSICS

The word *Pataphysique* had its origins in the mythology of P. H. in Rennes, where it was probably just a schoolboy exaggeration of Hébert's verbal mangling of the word *physique* (physics). The "oral tradition" recorded that P. H. was baptized in its essence, and Henri Morin had invoked its virtues in his play *La Chasse aux polyèdres*, written in the school year of 1889–1890. Once Jarry arrived in Paris, however, Pataphysics began to assume more concrete meanings for him: it gradually coalesced into a defense against everything epitomized by Hébert, and then became something of a personal poetic and philosophical credo.[1]

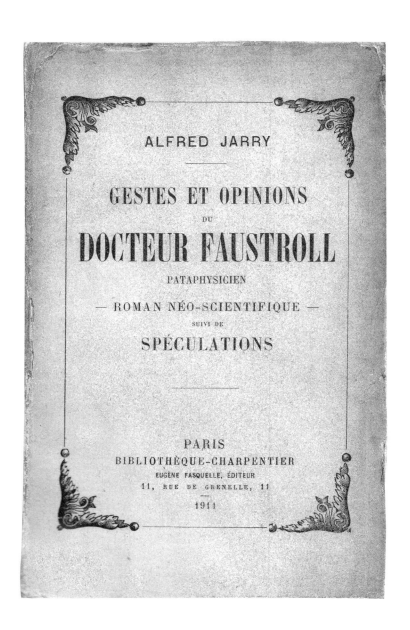

ALFRED JARRY

GESTES ET OPINIONS

DU

DOCTEUR FAUSTROLL

PATAPHYSICIEN

— ROMAN NÉO-SCIENTIFIQUE —

SUIVI DE

SPÉCULATIONS

PARIS

BIBLIOTHÈQUE-CHARPENTIER

EUGÈNE FASQUELLE, ÉDITEUR

11, RUE DE GRENELLE, 11

1911

3.1
The first edition of *Faustroll*, published
posthumously in 1911.

Jarry would later introduce his definition of the term with this statement: "An epiphenomenon is that which is superimposed upon a phenomenon." In nonspecialized language, an epiphenomenon is something that is the accidental by-product of something else. Biographically speaking, Pataphysics may be considered as the epiphenomenon of Jarry's attending the class of another teacher, Henri Bergson. His influence proved rather more expansive than Hébert's.

Jarry entered his class in 1891. In a few years Bergson would become the most famous philosopher in France; in the meantime he lectured on the history of philosophy at the Lycée Henri IV in Paris. He endowed this history with a personal slant, and his course commenced with the epistemological problems posed by the interaction of mind and matter. Otherwise, this course of Bergson's appears to have been quite as peculiar as his own philosophy; it traveled down all sorts of forgotten paths and eccentric dead-ends in the history of ideas, and any number of unusual theories were explored. Jarry was captivated: such an approach suited perfectly his jackdaw intellect, and he later wrote that Bergson's lectures were "precious above all others." Jarry followed these lectures for two years, and he transcribed them almost word for word. Uniquely among his schoolwork, he carefully preserved these notebooks, and early on entrusted them to Édouard Julia, a fellow pupil. Even though they are incomplete (the exercise books for the last half of the first year are missing), they total more than 700 pages of close writing.[2]

Ideas originating in Bergson's course would influence much of Jarry's future writing. He would often incorporate nonliterary modes within his works, but rarely without subjecting them to transformations of meaning and form. Philosophical concepts were no exception, and he habitually cited them from memory, with no great regard for accuracy. Jarry, I suspect, extended this cavalier attitude to Bergson's own philosophy, by appropriating elements from it which appealed to him, while rejecting its overall methods and conclusions. The most immediate effect of Bergson's teaching, though, was to provide the philosophical underpinning for the young Jarry's initial formulation of Pataphysics.

Shortly after arriving in Paris, Jarry had envisaged a treatise on the subject with the title *Elements of Pataphysics*. However, his notions for this new science soon ruled out a simple exposition of its subtleties. Even carefully skirting around its meanings was—and still is—apt to result in deeply unpataphysical solecisms. "Pataphysics," to paraphrase a modern exegesis by Ruy Launoir, "cannot be explained by non-pataphysical means." This is why only a small portion of Jarry's *Elements* was to appear eventually in *Faustroll*. It is also why this chapter is not intended as a complete exploration even of Jarry's own conception of this word's significance, let alone the subsequent elaborations of it by the likes of Daumal, Torma, Peillet, and Baudrillard, among others. Instead it is an attempt to outline a little of what Pataphysics may have meant for Jarry, and how it reflected his intellectual interests and his character, and perhaps influenced his life: its biographical implications, in other words.[3]

The few surviving pages of the *Elements* in *Faustroll* commence with this preamble and definition written in 1897, but based upon ideas originally formulated some four years or so earlier:

An epiphenomenon is that which is superimposed upon a phenomenon. Pataphysics […] is the science of that which is superimposed upon metaphysics, whether within or beyond the latter's limitations, extending as far beyond metaphysics as the latter extends beyond physics. And an epiphenomenon being often accidental, Pataphysics will be, above all, the science of the particular, despite the common opinion that the only science is that of the general. Pataphysics will examine the laws governing exceptions, and will explain the universe supplementary to this one; or, less ambitiously, will describe a universe which can be—and perhaps should be—envisaged in the place of the traditional one, since the laws that are supposed to have been discovered in the traditional universe are also correlations of exceptions, albeit more frequent ones, but in any case accidental data which, reduced to the status of unexceptional exceptions, possess no longer even the virtue of originality.

DEFINITION. *Pataphysics is the science of imaginary solutions, which symbolically attributes the properties of objects, described by their virtuality, to their lineaments.*[4]

This brief but elegant presentation of a new mode of thought is also a program for its application: Pataphysics will examine and explain. Although rigorously logical, and describing itself as a science, it begins with a critique of the limits of scientific induction, and then introduces a number of interlocking concepts: epiphenomenalism and the exceptional, the desirability of a "supplementary universe," imaginary solutions, and the implied superiority of "virtuality" over the actual.

Such a summary may seem to ignore an obvious characteristic of Jarry's text: his unruly logic is not entirely straight-faced. So it is quite legitimate to ask whether Pataphysics should be taken "seriously"? The answer may be found in a pataphysical principle omitted from the definition in *Faustroll*. A character in *Caesar-Antichrist* elucidates, in so far as Jarry cares for elucidation:

Axiom and principle of the identity of opposites, the pataphysician, clamped to your ears and your retractable wings, flying fish, is the dwarf atop the giant, beyond metaphysics.[5]

Thus Pataphysics incorporates the "principle of the identity of opposites," which is a philosophical idea with a history that goes back to Heraclitus. Jarry had subscribed to it even at Rennes, and may have encountered it in Coleridge, who averred his favorite proverb to be "Extremes meet." Even were this the case, Jarry certainly rediscovered it in Doctor Mises's "Comparative Anatomy of Angels," a text which he first referred to in 1894. Dr. Mises was a pseudonym initially employed by Gustav Theodor Fechner, the German scientist and philosopher, for his supposedly less serious writing, but later for works much harder to categorize. This text proved highly influential on Jarry's early ideas for Pataphysics, and one consequence of the "equivalence of contraries" was that distinctions between the serious and the comic were henceforth to be considered invalid. Jarry was introduced to Fechner's work in Bergson's lectures, and incorporating Fechner's maxim into Pataphysics also ensured it would remain quite distinct from the philosophy of Jarry's teacher, since Bergson acknowledged his own thought to be "frankly dualistic." Although Jarry's formulation of Pataphysics may well have many connections with Bergson's ideas, these connections were as often adversarial as approving.[6]

To return to Jarry's text preceding his definition. … The first thing to note is that Bergson was highly critical of epiphenomenalism, a theory which proposed that consciousness was no more than an accidental side effect of the state of the brain. Jarry, on the contrary, was so taken by this idea that he extended it to matter as well, by adopting the principle of the *clinamen*. This theory, from Lucretius's *De rerum natura*, cropped up in Bergson's lecture on determinism. Lucretius maintained that the original condition of the universe was that of an endless and uniform vertical rain of atoms into the void. A small random swerve (*clinamen*) by one of them was enough to cause an initial collision and initiate the creation of matter, and thus the universe. In Jarry's Pataphysics, a science of exceptions, both matter and mind are epiphenomenal, and are therefore immune from explanation by physics or metaphysics respectively.[7]

Jarry's digression on epiphenomena leads to the actual definition of Pataphysics. By a science of imaginary solutions Jarry appears to imply that theories should be valued for their originality, independently of meaning or efficacy. This is followed by the statement that Pataphysics, presumably as a part of its program to describe the universe supplementary to that of physics, "symbolically attributes the properties of objects, described by their virtuality, to their lineaments."

A simple reading of this would be that objects, in the widest sense, mental as well as material, should be imagined in their totality. But the word *virtuality* has a particular meaning in the philosophy of Bergson, which I suspect connects Jarry's proposition with his professor's idea of "duration." It is highly probable that Jarry had at least read Bergson's first book, *Time and Free Will, An Essay on the Immediate Data of Consciousness*, published in 1889, where this imaginary solution made its first appearance in print, since Jarry's own works refer often to this concept (he had originally been introduced to it in Bergson's lecture on "Habit").[8]

Conceptions of time are central to Jarry's works—sometimes explicitly, as in his treatise on how to construct a time machine; at other times hidden, in works that explore subjective states and modes of perception (*Days and Nights, Absolute Love*, for example). Time was likewise at the core of Bergson's philosophy. He believed that the confusing of time and space had given rise to most of the problems of philosophy, and had resulted in theoretical positions inimical to "common sense," notably in Kantian idealism, whereby the actuality of the external world is held to be only imperfectly perceptible to the mind. The time described by (Hébertian) physics, according to Bergson, was actually a form of space, since it is divisible, and one can envisage the idea of divisibility in one's mind only by assigning it spatial dimensions. (A doubtful assertion that is typical of Bergson's reasoning.) Real time, on the contrary, he considered to be a succession constructed from the instants of physical time by consciousness, perception, and memory. This is what he called duration.[9]

Bergson's duration appeared to be rather difficult to explain. "Duration," he wrote, on one of the rare occasions when he advanced a direct description, "when restored to its original purity, will appear as a wholly qualitative multiplicity, an absolute heterogeneity of elements which pass over into one another." More simply, it may be imagined as a flux of matter and memory where the actuality of objects is indistinguishable from their more subjective resonances: meanings, associations, and significance. These are the qualities which, for Bergson, constitute "virtuality." Now this is very close to Jarry's definition of Pataphysics.[10]

In pure duration, says Bergson, memory is able, by an act of will, to actualize the virtual past and project it back into the present. Bergson asserts not only that this fluid psychic state, in which reality is intensified and augmented, is "scientifically unknowable," but that its essential qualities are inexpressible. Language, he says, tends toward fixity, the opposite of duration; thus duration may be imagined only by a symbolic representation, and even then, imperfectly.[11]

Existing in duration, if nothing else, must be an intensely subjective state of being, and Bergson's description of how it might possibly be evoked resembles both Mallarmé's conceptions of Symbolist poetry, and Rimbaud's idea that a poet must become a "seer," a state in which he is able to willfully substitute the exotic for the banal, a mosque for a factory, and observe carriages traversing roads in the sky. This in its turn can be related to an idea from Taine that featured in another of Bergson's lectures, and which Jarry cited in his novel *Days and Nights*. Jarry misattributed it to Leibniz, and anyway only approximated its actual formulation: "Perception is only a hallucination that is true," is how he remembered it. Rimbaud's method of the poet making himself a seer by a "prolonged, determined and rational derangement of all the senses" is very close to this "supplementary" world where perceptions and hallucinations are indistinguishable, and the flux of constant becoming throws up objects with all their associations intact. It should be noted, however, that although Jarry was to use similar means to those of Rimbaud (drink and drugs), he could not have known of this theory of his. The seer letters were not published until 1912, and Rimbaud's biographer and brother-in-law carefully concealed their import up until that time.[12]

For Bergson, freedom could reside only in duration: free will could exist only if causality and determinism were done away with. Since duration consists of an ever-changing heterogeneity, no situation may exactly recur, and so nothing may be predetermined. The free act of the individual, defined as self-expression, is then able to emerge as an exception in a state in which everything is always exceptional, just as Pataphysics proposed. "We are rarely free," Bergson wrote. "The greater part of the time we live outside ourselves, hardly perceiving anything of ourselves but our own ghost, a colorless shadow which pure duration projects into homogeneous space. Hence [...] we live for the external world rather than for ourselves; we speak rather than think, we 'are acted' rather than act ourselves. To act freely is to recover possession of oneself, and to get back into pure duration."[13]

The concept of duration was intended by Bergson to resolve problems in epistemology and return philosophy to "common sense." It resulted in an ever more complex metaphysics that became distinctly remote from this goal. Physics, too, was prone to similar imaginary solutions. In the 1890s this most tangible of sciences was being forced into ever more extreme and counter-intuitive theories in order to explain observed phenomena. Thus, in Jarry's day, the universe was supposedly filled with an invisible and undetectable substance called "luminiferous ether," which had been proposed to explain the wave propagation of light. According to physicists, in

Jarry's words, it consisted of a "perfectly elastic and infinitely attenuated solid." This ultimately insubstantial substance, rather reminiscent of today's "dark energy," was the chief component of a theory of matter proposed by William Thomson, Lord Kelvin of Largs, by far the most celebrated scientist of the period. According to Kelvin, matter consisted only of vortices within the ether. Bergson despaired of such theories. Physics, he believed, was being taken to such levels of abstraction that "concrete existence was tending to vanish into algebraical smoke." Jarry, on the contrary, could not have been more delighted. That reality was tenuous conformed perfectly with Symbolist aesthetics and his own intuitions. Nothing could be more poetic; and Kelvin makes frequent appearances in *Faustroll*.[14]

Thus Jarry absorbed the more extravagant solutions of both physics and metaphysics into his new science. Here was a new space inhabited by a new matter enduring within a new time: a supplementary continuum lying to one side of everyday life. Jarry called it Ethernity in *Faustroll*; elsewhere it became The Absolute. Nevertheless, the imaginary solution *par excellence* was literature, and the real beauty of all these concepts lay in the fact that they were ripe for poetic transmutation. Kelvin's theories featured in *Faustroll* precisely because it was a work of literature and not of theory: Jarry was a poet above all else. He plundered theory for Pataphysics, but he plundered everything for his writing, including Pataphysics itself. Indeed, if one were to reduce Pataphysics to literature, then the definition proposes a literature as far beyond Symbolism (metaphysics) as this was from Naturalism (physics), one in which expression is imbued with its opposites, tragedy is inseparable from irony, the hoax from the heartfelt, a literature at once frivolous and hermetic: in sum, all the literary faults of which Jarry was to be accused.

This chapter may, after all, have attributed to Bergson too great an influence on Jarry during his first years in Paris. He poked fun at his professor in *Faustroll*—the list of dualities symbolized by the words "Ha Ha" includes "magnitude and duration," and whatever Bergson's influence, the implications of Jarry's definition remain. The qualifier "symbolically" indicates that Pataphysics is a science of interpretation, of will and representation, or, more especially, of imagination in both its literal and figurative meanings. It is a method for augmenting actuality with the virtual, whether in Bergson's sense or otherwise, and this alone would ally it with the poetic theories already cited.[15]

In this interpretation, Pataphysics was an appeal for an intensification of existence, for a supplementary universe in which imagination would have a reality equivalent to that of the actual. Such a proposal might not initially appear a particularly original poetic credo, but Jarry's statement of it in philosophical and, especially, scientific terminology was not only distinctly novel, but laid the foundations of its future influence. Jarry would reinterpret this first poetic version of Pataphysics with a more "scientific" formulation, and it is this variant of the "science" that would lend itself more easily to elaboration by others. His literary contemporaries considered science a rather vulgar activity, but physics and mathematics employed symbols too, and Jarry recognized the literary and imaginative potential of their increasing abstraction. As time passed and Jarry's circumstances altered, Pataphysics would indeed assume subtly different meanings. Initially, however, in his first conception, it may be seen as an unusually systematic mapping of the realm of the poetic imagination, a symbolic cartography that was both representation and idealization. It included previously neglected regions that were ripe for exploration, and it was Jarry's idea to substitute the map for the territory: "he wanted his life to conform to his literary program," in the words of Rachilde—a predilection that was likely to bring travelers in this realm up sharp against the conventions of the everyday.[16]

Couching an appeal for the superiority of a poetic universe in the language of rationality was itself an eminently pataphysical procedure. Pataphysics was able to seamlessly assimilate contradictions, or at least relegate them to the status of unimportant ambiguities. As a representation, it reflected Jarry's contrary nature; it was an almost inevitable product of his temperament. As a willful philosophy, it may be seen initially as his attempt to resolve these contradictions by elevating them into a basic principle and then codifying them as a discipline. The epiphenomenon of this approach was the creation of a conveniently unanswerable rationale for his contrariness. Pataphysics, therefore, could be either (or both) a tool for psychic integration or a license for dissipation; and Jarry's life would unfold between these options.

4

1891–1893

The refinements of Pataphysics lay a little in the future when Jarry, aged seventeen, first arrived in Paris. This city was already the undisputed cultural center of the world, and would remain so at least until the 1930s. Momentous social changes were in the air. Intimations of the coming century were unmistakable, and either feared or keenly anticipated. An enormous cast-iron construction rose up from the center of the city. The Eiffel Tower, completed in 1889, was then the tallest man-made structure in existence.

Depending on one's tastes, inclinations, and social situation, the 1890s were either the *Belle Époque*, a virile culmination of French culture promising a yet more glorious future; or the *fin-de-siècle*, the last gasp of an enfeebled civilization on the verge of extinction. For some, a time of extravagance; for others, especially the rapidly expanding working classes, one of daily struggle. Wealth and poverty were bound together in close proximity, and political upheavals were the frequent outcome—only twenty years had passed since the brutal suppression of the Paris Commune, when the state liquidated between 10,000 and 50,000 of its own citizens in a more or less perfunctory manner. The very vagueness of the figure was symptomatic of its indifference. Culturally, however, the 1890s were particularly propitious times to be young and Parisian, as Jarry and his friends were well aware. One of them, Francis Jourdain, called his memoirs *Born in '76*, since this meant having the good fortune of being twenty in 1896. And in Paris, because "we loved Paris as we loved life itself."[1]

The French capital was not only a political and cultural hothouse, it was also the European capital of pleasure. The toleration of lifestyles considered deviant elsewhere in Europe attracted rich dissolutes, along with penurious artists and writers who here perfected the bohemian life, that precarious combination of poverty and excess. Tiny hands were frozen, in the sentimental versions of this existence immortalized by Murger and Puccini, but its romantic assumptions could also prove fatal. Artists and poets were indeed starving in garrets. For every Mallarmé or Huysmans, a teacher and a civil servant respectively, there were others following an existence decreed by bohemian tradition. Most abandoned the struggle; but some were destroyed by it.

One of the more boisterous centers of bohemian Paris was the Latin Quarter, and it was here that Jarry's mother took an apartment. Her son was to spend a substantial portion of his life within a few hundred yards of this first address.

...

Paris — Lycée Henri IV. — Façade.

4.1
The Lycée Henri IV. The main staircase.

4.2
The school courtyard, site of the *bizuthage*. In Jarry's day it probably lacked lawns and planting.

4.3
The *lycée* exterior.

Madame and Alfred Jarry arrived in the capital in June 1891 and took lodgings at 11, rue Cujas. She presumably chose this neighborhood not for its literary associations, or the famous cafés lining the nearby Boul' Mich, but for its proximity to the Lycée Henri IV. Here Jarry was to sit the examinations to enter the prestigious (and oddly named, to English ears) École normale supérieure. He failed them. This was hardly surprising: entry was exceptionally difficult; only twenty-five humanities students were accepted annually from the whole of France. Successful candidates usually came from a special cramming class at the Lycée Henri IV, which Jarry joined later in the year. Thus, in October he entered the class known as the Rhétorique supérieure, or to its pupils as the *khâgne*, whose specific task was to get its pupils through the ENS exams. Here he found another school culture as rich as that of Rennes, with its own language and customs. The forbidding appearance of the school, once a monastery, implies much about its modes of tuition and discipline.[2]

As in Rennes, Jarry was once more the provincial in the big city, but this time quite literally so. He knew no one in Paris, and his accent marked him out. He even looked like a Breton, or at least his features conformed to Parisian prejudices in this respect. Bretons were thought of as round-faced, small, stocky: peasants, in other words. Nevertheless, he made friends quickly, and it is not surprising, given the high-pressure class he was attending, that a number of them became moderately celebrated authors and critics in later years, including Albert Thibaudet, Louis Laloy, Jean Chantavoine, and André Rivoire. He made other friends with whom he remained in contact after leaving Henri IV, the most significant being Édouard Julia, François-Benoît Claudius-Jacquet, and Léon-Paul Fargue, all of whom will reappear later in this narrative.[3]

Another classmate was even more the provincial than Jarry, and with a more outlandish accent. The future poet Gandilhon Gens-d'Armes came from the Auvergne, and spoke its dialect; he was the only one of Jarry's contemporaries to leave a substantial memoir of him from this period. This, he says, was because their peers were old before their time, and even out of class were too engrossed in their schoolwork to pay attention to frivolities such as Jarry's paradoxes.[4]

Jarry, according to Gens-d'Armes, was a conscientious pupil, but he was unable to restrain his irony—even when acknowledging the appreciation of his teachers. Gens-d'Armes recalls the Latin master, Monsieur Edet, congratulating Jarry on his written composition: "Very stylish Latin, Monsieur Jarry, excellent! Perhaps you could tell us which author has particularly informed your style?" "Aristophanes," Jarry replied, to derisive laughter in the class, but he went on to explain that he was, of course, referring to the Latin footnotes to the Greek author's text, where the editor glossed over the obscene passages to be found in the original. Monsieur Edet was not amused.

One of the rituals of the *khâgne* was an initiation reserved for new pupils. In the *bizuthage* they must improvise a speech on some unlikely topic decided upon by their elders. Mounting a sort of bollard in the school courtyard, Jarry confronted his audience, who, after some discussion, settled upon: Turkestan.

"Turkestan! A magnificent subject, and fortunately one with which I am perfectly conversant. The Orient, my friends, the unfathomable Orient …" In a moment he was discoursing on the Turks,

Istanbul, Pierre Loti, Aziyadé. ... Recalled to the subject at hand, he protested: "The subject! What else am I discussing? Since when is a digression out of order? Why, Cicero himself in the *Pro Milone* ... Seneca too was of the same opinion ... and we must not forget Quintilian, gentlemen. ..." Turkestan made a reappearance for a few seconds, only to be followed by a rapid sequence of topics strung together with intricate and faultless eloquence, the terrestrial Paradise, Genghis Khan, Persian poetry, Mehmed II, Saint Sophia, the Suez canal, whatever else could be imagined. The audience was submerged, and then the bell rang. "Gentlemen, we have only managed to consider the most preliminary aspects of this vast subject, albeit not too inadequately. We shall return to the subject tomorrow, at the point where this swinish bell is forcing us to stop."

He never did return to it, but henceforth I found Jarry's mental processes disturbing. When he let himself go he seemed in thrall to a torrent of words outside his control. It was no longer a person speaking, but a machine controlled by a demon. His staccato voice, metallic and nasal, his abrupt puppet-like gestures, his fixed expression and uncontrollable flood of language, his grotesque and brilliant turns of phrase, ended up provoking a feeling of disquiet. He was informed, intelligent, and discriminating; he was a good person, secretly kind, perhaps even shy beneath it all [...] but his originality resembled nothing short of a mental anomaly.[5]

In this account, written a decade later, Jarry appears already to have assumed the vocal manner-isms of Ubu. Yet when Charles-Henry Hirsch met him not long afterward, he remembered a "soft-spoken and thoughtful adolescent," whose life was "prudent and self-disciplined." There is no contradiction: when Jarry performed, he assumed the Ubuesque; it was a disguise reserved for more public occasions. It had the additional advantage of cloaking Jarry's provincial accent, which is perhaps why he more often assumed it in the company of strangers.[6]

As we have seen, Henri Bergson taught philosophy and its history at Henri IV, and Jarry's extensive notes on his course prove he could be studious when so inclined. He also had engrossing outside interests. In a rare autobiographical aside he later noted that "he got carried away [...] by theories it was impossible not to feel all around him: anarchism, Ibsenism, etc." His enthusiasms also included more popular entertainments, especially the circuses and pantomimes, elements of which he would later incorporate into his own stage productions. So far as his own writing is concerned, there is nothing that can be assigned definitively to this period other than a brief text whose title and location suggest it was written then, despite its nonexistent date: "Mémoire expli-catif du terrible accident du 30 février 1891." An exercise in absurdity, it describes Paris sweltering in a heat wave, the Seine cluttered with blocks of ice large as pumpkins, while fish float upon the water and, faint with thirst, emit horrible shrieks from the third story of the Eiffel Tower.[7]

...

In April 1892, the future poet Léon-Paul Fargue became a pupil at Henri IV. He and Jarry became close friends, and almost certainly more than friends. It is generally assumed that this was Jarry's first serious homosexual relationship (a topic that is covered in a little more detail in chapter 7). Fargue registered at the school under his mother's name of Aussudre, because he was born illegitimate and was not recognized by his father until after he entered the school. His parents did not actually marry until 1907. These inconvenient family relationships perhaps lie at the root of Fargue's endless reinvention of his past. To put it more bluntly, he was a confirmed liar. His close friends were well aware of this; Francis Jourdain, for example, recalled that his "reputation as a mythomaniac, mythologue, mythophiliac, and mytholaster was firmly established. […] It was no easy matter to navigate the labyrinth in which Fargue pursued truth in order first to capture and then misrepresent it. Fargue never told the truth to anyone."[8]

Fargue's reports from his previous school had been far from complimentary. His history master was especially harsh: "Detestable pupil, the class would be well rid of him"; and his languages teacher noted that Fargue's only successful activity seemed to be discovering ingenious ways of squandering his abilities. Being two and a half years younger than Jarry, he had yet to sit his *bac*, although he later claimed they were in the same class.[9]

According to Fargue, Jarry was "already a poet, very much the artist, and as a person, affectionate, even sentimental. He spoke rapidly, in a clear and attractive voice; there was nothing of that false curtness or the Ubuesque mannerisms that he adopted later on." They wandered all over the city, especially through its more unknown and decaying districts. This is a Parisian tradition of course, but they were not exactly dandyish *flâneurs*: Jarry sported an "unreasonably large round hat, a veritable observatory, which was certainly bought in the provinces," and a cape that, on account of his small stature, fell to his feet. "We felt as if we were making great journeys of exploration. One of our favorite excursions was along the banks of the Bièvre, still an open river then, an amazing place that reminded us of the drawings of Victor Hugo. We found a wonderful observation post by pushing through a fence into an enclosed yard guarded by large dogs (chained up luckily). We spent long periods there, motionless, watching clumps of tanner's bark glide through the filthy water, imagining it was some river from Hell."[10]

Other times they traveled through the city by *impériale* (a horse- or motor-driven double-decker bus with an open top), and found sources of reverie in the bizarre shop signs—a giant silver thimble, a locksmith's enormous key—and in briefly glimpsed scenes in passing windows: "We leafed through the boulevards as if through a book." It may be no coincidence that the hiatus in Jarry's philosophical note-taking coincided with Fargue's arrival at the school.[11]

Fargue was Jarry's first truly Parisian friend, one already familiar with the art and writing of his day, and he even had some literary connections. It may have been he who introduced Jarry to the work of the new generation of writers, the Symbolists, although a number of his other friends shared this enthusiasm. Claudius-Jacquet was one, and Édouard Julia, with whom Jarry spent many hours studying in his parents' book-lined home; and it was Thibaudet who first showed him the poetry of Rimbaud. Jarry immersed himself in the works of Mallarmé, Schwob, Quillard, Maeterlinck, Verhaeren, and Saint-Pol-Roux. At the Sainte-Geneviève library, near Henri IV, he read the ephemeral little magazines of the past ten years: *Scapin*, the *Décadent*, as well as those still being published, in particular the *Mercure de France*. And the bookshops: there was Vanier's, the famous publisher of the Decadent poets, of Verlaine and Rimbaud; and Edmond Bailly's, "whose windows," Jarry wrote, "sandwiched the earliest books of Régnier and Louÿs between pastels by Odilon Redon." He was overawed: "that phrase from Revelation would not be too far-fetched: 'The heaven departed as a scroll when it is rolled together; and every mountain and island were moved out of their places.'"[12]

In June 1892, the eighteen-year-old Jarry sat his exams once more. His results the previous December had put him in the top half of the class, but although his examination scores had improved (except in philosophy, despite all his note-taking) they were still not good enough for him to enter the ENS. Fargue may or may not have passed the first part of his *bac*, according to whether one believes him or no; one assumes not. The two of them then spent part of the summer vacation visiting art galleries. Fargue at this time envisaged a future as an artist rather than a poet. His father had founded a ceramics and stained-glass business, which produced works designed by Maurice Denis, Carlos Schwab, Gauguin, and Filiger: the major names of the new generation of painters associated with Symbolism, the Nabis, and Post-Impressionism. One can still see examples of his work at the famous Brasserie Lipp. Fargue "knew everyone."[13]

> We began looking at art, both in studios and galleries. At Durand-Ruel we met Gauguin around
> 1895. […] We often went to Le Barc's gallery, he was the first to show Lautrec, Bonnard,
> Vuillard, Roussel, Sérusier, Ranson and others whose works are now forgotten but who never-
> theless enchanted us, such as Jan Verkade and Filiger. There was nothing like it in Paris then,
> apart from Père Tanguy's shop. […] Pointless to describe Père Tanguy, everyone nowadays
> knows the portrait of him by Van Gogh. He had part of a small cobbler's shop in the rue Clauzel
> painted a pale duck-egg blue. In one window were customers' shoes awaiting collection, prices
> marked with chalk on their soles, and tins of shoe polish. The other was crammed with paintings
> by Van Gogh, Cézanne, Maximilien Luce, Gauguin and Émile Bernard, among others. They were
> priced between 30 and 100 francs. Once when visiting his shop he told us: "I have something new!"
> It was Cézanne's *Man with a Pipe*. "How much is it?" asked Jourdain, out of interest. "Oh, I
> couldn't let this one go for less than 200 francs!" But we hadn't a sou between us.[14]

This account compresses events from 1892 and 1893, the latter being the actual date of their first meeting with Gauguin, and introduces a number of figures who became important to both Fargue and Jarry. Francis Jourdain recalled first meeting Fargue when the latter was still at Henri IV. They had met through the artist Fabien Launay, who had encountered Fargue at an exhibition at Le Barc's: "An astonishing fellow!" Launay reported. Typically, Fargue had told him he was a student, not a schoolboy.[15]

Jourdain, nineteen or twenty at the time, already knew personally most of the artists mentioned by Fargue. His father Frantz was a famous modern architect and designer with many literary and artistic friends. Among his varied activities in later life (art critic, artist, furniture and ceramics designer, Communist activist), Francis Jourdain was the art director for Jean Vigo's masterpiece *L'Atalante*, and perhaps also for his previous film (no one is credited) *Zéro de*

Conduite, which would help explain the eerie resemblance of the physics teacher featured in it to F.-F. Hébert. Jourdain left vivid memoirs of his youth, and was another keen wanderer of the byways of Paris, one of his favorite locales being the Bièvre.[16]

Soon Fargue and Jarry met some of Jourdain's other friends from the Lycée Condorcet. It was Jourdain who initially directed Fargue and Jarry's tastes in art, and it was he who was the focus of a group which, apart from Fargue, Jarry, and Launay, included the poet Maurice Cremnitz, the painters Georges Bottini and Léonard Sarluis, Maurice Thomas (who became the prolific film director Maurice Tourneur), the future collector of the Impressionists, Louis Rouart, and the writer and critic Gaston de Pawlowski. They were all more or less the same age, and apart from cultural pursuits, some (Launay, Bottini, Pawlowski) shared Jarry's enthusiasm for cycling and frequented the velodromes around Paris. Some, too, were openly homosexual (Cremnitz and Sarluis). Mostly they were to be found in the cafés and cabarets of Montmartre—a little too often, perhaps. Both Launay and Bottini died young of illnesses exacerbated by the consumption of immense quantities of alcohol. Their paintings were then neglected for many years, but appear to be undergoing a reevaluation at the present moment.[17]

In a matter of months, since arriving in Paris, Jarry had acquired a rapid conversance with the art and writing of his most immediate contemporaries. Not only that, but all this literary and artistic fervor was on his very doorstep, in close proximity to the *lycée*. It should be no wonder that his schoolwork suffered some neglect. But his most important literary discovery was not a contemporary, but an author who had died, aged twenty-four, just a few years before Jarry was born.

4.4
Félix Vallotton, The Comte de Lautréamont.
An imaginary portrait, since no likeness
of the author was then known.

One could hardly envisage a more perfectly malign influence on the young student than the works of Isidore Ducasse, the self-styled Comte de Lautréamont. Quite when Jarry came across *Les Chants de Maldoror* is uncertain. Fargue claims to have introduced Jarry to his writing, but their fellow pupil Thibaudet was also an enthusiast, and the authors Léon Bloy and Remy de Gourmont had alerted their readers to his works in the *Mercure de France* (in January and February 1891 respectively).[18]

Lautréamont's text was first published in full in 1869 and reprinted twice before Jarry read it, yet censorship problems meant it remained a rare book, and it was not made more generally available in France until 1920. The book's influence on Jarry was profound. Its casual jeering blasphemy and contemptuous dismissal of all morality, whether divine or man-made, was extraordinary enough, its overblown rhetorical style even more so. Yet what made Lautréamont truly unique was the way in which he repeatedly brought the reader up short with a directly addressed remark, or by some deliberately inappropriate and sardonic observation: it was this ironic autophagy that constituted the chief innovation of *Les Chants de Maldoror*.

> It is a magnificent, almost inexplicable stroke of genius, which from now on belongs to that list of works which forms […] the only possible reading of those whose ill-made spirits will not lend themselves to the joys of the commonplace; or of conventional morality. […] How many carefully considered and honest pages of good and simple writing would I give for these shovelfuls of words and phrases beneath which he seems to have wanted to inter reason itself.[19]

Maldoror, despite this eulogy by Remy de Gourmont, was still little known outside the core of Symbolist writers, and the full extent of its impact on Jarry's inner life and opinions remains a matter of conjecture, although it would hardly incline him toward conventionality. In contrast, its immediate effect on his writing is obvious: parts of his first book were grotesquely Maldororian in style. A more lasting and constructive influence was Lautréamont's use of irony and humor in an apparently serious work. The key mechanism he employed, as we have noted, was the direct address to the reader, but Jarry was to find a way of burying this subversion at a deeper level in the text. Henceforth, the humorous and the serious, comedy and tragedy, would coexist in his work. It is also hard to resist a comparison that Jarry himself may have noted: between the persons of Ubu and Maldoror. Both are unrestrained and tempestuous beings bent only on pitiless self-gratification and revenge.

...

At about the same time that Jarry re-registered at Henri IV in September 1892, so as to make a further attempt on the ENS, he and his mother moved from the rue Cujas. His mother took an apartment at 84, boulevard de Port-Royal, to the south of Henri IV, but she also rented two rooms for Jarry close by, which became the first of his several unusual residences. Here he, and Fargue, were free to read, write, receive friends. Jarry named it the *Calvaire du Trucidé*—literally, Calvary of the Slaughtered.[20]

4.5, 4.6
Jarry's "Calvary." The door to Jarry's rooms in the alleyway; view down the alleyway to the boulevard de Port-Royal.

In the mid-1970s it was still possible to walk down this alleyway where Jarry's tiny apartment had once been. It was a strange situation, a row of three-story houses which should have been looking out on to a street but instead faced, at a distance of only four or five feet, the twenty-foot-high stone wall that surrounds the Val-de-Grâce hospital. The whole frontage of this short terrace of houses was consequently overshadowed, and the alleyway in deep gloom whatever the time of day. Jarry's rooms were on the first floor; visitors were directed to follow the bloody handprints up the tortuous staircase, and his permanently nocturnal apartment was the perfect habitat for Jarry's new companions: owls, free to fly about, or sleep, as they wished. He explained their attraction: "the unthinking presume they are malefic, since they sleep during the day and awaken at night, and their crooked beaks are preposterously shaped and utterly inconvenient." Almost certainly they had been tempted across the wall from the hospital gardens with offerings of raw meat, and did not live there permanently. Arnaud reported that the owls of Val-de-Grâce were still on good terms with the local residents in the 1970s, and would perch on the wall surrounding the gardens. As for their nocturnal habits, Jarry too had already adopted them, according to Rachilde. She says he mostly slept during the day and went out at night.[21]

Jarry took his meals at Chez Ernest, a cheap café on the rue Saint-Jacques, then a lively thoroughfare in a predominantly working-class part of the city. The clientele and owners soon became firm friends, a regular part of his daily life, and they were also to play their part in the performances of *Ubu Roi*. The café, close to the southern exit of the alleyway in which the Calvary was situated, was patronized by painters, writers, "thinkers" … and the sewermen from the Compagnie Richer, whose odor tended to deter more respectable customers from entering the establishment. Jarry's grace before eating found favor with his fellow diners, we are told: "We offer our thanks to Divine Providence for furnishing us with two eyes, just in case we lose one, but with only one mouth, since it's not so easy to miss a hole." The joke depends rather on "lose" and "miss" being the same word in French.[22]

Fargue had also re-registered at Henri IV, and there is a class photograph of him that dates from this time (Jarry is of course not shown, since it was a different class). Fargue had by now acquired his companion's literary interests, and judged that his endeavors justified an appearance in print. "Luckily," he recalled, "Cremnitz had the particular great good fortune to be on friendly terms with the editor of a review, whose third issue had just appeared: *L'Art littéraire*. This person, a character to whom we would not normally have been drawn, was called Louis Libaude, a civil servant what's more, an official auction valuer who specialized in the sale of horses."[23]

Libaude, whose literary pen name was Louis Lormel, aroused strong antipathies in some. Around 1905, he became an art dealer, and John Richardson, in his biography of Picasso, described him then as "a Dickensian villain who had swindled so many local artists that when he did the rounds of the studios on the Butte [Montmartre], he slunk along in the shadow of buildings and carried a revolver for fear of attack." Jourdain, for his part, remembered him as having "the far-from-pleasant countenance of a vaguely crapulous Jesuit."[24]

Fargue's recollection was inevitably incorrect; he must have met Lormel before the third number of *L'Art littéraire*, published in February 1893, since his first published text, a sonnet,

PARIS — Rue Saint-Jacques - Bazar du Val de Grâce

4.7
The rue Saint-Jacques in Jarry's day (and the cyclist
bears more than a passing resemblance to him).
Chez Ernest is the second shop front on the left past the
"Bazar," and the exit from the alleyway was two doors
beyond that. In the distance, the last building on the left,
at the end of the street, is no. 84, where Jarry's mother
lived, since this is the corner of the rue Saint-Jacques
and the boulevard de Port-Royal.

4.8
Léon-Paul Fargue (top left, with hands on hips)
at the Lycée Henri IV, circa 1892.

4.9
The earliest surviving image of Jarry, from a class
photograph taken at the Lycée Henri IV in the
spring of 1893.

actually appeared in this issue. Jarry had similar ambitions, but somewhere a little more prestigious perhaps? And in the event, it could not have been simpler.

The Paris newspaper *L'Écho de Paris* issued a weekly literary supplement edited by two prominent authors of the day, Marcel Schwob and Catulle Mendès. Every month there was an open competition by anonymous submission, with a 100-franc prize for four winners (one for poetry, three for prose). In February, Jarry submitted an untitled poem, later to be included in his first book *Les Minutes de sable mémorial*. He was jointly awarded the poetry prize, and his poem appeared on March 19, 1893. The following month he won one of the prose prizes with "Guignol," also to be incorporated into *Minutes*, and later into *Ubu cocu*. Thus was the person of Père Ubu first revealed in print, and here he also uttered the words "Pataphysics is a science which we have invented, and for which a crying need is generally experienced." A momentous event, and it is worth underlining that Mendès and Schwob, both well qualified to judge this anonymously submitted text, easily recognized its literary merit. The general subversion of the Ubu texts lies in the contrast between the vulgarity of their content and their elegant and self-knowing literary style, on this occasion certainly the exclusive work of Jarry.

Jarry appears to have assumed that it was Mendès who was chiefly responsible for his promotion to published author, and he did not forget, as effusively inscribed copies of his future books bear witness. Jarry and Schwob also became friends and he began to frequent the latter's home, two tiny rooms overflowing with books and papers. He presumably also attended the regular meetings of contributors to *L'Écho* at the Café d'Harcourt on the boulevard Saint-Michel. Entry into literary circles appeared easy for him.[25]

...

Most accounts of Jarry's life assume that during the early months of 1893 he suffered a long unspecified illness. The source is his sister's *Notes*, which state succinctly: "[he] falls ill, his mother and sister came to him, his mother remained at his bedside for forty days during the winter, she saved him, then died herself nine days later." Jarry's mother died on May 10, which would mean an illness beginning at the end of March (not exactly midwinter).[26]

At almost the same moment, Fargue was dispatched by his parents to Coburg in Germany, the pretext being to polish his German so as to improve his chances in his *bac*. A strange decision during term time, and in fact there were more urgent reasons. His parents had become increasingly concerned about his "friendship" with the older Jarry, and there were some legal difficulties too about Fargue's registration at the school because of his illegitimacy. The trip to Germany was a punishment, as epistolary sermons from his father made plain: Léon-Paul was to buckle down and work at his German, never mind if he was bored out of his wits. Within days, however, he was in trouble again. Fargue senior wrote to forbid him from seeing "a young man who is too old for you." After two months Fargue was summoned back home, although his father balked at his returning to Henri IV. Whether he actually did or not, it made no difference: in July he failed his *bac* with spectacularly poor marks.[27]

Jarry and Fargue had corresponded during the latter's absence, although not all that frequently. Jarry kept Fargue's letters, but Fargue did not keep his, or at least they have never been found. Fargue's correspondence is revealing, being almost the only firsthand evidence regarding their relationship. Although these letters are warm, nothing in them implies a more intimate association than an enthusiastic literary friendship, though this may have been simple discretion in the circumstances.

Fargue's first letter to Jarry, dated April 16, would have arrived during his mortal illness. Nevertheless, Fargue's next letter (May 5) thanks him for his reply, which at least shows that Jarry was well enough to write back. Fargue asked Jarry to send him his writings, and to describe in detail events at the offices of *L'Écho de Paris*. Jarry had met Mendès and probably Schwob during his absence, and his being invited to spectate at their editorial meetings rather eclipsed the literary introductions that Fargue had so far engineered. Fargue wanted news of exhibitions, of events at Henri IV, of mutual friends. He had returned to Paris around May 23, and his last two missives were short telegrams arranging to meet Jarry in the reading room of the Sainte-Geneviève library. It was too risky to meet at school; news might get back to his parents.[28]

• • •

In a telegram to another school friend, Édouard Julia, on May 6, 1893, Jarry declined an invitation to a dinner in honor of Mendès—and presided over by Schwob (to whom Julia is asked to present his especial apologies)—because of his mother's bronchitis, as he felt unable to leave her until she was out of danger. On the 10th she died, at the age of fifty.[29]

There is almost nothing more to say. The depth of Jarry's affection toward his mother can hardly be doubted, but he never confided his feelings about this sudden bereavement to anyone, or at least to anyone who has left a record of it. The loss of his letters to his sister is particularly significant at such moments. There was a memorial service the next day, the notice of which he preserved in his papers. Caroline was buried in the Quernest family tomb in Rennes. Various commentators have discerned signs of Jarry's grief in passages from *Minutes*, but they require fairly determined reading to yield such results. It cannot be a coincidence, though, that his next published text was "Lieds funèbres" (Funeral Lieder), written in May and published by *L'Écho* in June, Jarry again winning one of the prose prizes. This was followed by a fourth prize and the publication of "Opium" in August.

In July the entrance examinations for the ENS made their annual reappearance, and once again Jarry failed, once again with higher but still inadequate grades. It was his last attempt, and he did not return to Henri IV. His burgeoning literary career already offered more than academic qualifications.

• • •

Following the debacle of his exam results, Fargue's parents seem to have given up on him, and allowed him to pursue his interest in painting. In late August or September 1893, Fargue and Maurice Thomas headed off to the artists' colony around Pont-Aven in western Brittany. They took rooms in an annex to the Pension Gloanec, made famous by its association with Gauguin, who was then in Tahiti. The countryside around Pont-Aven was teeming with artists: a current website lists twenty-three active at this time, and these are only the better known among them. Fargue settled down to painting and his letters to his mother stress how hard he is working, while making repeated appeals for funds.[30]

Fargue and Thomas made the acquaintance of one of the least sociable of the Pont-Aven artists, but one in whom Jarry and Fargue already had an interest after seeing his works at Le Barc's: Charles Filiger. Something of a recluse even then, Filiger in later life became increasingly isolated, convinced that art dealers were in league to exploit him. It may be that this paranoia was already taking hold. He needed careful handling.[31]

Filiger's letters to Fargue have recently come to light. The first of them, after Fargue's initial visit to Filiger's studio, is warm and affectionate. He thanks him for his visit and regrets not giving him a painting he had admired. What next occurred is uncertain, except Fargue evidently took advantage of his kindness—at least Filiger thought so. His next letter, and another to a friend, asserted that not only had Fargue "extorted money" from him, but he had taken away a number of paintings which he proposed to offer to Le Barc. Filiger demanded their immediate return and informed Fargue that he was writing to Le Barc to tell him that he had not sanctioned this arrangement. "As for the rest, I trust you will treat me with more respect when you return to Paris." The trip ended badly for Fargue and Thomas. According to Filiger they fled Pont-Aven at night so as to avoid paying their hotel bill. They were detained by the gendarmerie while attempting to board a train at Quimperlé railway station.[32]

· · ·

September 8, 1893 was Jarry's twentieth birthday, and he returned to his father's house in the rue de Bootz in time for it. In celebration, Anselme spent 200 francs on tailored clothes for his son, including an overcoat for 70 francs. The fabric was chosen, fittings were made, and the result was presented to Jarry in early October. Now a Parisian, he declined the overcoat on the grounds that its cut was too "vague," and returned it to the tailor for modifications. These too failed to meet with his approval and he asked for further changes, which the tailor refused to undertake, whereupon Jarry's father declined to pay for it. Eventually, after a court judgment and the appointment of bailiffs, Jarry senior was persuaded to settle the bill, with extras to compensate for the tailor's inconvenience. Jarry was not to be so fastidious about his apparel for long, although most of the few photographs of him at this period have him in wing collars and cravat.[33]

Jarry and Fargue had both returned to Paris, and they resumed their rounds of the art galleries, the most important exhibition being the first presentation of Gauguin's Tahitian paintings at Durand-Ruel in November 1893. This is when Jarry and he met for the first time; Fargue was now writing art criticism for *L'Art littéraire*. They also called in at Ambroise Vollard's gallery nearby, and wrote the very first reviews it received. Vollard would play a role in the Ubu cult a few years later, and presumably he and Jarry remained on friendly terms from this first meeting.[34]

In October Henri Morin moved to Paris to attend the École Polytechnique. He visited Jarry at the Calvary, where he could see no sign of any literary activity. "He did not receive many visitors. [...] The only inhabitants were 2 or 3 pairs of owls dozing on the furniture, which was liberally covered with their droppings, a fact that seemed not to concern him." Not only droppings: others recalled chunks of raw meat dropped from a beak and falling to the floor with a dull thud, there to remain indefinitely stuck. The profusion of owls may be an exaggeration, and anyway, Jarry had kept on his mother's apartment after her death and was probably living and working there most of the time. In November he finished a translation of Coleridge's "The Rime of the Ancient Mariner."[35]

...

On November 9, 1893, Alfred Jarry went to the theater, and the evening's entertainment proved most instructive. One of the central tenets of Symbolism was that of "synthesis," which derived especially from Wagner's conception of the *Gesamtkunstwerk*, or "total artwork." Many of the Symbolists were great admirers of the German composer, and they shared his opinion that the obvious place for a synthesis of art forms to occur was on the stage. However, the earliest attempts to found a Symbolist theater in Paris had been only partially successful.

French theater history records that in 1893, Lugné-Poe and Camille Mauclair decided to take over Paul Fort's ailing Théâtre d'Art; and that they renamed it the Théâtre de l'Œuvre. In fact, they had decided to mount a single performance of Maeterlinck's *Pelléas and Mélisande*, and the founding of a new theater company, the Œuvre, followed unintentionally. *Œuvre* in French has similar meanings to "work" in English: work as a task, and a work of art; and Pierre Bonnard's logo for the new venture depicted a laborer with a pickaxe rolling up his sleeves and about to hack away at … an exquisite piece of dramatic art, perhaps? Francis Jourdain cannot have been the only one to interpret the pile of stones behind the toiling workman as an anarchist barricade.[36]

Fort's attempts at producing a Symbolist theater had suffered from a lack both of funds and of professionalism—hardly surprising, since he was only eighteen when he founded his company. Its innovations (on one occasion the audience was doused with different perfumes during the performance) failed to disguise its amateurism, which restricted it to a somewhat specialist audience. The magazine *La Plume* informed its readers that it was patronized by wild-haired revolutionaries and by "decadento-instrumento-maeterlincko-symbolist poets, neo-traditionalo-pointillo-impressionist or non-pointillo-impressionist painters."[37]

Lugné-Poe, however, had trained at the Académie, and had practical experience in both amateur and professional companies. He thought it should be possible to create a theater that at least partially pursued Fort's Symbolist aims, but with a wider repertory, and a practical expertise which could attract a more varied public. Tidings of the new theater provoked extravagant expectations among Jarry's friends: "Sensational news. [...] Beside the names of Ibsen and Maeterlinck, the newspaper announcements carried other names unknown to us, more Scandinavian than even we could have hoped for, magnificently impossible to pronounce, men of mystery who promised distant fjords and new truths which would change our old world. We quivered with impatience and expectation. Already we thought we could discern the distant rumbling of storms, low growls against which we would pitch the clear cries of our youth. We hardly knew who was to be the enemy; we would be fighting a vague yet noble cause, whose greatest virtue was that it was our own, that it was today's cause, and tomorrow's too … the obscure offspring of Princess Maleine and Ravachol." The languorous heroine of Maeterlinck's first play and the recently executed anarchist bomber would have made a rather unlikely romantic couple, and this association of anarchism with Symbolism will be discussed in more detail in the next chapter.[38]

Lugné-Poe's immediate successes were indeed the introduction to France of plays from the frozen North, the "unpronounceable" Björnstjerne Björnson, and especially Ibsen, then barely known outside Scandinavia. The Œuvre, however, was in competition with Lugné-Poe's old employer at the Théâtre-Libre for the presentation of Ibsen's plays. These were effectively the only two professional companies presenting modern drama in Paris, with the former specializing in Symbolist theater, the latter in realist or "Naturalist" works. Other smaller avant-garde or progressive ventures tended to be short-lived or purely amateur. The Œuvre usually gave only two performances of each production: a dress rehearsal open to an invited audience and friends, followed by an opening night for an audience of subscribers (a ruse to evade state censorship). In the Œuvre's case, this meant its plays were seen by around 2,000 people, which therefore constituted the total audience for this type of theater in Paris in the 1890s. The exact size of the audience varied according to which auditorium the Œuvre was using, since it was a company with no permanent venue.[39]

Lugné-Poe wished to capitalize quickly on the success of the Œuvre's first Ibsen, a strangely somnolent version of *Rosmersholm*. The next production turned out to be one in which all the artistic, political, and philosophical obsessions of the period were stirred together into one great volatile mix, and the events surrounding it vividly evoke the ideological ferment within which Jarry would launch *Ubu Roi*. Jarry's play would be performed by the same company three years later with even more explosive results, but *Ubu Roi*, though celebrated in theatrical history for the turbulent reception it received, was by no means the first play to cause a riot at the Œuvre.

Ibsen had offered Lugné-Poe *An Enemy of the People*. It was impossible to drape a Symbolist cloak over this drama; it demanded a rigorously Naturalist implementation. The Symbolists' interpretation of the anarchist cause, however, provided Lugné-Poe with a means of approach. The play's climax occurs in the penultimate act when Dr. Stockmann, who has exposed the contamination of the town's waters, faces a violent mob of townsfolk who denounce him, not because he is mistaken, but simply to protect their own financial self-interests in the spa. Stockmann's speech contains statements which can be interpreted as supporting an antidemocratic and "Socratic" version of anarchism: that the ignorant and self-centered masses would be better off being ruled by benevolent individualists. In the play, these sentiments merely serve to further inflame the riotous crowd on stage.

It was a tradition at the Œuvre to preface new works with an introductory lecture, and Lugné-Poe approached Laurent Tailhade, in full awareness of his fervent anarchist sympathies and considerable oratorical abilities. Tailhade was a rather astonishing individual, an energetic fulminator who carried invective to unsurpassed extremes in an unceasing flood of poetry, pamphlets, newspaper polemics, lectures, and speeches. Consequently, he fought many dozens of duels throughout his life, and was never short of personal enemies. Provocation enough, but word had got out, or was given out, that the play was sympathetic to anarchism.

Tailhade took his place behind a lectern on stage, and in the still-prevailing anti-German atmosphere, began by insulting the French audience, writers, and critics, including the most reactionary of them all, who was certainly there: "Francisque Sarcey, the gigantic Megatherium of intellectual non-receptivity." He then compared French theater unfavorably with German (Wagner) and Scandinavian drama, in other words: Ibsen. Invective against the church and the family followed, but Tailhade reserved his real venom for the bourgeoisie, at the point where he finally turned his attention to the play in question. According to him, Stockmann's brother and enemy, the mayor in the play, embodied the cowardly bourgeois *arriviste,* those "greasy vermin whose appalling stupidity numbs everything it touches," who furthermore possessed "the fetid and carnivorous soul typical of so-called 'honest men.'" This phrase was to be quoted in outraged editorials across Paris, and in the auditorium near pandemonium ensued. Tailhade had to wait almost half an hour before resuming; Lugné-Poe mounted the stage beside him to plead for quiet, but to no avail. Bombarded with vegetables and coins, "Tailhade deserves credit for enduring this tempest with magnificent *sang-froid.* Not an inch of his face moved. Arms crossed, he disdainfully looked over the waves of fury breaking at the footlights," as Léon Bloy recalled.[40]

Jarry was certainly present, not only because of the "Ibsenism and anarchism" that were his particular interests at the time, but because a number of his friends played walk-on parts. The Œuvre's budgets were minuscule, and the crowd scene presented a problem. Lugné-Poe asked everyone he could think of, including Jourdain and his friends, to help out and take part in it (their payment consisted of free seats for the rest of the season).[41]

The performance itself proceeded with constant interruptions from the various factions. Jourdain and his fellow extras patrolled the auditorium and corridors during the early acts and the intervals, defending the cause of "Ibsen, Liberty, Lugné-Poe, the Individual, the Spirit and Revolt. We acquitted ourselves of this self-imposed mission with such enthusiasm and intransigence that, while we were unable to impose silence on our adversaries, we unfortunately complicated the task of the actors." Then came Stockmann's speech; cries of "*Vive l'anarchie!*" rang out around the hall, and renewed disputes broke out among the audience, with supporters and opponents coming to blows.[42]

The play staggered to its conclusion, and the departing audience was confronted by police outside the theater, attempting to pick out the jubilant anarchist sympathizers. A couple of days later the prefecture opened a file on the company, and began sending undercover officers to performances. Jarry later celebrated Tailhade's performance in chapter 22 of *Faustroll* where, as "Friar John," he delivers an allegorical sermon at the end of which he slaughters the *mufle*, Tailhade's word for boors, philistines, the bourgeoisie: "he winkled it from its shell with the forked tip of his sword, and chopped its fundament into as many pieces as there were people present in the nave."[43]

...

The December 1893 issue of *L'Art littéraire*, its thirteenth, carried a new editorial byline: A.-H. Jarry, L.-P. Fargue, and L. Lormel. Fargue had at last introduced his companion to Lormel, and the latter had effectively ceded control of his review to the two younger poets (Lormel was born in 1869). The magazine had been publishing the coterie around Jourdain—Cremnitz, Launay, etc.— along with pieces extracted from more famous authors. It was a simple four-page broadsheet until early 1894, when it assumed a more conventional magazine format. Many of its contributors were frankly second-rate, and paid for the privilege of being published (much of the surviving correspondence between Lormel and Jarry is concerned with extracting these fees from his collaborators). For a while Jarry paid his subs, and even paid Fargue's too, but he soon fell behind.[44]

The editors and contributors met at the Café Procope on the rue de l'Ancienne-Comédie. Lormel gives us a portrait of Jarry at these discussions: "small and febrile, dark-haired and pale-featured, his dark eyes shining in his motionless face, carefully enunciating—in the bizarrely accented pronunciation of Père Ubu which he so often enjoyed adopting—some paradox which he then sought to demonstrate by recourse to his great erudition. He aimed to amaze and disconcert. His was an inherently complex nature, and his mental processes were as different from the average Frenchman's as those of a Chinese mandarin; he loved archaic traditions, strange events, inexplicable facts."[45]

Jarry's first contribution to the magazine was a poem, but soon he began writing art and theater reviews. He was also able to publish more difficult texts in the hope that these might be noticed and gain him access to more prestigious publications. In this he was to be successful, and Jarry's tenure as editor of *L'Art littéraire* was brief. When a better offer appeared he moved on, and Lormel's magazine then went into a rapid decline before being absorbed by another review at the beginning of 1895. Lormel was not pleased with his former collaborators, and he took his revenge a few years later in a brief fictionalized memoir of the magazine's editorial gatherings. Here the "inseparable" Jarry and Fargue appear as Death's-Head and The Androgyne respectively, nicknames which he probably found in Jarry's "Haldernablou." Lormel makes snide references to their "unacknowledgeable relationship," and describes Jarry discussing masturbation "from personal experience." Jarry returned the compliment by devoting a chapter to him in *Faustroll*, in which he is characterized as "*Baron Hildebrand de la mer d'Habundes*," which can be roughly rendered as "Baron of the Isle of Cack and of the Sea of Abundant Crap," and derives, we are told, from an agreeable Rabelaisian proverb: "A squitty arse never lacks for shit."[46]

Now, though, at the end of 1893, Jarry was poised to enter the heart of the Parisian literary avant-garde, the headquarters of Symbolism, that new writing which in his own words had been a "revelation." But Symbolism did not easily submit to definition, nor were its relations with the "anarchism and Ibsenism" espoused by Jarry entirely obvious.

5

ISMS OF THE 1890S

Symbolism, anarchism, idealism, Ibsenism. … We have seen how these causes were deemed one and the same by Lugné-Poe and his friends, and among many of those associated with Symbolism; but just how might a synthesis be constructed out of such contradictory elements? The task fell largely to the writer Remy de Gourmont.

It was Gourmont too, after Mendès and Schwob, who was to play the most important role in introducing Jarry into literary circles. Something of an ultimate "man of letters," Gourmont possessed a breadth of interests and learning that made him a perfect patron for the young poet. Not only was he an established poet, novelist, essayist and critic, even a book designer and typographer, he was also the behind-the-scenes editor of the most influential literary magazine of the period, the *Mercure de France*. This magazine was central to the Symbolist movement; all its best authors were published there, and Gourmont was its principal literary theorist. His elucidations of what they stood for attempted to align the movement with radical social and political thought, but in his eagerness to persuade, he tended to cast his net a little too wide.

"Symbolism," he wrote, "can be literally translated by the word Liberty, and for those of a more violent disposition, as Anarchy. Liberty in Art is so stupefying a novelty that it remains misunderstood, and is likely to remain so. […] In order to understand in what respect Symbolism is a theory of Liberty, and how this word, apparently so strict and precise, on the contrary implies an absolute freedom with regard to both ideas and forms, one must invoke the ideas of Idealism, for which Symbolism is no more than a synonym."[1]

Gourmont defined idealism in terms of the transcendental idealism of Kant, exactly that idealism which Bergson had labored so hard to refute by means of duration. To summarize briefly: Kant held that the world can be known only provisionally, at best as a correlate or a representation (and thus, implies Gourmont, as a symbol) because it is experienced, and therefore mediated, by the senses, and then ordered by our mental processes into time and space. "Things in themselves," being outside such structures, are unknowable. From this circumstance Gourmont concluded that "what surrounds us, what is outside us, exists only because we ourselves exist. […] What you call dream or fantasy, is therefore the true reality for those of us who conceive these dreams and fantasies, and there exists an unlimited freedom in the domain of literature, a literary anarchy. This then is the present enviable state of literature. We must guard against the rule-makers; accept no formulas; surrender to our temperaments, be free, and remain so."[2]

Gourmont was certainly a remarkable man of many achievements, but this analysis, so diligently fitted together from such differing fields of discourse—cultural, philosophical, and political—resulted only in theoretical confusion. The same held for the majority of attempts to align Symbolism with anarchism. Lugné-Poe's production of *An Enemy of the People* had shown the Symbolists' enthusiasm for the anarchist cause, and Gourmont was not alone in invoking "idealism" to perform the trick of reconciling such apparently antipathetic movements. Nor was he alone in substituting one meaning of the word for another so as to perform this philosophical sleight of hand.

The word "idealism" encompassed so many different meanings that it readily lent itself to such stratagems, and it is a poor excuse that these were often unintentional. Gourmont supposed himself to use it in a strictly philosophical sense. For Mallarmé and his followers it was a quest for the Idea, a search for some concept of impossible perfection. Otherwise the word tended to assume variants of its common usage: a sanguine assessment as to how society might turn out should humanity at last conform to its innate altruism, a conviction that progressive values in aesthetics and morality must somehow coincide, or even just a vague optimism regarding human nature. These last interpretations allowed many of its Symbolist supporters to imagine themselves in an alliance with a rather fluffy version of anarchism, in which the decapitation of the state would usher in an era of liberty, fraternity, equality, etc.

5.1
Laurent Tailhade and his companion caught in the explosion at the Foyot, from the *Petit Journal*, April 16, 1894.

Anarchism, however, could never go along with a strictly idealist conception of Symbolism. Anarchism is idealist only in the popular sense of the word, since a politics of action aimed at overturning something as tangible as the power of the state could have no truck with a philosophy verging on solipsism. Furthermore, in terms of a cultural alliance, cooperative anarchism generally had little sympathy for the Symbolist aesthetic, which was individualist to the point of elitism. The mainstream of anarchist thought in fact tended to endorse Naturalism—Symbolism's avowed enemy—with its depiction of the wretched existence of the rural and urban poor, and Kropotkin cited Zola as a notable ally.

Anarchism knew better what it was against than what it was for. The ills of the world, particularly the degradation and exploitation of the working classes in capitalist societies, proceeded from the centralized state imposing its will on its subjects. This conviction connected the various strands of anarchist thought, but as a movement anarchism was profoundly divided when it came to practical considerations such as means and aims, namely how to abolish this state, and what to replace it with. When Kropotkin wrote the entry on anarchism for the famous 1911 edition of the *Encyclopaedia Britannica*, he distinguished seven main factions, all of which were cooperative, apart from two: literary anarchism and individualist (or philosophical) anarchism.

The first of these two simply denoted literary sympathizers (Kropotkin included Ibsen among them). The Symbolists, however, were more particularly attached to the works of an anarchist from the individualist tendency, who was probably the movement's least representative thinker. Max Stirner was a sort of "outsider" anarchist, and the *Mercure de France* began serializing a translation of his most important book, *The Ego and Its Own*, in May 1894. Kropotkin (in the article cited) devoted a paragraph to Stirner, and both his analysis and conclusion seem particularly damning here. Stirner, he wrote, "advocated, not only a complete revolt against the state and against the servitude which authoritarian communism would impose upon men, but also the full liberation of the individual from all social and moral bonds—the rehabilitation of the 'I,' the supremacy of the individual, complete 'amoralism,' and the 'association of the egotists.' [...] It is thus a return toward the most common individualism, advocated by all the would-be superior minorities, to which indeed man owes in his history precisely the state and the rest. [...] This is why this direction of thought, notwithstanding its undoubtedly correct and useful advocacy of the full development of each individuality, finds a hearing only in limited artistic and literary circles."

Nothing could be clearer.

Gourmont attributed a "violent disposition" to anarchism, and this was certainly borne out by current events in France. However, by employing the word in its popular sense, he misrepresented the ideas not only of its key thinkers, but even of Stirner. At the moment when he was writing there was an upsurge of anarchist attacks in France, known by activists as "propaganda by deed." These assassinations and bombings were, however, consistently repudiated by the leading figures in the movement, including Kropotkin and Jean Grave, editor of the most important French anarchist journal of the time, *La Révolte*, to which Gourmont himself subscribed.[3]

The "deeds" of the early 1890s constituted a violent backdrop to the politics of the period, and were a constant reminder to the establishment that the ideals of the Commune were not forgotten. Events were set off on May 1, 1891. The army fired on unarmed mill workers and their families at Fourmies, who were demonstrating for an eight-hour day. Nine were killed, including four young girls. The same day, three anarchists were arrested after a shoot-out following a demonstration in Levallois and were subsequently sentenced to long prison terms. In March 1892 the anarchist Ravachol placed bombs in an army barracks, and the houses of the Advocate General and the judge who had presided at the trial of the Levallois anarchists (there were no injuries). He was arrested at the Restaurant Véry in the boulevard Magenta when a waiter overheard him discussing the explosions. The following month a supporter bombed the restaurant, killing two people. Partly as a result of this act, in which he had no hand, and for crimes that predated his anarchist activities, Ravachol was condemned to death and guillotined on July 11, 1892, when his nonchalant defiance at his execution transformed him into a martyr. Lugné-Poe's production of *An Enemy of the People* therefore appeared in the context of this event. In revenge for Ravachol's death, Auguste Vaillant threw a *marmite* into the Chamber of Deputies from the public gallery on December 9, 1893. The device caused no fatalities, slightly injuring one deputy. The same evening, Laurent Tailhade pronounced his famous assessment of this act during a private dinner held by the editors of *La Plume* and attended by Mallarmé, Verlaine, and Zola: "What matter a few vague humanities if the deed itself is a thing of beauty." Variants of this remark saw him pilloried in the press. Vaillant was executed on February 5, 1894, and he in turn was avenged by Émile Henry, a friend, or at least an acquaintance, of Félix Fénéon. Henry detonated a bomb at an apparently random target, the Café Terminus, on February 12, 1894, killing one person and injuring twenty. A few weeks later, on March 4, an explosion wrecked the Foyot, a restaurant across the road from the Senate and thus an establishment mainly frequented by ministers. Ironically, the only seriously injured party was the outspoken Tailhade, who lost an eye (it did not alter his convictions). The anarchist attacks culminated on June 24, 1894, when the President of France was stabbed to death in Lyon by the Italian "propagandist" Casério.[4]

The government's subsequent repression culminated in the famous "Trial of the Thirty" in August 1894 when, much to the authorities' surprise, most of the accused were acquitted. This was not a little to do with Félix Fénéon's phlegmatic and expressionless ripostes from the dock, which reduced the proceedings to simple farce. A typical exchange: when the prosecutor asked him why he had surrounded himself with the anarchists Cohen and Ortiz, he observed: "one cannot be surrounded by two persons, three at least are required." When the judge dramatically retired after mistakenly opening in court a package containing excrement, Fénéon's comment was audible throughout the chamber: "not since Pontius Pilate has a judge washed his hands with such ostentation." In England, Wilde's witticisms earned him hard labor, but in Paris Fénéon's had him acquitted. In the end, only three common criminals were found guilty from among the thirty so-called anarchists. One of them, a butcher's apprentice, had been accused of stealing a pork chop from his employer. … The outcome was beneficial. The very public failure of this trial brought an end to the cycle of revenge attacks and marked the effective cessation of anarchist violence in Paris. Fénéon returned to literature.[5]

Symbolism bore a superficial resemblance to anarchism; it was united by what it opposed: "We are rigorous anti-Naturalists. It is not a matter of joining a group, no orders have been given, no crusade organized, we have aligned ourselves as individuals against a literature whose base-ness makes us want to puke." It was definition by exclusion, except that Gourmont proposed that the common enemies of Symbolism—conformity, Naturalism—implied what they must therefore support: idealism, again. A circular argument, idealist because anti-Naturalist, anti-Naturalist because idealist. Certainly the majority of the avant-garde writers and artists associated with Symbolism would have described themselves as "idealists," and were in broad sympathy with anarchism, if only as a movement that exemplified the principle of revolt in its broadest sense, and because, above all, they shared its anti-bourgeois sentiments. Such vague attachments fortu-nately spared them the arduous tasks of political organization. Yet even Oscar Wilde described himself as a socialist, and there were others among the Symbolists who were anarchist activists in the true sense: Fénéon, Mirbeau, Quillard, Tailhade, for example, all of whom were soon to be among Jarry's closest friends.[6]

As for Symbolism itself, this evaded definition altogether, as befitted an aesthetic devoted to evocation and suggestion, rather than exposition. Historically, it had played a vital role in the renewal of literature since the late 1880s, it reinvigorated the effusions of the Decadents, and its influences combined to create a new writing, at once cerebral under the influence of Mallarmé, and vehement after the newly discovered poems of Rimbaud (to instance only the names most readily recognizable to English readers). Yet a critical diagnosis of Symbolism finds itself in a paradoxical situation: the symptoms are relatively easy to identify, but no obvious pathology connects them. A "symbol" commonly refers to the representation, ideal or otherwise, of an abstraction. This may well describe some Symbolist poetry, but it is by no means exhaustive. Symbolism seemed to have no real agenda, only a set of mannerisms. It was characterized by bizarre imagery, idealized medievalism, metaphysical speculation, obscure vocabulary and often arbitrary Capitalizations: the elevation of the Dream, the Idea, and the Absolute over reality (small "r"), and Art above all else. Even so, a new generation of writers had rallied to this equivo-cal movement, its very ambiguity being doubtless part of the attraction: it offered fraternity but required no commitment to a program, either artistic or political.

Jarry certainly shared many of these vague attachments. His allegiance to the anarchist cause was pataphysical, which on this occasion means: symbolic (i.e., nominal). His "Visions of the Present and Future" appeared soon after Henry's attack on the Terminus, which for many sympathizers was an outrage too far, and Jarry condemned the absurdity of its motives. The politics of the day was never to be one of his immediate concerns.

Symbolism conformed perfectly with Jarry's interests as a writer, and many of its practitio-ners shared his impossibly wide reading, scholarship, and enthusiasms. For most of its devotees, however, art was one thing, and life another. The otherworldliness of Symbolism and Idealism were all very well in small doses and for artistic effect, but the incorporation of such concerns into one's mode of living might have more serious consequences.[7]

6

1894–1895

Such was the cultural and political milieu that Jarry entered, in the early spring of 1894, by keeping an appointment with Remy de Gourmont. This meeting, potentially as momentous for Jarry as his encounter with Hébert, initiated a collaboration which, had it been a little more long-lived, could have meant Jarry's later life turning out very differently. Gourmont, although fifteen years his senior, was someone who could fully appreciate both Jarry's originality and his scholarship, and he was probably also one of the few whose advice was valued by Jarry himself. They had much in common. Until recently Gourmont had been a librarian at the Bibliothèque Nationale, yet he was not an entirely bookish individual. In 1891 he published a rebuttal of patriotism, in which, with regard to the question of Alsace-Lorraine, he observed: "Personally, in exchange for these forgotten territories, I would not deign to give either my right little finger, which supports my hand when I am writing, nor my left, which I use to tap ash from my cigarette." A newspaper campaign led to his dismissal, and this campaign was conducted in *Le Figaro* by a certain Fouquier, who would later appoint himself the chief critical enemy of *Ubu Roi*.[1]

6.1
Remy de Gourmont (top) and Arthur Symons (left),
around the time they first met Alfred Jarry. The third
person is the sexologist Havelock Ellis, whose
works were published by the Mercure. Photographs of
Gourmont are uncommon because of his later illness;
this is from Symons's *Colour Studies in Paris* (1918).

6.2
The fork of the rue de Seine (to the left) and the rue de
l'Échaudé in about 1919, by Eugène Atget. Although
the photograph was taken some years after the Mercure
moved, these streets would not have much altered.
The Mercure's offices were in the fourth building on the
left side of the road.

Gourmont happened to have another visitor on the day that Jarry called, the English poet Arthur Symons, who described their encounter with Anglo-Saxon condescension.

> I met Jarry in Remy de Gourmont's rooms in la rue du Bac, one afternoon, when, in the middle of our conversation, someone knocked. Gourmont went out and returned with Alfred Jarry, a small, nervous, sad youth, with a square face, and black savage eyes, and, as he spoke, we noticed a kind of pose in the way he weighed his words: for he was face to face, for the first time in his life, with two writers, before whom he assumed a surprising humility. He laid on the table with hieratic gestures a huge portfolio, which contained some of his prose and some of his amazing designs. [...] After he had gone Gourmont and I began laughing at his meager appearance and at some of his prose; but the prose turned out much better than we had imagined.[2]

Jarry had arranged this meeting solely on his own behalf; there was no sign of Fargue. However, Gourmont soon met Jarry's friend and the three of them discovered a shared passion for Épinal prints—large, crudely printed colored woodcuts, often religious in nature—which were threatened by advances in printing technology. Fargue and Jarry proposed a collection of prints with a foreword by Gourmont, to which he agreed.

Meanwhile, on February 4, Jarry's grandfather had died, leaving him a negligible inheritance. Once again, information on his family attachments is lacking, and it is not known whether he attended the funeral in Saint-Brieuc.

Jarry was still living at the Calvary, at least part of the time. Accounts of its extravagant interior decoration depend on a single anecdote from Georges Rémond, but it is more likely that the décor was improvised for this specific occasion, since a certain amount of preparation had obviously been undertaken. Jarry had met a new set of friends when sharing a table at Chez Ernest, various more or less flamboyant bohemians who have left little trace apart from their bit parts in Jarry's life story: Rémond himself, Octave Fluchaire, Sosthène Morand, Sior Carlo, Don Beppi ...[3]

Eventually he deemed them worthy to be received at his apartment, but first they "must of course undergo the proofs, agonies, and torments of initiation." They assented, and Jarry led them from the café along the dark and twisting alley to the Calvary. Here black drapes decorated with skeletons covered the walls from floor to ceiling, the shutters were closed, and the room was lit only by a veiled oil lamp and a night candle placed inside a papier-mâché skull. Three-legged painter's stools stood about the table upon which an owl blinked beside an open Bible. Behind the door, for some reason, was a pair of dumbbells.[4]

Jarry stood upon a stool and bade them sit. He placed the owl on his right hand, gripped the Bible in his left, and "in a desolate voice" intoned some verses from Leviticus each of which ended with the words "and he shall be unclean." Replacing the owl, now emitting plaintive shrieks, he pronounced in a loud and forceful voice: "While mandrakes lament, and passionflowers relent, the white lumbricus of burials returns to its lairrrrrrr." The light went out and simultaneously, "by some strange miracle or due to careful planning," the stools suddenly collapsed, tipping the inebriated initiates abruptly and painfully on the floor. Meanwhile the screeching owl flew manically about the rooms casting shadows from the skull-lamp, Jarry all the while crying, *à la* Lautréamont, "Zibou, Zibou, don't make such sounds!"[5]

Morand was enraged; he leapt at Jarry and pushed him over, and the skull was smashed when he attacked the owl. On relighting the lamp, he seized the Bible and read: "In those days Christ said to the Apostles: Those who shit on their fellows shall be the first to be shat upon." Stepping over the prostrate Jarry, he led the victims from the room, slamming the door behind him in fury. "Then," according to Rémond, "he looked at us with a strange expression and, raising his fingers to his nose, exclaimed, 'What's this! Ah! The filthy pig!'" Jarry had coated the door-knob with something unmentionable, and the initiation was complete. Later he was forgiven his joke and they all turned up to root for *Ubu Roi*.

...

The portentous verses proclaimed by Jarry from his perch are the first and last lines of his poetic drama "Haldernablou," a Maldororian rendering of Jarry and Fargue's liaison. It was destined, perhaps deliberately, to be the cause of discord between them. A dense and obscure text, it combines the gothic atmosphere of his prank at the expense of Rémond and his friends, with the irony, rhetoric, and bestiary of Lautréamont, and the pretensions of Symbolism. Although it was an adolescent work, in which plagiary tends toward unconscious parody, it was one in which a new voice was struggling to appear, and was probably one of the pieces he had shown Gourmont—Jarry dedicated it to him when it was published.

"Haldernablou" was written in the first couple of months of 1894 and Jarry sent it to Alfred Vallette, the editor of the *Mercure de France*, with the title "Histoire tragique du page Cameleo." This version differed from the published one only in respect to its title and the names of the two principal characters. In the first version they were Duke Henrik (an Ibsenized version of Henri, from Alfred-Henri Jarry), and Cameleo, his page. Léon-Paul Fargue's nickname was Cameleo, from *caméléon*, "chameleon," referring to his first name, but also to his changeable nature and cavalier approach to veracity.[6]

In an inexplicable act of cultural vandalism, nearly all of the Mercure's archive was deliberately destroyed in the 1940s; thus Jarry's first letter to Vallette is lost, as are all the latter's replies. Judging from his second, of March 4, the text initially received a lukewarm reaction, but not an outright rejection. Undeterred, Jarry was sending something else instead: his translation of "The Rime of the Ancient Mariner." Jarry's letter, as Besnier points out, follows the established model of the letter from the young poet to his respected elder: "what young poet does not dream of one day writing for the *Mercure*?" He also apologizes that the title of "Histoire tragique" is too close to that of a recent work by Gourmont, and suggests changing the title simply to "Cameleo"; later it became "Haldernablou."[7]

Jarry's third letter to Vallette, of March 6, 1894, implies that Vallette had changed his mind and accepted "Cameleo" for the *Mercure*, although he was unable to publish it for a few months (it was scheduled for July)—perhaps Gourmont had interceded on Jarry's behalf. This letter of

Jarry's also offers the tactful observation: "I have not mentioned in my letter the question of buying shares in the *Mercure*, in the belief that in so doing I would appear to be trying to pass too rapidly through a door which anyway is not open to everyone." As with *L'Art littéraire*, authors were encouraged to take a financial stake in the magazine, and Jarry did indeed soon do so, taking four 100-franc shares on April 3. So by then we may assume that he had passed through the door that led to the celebrated Tuesday afternoon salon at the offices of the *Mercure*. Four hundred francs was a substantial admission fee.[8]

Despite his mother's death, and with it her academic ambitions for Jarry, he continued in his attempts to enter higher education, but this was probably more to avoid his looming military service, and possibly to secure the continuance of an allowance from his father, for he seems otherwise to have had no financial means. In March Jarry sat the exam for the License-ès-Lettres at the Sorbonne, but failed. He then made a very half-hearted last attempt at the entrance exam for the ENS in July, after which it was too late to avoid conscription.[9]

Jarry's next letter to Vallette, of May 27, bears the address of the rue de Bootz in Laval. He had been recalled to the family home by Charlotte to attend the last hours of his uncle Julien-René. This letter explains the changes to "Cameleo"; Jarry writes that, after consulting Gourmont, he wishes to change the title and names of the characters in his play because "the 'page Cameleo' has implored me to debaptize him." Therefore he asks that the new names of Haldern and Ablou be substituted, and as a title "simply 'Haldernablou,' in a single word the horror of the doubly coupled beast."[10]

Cameleo Fargue had good reason for his discomfort. Despite its obscure style, "Haldernablou" is a comparatively overt description of a homosexual love affair, although the hero (obviously Jarry) expresses horror for the physical aspects of love. The page Cameleo (renamed Ablou) is portrayed as distinctly subservient to his master (now called Haldern, a translation of Jarry's second name, Henri, into Breton), and he must endure Haldern's expressions of his diffidence in this regard: "Love exists outside of sex; I would like someone who was neither man nor woman nor yet a monster, a devoted slave and one who could speak without breaking the harmony of my sublime thoughts, one for whom a kiss were a demonic depravity." More ominously, the text ends with Ablou's death, or more ambiguously, with the death of their association. Haldern again: "I will kill him: because I despise him for being impure and venal—because beauty, if it is not to fall from grace, must elect none other than an equal beauty, even for a slave, because his lingering pride will ruin our love affair; because theology rightly says one must destroy the beast with which one has fornicated. […] He will never speak again—and that is the only thing about him I will regret."[11]

Despite his "debaptism," Fargue must have realized that his identity would be immediately obvious to his friends and acquaintances, not least those at the *Mercure*. Unfortunately, he was in no position to ask favors of Jarry. Laval was more than halfway to Pont-Aven, and Jarry expected to travel on there before returning to Paris. He had therefore asked Fargue for a letter of introduction to Filiger, which means that Fargue had been uncharacteristically reticent about the events of the previous summer.

The rue de l'Échaudé, a dark and narrow thoroughfare off the boulevard Saint-Germain, was an insalubrious street in the 1890s, being chiefly known for its brothels. On Tuesday afternoons, usually between November and the onset of the summer, the two second-floor rooms occupied by the *Mercure de France* were opened to an invited group of artists, writers, composers, critics, and aspiring *littérateurs*. A third room was a bedroom, since this was also the home of Alfred Vallette and his wife, Rachilde. "One entered a dark red room in which Rachilde reigned over a pandemonium of smokers," recalled Paul Valéry, "a fermenting mix of striking personalities who here enjoyed total freedom of thought and expression: theories, gossip, propositions, or opinions, whether aesthetic, religious, political or philosophical." As we noted in the Preface, this was undoubtedly one of the most important salons in Paris, if not in Europe. Here were to be found many of the most significant figures in the arts of the day; and this makes Rachilde's recollections of her role as hostess all the more surprising:[12]

> Every Tuesday, we received men of letters, some very bohemian, others established or *arrivistes*,
> poverty-stricken geniuses, or amateurs too rich to have any talent. Since there were hardly
> any women present, I resigned myself to the task of being a simple pourer of tea, speaking little,
> listening a lot, always enjoying myself, never understanding what I wanted to understand, to
> the point where Oscar Wilde once asked: "That enigmatic creature in the black woolen dress, can
> she really be the author of *Monsieur Vénus*?"[13]

In fact, in the early years at the *Mercure* she was probably the best-known author of them all. The successful prosecution in Belgium of *Monsieur Vénus* in 1884, during which Rachilde had been accused of inventing a "new vice," had made her a celebrity (she escaped prison only by remaining in France), whereas the likes of Gide, Valéry, and so on were still hardly published.

The citation above is from the beginning of Rachilde's memoir of Jarry, written some thirty years after the event. It is typical of this peculiar book, in which she presents herself as a modest, naïve, and censorious creature, who never really understood the person whose most constant friend she became. Arnaud concluded she neither liked Jarry nor his works, but this seems improbable. Vallette and Rachilde, and their daughter Gabrielle (born in 1890), soon became a sort of substitute family for Jarry, and it was certainly Rachilde to whom he was closest; they would not have taken on this often demanding responsibility if they had not felt a genuine affection for him. It is patently true though that Rachilde did not rate his writing very highly, as will become obvious, and so the assumption of a rather frivolous persona in her book allowed her to write an anecdotal account of Jarry while avoiding an assessment of his works. This did Jarry's posthumous reputation few favors at the time (1928), since it was precisely such an assessment that was then sorely needed, but Rachilde was a novelist and her book is really a *roman à clef* which happens not to disguise the names of its characters. It appeared in a series called *La Vie de Bohème*, which adequately summarizes its plot, and it has many faults, not least a fictitious ending

(Rachilde allows the inattentive reader to believe that Jarry's famous letter of May 28, 1906, cited on p. 333, was his last). Even with its faults it remains a major source for any biography of Jarry, and a valuable portrait despite its partiality.[14]

Rachilde, moreover, had another motive for passing over Jarry's writing in silence. Both she and her husband became both politically and artistically reactionary as they grew older, and they could not abide the new generation of authors who came to prominence after the First World War. In 1921, for example, they refused to subscribe to the memorial for Apollinaire (whom they had published) because its committee comprised too many "dagos, Cubists, Bolsheviks, Dadaists and other sorts of Boches." This from the editors of what had been the greatest publisher of foreign literature in France … Rachilde quite rightly considered Jarry as "the precursor of all the buffoons of the present-day world of letters" (by which she meant Dadaists, Surrealists, etc.), and it was something for which she could not forgive him.[15]

…

6.3
Félix Vallotton, portraits of Vallette, Rachilde,
Gourmont, early 1890s.

Like many another Parisian with literary ambitions, Jarry and Fargue had set their sights on joining the brotherhood (for such it mainly was) of the Mercure. Here they could meet all of the most progressive young authors of the new generation. And young they were—the prevailing hirsutism of the period makes them appear older, but most were in their twenties. The magazine itself was effectively run by a triumvirate: produced by the ever-practical Vallette; personified by his wife, the lively "man of letters" (this was Rachilde's own description of herself on her card); but behind the scenes, in Camille Mauclair's words, its "sage and oracle" was Remy de Gourmont.[16]

The first issue of the *Mercure de France*, capriciously dated December 25, 1889, appeared on January 1, 1890. It was founded by a collective of a dozen authors, one of whom, Jules Renard, put up most of the money. Vallette was persuaded to be its editor. It had 32 pages, but was a rapid success; within four years it was 96 pages, and by 1904 each of its monthly issues was at least 288 pages long. Literary contributions were but a part of this bulk; it also contained reviews of the arts, humanities, and social sciences from across Europe, and quickly established itself as the essential French journal for anyone interested in these subjects. The publishing arm of the *Mercure* followed soon afterward and was equally well received. For the first few years it published beautifully designed limited editions at their authors' expense, and this was how Jarry's first two books were to appear. By the turn of the century, however, it had an extensive list of standard paperback editions of contemporary and classic French literature, and of translated literature from around the world. The review ceased publication in 1965; the publishing house still exists.[17]

An *entrée* to the Mercure meant acceptance into the most avant-garde faction of French literature in Paris, and Jarry appears to have accomplished this with little difficulty. According to Fargue, he and Jarry were originally invited to the Mercure because Vallette kept an eye on the smaller literary reviews and had noted their contributions to *L'Art littéraire*, but in fact Vallette wrote a weekly survey of these publications for the *Écho*, and may therefore have come across Jarry in its offices. Symons recorded that Jarry was introduced to Vallette and Rachilde by Gourmont, and both versions may well be correct. Fargue's evocation (edited here) is engaging:[18]

Only someone from my own generation can understand the true import of these simple words: To be invited to the Mercure! We turned up, hearts pounding. The Mercure in those days was in the rue de l'Échaudé, three rooms on the second floor, a small reception room, a bedroom and an office-library. Vallette opened the door himself, dressed in a short jacket and slippers. He was of a stocky, rather round build, and had a slightly military air, short hair and a square moustache. He was gentle, obstinate, self-possessed. He had a horror of pretension, deception, and admired straight talking. He was one of the most reasonable men I ever met.

In those days we were two nervous and timid novices, and he, the Director, the director of the Mercure, was Jupiter himself. Nevertheless, he put us at our ease with a cordial smile and immediately engaged us in a discussion of "the great literary subjects" of the moment. He made it obvious that he was interested in our youthful opinions. At last, we had been invited to the Mercure Tuesdays!

These celebrated reunions took place at the end of the day's business. Almost instantly the little salon was thick with tobacco smoke. The air could be sliced like a loaf, one could barely see anything. All these famous persons seemed as if painted on a canvas of fog, and in the end Vallette was compelled to acquire some sort of machine to absorb the smoke. Only then was it possible to discern persons rather than the shapes of phantoms: Remy de Gourmont, a suspect shadow overtaking his cheek, already limiting his appearances and who would hide himself in the little library; Henri de Régnier, who loomed up Lohengrin-like, sharp and straight; Valéry, all nerves and energy, already the master of a conversational style bursting with ideas; Marcel Schwob, stuffed with literature and grimoires, a sagacious magician, organized, precise, smiling with an air at once mysterious and macabre; Pierre Louÿs, one of the handsomest faces of those days, a wave of hair above his forehead, a voice like satin, immaculately and fashionably dressed; Alfred Jarry, combative, who deployed sallies of wit as if flinging dice on a gaming board; Vielé-Griffin, spontaneous, polite, but quick to take offence; Pierre Quillard, ardent supporter of just causes …[19]

Fargue continues with brief portraits of Léon Bloy, Lord Alfred Douglas, Louis Dumur, Paul Fort, André Gide, A.-F. Herold, Charles-Henry Hirsch, Gustave Kahn, Jean Lorrain, Octave Mirbeau, Jules Renard, Jean de Tinan … and there were many others who "as soon as they appeared at the door were lassoed by Rachilde's enormous laugh." These others, contrary to Rachilde's assertion, did include a few women, among them the actresses Marguerite Moreno and Fanny Zaessinger, who became a good friend of Jarry, and Remy de Gourmont's unusual mistress, Berthe de Courrière, of whom more later.

Fargue recalled his nervousness on first entering the salon. Jarry too was nervous perhaps. If so, he disguised it well, although Rachilde's account should be treated with caution; as Besnier points out, it bears little relation to the polite letters Jarry had addressed to Vallette. Here is her first encounter with "that strange personage, who acted out for his own benefit the comedy of a literary existence pushed to the point of absurdity":[20]

That particular Tuesday […] I had placed a hank of silk over the wrists of a young provincial poet so as to unwind it, because I often embroidered another kind of canvas than did the Gentlemen of the Symbol during their technical discussions, which often became heated. An unknown made his entrance with the careful gait of a wild animal entering an arena and wary of being put through its paces in front of an audience. I had just time to hear my husband say "Alfred Jarry," and to reply with a more or less banal greeting, when Jarry suddenly and violently ripped the silk from the poet's wrists and threw it to the floor, snarling in a bizarre intonation in which he hammered out the syllables as if through the teeth of a rusty gear wheel: "Idiot! Why not take up spinning while you're at it?"[21]

Elsewhere she recalled that her first impression had been of his terrifying black eyes. Rachilde had then retrieved the hank of silk and proffered it to Jarry with a "Your turn now, Monsieur," to

6.4
Félix Vallotton, portraits of "The Mercureists" in the late 1890s. This page: Stuart Merrill, Jules Renard, André Gide, Francis Vielé-Griffin, Pierre Quillard, Léon Bloy, A.-F. Herold. Opposite: Marcel Schwob, Henri de Régnier, Pierre Louÿs, Édouard Dujardin, Louis Dumur, Paul Fort, Gustave Kahn, Octave Mirbeau, Laurent Tailhade.

which he meekly assented. They soon became close friends despite this tempestuous introduction, which Jarry, never ingratiating, had reinforced with further gallantries: "We have read your stories, Ma-da-me. We were under the impression that they were written by a man. We see now that this is not the case, and it is most regrettable." Rachilde, furthermore, confessed to a profound aversion to small men and disapproved of alcohol, although she admired "elegant deportment and harmonious gestures," and constantly stresses her predilection for good manners and refined behavior. This was a strange basis for their friendship. Similar reservations had surrounded her choice of a marriage partner. The combination of the stolid Vallette and the rather more vivacious Rachilde (a partnership which resembled that of Jarry's parents) was looked upon with some amusement by their friends, and not a little skepticism. Nevertheless, their marriage lasted until Vallette's death in 1935. Rachilde was thirteen years older than Jarry, and Vallette fifteen.[22]

Jarry came to monopolize the Tuesdays. His sheer manic ebullience, restless intelligence, and bizarrely inventive conversation soon dominated the room—but without arousing resentment. Jarry, at least at this period, knew when to stop; he would do so suddenly, conceding the floor with a disconcerting grin which was almost immediately extinguished, as if with the flick of a switch. "He was at his most brilliant in Rachilde's salon, his roguish energy, his hard and toneless voice, his nasal accent, all combined to add to his appeal." In fact *le parler Ubu* soon became a craze among the habitués. "It was the best period of Jarry's life," wrote André Gide, who regarded him with a bemused circumspection. "You could not invent such a character, I also met him at Marcel Schwob's and elsewhere, and always with tremendous enjoyment [...] he exercised a sort of extraordinary fascination over the Mercure at that time. Everyone, or almost everyone, attempted, some more successfully than others, to imitate and adopt his humor; and above all, his outlandish and relentless manner of speech, without nuance or inflection and with an equal emphasis upon every syllable, including the silent ones. A nutcracker, if it could speak, would sound no different. He expressed himself without the least reticence, and with utter disdain for decency or decorum." Jarry was indeed allowed to exceed the normal etiquette of the company. The rapidity of his speech, his wit and his aberrant charm, allowed him unusual liberties, and a cascade of paradoxes might be abruptly terminated by bluntness. Albert Mortier recalled the subject of literary "taste" becoming the topic of debate: "Taste," pronounced Jarry, "we shit on it."[23]

Marcel Schwob, having awarded a prize to "Guignol," was already familiar with the grotesque personage who lay behind Jarry's performance: Père Ubu. Jarry probably needed little persuasion to introduce this character to the rest of the Mercure, and he soon performed readings from early versions of *Ubu Roi* and *Ubu cocu*. In a letter to Jarry, Jean de Tinan recalled these readings being "accompanied by the laughter of Rachilde, the laughter of Moreno, the laughter of Fanny, the laughter of Vallette, the laughter of Schwob, the laughter of Herold, the laughter of everyone—[and delivered] in the sonorous tones of the admirable voice of the Master of Phynances!"[24]

Thus did the Ubu cult enter Paris, and Jarry modified the "Chanson du Décervelage" (Song of Disembraining), the rousing hymn from *Ubu cocu*, so that its bloody executions of bourgeois *rentiers* (landlords) now took place in the rue de l'Échaudé. The salon regulars soon knew it by heart, and the diarist Paul Léautaud found himself one evening among a group of them (Vallette, Rachilde, Tinan, Bruchard, Beck, Zaessinger, and of course Jarry) belting out its five verses from the upper deck of an open-top omnibus:[25]

> A carpenter was I, for many a long year,
> Rue Champs du Mars, 'swhere we was livin'.
> 'N my wife, she toiled too, as a milliner,
> So you see, m'dears, we never lacked for nuffin.
> When Sunday came round, 'n it weren't raining,
> Into our poshest gear we'd climb,
> And off we'd go to the disembraining,
> Ru' d' l'Échaudé, for a grand old time!
>> Roll up, roll up, and see the wheels whirl,
>> Roll up, roll up, and see the brains swirl,
>> Roll up, roll up, see the landlords' lips curl;
>> Hurrah! Horns up yer bum! Long Live Père Ubu![26]

Léautaud neglects to tell us where the troupe was heading, but henceforth Jarry had a ready-made circle of friends. The Mercureists went *en masse* to most productions at the Œuvre, and were regulars at the cabarets in Montmartre and the cafés of the Latin Quarter.

...

During the early months of 1894 Jarry was busy writing: criticism and then two philosophical essays (of a sort) for *L'Art littéraire*, more art criticism for *Les Essais d'Art libre*, and putting together *Minutes*. These labors were interrupted in mid-May when he was called back to Laval. His uncle's demise was imminently expected, but the crisis was prolonged and Jarry grew bored. "Bored with a household concerned only with an invalid [...] and if one goes out there are no books, no reviews, just the idle curiosity of the natives." This complaint to Vallette accompanied the final manuscript of the newly titled "Haldernablou," dispatched for publication in the *Mercure*. After a month of inactivity he decided that Uncle Julien no longer required his presence, and took the train to Pont-Aven, taking a room at the new, larger Gloanec (the Pension had gained additional premises since Fargue had stayed there).[27]

Almost immediately he received a letter from Fargue, who was understandably concerned to discover that Jarry was in Pont-Aven. He pressed him to return, on Gourmont's urging apparently, since the book of Épinal prints needed immediate attention. He also reiterated his plea for changes to "Haldernablou," and so had received no reassurance that these had already been made. There is a hint of desperation: "Gourmont is pressuring me to come and drag you back by the hair, but I don't know if I can do that." At the same time Fargue wrote to Filiger, in an attempt at reconciliation, and to inform him of Jarry's intended visit.[28]

6.5
The Hotel Gloanec, Pont-Aven.

At the Gloanec, Jarry renewed his acquaintance with Gauguin, who was in a bad way, laid up in bed in the hotel. He had returned from Tahiti with a native companion known as Anna the Javanese and a pet monkey, and a couple of weeks earlier they had been strolling through the nearby fishing port of Concarneau with the painter Armand Séguin. This exotic procession had attracted derision and the odd stone from the local urchins, and Séguin had administered a clip round the ear to one of the culprits. A group of local fishermen then laid into the artists with their clogs and Gauguin's leg was badly broken, his tibia left protruding through the skin. Pont-Aven was not always the artists' paradise it was made out to be. We do not know precisely what the relations were between Gauguin and Jarry, but they were warm enough for Jarry to be permitted to add his verses on three of Gauguin's paintings to the great compendium the latter was assembling with Forbes-Robertson, Roderick O'Connor, and Séguin, as a part of their search for the "divine source of all form." A few years later Gauguin devoted some pages of his home-produced Tahitian magazine to an enthusiastic appraisal of Ubu.[29]

The single extant letter from Jarry to a member of his family came to light only in 2008. It can be dated to around June 18, 1894, and was written to his sister Charlotte from Le Pouldu, a tiny hamlet near Pont-Aven. Jarry described his activities in a direct manner that is unique in his known correspondence. He thanked her for forwarding the *Mercure*'s proofs of "Haldernablou," and a copy of Gourmont's new book "with its magnificent dedication" (it has never been found); then describes cycling to Le Pouldu ("22 kilometers without touching the handlebars") in the company of Séguin, who then invited him to a Breton double wedding. Here he reproached Gauguin and Filiger for drinking too much alcohol; they explained it was safer to drink wine than the local water. On leaving the celebration he discovered that the local brats had stuck clog nails in his tires. The final paragraph, which Charlotte is told not to pass on to their father, concerns the exams for the ENS. Jarry tells her he missed the first sitting, even though he was still receiving his allowance from his father. He is unconcerned, since the second part is not until July 6, and the results would not be known until the end of that month. The letter ends: "Kiss Papa for me. With much love and lots of kisses, Alfred."[30]

Jarry's uncle succumbed on June 21, and Jarry returned to the family home. He stayed only until the funeral, and by July 1 he was back at the Gloanec. Jarry then called on Filiger. It was fortunate they had already met at the wedding, since he would otherwise have been confronted by a firmly locked door. Filiger's reply to Fargue's placatory letter had been cutting:[31]

I am replying, but for the last time—and you can be sure of that—to the last of your letters. I simply want to tell you that I am bored with your correspondence and I think you've already said everything you want to say? You talk too much, you write too much and you have too many friends, and I think it will all come back on you. As for your faults, tell them to someone who wants to know about them, for my part, I'm not interested. [...] You have annoyed me this past year, with your meddling. [...] So as to avoid the same thing happening all over again, I have made up my mind only to receive intimates, which is why your friend Jarry will be ill-advised to call on me; and I will treat anyone else in a similar manner. Useless to speak more [...] I am also writing to Gourmont to tell him the same.[32]

Both Gourmont and Jarry held Filiger's work in particular esteem (he had supplied frontispieces for two of Gourmont's recent books), and Filiger must have complained to Gourmont of Fargue's conduct, since Jarry wrote a letter to Gourmont containing bitter criticisms of his friend, though its actual content is unknown apart from a vague auction catalog description. For Jarry, these events and Fargue's endless dissimulation, and for Fargue the imminent publication of "Haldernablou," were reasons enough to end their relationship, which anyway was already fragile. Was there a final confrontation on Jarry's return to Paris? Fargue's friend Léon Pivet remembered violent arguments when they fought like dogs, rolling on the ground and throwing punches. After this final break occurred there was to be no more talk of the Épinal book. In fact Jarry and Fargue never again exchanged a word, nor acknowledged each other, even on the frequent occasions when they found themselves in the same room. Their relationship, regardless of its precise nature, had lasted only just over two years, yet one feels it was significant—a time of "shared experience of wild enthusiasms," to quote Jarry's exact contemporary Hofmannsthal. For a while Gourmont would take Fargue's place, at least so far as enthusiasms of an intellectual nature were concerned.[33]

· · ·

Despite their rocky introduction, Jarry and Filiger became friends nevertheless. A number of letters from Filiger over the next few years attest to his liking for Jarry, and again it is unfortunate that we do not have the other side of the correspondence, because one senses that after a while Jarry sought to maintain a certain distance. Filiger's letters unburden himself of difficulties in his personal and artistic life; both were fraught with seemingly insoluble problems and exacerbated by dire poverty. Charles Filiger was a tragic figure who suffered from depression and lack of motivation; despite decades devoted to painting, his output was pitifully small. His flight from Paris in 1890 was prompted by some sort of homosexual scandal, and he was in effect an exile who found the normal associations of everyday life impossible to maintain. He perhaps seized upon Jarry's friendship with rather too much enthusiasm. Their correspondence lasted a couple of years before Filiger retreated into a monastic existence devoted to his art, which was universally ignored. Jarry's essay on him appeared in the *Mercure* in September 1894. It aimed at suggestion rather than explanation which, Jarry informed his readers, was anyway absurd.[34]

Apart from researching his article on Filiger, what exactly had been the original aim of Jarry's trip to Pont-Aven? His first art review for *Essais d'Art libre*, published a couple of months before, had singled out works by Gauguin, Sérusier, and Filiger among others. It may be that he and Gourmont, or Jarry alone, already had the idea of expanding the remit of the anthology of Épinal prints to include works by the artists associated with Pont-Aven. Jarry appears to have been visiting artists' studios and sounding out their willingness to collaborate on the project that would soon become Jarry and Gourmont's luxurious art magazine *L'Ymagier*. Fargue was not party to this change of plan.

There were plenty of other artists to be found at the Gloanec or nearby, notably Séguin, who subsequently conducted an extended correspondence with Jarry, much of it concerning the pitiable state of Filiger. The English artist Forbes-Robertson was also there. During Jarry's stay he drew his portrait; he appears very much the young dandy, his tie pin depicting one of his beloved owls, though his long hair must have aroused comment in conservative rural Brittany.[35]

...

6.6
Eric Forbes-Robertson, *Alfred Jarry*, pencil drawing, Pont-Aven, June 1894.

6.7
Henri Rousseau, *Self-Portrait*, pen and ink, 1894. According to Arnaud, this drawing was made at Jarry's suggestion.

6.8
Henri Rousseau, *Portrait of Léon-Paul Fargue*, oil painting, 1896.

Fargue's evocation of Montparnasse in his *Le Piéton de Paris* recalled that, at this period, Henri Rousseau lived near the railway station in the avenue du Maine:

> We came across him by chance, Alfred Jarry and myself, while out walking, or in some café. After a while, not without carefully thinking it over, he took us to his studio. Soon he had painted both our portraits, one after the other. He portrayed me, with the pointed beard that I wore in those days, in front of a window beyond which passed a railway train encumbered by heavy smoke like the plume on a soldier's helmet. […] I do not know what became of this portrait, which he never gave to me. In those days he was in the habit of saying: "We have four great writers: Monsieur Octave Mirbeau, Monsieur Jarry, Monsieur Fargue, and Monsieur Prudent-Dervillers." (This latter was the local municipal councilor.)[36]

This account is pure fabrication: Jarry had already met Rousseau and reviewed his paintings. Rousseau's portrait of him was painted in 1894 and exhibited in 1895. Fargue's portrait, lost for many years, resurfaced in 2001, when it was put up for sale at Christie's. It is dated 1896. Fargue was one of many fabulists when it came to the life of Rousseau, but Jarry too could be culpable. A few years later he frequented a certain Dr. Saltas, who suffered a slight excess of credulity. Jarry's principal entertainment was to tease him with outrageous stories, which the Watsonish doctor duly recorded for posterity.[37]

> Jarry had spent the night at Les Halles with some friends, including an artist and his model. They were returning to his home across the Pont des Arts when they noticed an individual walking along the banks of the Seine. Jarry inquired of him what he was doing in such a place at that early hour in the morning. "I am a customs officer," he replied, "it's my job." Jarry looked at him intently, with a serious expression. "My dear fellow," he said, "you have the exact appearance of an artist and it is absolutely essential that you take up painting." Rousseau objected that he knew nothing of painting and doubted that he ever would. But Jarry persisted, and repeated that he was born to be a painter and nothing else, that he undoubtedly possessed genius, that it was often the case with artists that their vocation was writ large across their face, and to prove it he placed in front of him the artist's easel, while the barely dressed model placed herself at the foot of a tree, and he directed him to paint the tableau now before his eyes: Eve beneath the apple tree in the Garden of Eden, awaiting her victim, Adam, father to us all.
>
> So convincing was Jarry, so persuasive, that the unhappy customs officer was already beginning to believe that up to now he had neglected his true vocation. He took a brush in his hand and traced the outline of a woman, and then a tree on the canvas. The problem of the apples now arose, since it was obviously with an apple that Eve seduced the first man. The customs officer was nonplussed. Jarry then advised him to take up some red from the palette, and here and there he indicated where he should make some round shapes, advice which was carefully followed by his pupil. The tree, or at least what was supposed to be a tree, was now covered with little red balloons, two of which also decorated Eve's chest, according to the instructions of his satanic teacher.[38]

To cut a long story short, these activities attracted the attention of the constabulary, who escorted everyone to the local police station. Here Jarry's protestations that he had discovered a genius were treated with skepticism. Evidence was taken, and Rousseau later put before a court. Jarry spoke for the defense, and the judge realized the whole affair had been a practical joke, and acquitted the accused. Rousseau, we are told, was so grateful that through copious tears he offered to paint a portrait of the judge's wife as a token of his gratitude. He would not take no for an answer and eventually persuaded her to sit for him, thus beginning his artistic career.

Why should Saltas recount this impossible tale—Jarry was twelve years old when Rousseau actually began exhibiting—unless it came from Jarry himself, who would not have expected it ever to be published? (Saltas attributed it to an anonymous anecdotist.) The probable occasion of Jarry's meeting with Rousseau was a more prosaic encounter. In April or May of 1894, Jarry had visited the exhibition of the Salon des Indépendants with Charles-Henry Hirsch, one of the editors of *Essais d'Art libre*, for whom he was reviewing the show. The Indépendants had no selection jury and Rousseau had been showing there annually for several years. On this occasion he exhibited four paintings, among them what is now one of his most famous works, *La Guerre*. He was in the habit of hanging around within earshot of his exhibits. Observing Jarry and Hirsch discussing another of his works, *The Earthly Paradise*, he asked them what they thought of it. "Si-mp-ly su-bli-me," replied Jarry, "but who are you, Mon-sieur?" "Henri Rousseau, the artist." They would quickly have found things in common. Rousseau was also born in Laval, in the tower of the old city gates (which can be seen in the postcard in figure 14.8). The infant Jarry had walked through them every day *en route* to his primary school. Indeed, Jarry could have met him then; Rousseau, some thirty years older, had been a schoolfellow of Jarry's father, as he related in a letter to Jarry of June 1894.[39]

Jarry's review of the exhibition, published in June, singled out *La Guerre*, and later Jarry was to commission a lithographic version of it for his magazine *L'Ymagier*. Jarry did everything he could to promote Rousseau, who already had the beginnings of a reputation. Although Rousseau had been exhibiting at the Indépendants since 1886, he had garnered only a handful of favorable reviews, including one in the *Mercure* three months earlier. Such notices were hugely outweighed by less appreciative comments. The sincerity of Jarry's admiration for Rousseau's painting was often called into question, not least in the second edition of Chassé's book on Jarry. It is nowadays difficult to understand the controversy surrounding Rousseau's work, when exhibitions of it are mounted in major public galleries around the world, but he was the first self-taught artist to exhibit with the "professionals," and he had to put up with a great deal of derision for his presumption. Even artists one would have imagined to be sympathetic failed to appreciate his work. Sérusier recalled himself and Gauguin laughing at Rousseau's works in the Indépendants, and Gauguin remarking, "Well, at least he's not as stupid as Bouguereau." If Jarry did not actually discover Rousseau, he was certainly responsible for his being taken seriously: it was directly because of Jarry's influence that Apollinaire, and hence Picasso, later became his champions. Rousseau's eventual success has confirmed Jarry's judgment and opened the way for a more general appraisal of all forms of nonprofessional art, from the naïves to "outsiders."[40]

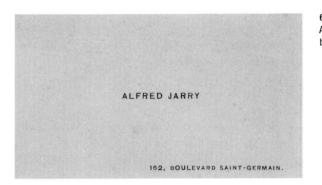

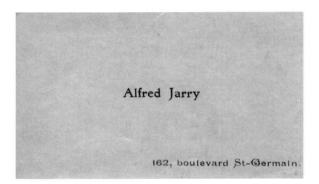

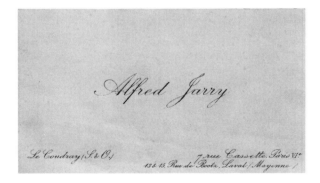

6.9
Alfred Jarry's visiting cards; the last must have
been printed sometime after July 1900.

At the end of June 1894, when Jarry was still in Pont-Aven, Rousseau wrote to him about his proposed portrait. His congenial and helpful tone suggests they were already close, and his letter contained news of Jarry's lodgings in Paris. The lease on his mother's apartment had run out and the rooms were to be let. Rousseau had been to rescue his most precious possessions, notably his "box of famous actors" (by which he meant Jarry's marionettes, including that of Ubu), and the Japanese lantern to be used in the background of the portrait. As for the rest, the concierge, Monsieur Donzé, and a neighbor would deal with it. Monsieur Donzé also attached a reassuring note that ended "the owls are well."

Jarry returned to Paris and took another apartment, at 162, boulevard Saint-Germain, on the corner of the rue de Buci, a building since demolished. This was a larger, two-room accommodation, unusually conventional for Jarry, and unlike his other residences it did not merit a poetic name (the more squalid the habitation, the more grandiose its description, according to sound pataphysical principles). He had visiting cards printed.

Rousseau's letter suggested he was impatient to get started on the portrait; this young critic was, after all, one of his few artistic admirers. Jarry later told Apollinaire that the artist needed only a single sitting and that he had measured him like a tailor for a suit. The portrait is lost, but a sarcastic review survives from when it was exhibited at the 1895 Salon des Indépendants (and famously given the title *Portrait of Madame A.J.* in the catalog, an error occasioned by the poet's exuberant coiffure):[41]

> Let us not forget those artists whose ingenious fantasies break the monotony that seems obligatory for all serious exhibitions of painting. Monsieur Henri Rousseau, monopolist of the baroque, has surpassed himself this year with an enormous portrait of a long-haired poet. […] Two owls are perched on the balcony before which the poet is seated. Various emblems surround him, which reveal that his habitual preoccupations should not be confused with those of the vulgar, and that he is absorbed in the loftiest deliberations. A quill behind his ear identifies him as a writer. His fixed and round black eyes, his profoundly black hair, and his formal clothes, also black, accentuate the seriousness of his thoughts. Some charming verses, inscribed in gold on the frame, underline the fact:
>
> O muses lapidarian, engrave your brow's isosceles
> Upon his eye-lids' reveries to ascertain he'll always please
> His avid readers whose sincerity's
> The source of pleasure's luminosities.[42]

The verses are presumed to be Rousseau's own. From another review it is clear that the "quill" is in fact the tongue of a chameleon perched on Jarry's shoulder. From this description, and their appearance in Jarry's illustrations to *Minutes*, it has been presumed that he kept chameleons as well as owls, but although Paul Fort mentioned this in passing he seems never to have been to Jarry's home, and none of his actual visitors ever reported seeing any. If, on the other hand, this was a pictorial reference to "Cameleo" Fargue, it may explain Jarry's later mutilation of the portrait, after their estrangement. According to Apollinaire he cut out and kept only the head, its edges scorched by burning. André Salmon, however, recorded that only the background survived, with an empty space for the head. It was the background alone that Saltas says he found in Jarry's room after his death, along with a stuffed owl and other detritus. He didn't bother to rescue it.[43]

···

Jarry returned from Pont-Aven in time for the publication of "Haldernablou" in the *Mercure de France*, and of the first act of *Caesar-Antichrist* in *L'Art littéraire*, both in their issues for July 1894. These important texts were effectively his first pieces of noncritical writing to appear, apart from the poetry and "Guignol" published in *L'Écho de Paris* a year previously. Jarry was also preparing his first book, *Black Minutes of Memorial Sand*, which was to be published by the Mercure in September, and with Gourmont, the first issue of *L'Ymagier*. These publications were produced to the highest private-press standards and *L'Ymagier*, moreover, would also have required extensive research. Jarry must have been spending much of his time in libraries, which rather contradicts Rachilde's assertion that he slept all day. Yet he still had time for more frivolous pastimes. A sack of dried chickpeas lay slumped beside his window, and his peashooter had been redeployed against the stovepipe hats of the bourgeois on the boulevard below. Multiple direct hits produced a gratifying drum beat.[44]

His new residence, despite its address, was not exactly luxurious. "He lived in a small old house that due to various unusual circumstances had somehow survived on the boulevard Saint-Germain." "Traditional" toilets were situated on the staircase. Jarry's rooms were decorated with "images of the saints [Épinal prints], crucifixes, censers and a mass of objects devoted to the cult, all from Brittany. […] Two stuffed owls hung from the ceiling. Jarry lived amidst all these dusty objects with his roommate, an ancient, and living, owl. A closed curtain covered one wall; Jarry had cut a hole through it to his bedroom so as to make a puppet theater, in which he presented *Ubu Roi* to invited audiences."[45]

Since Henri Morin was then in Paris, he may well have assisted with these presentations of *Ubu* (there are no descriptions of them). What we do know is that, according to Henri, at some point in 1894 he gave Jarry permission to do whatever he wanted with the Hébertian texts written by himself and Charles, providing only that he change the names of the characters (although this statement is contradicted by the fact that Jarry had already used the name "Ubu" the previous year in "Guignol"). As for the exact nature of Morin and Jarry's relationship, a certain ambiguity persists. Rachilde knew Henri Morin, and later wrote: "Not only do I know what underlay this friendship, but I have absolute proofs from very interesting witnesses […] but out of literary sadism I will not discuss the matter." A sexual element to their relations might explain Henri's reluctance to speak of Jarry's plans to his brother even though they were in regular contact.[46]

A momentous month: October 1894 saw the almost simultaneous appearance of Jarry's first book, *Les Minutes de sable mémorial*, and the first issue of *L'Ymagier*; Jarry was only just twenty-one.

The full title of the English translation of Jarry's first book is *Black Minutes of Memorial Sand*, a compromise because most of the words in the French title have at least two meanings: a presentiment of the book's complexities. It was published by the Mercure de France at the author's expense: having the Mercure's imprimatur was considered an honor in itself. It is unclear where Jarry could have got the money to finance this luxurious publication unless from his father. *Minutes* was designed by Jarry and printed by Charles Renaudie, whose small print shop was situated around the corner from the Mercure in the rue de Seine. It was bound in plain wrappers bearing neither the author's name nor the book's title; the only decoration was a small heraldic crest printed in gold. Although it conformed to the tradition of the poet's first small book of "precious" verse (it measures approximately 5¼ by 4½ inches), it was nevertheless extensive: 236 pages on fine paper with woodcut decorations, many by Jarry himself, and printed in various colors. There were 197 copies on Arches paper, 19 on tinted Ingres, and one author's copy on multicolored papers, which Jarry attempted to sell not long afterward.[47]

6.10
Les Minutes de sable mémorial, 1894.

The book is deeply Symbolist in both design and content (with the partial exception of "Guignol," although Ubu is here given something of a makeover). Jarry had no intention of making things easy for the reader, and even the title page required an act of decipherment. The next page carried the announcement of two forthcoming books: *Caesar-Antichrist* and *Elements of Pataphysics*. *Minutes* collects together nearly all of Jarry's noncritical writing from the past eighteen months, and in consequence contains a wildly disparate variety of texts: poems, prose poems, prose texts, plays, etc.

A sort of manifesto prefaced the book, although Besnier remarks that it resembles less an introduction than a declaration of war on the reader. Jarry muses upon his various possible relationships with this wretch. For example:[48]

> 3rd Case: if, against all probability, he is equal with the author, the latter at least surpassed him in
> the past when he was writing the work, that unique moment when he saw EVERYTHING
> (but was far from spelling it out, as explained above, for this would merely have been (cf. *Pataph*.)
> brutishly passive association of ideas, disdain (or lack) of free will or of intelligent choice, and
> sincerity, anti-aesthetic and contemptible).[49]

The reference to Pataphysics, abbreviated as if it were an acknowledged discipline, is a typical Jarry touch. Elsewhere the introduction is more obviously Mallarméan: "To suggest rather than to state, to make a crossroads of each word in the street of sentences."

Jarry used *Minutes* as his introduction, or to offer his thanks, to numerous writers, artists, and critics. There are known copies inscribed to Berthe de Courrière, Gourmont, Mendès, Lugné-Poe, Gustave Kahn, Arthur Symons, and to foreign literary reviews, including *The Yellow Book* in London. The copy for Catulle Mendès was particularly fulsome. Jarry had it specially bound, and decorated the cover with a drawing of the three *palotins*, Ubu's henchmen. The inscription read: "To Catulle Mendès, from his admirer since very ancient times. Alfred Jarry," and inside was a second inscription: "This book contains many of the first things I had published thanks to Maître Catulle Mendès, and which probably could not have come into being without him. Alfred Jarry."[50]

Reviews were few, and mostly uncomprehending, with some deploring the influence of Lautréamont. Jarry asked his friend Édouard Julia to review it in *L'Art littéraire* but it closed before he could do so, which the latter may not have regretted. Gourmont, naturally, was more enthusiastic; his review in the *Mercure* (the publisher's own magazine) of this "huge little book" tackled its impenetrability:

> Why obscurity in literature? Monsieur Jarry's preface […] suggests that obscurity is often no
> more than the shadow cast by our ignorance or idleness. A work of art can be recognized
> by its new metaphors; and all new metaphors are obscure: any written work of art worthy of
> the name must be obscure. For myself, thank God! if there are not so many new things here,
> there are plenty of obscure ones, and these are the most beautiful.[51]

His conclusion: "a gratifying debut, not all of it pleases me, but what does please me pleases me greatly, it is a stem whose first flowerings allow one to look forward to a future of beautiful holly-hocks and passionflowers—in the shadow of hanged men and beneath the outspread wings of gold-breasted owls." The review ends with Gourmont inviting his readers to spend some of "the long evenings of the coming winter" devoting time to the interpretation of the escutcheon on the cover.

There were also a few letters of thanks. Max Elskamp, the Belgian poet, congratulated Jarry, particularly on "Guignol": Ubu was already coming to the fore. Régnier likewise found Ubu the most interesting part of the book, and he noted in his memoirs that the book as a whole "attested to the author's singularly bizarre intellect in which hermeticism was mixed with buffoonery, by turns satisfying and preposterous." Henri Mazel looked forward with enthusiasm to the rest of *Caesar-Antichrist* (a part appeared in *Minutes*), but Filiger was among the puzzled: "I wasn't able to understand it all but I admire the originality of these extraordinary tales, and I am grateful that you thought of me." Jarry's disregard for the reader had its inevitable consequence. Both *Minutes* and his next book, *Caesar-Antichrist*, took several years to sell their tiny print runs, although 250 copies was a pretty standard run for books of poetry in the 1890s.[52]

Jarry may well have been disappointed with the overall reaction to *Minutes*, but he had taken the most radical literary forms of his day and pushed them to a point where they effectively imploded, with only Ubu emerging from the ruins. The tactful response of Mallarmé, however, was all he could have asked for (although it has to be said that Mallarmé was known for his generous verdicts on books he received):

> You have already accomplished the first thing that is necessary in order to set forth, my dear poet: that of stepping back from the infinite possibilities of the old literary landscape in order to place your feet firmly on virgin territory that is all your own, and then allowing yourself to dispense with the rest—this in the exceptional book which I have just closed, *Black Minutes of Memorial Sand*; in other hands, it would have remained on the level of the quaint, but in yours it attains that of the luxuriantly Unusual.
>
> Your hand; and many thanks to our dear friend Gourmont for the delectable *Imagier*, for which I will try and drum up a customer or two, if I can.
>
> Yours,
> Stéphane Mallarmé[53]

The postscript of this letter reads "À bientôt" (See you soon). Since before their separation, Jarry and Fargue had been regular guests at another famous literary salon in Paris, that of Mallarmé. Like the Mercure's, it was held on a Tuesday, but later in the evening, from around 8 p.m., so Jarry would have gone there afterward. Mallarmé was the undisputed leader of the Symbolist movement, soon to be elected Prince of Poets by his contemporaries. He lived outside bohemia in the rue de Rome, and his Tuesdays were more cerebral occasions than those of the Mercure—Ubu-speak was not deployed there.[54]

6.11
Stéphane Mallarmé in his salon on the rue de Rome.

6.12
L'Ymagier, the first five issues.

Mallarmé's evenings had begun in the 1880s for a few select friends: "In that room we passed many unforgettable hours, undoubtedly the finest we will ever know, amidst the graceful seductions of his words, disciples of a sort of disinterested cult of ideas whose religious fervor was that of the mind." This religious awe was common among his audience, but as the tiny room became more crowded over the years, early devotees such as Dujardin, Fontainas, Mauclair, and Régnier came to regret the master's increasing fame.[55]

By the time Jarry attended, the salon was distinctly packed, although the company was just as distinguished, especially in retrospect: Mallarmé's choice of guests was judicious, and those yet to be recognized would be so soon. Between their feet wandered Mallarmé's cat, whose lineage could be traced to one belonging to Baudelaire, and the discourse was swathed in clouds of smoke: a large jar of tobacco sat upon the central table, with packets of "Job" cigarette papers scattered about it. Through the fog could be discerned a small but select collection of paintings (Manet, Monet, Whistler, a portrait by Guys which had also once been Baudelaire's) and sculpture (Rodin, Gauguin). Otherwise the later Tuesdays were conducted with almost bourgeois ceremony. Conversation was general until around 10 o'clock, when the poet's daughter and wife would enter bringing "grog" (rum and hot water with a squeeze of lemon), which would be briefly passed around, whereupon the ladies retired (it was an all-male affair). Then, in Symons's words, Mallarmé would rise from his rocking chair "to stand leaning his elbow on the mantelpiece, while one hand, the hand which did not hold the cigarette, would sketch out one of those familiar gestures which gave the impression each time of his *entering* the conversation, just as one enters on stage. One of the best talkers of our time, Mallarmé's intelligence moved with the half-apologetic negligence of the perfect acrobat. He seemed to be no more than brushing the dust off your own ideas, settling, arranging them a little, before he gave them back to you, surprisingly luminous. It was only afterwards that you realized how small had been your own part in the matter, as well as what it meant to have enlightened without dazzling you. Here was a house in which art, literature, was the very atmosphere."[56]

More general discussions followed, and one visitor recalls Mallarmé and Jarry, at two in the morning, "employing endlessly inventive images" to elucidate the architecture of the sonnet for the two remaining guests, Jarry and himself. It was a matter of the quatrains being the columns that supported the pediment whose sides were the tercets (but our witness may not have recalled their conversation with much accuracy). Jarry remembered it, though. When he came to write the chapter of *Faustroll* dedicated to Mallarmé, the doctor observes "two distant columns, the isolation of two prismatic trinities of Pan pipes, splayed out in the spurt of their cornices the quadrigate handshake of the sonnet's quatrains."[57]

...

L'Ymagier, like *Minutes*, was a handsome production printed by Renaudie on various fine papers. Measuring approximately 11 by 9 inches, the first issue had 70 pages. The editorial announced that it would appear every three months and form an annual of between two and three hundred pages containing around 200 prints, and at least 8 large Épinal prints that had been specially pulled (and twice folded, to Jarry's distress). *L'Ymagier* also contained careful reproductions of late medieval woodcuts, and tipped-in prints commissioned from contemporary artists, all accompanied by commentaries from Gourmont and Jarry. The contemporary artists featured were chiefly those associated with the Nabis group in Pont-Aven: Bernard, Filiger, Gauguin, O'Connor, Roy, and Séguin; Rousseau also made an appearance, as did the pictorial efforts of the editors. There were also a few other artists who seemed rather out of place in this company (Forbes-Robertson, Espagnat, Whistler).

The characteristic shared by most of these various elements was "primitivism," valued because it allowed for immediate and unmediated forms of expression, direct and untainted by cultural preconceptions. Primitivism is a theme which runs through many of Jarry's works and enthusiasms: his promotion of "popular" theatrical forms such as pantomime, marionettes (which are "rudimentary" beings), his appreciation of childhood experience (another form of the primitive and rudimentary), and the productions of the untutored such as Rousseau. Jarry later told Gourmont that Rousseau "painted with the grace, purity and immediacy of the Primitive." All these were qualities that Jarry himself carefully preserved in the intentional crudity of *Ubu*, and both *Minutes* and *L'Ymagier* promoted deliberately unsophisticated imagery. Jacquelynn Baas in her history of the woodcut notes their unconventionality (but she perhaps misinterprets Jarry's intentions): "when one considers that Vallotton's relatively elegant woodcuts were considered barbaric by many bibliophiles at this time, the value of Jarry's crude blocks to his anti-establishment purposes is unmistakable." More than that, the "primitive" conferred an authenticity that served as a lever for overturning cultural conventions, and signaled a quest for universal meanings. These are themes that would be taken up wholesale in the following century in the arts, anthropology, and psychology.[58]

Such concerns had come to the fore in the paintings of the Nabis group, most of whom were ex-pupils of the Lycée Condorcet, as we have noted. The group's inception can be dated from 1888, when Sérusier brought back from Pont-Aven his painting *The Talisman*, and showed it to his fellow artists at the Académie Julian. This tiny landscape, veering on the abstract, was painted on a cigar box lid under the direction of Gauguin, and demonstrated that a painting is simply "a flat surface covered with colors assembled in a certain order," in the words of Maurice Denis two years later. Such experiments led Sérusier and his friends to discard the "tricks" of representation: perspective, illusionism, figurative coloration, etc. They were soon to transfer these ideas to stage design with Lugné-Poe. This art was, above all, a search for a new simplicity, and given the often religious imagery of the Breton countryside, with its roadside shrines and calvaries, their paintings often resembled the pre-Renaissance primitives. So while the Nabis in one sense looked backward (like *L'Ymagier*), they were also the future for an art of painting outside the constraints of strict representation, and were thus the real precursors of modernism. More to the point, for Jarry and his friends, Gauguin and his followers were the authentic Symbolist painters. Previous Symbolist artists had remained in thrall to appearance, either by subject matter (Post-Impressionists, etc.) or execution (the academicism of the artists around the Rose+Croix, for example), whereas the Nabis esteemed imagination, deformation, and subjectivity. They were Symbolist therefore in the Mallarméan sense, seeking suggestion before representation, and in Gourmont's: idealist, anti-Naturalist. For all these reasons their paintings were controversial, even to their contemporaries. In 1889, the youthful Gide stopped at an inn during a walking tour of Brittany. "A servant showed me into a whitewashed room, and left me sitting with a glass of cider before me. A number of unframed canvases with their faces to the wall were all the more conspicuous because of the scarcity of furniture. No sooner was I alone, than I ran up to the pictures and gazed at them in increasing amazement; I thought them simply childish daubs." He decided to stay the night, took a room, and waited for dinner: "I wanted to see what kind of artists were capable of producing such amusing freaks." He was in Le Pouldu, and the artists were Gauguin, Sérusier, and Filiger. Gide should be forgiven his reaction because of his age (he was nineteen), but it was one that then would have been almost universally shared.[59]

L'Ymagier therefore, despite its archaic appearance, was also an avant-garde publication supporting the latest innovations in the visual arts. Contextualizing the art of the Nabis within the tradition of medieval printmaking was a part of its program. The magazine was also simply the repository for some of the passions of its editors. Gourmont's introduction outlined their interests: images, religious or mythological, with only as many words as were necessary to explain these "emblematic dreams." *L'Ymagier* would trace the development of the woodcut through the history of printed literature since the fifteenth century and its parallel history which flowed alongside, that of the oral traditions of popular culture: stories, legends, songs. (Neither editor seemed tempted to reconcile their admiration for popular folk imagery with their notion of art as an essentially elite individualist expression, a variant of the same contradiction that allowed the Symbolists to adhere to anarchism.) Each issue was to be thematic, the first being devoted to the Passion; reproductions would be as precise as possible, often taken from original blocks. The essay by Jarry which accompanies the depictions of the crucifixion is perfectly serviceable but slyly oblique and not particularly reverential, tendencies that became more noticeable in future issues. Gourmont too allowed his tongue to approach his cheek. His introduction in the first issue considers the joy of a Breton peasant discovering in a peddler's basket, "for the price of a clipped sou," certain poignant and symbolic engravings—that in fact depict the spiritual condition of those in states of mortal sin. An unlikely cause for merriment among the pious, one would have thought.[60]

These small mischiefs apart, the review was a serious and immaculately printed presentation of the iconography it intended to explore and, by implication, to rescue from its imminent demise due to the industrialization of printing. In this, *L'Ymagier* was at least partially successful. The woodcut had been something of a forgotten medium (although Vallotton had recently begun using it), but it was soon taken up by the likes of Munch, then in Paris, and later by the German Expressionists. *L'Ymagier* took some of the credit for this renaissance. It was a remarkably ambitious enterprise, thus it was all the more surprising that an established author such as Gourmont should have entrusted such a recent arrival as Jarry with its co-editorship. Nevertheless, the almost excessive warmth of his letters to Jarry around this time testify to the esteem in which he held his collaborator.[61]

As with *Minutes*, the first issue of *L'Ymagier* served as Jarry's avant-garde calling card. He notably used it to make his initial contact with Lugné-Poe. Jarry's self-conscious letter of October 30, 1894 complimented the theater director on the Œuvre's second season and dangled the prospect of reviews in the magazine for the next one.[62]

The two editors must have thrown themselves immediately into work on the second issue, which was to be accompanied by a "*Collection L'Ymagier*," whereby connoisseurs could purchase separately editioned prints from the magazine. Gourmont, at Jarry's urging, visited Rousseau's studio. Despite the artist informing him that he had learned his trade by painting murals in bakeries, Gourmont agreed they should include a lithograph of *La Guerre* in no. 2. It was the only print made from Rousseau's work in his lifetime.[63]

There was another person behind the scenes at *L'Ymagier*, however. The magazine was almost certainly financially underwritten by Gourmont's mistress, Berthe de Courrière; it was her address, shared with Gourmont, that appeared on the review, and to which callers were invited between 2 and 3 p.m., except on Fridays. During the preparatory work on *L'Ymagier* she had swamped Jarry with bizarre ungrammatical telegrams, some of which he later incorporated into his novel *Visits of Love*:[64]

6.13, 6.14, 6.15
Woodcuts from *Le Miroir du Pécheur*, as published in *L'Ymagier* 1. The soul of a man in mortal sin; The soul of a man who has fallen back into mortal sin; The soul of a man who regrets having offended God.

Saturday 15 September 9.15 a.m.

If you receive this note in due time, would you come right away, about 10.15? (not before, please).
In accordance with that law whereby the same idea, if it arises, does not arise twice running,
I should not wish to be the cause of any delay.

If you should not receive this this morning, tomorrow, Sunday, about 4.30.

Saturday 15 September 11 a.m.

Did you receive the message I have sent you this morning?

Since I very much wish to see you, I would ask you, if you receive this, to be so good as to visit
me, this afternoon, about four (I mean four o'clock, as in process-servers' affidavits).

I apologize for this absolutely [*sic*] accidental profusion of correspondence.

Saturday 15 September 2.30 p.m.

It would seem to me a great pity not to see you today. Will you come about four (not before)?
We'll converse, and if I am obliged to go out, not having been able to do everything I need to do
during the day, you will, won't you, resign yourself to accompanying me? [65]

The following Saturday the barrage resumed with a telegram at 8.15 in the morning: "I will do all I can to try and come by your house this morning between 10 and midday. I would like not to see too much mess, and to find you in the raiment to which my eyes are accustomed. But do not positively wait for me, and go to the printer all the same." A year or so later the intentions behind these unusual communications would be revealed.[66]

In the meantime Jarry was preoccupied with a more serious problem, his looming military service: an effective imprisonment likely to absent him from the capital for three whole years at the very moment when all doors appeared to be opening for him. Since August, Jarry had been attempting to influence the authorities to allow him to serve in Paris, instead of Le Mans to the south, which is where he was initially to be dispatched. Jarry's sister persuaded the Deputy at Laval to intervene with the Minister of War, but his initial attempts were rebuffed. Eventually the general compromised, and Jarry was sent to the Corbineau barracks at Laval, which at least meant he knew people in the town, including his father and sister. Conscripts were assigned to particular branches of the army by lottery. Jarry preserved his ticket, no. 88, perhaps because the crudely drawn image was rather reminiscent of an Épinal print. He was inducted into the 101st Infantry on November 13, 1894.[67]

Before submitting to this ordeal Jarry had himself photographed, well knowing that his abundant locks would be the first casualty of his military career. The result is what is now the best-known image of Jarry, which is usually attributed to Nadar, although if this is the case it must have been taken by one of the studio's photographers, since Nadar himself had by then moved to Marseille. This photograph is usually dated to 1896, soon after Jarry's time in the army, but the length of his hair, which perfectly accords with descriptions of Rousseau's portrait of 1894, makes this very unlikely, and Léandre's drawing from December 1896 (figure 8.13) clearly shows it still much shorter.

...

Three years of army life lay ahead. Open resistance was useless; the military was well practiced in breaking stubborn cases. Later Jarry told the gullible Dr. Saltas that he had been discharged for "precocious imbecility." Although his records do not show this as the official reason for his release, it was in fact a fairly accurate description of his mode of survival. Jarry chose subservience, but subservience taken to the point of parody: the pataphysical solution to the problem of obedience.

6.16
Alfred Jarry, photograph attributed to
Nadar, probably from late 1894.

He submitted to army discipline totally and phlegmatically, although he could not quite resist allowing his superiors the suspicion that this capitulation was not entirely sincere. The army's weak point was its obsession with the precise observance of regulations, and Jarry took this to new heights of pedantry. Such behavior proved difficult to fault, since it was not easy to justify punishing someone for their very fastidiousness. Jarry was never insolent; instead he assumed a bluff and affable naïveté, cloaked in Ubu-speak, that was disconcerting because, in the absence of more concrete infractions, a mannerism of speech could hardly be punished with severity. This new variant of freedom, freedom through slavery, was a theme Jarry would later explore in his play *Ubu enchaîné*. When eventually he was discharged, it was with a good record, despite his constantly receiving minor punishments.[68]

LAVAL (Mayenne). — La Caserne Corbineau.

J. Sorel, Edit., Rennes

6.17
Laval. The Corbineau barracks.

One of Jarry's sergeants, Gaston Roig, described his induction. On the parade ground the captain held forth at length, offering the confused and disoriented recruits his congratulations: because Providence had granted them the privilege of serving their country beneath the fluttering standard of one of the most famous regiments in the whole of France, etc. He then passed along the ragged line of conscripts inquiring of each their name, birthplace, occupation. He paused a while before speaking to Jarry; Roig presumed he was surprised by his stature, which only barely conformed to the military minimum, and by the long hair brushing his shoulders.[69]

"Your name?"

"My na-me-is-Al-fred-Jar-ry, Mon-sieur; or-ig-i-nal-ly-fr-om-Laval,
    now-a-man-of-let-ters-in-Pa-ris."

"Very well, my friend, but you must have heard what I said a moment ago to your neighbor.
    From now on you must call me mon capitaine, and not Monsieur."

"Cer-tain-ly-Mon-sieur, hence-forth-I-will-call-you-mon-ca-pi-tai-ne."

Apart from Roig's account of Jarry's time in the army, we have Jarry's own in his novel *Days and Nights*, which he began during his service. On this occasion it is perfectly legitimate to use his fiction as a direct biographical source, since Jarry later gave an annotated copy to his friend Édouard Julia in which he pointed out the factual elements in the book.

Jarry's attitude to the army was not entirely without contradictions. He was certainly mortified at having to spend his time employed in tasks that were not only deliberately pointless but also deliberately interminable, endless spit-and-polish. Far worse, however, was the insult to his individualism. His distaste for the common soldiery is expressed early on in *Days and Nights*: "He had only once seen a soldier in close proximity: by chance, in a third-class carriage near Brest, repatriated, naked under his greatcoat and breeches. Dirty skin was visible through the holes in his pockets. He smelt of shit, fever, sperm, boot polish and rifle grease." His animal nature was no accident. Jarry concluded that it was the army's explicit intention to reduce its soldiery to the state of simple beasts:[70]

> "Discipline, the principal strength of armies," according to the training manual, demands from the soldier an unthinking obedience and allegiance at all times. It must first suppress the intelligence, and then substitute just a few animal instincts based upon that of self-preservation, lesser wills subsumed into the will of leader. [...] This annihilation is achieved by known procedures and by machinery with more or less fixed gears.[71]

Jarry determined to survive his time in the military through a more "noble" form of self-preservation: "to preserve one's self and maintain one's individuality against outside forces." The problem of subservience and obedience thereby arose, but although the soldiery were a mindless mob, their superiors were so in name only, thus nothing could be lost by feigned submission. The ineptitude of the officers is one of the targets of the novel, and also of his later journalism: not only the ineptitude of the officers, but especially that of the medical staff. Jarry later promoted the novel as exposing "appalling details of military medicine," and parts of it report near-criminal incompetence. Yet despite his contempt for the military machine as a whole, there were certain aspects of its training which he enjoyed and excelled at. He was an enthusiastic swordsman, and an excellent shot, but these achievements could not outweigh his deficiencies in other respects.[72]

Although Roig was sympathetic, and became a good friend to Jarry over the coming months, his corporal, Bouilly, was a different animal altogether. He was a fierce, red-faced, little man with a fetish for discipline. The slightest infraction had him threatening his charges with Biribi (the African punishment battalions), accompanied with references to the "rustic origins of their genealogy" and other choice observations. The classic military bully. After Jarry's exchange with the captain at his induction, Bouilly had marked him out: "Another wastrel from Paris. And in my squad, of course."

6.18
Caricature of Jarry as a conscript, drawn to accompany
the memoir of Gaston Roig.

After the induction, statistics:

Hair: *brown*; eyebrows: *brown*; eyes: *brown*; forehead: *straight*; nose: *average*; mouth: *average*; chin: *round*; face: *oval*. Height: 1.61 m.

Next, the haircut. And uniform: Jarry was only five foot three and a half inches tall, and he had very small feet (he often wore Rachilde's shoes in later, poverty-stricken times). Consequently none of the uniforms or boots fitted.

Drill: according to Roig, "military training was incapable of altering the quiet serenity which characterized Jarry's sojourn beneath the flag." Jarry applied himself. Left foot forward, make a line, little finger aligned with the trouser seam, all quickly mastered, and all to no avail. Jarry was just too small; his uniform was baggy, and his boots flapped at the end of legs too short to achieve the regulation military stride. He was out of proportion with the long infantryman's rifle, and looked ludicrous on the parade ground. Bouilly, however, saw no reason for him not to conform to military norms, and was exasperated by Jarry's strange docility, beneath which he sensed both insolence and contempt. Jarry became the principal butt of his abuse when, having been given a punishment accompanied by Bouilly's customary insults, Jarry replied courteously, and of course mechanically: "Certainly Corporal I will sweep the dormitory and refill the water jugs so that I will not be sent to Biribi, as you have so correctly observed." Eventually, though, Bouilly admitted defeat; Jarry's attempts to keep up during drill were demoralizing the whole company, and he was excused parades.

After a while, Roig allowed Jarry the use of his officer's quarters, and here he wrote: notes for *Days and Nights*, articles for *L'Ymagier*, correspondence. In Roig's room too, they drank. Roig is the first to mention Jarry's appetite for alcohol, seemingly acquired from the canteen during parades when he was given the most menial tasks: peeling potatoes, washing dishes, cleaning floors. The corporal in charge of these minor punishments shared his colleagues' perturbation at Jarry's contentment during their execution, and heaped even more upon him. Roig tells us that Jarry frequently returned to his dormitory with a list of punishments as long as when he set out—which he proceeded to undertake with the same irritating equanimity.

Sweeping the parade ground was his main occupation, however. Jarry explained the theory: "It is no mere gesture toward the rhetorical that this object, which in the civilian world is commonly known as a broom, is here referred to as a 'brush.' This is because it is only suited, at best, for sketching out decorative motifs in the dirt, and for roughly outlining the design of some future sweeping project, one which is likely to remain in the realms of the improbable." As for practice: one evening, around five o'clock, Roig says he was passing the time of day with the sergeant of the guard. This was a man notorious for the precision of his instructions, even regarding such matters as sweeping the courtyard. Suddenly the sergeant stopped in mid-sentence, his eyes bulging in stupefaction (so Roig assures us). He was staring past Roig at he knew not what. "What the fuck are you doing there, dammit!" Roig turned round. Jarry was standing behind him, marooned in his enormous uniform, rigidly at attention, broom across his shoulder. "Didn't you hear what I ordered you to do earlier?" "Yes, Sergeant." "Well?" "Sweep the parade ground,

Sergeant." "Well, dammit! Sweep the parade ground then, that's not too difficult to understand!" "Of course, Sergeant …" Jarry replied, "*but in which direction?*"

Roig and Jarry passed the winter evenings in his room, talking, drinking. Roig had literary ambitions and was keenly interested in news from the Mercure. Unfortunately his enlistment ended in April 1895. They remained friends, and Roig attended some of the marionette performances of *Ubu* at boulevard Saint-Germain, and later the première of *Ubu Roi* itself.

Jarry quickly made other friends in the barracks, and became something of a minor celebrity in this tiny universe. His comrades envied his successful evasion of so many of the rigors of military training, and when he needed assistance with his menial duties he never lacked for volunteers. Among these malingerers was Maurice Dide, who appears in *Days and Nights* under the pseudonym Nosocome. Dide was a medical intern, and the novel describes his various methods for fooling the doctors into granting him medical leave or vacations in the sick bay. It is impossible to know how much use Jarry made of these ruses, though the novel implies that he spent a certain amount of time in the infirmary as a patient. Perhaps he was actually ill? He mentions the return of influenza, which may have been the illness he suffered the previous winter when he was nursed by his mother.

…

Jarry's military service was at first arduous, but after a few months he became something of a part-time soldier. According to Charlotte, one of the regimental doctors was a friend of their father, and he got Jarry permits for Paris. On one occasion, though, Jarry went instead to Rennes to take part in a bicycle race, and was spotted by the barracks' commandant. Luckily he, too, was a friend of Anselme's: "Bugger off to Paris next time, at least I won't bump into you there." After Roig left the service, Jarry took the commandant's advice and contrived more and more frequent trips to Paris. Even during the early months of 1895 he was able to sustain his literary activities around *L'Ymagier*, and from the late summer appears to have spent extended periods in the capital.[73]

L'Ymagier indeed came out with commendable regularity over the following months. The second issue must have been finished before Jarry's induction, and appeared in January 1895. Jarry contributed his text on "Monsters," illustrated by woodcuts donated by Paul Fort. The third number followed in April, containing, among other things, a piece by Jarry on the Virgin and Child, and the lithograph of Rousseau's *La Guerre* (publication coincided with Rousseau's exhibiting his portrait of Jarry at the Salon des Indépendants). For the next issue, in July, Jarry wrote a scholarly disquisition on a thorny theological dispute: how many nails were employed to crucify Jesus Christ, three or four? This essay had only five plates to nine pages of text, and so was rather at odds with Gourmont's assertion that the words' only function in *L'Ymagier* would be to explain the imagery; its inclusion could only have been a bit of black humor on the editors' part. Jarry's main source was a learned tome by Cornelius Curtius, *De clavis dominicis*, and his personal copy of the book, from 1634, recently came to light, showing that his library was not so reduced as it was later to become.[74]

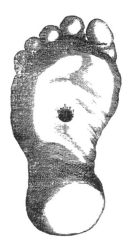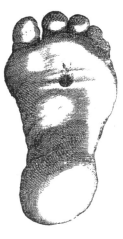

6.19
Illustration for Jarry's article "Les Clous du Seigneur" (The Nails of Our Lord), *L'Ymagier* 4.

Jarry's trips to Paris were not entirely taken up with arcane literary activities. As early as February 16, 1895 he had made an appearance in the capital, since he was at the famous party thrown by the Natansons, the owners and editors of the *Revue Blanche*, to unveil a series of paintings commissioned from Vuillard. Jarry came with the recently released Fénéon, who was now the principal editor of this review, the first record we have of their friendship. The bar was manned by Toulouse-Lautrec, four and a half feet tall, and by fellow-artist Maxime Dethomas, a full two feet taller. These two applied themselves to the prostration by cocktails of some 300 guests, who included just about every notable writer and artist of the day, but especially those associated with the *Mercure* and the *Revue Blanche*.[75]

When Vuillard, accompanied by Bonnard, arrived late at his own party, he was confronted by a crowd of semi-coherent inebriates. Bodies lay flat out on improvised beds in adjoining rooms. Vuillard was soon among their number; Fénéon gave up his place to him before being guided unsteadily from the party by a chambermaid. Vallette and Rachilde managed a slow and erratic waltz until the early hours by tightly gripping each other's shoulders. Lautrec's potions had a near-instantaneous effect on some, according to Jourdain: "'Let's get to work,' said Lugné-Poe, as he collapsed on to a bed to which sleep nailed him for the next ten hours." He was soon followed by Bonnard, discovered unconscious on the tiled floor of a toilet, his teeth chattering uncontrollably. By dawn an unusually sober Lautrec surveyed the ruins; he had served over 2,000 cocktails. This may have been when Jarry and he first met. A copy of *Caesar-Antichrist* inscribed to Lautrec survives, and Lautrec helped to paint the backdrop for *Ubu Roi* according to Lugné-Poe.[76]

···

In 1895, during the temporary hiatus in the Dreyfus Affair, another scandal engaged the attention of Parisian literary society, and also brought Jarry a new acquaintance: Lord Alfred Douglas. The narcissistic Bosie was in Paris, apparently delighted with his newfound celebrity as the *homme fatal* responsible for the downfall of Oscar Wilde. *Days and Nights* depicts both Jarry and Douglas taking part in some sort of imbroglio at the studio of Léonard Sarluis. The novel dates this event as occurring before the start of Jarry's military service in November 1894, but it more probably took place when Douglas resided in Paris six months later. When Douglas first visited the Mercure, they were initially sympathetic, and he was welcomed to the Tuesdays; later Wilde would appeal to Vallette not to publish Douglas's account of their relationship. The Mercureists rallied speedily in support of Wilde; a "Defense of Oscar Wilde" by Hugues Rebell came out in the August issue of the review. It ended with the hope that Pentonville Prison (Wilde had not yet been moved to Reading Gaol) should suffer the same fate as the Bastille. Elsewhere Lormel, Lorrain, Mirbeau, Régnier, Tailhade, and the critic Henry Bauer all published articles vehemently condemning the actions of the British state.[77]

When Jarry and Fargue had separated, most of the group around Jourdain had sided with the latter, and thereby earned themselves a passing insult in *Faustroll* when Jarry referred to "young men with red hair, equally cretinous in their speech and their silence." A new group of friends soon took their place, and they are identified in Édouard Julia's copy of *Days and Nights*. Gathered in Sarluis's studio were Douglas, Henri Albert, the acerbic translator of the complete works of Nietzsche for the Mercure, Fanny Zaessinger, the only female, Ernest La Jeunesse, and Léonard Sarluis himself.[78]

Sarluis was an unusual figure, an artist who has more or less disappeared from art history. After an exceedingly cloistered upbringing in The Hague, he appeared in Paris as an art student in 1894 and was an immediate sensation, not least because of his great wealth and remarkable personal beauty. Pawlowski tells us that when Sarluis toured Italy, fruit vendors in Naples refused his money: "Angels do not pay!" The professional debauchee Jean Lorrain wrote in his newspaper column that "some sort of Dutch cherub has arrived in Paris, he has the smile of the Mona Lisa and the talents of Raphael." Not a judgment with which many would concur. Sarluis's paintings were huge—the studio at this moment was dominated by his twelve-foot-high *Nero and Agrippina*—but they were effeminate and just a little nauseating: decadent parodies of Raphael that were old-fashioned even in the 1890s. His style remained unchanged until his death in 1949. His only concession to modernity was that the Botticellian braids of his Salomés were gradually transformed into flappers' bobs from the 1920s onward. In Paris, he quickly found himself a place at the Café Napolitain, where "La Jeunesse was his mentor, and Oscar Wilde his god." It was the former who was the victim of events in his studio.[79]

La Jeunesse, a lifelong friend of Jarry's, was, in contrast to Sarluis, famously ugly, a fact which his self-portrait makes little attempt to conceal. He had other physical abnormalities: an exceptional growth of body hair and a falsetto voice. In compensation he was corrosively quick-witted. An extravagant creature all round, not least in his dress, he was popular on the boulevards,

6.20, 6.21
Ernest La Jeunesse, caricatures of Léonard Sarluis
and of himself, from *Talentiers*, 1896.

and close to Wilde and his circle. Later on, Apollinaire wrote an affectionate account of him in *Le Flâneur de deux rives* in which he described his rooms filled with a fantastic profusion of books, enamels, objects in ivory, ancient Greek gems, African statues, and ornamental canes. He appeared content to fritter away his entire existence in cafés, in particular the Napolitain, and earned himself a reputation as a masochist by seeming to collude with Jarry as the butt of his jokes. An unusual relationship, to which Jarry referred in his dedication in La Jeunesse's copy of *Ubu Roi* (one of the few on *Hollande*): "This copy is to glorify Ernest La Jeunesse, worthy to be glorified, except when inclined to make a complete ass of himself in public." La Jeunesse published his most famous book, *Les Nuits, les ennuis et les âmes de nos plus notoires contemporains*, in 1895, a selection of caustic parodies of the more respected authors of the day which were nicely characterized by Armory as "anthumous obituaries."[80]

Fanny Zaessinger presents a different enigma. Small, beautiful, evidently spirited, she crops up with some frequency in Jarry's company for several years, even visiting him in Corbeil when he moved out of Paris. André Lebey, for one, often ran into the pair of them around Montmartre. They were close, but it was also a brief friendship and the reason for its brevity remains a mystery. Fanny appeared in Paris in the early 1890s and disappeared around 1898. In between she acted, often at the Œuvre, modeled for Lautrec and Léandre among others, and was "associated" with various writers and artists. Her date of birth is uncertain, but she was in her early twenties; no image of her is known, though many from her modeling days certainly exist, but remain unidentifiable. Her life after her sudden disappearance is a complete historical blank. There are no known letters, no notion of what she did subsequently, or of when or where she died. Yet Fanny was a young lady who made quite an impression on most of those she met, even upon Colette, who was not one to be easily taken aback:[81]

> When I saw her in my flat, Fanny with her soft chestnut hair tumbling on her shoulders, when I saw her toss her page's toque on my bed, caressing all the objects in the room with her lovely, tip-tilted fingers, when I saw her casually open her dress and reveal her eager breasts and stick out her tongue at my mirror, when I heard her divulge to Willy, to me, to the birds at the open window, her preferences in the way of voluptuous practices, then the blood of "Madame Colette's daughter" was roused.[82]

So what occurred in Sarluis's studio? Jarry's description in *Days and Nights* is carefully ambiguous. Lots are drawn to see who should pose naked, but the result has been fixed in advance and falls on La Jeunesse …

> who refused to comply. Sengle [Jarry] held him by the shoulders—with his fingertips—and Huppe [Fanny] stripped him. […]
>
> Severus Altmensch [La Jeunesse] was naked, but for his feet, which seemed more deformed for being only guessed at, encased in their built-up boots. Hollow-chested, belly jutting as the

tip of a tetrahedron, arms like two laths, legs of a faun—a faun in an etching, castrated out of decency—and every limb protruding as if disjointed. A vicuña's or llama's curly astrakhan luxuriated everywhere, a wool resembling suint; and with his claw-sharp nails he combed his enormous belly's triangular pubis toward his chest, point upward.

Huppe willingly did her best to oblige him; Severus uttered little cries, simpering and biting at her breast. Her efforts came to nothing since he was a masochist, a fetishist and a clerk of court, and he writhed on the carpet while sucking the beak of a stuffed peacock.[83]

In the novel everyone ended up naked, although Jarry's annotations to Édouard Julia's copy had only La Jeunesse being stripped. Events were then interrupted by the ring of the doorbell and the arrival of Cremnitz; whatever followed is left unstated.

Afterward they may well have repaired to the nearby Chat Noir. Montfort noted that Sarluis, La Jeunesse, Jarry, Tinan, and Douglas were often to be seen together at the famous cabaret during Wilde's trials, which began in April 1895. All of these companions of Jarry were famously fastidious in dress, but he was surviving on very little, perhaps an allowance and some military pay, and his appearance tended toward the ragged. He was still enveloped in his absurd black overcoat, now offset by a white scarf, but his battered and overlarge shoes, perhaps army boots, proclaimed his straitened circumstances.[84]

Fargue and his gang were often there too, and some of them at least still spoke to him. One evening Jarry appeared and sat at a table on his own, until Cremnitz or Bottini went over to him. The Chat Noir was famous for its shadow-puppet theater, a medium bound to appeal to Jarry, and he made the acquaintance of many of its most celebrated habitués, the comic writer Alphonse Allais among others, as well as with its larger-than-life patron, Rodolphe Salis. Salis died early in 1897, so these were, in fact, the last months of the most famous cabaret of the period.[85]

...

Jarry's father died after a brief illness on August 18, 1895, and according to Arnaud, Jarry did not attend the funeral; he was probably in Paris. The solicitor in charge of administering his father's estate wrote to Jarry there on the 25th, urging him to return to Laval within a week or so, but Jarry, busy preparing *Caesar-Antichrist* for publication, was content to avoid the proximity of the barracks and to allow his sister to represent his interests. He remained principally in Paris until at least late September, and Roig, who bumped into him in the street around this time, was surprised to see that he didn't even bother wearing his uniform.[86]

In September an abbreviated version of *Ubu Roi* appeared in the *Mercure* as the "Terrestrial Act" of *Caesar-Antichrist*, and the next month the book itself was printed. Whereas *Minutes* was primarily a book of poetry, *Caesar-Antichrist*, which resembles its predecessor in format and production, was a play, and a play that might be described as ultra-Symbolist. Using a stupefying mixture of symbols from personal, mathematical, iconographic, and religious sources, Jarry constructed a universe of meanings that led: where eventually? He was continuing to push

Symbolism to extremes, and pursued its demoralization by once again incorporating elements too heterogeneous for it to absorb, notably the grotesque figure of Père Ubu. There were fewer reviews even than for *Minutes*; when the Heraldic Act had appeared in the *Mercure* the previous March it had been seen as so obscure that even an avant-garde journal such as *La Jeune Belgique* had been lost for words. Its reviewer cited two scenes before commenting: "Mammamouchi: apogrousalabos triphocaran tatalababa colocopicsoné zoufzouf lapatapoum bottocu pampam." Dadaist sound poetry before its time, but the book publication brought congratulations from friends (Kahn, Quillard), and Mallarmé once again obliged with an enthusiastic letter.[87]

6.22
César-Antéchrist, 1895.

The fifth issue of *L'Ymagier* also came out in October, although Jarry's name does not appear except on the masthead. His only contribution was his drawings of devotional biscuits from Brittany, signed with the pseudonym "Alain Jans." It was the end of his collaboration with the magazine he had co-founded.

Jarry had to return to barracks before the publication of *Caesar-Antichrist*, since on November 5, 1895 he wrote to Vallette asking him to delay distribution of it no longer, and to send out review and presentation copies—he was to write and sign Jarry's dedications himself but using Jarry's name, a fact that bibliophiles ought to note. One of the two copies on special China paper was for Gourmont, and Jarry also asked Vallette to use the *L'Ymagier* address, Gourmont and Courrière's residence, for correspondence. Why then did Gourmont prevent the *Mercure* from reviewing Jarry's book? In the interim, probably some time in mid or late November, the affair of "The Old Lady" came to a head, a farce that was to have unfortunate consequences.[88]

...

6.23, 6.24, 6.25
Alfred Jarry, drawings of biscuits from *L'Ymagier* 5.

La Vieille Dame, The Old Lady, was the Mercureists' nickname for Berthe de Courrière, who was forty-three in 1895. The formidable and also distinctly ludicrous mistress of Remy de Gourmont, Berthe Courrière (the "de" was her own addition) had had a picturesque career. She came to Paris in her twenties and was the mistress successively of several government ministers, of the ill-fated right-wing politician General Boulanger, and of the sculptor Clésinger—her monumental physique made her the perfect model for his large statue of the Republic exhibited at the Exposition Universelle of 1878. He left her a fortune on his death in 1883, and three years later she met Gourmont. He indulged her passion for the occult with séances and table-turning at her flat in the rue de Varenne, and appears to have tolerated a series of ardent liaisons with several more or less disreputable priests. A black mass that ended badly resulted in a short stay in a psychiatric hospital, and her relationship with the heretical ex-abbé Boullan made her the model for Madame Chantelouve in Huysmans's novel *Là-bas*. In 1890 she was arrested in Bruges when police discovered her almost naked in the street near the house of another ecclesiastic with whom she was involved, this one a famous exorcist whom Huysmans depicts in his novel as having a crucifix tattooed on the sole of each foot so as to trample the Cross with every step. Later on, she had a prolonged affair with Gourmont's brother. These adventures had earned her a reputation as a voracious sexual predator among the writers of the *Mercure*.[89]

And the "affair"? … no more than a practical joke played on Jarry by two of his friends, Jean de Tinan and Rachilde, or so the latter would have us believe. Essentially there are two very biased accounts of it: by Rachilde, and by Jarry himself. Jarry, in his novel *L'Amour en Visites* (*Visits of Love*), exaggerates for literary effect, and perhaps further to wound his ex-patron Gourmont. Rachilde, however, plays down her role in the affair in her book on Jarry—no doubt because, in this matter, she seems to have been driven by motives that appear to pass beyond the mischievous into rather more unfriendly territory.

Rachilde did not disguise her dislike for Courrière. She claimed to put up with her only for Gourmont's sake, but neglects to mention that he had persuaded Berthe to put money into the *Mercure*. Rachilde's account began with a description of Courrière's habitual costume at the Tuesdays: a rough cloak like those worn in religious orders, a full skirt made of something resembling sackcloth, over her arm a plaited rush shopping bag from which she was inseparable, and which was reputed to contain consecrated hosts she would toss to stray dogs in the street. A bright blonde wig was visible beneath her hood, and around her neck she wore a homemade necklace of cockerels' feathers, frequently bedraggled by rain. From beneath her skirts projected a pair of men's sandals, her large feet being deemed particularly risible. Berthe's skin, furthermore, had a permanent sheen, from being rubbed daily with unrectified Vaseline. This get-up, Rachilde continued, outraged the young novelist Jean de Tinan, the most dandyish of the Tuesday celebrants, prone to silver-buttoned black satin waistcoats and a bunch of violets in his buttonhole. And so, one day he had an idea. Rachilde should persuade Courrière that Jarry harbored a secret passion for her, Berthe would pounce, both would take offense, and thus would Rachilde's salon be disencumbered of both of its worst "monsters" in one go. Rachilde therefore attributed the blame to Tinan, whose death twenty years before she was writing made him a convenient scapegoat, and

6.26
The only known photograph of Berthe de Courrière,
from *Comœdia*, November 13, 1921.

6.27
Photograph of Jean de Tinan by Pierre Louÿs, 1897.

went to some lengths in her memoirs to imply that Tinan disliked Jarry. However, this may be easily disproved with reference to letters Tinan wrote to his friend André Lebey.[90]

Here Tinan's admiration for his sartorial opposite, for both his person and his works, was almost gushing. In one letter, from August 1895, only three months before he was supposed to desire Jarry's banishment, he writes, for example: "Ah the last issue of the *Mercure*! Your friend Jarry's woodcut! When such things are to be seen then life is worth living. And the 'Père Ubu who has drunk too much!' And the word 'Sloven,' which evidently haunts your friend Jarry, and the fifth letter of the word '*merdre*,' etc., etc." Furthermore: "his imagination surpasses all of ours," and a month later he regrets that Lebey does not know Jarry well enough to make an introduction: "at least he's not banal!"[91]

But Rachilde seemed bent on this intrigue, and on involving Tinan. He was an enthusiastic romantic and an inveterate boulevardier, to such an extent that it was something of a mystery to his friends how his many love affairs and late-night escapades left him any time for writing. When these liaisons came to their usually disastrous conclusions, he was often laid low by nephritis. The illness was serious, and he had only three years left to live. Like many at the Mercure, Tinan was well known to be besotted with Fanny Zaessinger, and so Rachilde told him that Fanny had designs on Jarry. Tinan's jealousy would surely have been short-lived, since Jarry did not exactly disguise his sexual indifference to women. Rachilde then decided on another tactic, and proposed an unusual mission to The Old Lady. Berthe de Courrière was generally credited with Huysmans's conversion to Catholicism—once she had convinced him of the reality of black magic, he had fled straight into the embrace of mother Church. Another conversion must now be attempted. Jarry, she suggested, had strayed onto paths that led to perdition, and it might be a "good work" to return a young man to the true path of worship: women. An unorthodox Christian duty perhaps, but no more than some of Courrière's other religious activities.[92]

Events took their course, and Rachilde had the grace to preface her account with a (too light-hearted) profession of shame. She told Berthe that she had noticed that Jarry assumed a distracted air when she spoke, and that he had complimented her singing voice, and that beneath Jarry's brusque manners and dishevelled exterior … and so forth. Berthe responded by intimating to Jarry that he seemed to need looking after—buttons sewn on and other services—a fact which Jarry revealed to Rachilde in tones of real horror. She assured him that Berthe's eccentricities at the Mercure hid a tender sensibility and that in domestic circumstances she might be transformed, just like one of those princesses in *The Arabian Nights*.

"No, Ma-da-me," replied Jarry, "we do not believe in such transformations. Men of genius are welcome to sleep with their cooks, but we would not wish genius upon our own person at such a price. We do not love women at all, and if we ever did, we would require her to be our equal, which is saying quite a lot! We are Breton, not Norman!"[93]

It is Gourmont who is being referred to here (Courrière looked after his household, and he was from Normandy). Despite his literary reputation, Gourmont's relationship with Courrière laid him open to a certain amount of ridicule, a fact of which he must have been aware, and which perhaps made him all the more sensitive to the "joke."

Berthe, though, had taken the bait, and she began her pursuit with literature. She lent Jarry a book, which he neglected to look at for a month or so, but when he eventually picked it up a manuscript fell from between its pages. It was a bizarre and astonishing declaration, couched in the worst excesses of Symbolist style, entitled "Tua res agitur" (This concerns you). A very brief extract of its several pages is quite enough for anyone, although Jarry later included all of it in *Visits*:

> Come, there is none to equal me. I know the despair of Orpheus and the anguish of his plaints. The vulture will cease to devour Prometheus and Pygmalion will no longer animate a futile shade.
>
> Come, I shall give you time and eternity, I know the secret of beyond, you will not uselessly implore the deaf gods, and your dreams will not shatter on the limits of the possible.
>
> Come, and you will prevail; come, that I might carry you off to limitless space. I have won over all the Chimeras, I shall give you an unending dream.
>
> My arms are strong enough to carry you, my heart stout enough to sustain you, my spirit mighty enough to initiate you.
>
> [...] Come, you will be the Conqueror, if you can but understand, and dare.[94]

Rachilde's account effectively ends here, and so she avoided any mention of the consequences. According to Jarry in *Visits*, the telegrams of September 1894 followed this unconventional declaration, and here his and Rachilde's accounts contradict one another. The problem is one of dates. The dates on the telegrams are not in doubt, since they still exist. Jarry's version (admittedly in a novel) has them being sent after he read "Tua res agitur," thus the whole business would have begun in August 1894 at the latest. However, Rachilde says Jarry received "Tua res agitur" as a result of the conspiracy by herself and Tinan at the Mercure, and Tinan only first began attending her salon in the spring of 1895. The simplest explanation is that Tinan had nothing at all to do with it.[95]

Whatever the exact sequence of events, they unfolded toward their inevitably unhappy conclusion, probably during Jarry's occasional stays in Paris in the summer of 1895 when, as coeditor of *L'Ymagier*, he could hardly avoid seeing Berthe. Eventually she inveigled Jarry into visiting her rooms, which were hung with tapestries, redolent with incense (and the smell of rancid butter, according to one visitor), crammed with Clésinger's plaster casts of her body parts, and decorated with a fantastic plethora of ecclesiastical objects. Jarry's description in the chapter of *Visits* devoted to her was willfully cruel:[96]

> The Old Lady is old, as her name indicates; statues of her half a century ago—when celebrated prefaces proclaimed the luster of her beauty—attest to the fact that the meaning of the word beauty oscillates over time from one pole to another.[97]

He reproduces her conversation:

> THE OLD LADY: I've changed my dress five times in your presence and you haven't even looked at me. I have dresses slit at the side so that they reveal a glimpse of my yellow drawers underneath, and only one fastener need be undone and the whole dress slips off. And I've had them specially made for adultery. I never wash except with Vaseline. I get it cheap from a pharmacist in the suburbs who also supplies me with anti-herpetic ointment. Thus I've been able to preserve the softness of my skin. Oh! Don't look at me like that in the light. They're only little red pimples.

… and then descends to gratuitous vulgarity, after a swipe at Gourmont (Lucien is Jarry's pseudonym on this occasion):

> THE OLD LADY: […] I am naturally chaste, and it is so long since that happened to me that it is exactly as if I were a virgin.
>
> LUCIEN: But if I may be indiscreet, how about The Old Man?
>
> THE OLD LADY: Oh. I beg you, let us cast a veil …
>
> [*She rubs her bristly chin on Lucien's knees.*] They say that in the brothels, some of the women have obliging little tricks that are quite extraordinary. […] Would you like me to put my false teeth in a glass of water so as to extend to my whole palate the softness of my lips?

Jarry had excelled himself, and the immoderation of this very personal hatchet job is unique in his writing. He never again resorted to such personal insult, and the fact that he felt the need to do so reveals something of the injury he felt, although it does not really explain why.

This was not the immediate cause of the rupture with Gourmont, however, since the book did not appear until 1898 (at which point Gourmont threatened legal action, according to Rachilde). The precise circumstances are unknown, and given that Jarry actually refused Gourmont's mistress's advances, the only apparent explanation for their break before the appearance of *Visits* is some verses penned by Jarry in December 1895. Jarry must have become aware that some of the Mercureists were following the various acts of this drama with amusement. He'd been "had," and his response was "An Inscription to be Placed at the Start of the Noble History of the Old Lady," a scurrilous poem that galloped through a chronicle of Berthe's previous *amours* while exploiting the French rhyme between Vaseline and Messalina.[98]

Gourmont could not ignore this poem circulating around the Mercure, along with Berthe's declaration to Jarry, which he had shown to Rachilde, and so probably to others. He ended both his friendship and his collaboration with Jarry. Jarry's name disappeared from the masthead of *L'Ymagier*; there were to be three further issues edited by Gourmont alone. He never again referred to Jarry in print, and so he was omitted from Gourmont's important survey of Symbolist literature, *The Book of Masks* (two volumes, 1895 and 1896). More importantly, Jarry lost his principal literary ally. Arnaud points out that because the production of *Ubu Roi* was to occupy Jarry for most of 1896, he had no need of Gourmont's assistance; but later, when he wanted to publish non-Ubuesque works, it would have been invaluable. After *Days and Nights*, however, the Mercure published no more of Jarry's novels, and after *Visits* appeared, not even the magazine of the *Mercure* was open to him (although one article was smuggled in under a pseudonym). Even though Jarry's quarrel with Gourmont is generally thought to be the reason why his works ceased to appear in the *Mercure*, one cannot but suspect that this was not the whole story. Vallette and Rachilde had serious reservations about Jarry's writing, and the argument with Gourmont sufficed as a convenient excuse not to publish him. Vallette's obituary of Jarry would support such a supposition.

Jarry certainly did nothing to prevent the ending of his relationship with Gourmont. He might easily have repaired it, at least until he circulated the "Inscription." The risks were high; he could have burned all his boats at the Mercure. Besnier sees here a deliberate "Oedipal" assassination, although it all looks rather too accidental and hotheaded to support such an interpretation. Jarry continued to be a regular at the Tuesdays, but Gourmont now rarely came. Their quarrel happened to coincide with his withdrawal from literary society because of his worsening illness. The cloud on his cheek mentioned by Fargue had become a tempest; his face was disfigured by lupus, and cauterization froze it into an expression of disdain, his bottom lip left hanging and paralyzed. Part crippled also, he became a virtual recluse among his books, garbed in a monk's habit and cap. His situation was not quite as tragic as it sounds, since his solitude was broken by the many literary visitors who managed to negotiate their way past his "Cerberus": Berthe. She remained with him "faithfully" during his affliction. There was a final bizarre postscript. When Gourmont died in 1915 she had him buried in her ex-lover Clésinger's sepulcher in Père-Lachaise. She joined them both on her own death a year later.

It is unlikely that Jarry ever discovered the truth of the Old Lady affair, or the part played in it by Rachilde and Tinan, if the latter was involved at all. Jarry was not particularly forgiving, as the cases of Lormel, Fargue, and Gourmont have variously shown. Yet his friendship with the conspirators was unaffected; Rachilde remained his close friend, and his cordial relations with Tinan not only continued, but if anything became warmer. There is an ordinary copy of *Ubu Roi* dedicated to him, but when the facsimile edition appeared in 1897, Tinan received the first copy of only ten on Chinese paper. Nor did Tinan's enthusiasm for *Ubu* diminish, as is demonstrated by the letter already cited on page 74, which he later published with little variation as an article in *Le Centaure*.[99]

...

Late in 1895, a friend from the army reappeared in Paris: Maurice Dide, the medical intern. A chapter in *Days and Nights* provides a transcript of a hashish session at his apartment on the quai d'Orléans. Two others participated, probably Gaston de Pawlowski and Albert Haas, a German writer passing through Paris. It is safe to assume that Jarry was in Paris by late November or early December 1895, and that this was when the Old Lady affair came to a head, because we next find him in the Val-de-Grâce military hospital, over the wall from the Calvary. He would surely have been hospitalized in Laval had he fallen ill while at the barracks.[100]

On December 14, 1895 Jarry was discharged from the army, twenty-three months early, on medical grounds: gallstones. This was an unusual condition in one so young, and conveniently hard to diagnose in Jarry's day, when the only symptom was pain around the liver. He later told Tailhade and Guitry, among others, that he had swallowed various "poisons" in order to be invalided out of the army, and that these were what caused the occasional skin eruptions on his face—a claim that previously has been treated with a certain amount of skepticism. However, an early biographer, Lebois, was more specific. According to him, Jarry swallowed a dose of picric acid. This substance would have been easily obtainable, since the army employed it both as an explosive and as an antiseptic, and on this occasion Lebois's statement has some independent verification. Jarry told Guitry he had swallowed yellow fabric dye, another common use for picric acid. Furthermore, the symptoms of picric acid poisoning are close to those for gallstones (liver damage and abdominal pain), and for jaundice (yellowing of the skin). It can also cause various forms of dermatitis. Jaundice, moreover, is a secondary condition often caused by gallstones and thus, in Jarry's day, a yellow complexion constituted one of the few visible symptoms of both of these complaints. Jarry's sallowness was remarked upon on more than one occasion, as were his skin problems. Since Dide, now in Paris, had previously used his medical knowledge to show Jarry how to fake various ailments, it does not seem quite so unlikely that Jarry may indeed have risked this perilous means of extricating himself from the army.[101]

Other unknowns surround his demobilization. Rachilde says Courrière pulled strings to get him out (having known a general or two in her time), and this when he was writing the "Inscription." … And, according to his discharge papers, the army were under the impression that he was a student at the ENS.[102]

Jarry survived the army; he even rather got the better of it. Besnier describes *Days and Nights* as a demonstration of the application of Pataphysics to the vicissitudes of the everyday. The novel sketched out a theory of desertion in its widest sense: of how to evade reality by means such as dreams, drugs, hallucination, variants of the "other worlds" evoked in Jarry's description of Pataphysics. In these difficult circumstances, his "noble mode of self-preservation" was simply the practical implementation of this theory, this "science." The distinction between fiction and reality becomes a little blurred here, and not for the last time.[103]

Despite Jarry engineering a fairly easy time of it, the rigors of military service should not be underestimated. It was a brutal imposition at a critical moment in a young man's life, and many were broken by it (Fargue was traumatized by the experience, for example). Suicides and self-mutilations were not uncommon. In various ways this *was* a formative experience for Jarry, and the fact that it coincided with his break with Gourmont made it all the more emphatic. It may have initiated his addiction to alcohol, a taste which coincided with one for unconstrained liberty: a predilection, and a combination, that was perhaps impractical.

Jarry returned to Laval in late December to finalize the liquidation of his father's estate. Anselme's debts were covered by the sale of two properties. Charlotte's share included the remaining property at the rue de Bootz, and Jarry's was a lump sum of more than 15,000 francs. 1895 had been momentous, and he had already laid the foundation for his activities the following year, which was to prove an even more pivotal year in Jarry's life. His sudden wealth made possible ambitious plans for 1896, but these could not be realized while he was still in the army. Thus perhaps the drastic measure of poisoning himself in order to regain his freedom.[104]

MISOGYNY AND NOSTALGIA

The reasons for the fury of Jarry's rejection of Berthe de Courrière are not entirely obvious. His private life was evidently a touchy subject, and unless some further correspondence surfaces, it is likely to remain an obscure one. Jarry was exceptionally discreet about this aspect of his life, and although his sexuality presents contradictions as strong as any others, one is largely reduced to speculation with regard to it.

7.1
This tin or pewter plate was given to Rachilde by Vallette and inscribed by Paul Verlaine. Subsequently inscribed by Jarry to Rachilde: "In bourgwaus socilliety my dear little Monsieur Vénus, you will always go barefoot," with a drawing by him of Père Ubu. Rachilde's reply reads: "I have both glory and paper and never go on foot anymore." (From *La Brèche, action surréaliste*, November 8, 1965.)

7.2
Claudius-Jacquet (center) around the time he knew Alfred Jarry.

CHAPTER 7

Jarry was widely considered a misogynist, yet his firmest and most long-lived friendship was with a woman, Rachilde. He also had various other female friendships—it is impossible to know if they were ever anything more—notably with the mysterious Fanny Zaessinger, who was certainly not overburdened with inhibitions. Rachilde recorded a number of Jarry's reflections regarding the "different sex": "The honor of women is something essentially negligible since they have no soul. Their virtue is a matter of temperament: which they either have, or they lack … and we are not referring to their virtue!"[1]

Some were more personal: "Ma-da-me, you are a thoroughly low character! You are merely a negligible quantity of atoms stuck together, but we grant you one quality at least: you do not cling!" Rachilde observed that Jarry's "compliments always had a certain savor," and that he "made a show of a profound disdain for women in general, and literary ones in particular." Many at the Mercure understood that his more abusive pronouncements were coded. Tongue in cheek despite their truculence, they performed what Bergson almost concluded was a component of humor: to discover whether the listener was "one of us." The "us," his audience, was able to laugh at what it took most seriously, and Jarry constituted a kind of initiation for newcomers to the salon. Even so, his asperity toward women often seems unfeigned.[2]

During his late adolescence and early twenties Jarry undoubtedly considered himself homosexual, or "Uranian" in the then prevailing parlance. His many homosexual friends and acquaintances assumed the same. Wilde, for example, presumed as much, likewise Lormel. And how else should one interpret a postcard such as this, received from the precious aesthete and minor diplomat, the poet J.-M. Levet, and posted from Biskra: "Henry Jean Marie Levey [*sic*] thinks it his duty to inform Monsieur Alfred Jarry that he has acquired an Arab nomad for 1 fr. 30—one franc thirty centimes—the veritable phynance-stick and he will not relinquish him for all the gold of Poland and Aragon."[3]

Other instances of Jarry's friends taking his homosexuality for granted could be easily cited. However, Jarry, the hard-drinking athlete, did not much resemble the contemporary literary trope of the limp-wristed Decadent poet personified by the likes of Wilde and Levet. Furthermore, Jarry's inclinations appear to have been more cerebral than physical, since his early writings display an aversion to physical relations in the context of homosexuality, or in any other context for that matter. Outside of his various possible homosexual relationships, with the likes of Levet, Sarluis, and "Bougrelas" (who will make his brief appearance in the next chapter), there are three which seem particularly significant: Morin, Fargue, and Claudius-Jacquet.

In the case of Henri Morin, we are left only with Rachilde's assertion that she will not disclose what she knows out of "literary sadism." This comes close to confirming that there was something worth disclosing. When her book on Jarry was published, Henri Morin was still alive, which may explain her reticence.

With Fargue, there is a modicum of certainty. Around 1940, the author Auriant, a Mercureist of many years' standing, was speaking of times past with Rachilde. His diary records that they recalled some sort of violent scene between Jarry and Fargue, perhaps even that of their final separation. Auriant wrote down this conversation:

> I got Madame Rachilde on to the question of A. Jarry. This time she said: "L.-P. Fargue should have known." I [Auriant] said to her: "He probably wouldn't have asked." "But he certainly confessed to me." "What did he tell you? that he was Jarry's lover?" "Yes, when I asked him what he'd done to provoke this scene, and then he went into so much detail that I had to ask him to desist. When I told Monsieur Vallette, he answered: 'Are you surprised? You'll come across plenty of others.'" [4]

As for Claudius-Jacquet—who seems to have been the one real object of Jarry's affection—almost nothing is known of this relationship; not even whether Jarry's feelings were reciprocated. The emphatic celibacy of the novel in which Claudius-Jacquet appears, *Days and Nights*, perhaps suggests not. He left Paris for good at least by 1900, and all that survives are a number of Jarry's letters and cards to him. Uniquely warm despite their brevity, they communicate much. The only known reply to these messages, or at least the only one Jarry preserved, was occasioned by Jarry sending him a copy of *Messalina*. After some words in its praise, Claudius-Jacquet announced "news which will somewhat amaze you without really amazing you, knowing how well you know me": his marriage. Jarry continued to write him the occasional postcard, henceforth more carefully tempered. He was the only person, apart from his sister, whom Jarry addressed with the familiar *tu* in the whole of his correspondence. [5]

Parts of Jarry's prose fiction do seem to trace a sexual journey of some sort, but whether he himself alighted at the stops indicated is not known. The itinerary is fragmentary, but it may be briefly outlined.

Jarry's first book, *Minutes*, contains the openly homosexual text "Haldernablou." The circumstances of its composition have been described above, and its distaste for a sexual expression of homosexuality is unmistakable. Jarry's next two books, *Caesar-Antichrist* and *Ubu Roi*, are devoid of overt sexual content, but 1896 would see the publication of "The Other Alcestis," a series of short prose texts which contains one of Jarry's most misogynistic tirades, put in the mouth of Queen Bilkis and aimed at the Homeric Helen:

> Behold this body artificially strangled around the middle which dares, when recumbent, to mimic the sign of infinity; on the upper part are the two bruised and excoriated organs which decompose and dissolve when an unconscious being, before acquiring the nobility of grinding bones, must begin living on putrefaction—having hatched in blood and sanies from a ruptured tumor because some man has inconsiderately urinated on the clump of mold that conceals the shameful suppurating wound of the inferior swelling. [6]

Later the same year, as recounted in chapter 8, there would be a similar rant about women actors playing the roles of boys, then the custom on the Parisian stage. The intensity of Jarry's pronouncements suggests that some real incidents may lie at the root of his distaste, and if he did have youthful heterosexual experiences they perhaps resemble those in the early chapters of *Visits of Love*. Much of this book was written before or at the same time as *Days and Nights*, and narrates an apparently conventional bourgeois "sentimental education." "Everybody has a try at the traditional visits," the author remarks on the first page of the novel: Jarry too then, presumably. These "visits" consist of a succession of assignations: with the family's housemaid, with a prostitute, the Old Lady, a duchess, the young cousin, the fiancée. How many of these—mostly fruitless—encounters are autobiographical in origin? The Old Lady, certainly. The prostitute, possibly: the caller here is a soldier aged twenty-one, Jarry's age when he joined the army, and such adventures were surely commonplace, even expected? As for the others, it is impossible to know. Jarry's relations with his relatives remain obscure, cousins included, and it seems unlikely there was ever a fiancée even distantly in prospect. Overall, *Visits* leads one to believe that Jarry may well have had similar heterosexual experiences to some of those described, although since they are again couched in defensively aggressive misogyny they were perhaps more wounding in real life than on the page. The only references to homosexuality in the novel are so rarefied and obscure that they are easily missed (in the visit to the doctor). Perhaps the most adequate summary of this book is Jarry's own. He dedicated a copy of *Visits* to Rachilde, who had recently published a novel, *L'Heure sexuelle,* under the pseudonym Jean de Chilra:[7]

> To Rachilde and to Jean de Chilra
> these XI hetero … doxical moments
> in the autosexual hour of
> Monsieur Ubu
> Alfred Jarry[8]

Around 1896, a gradual change is perceptible in Jarry's attitudes. His misogyny becomes moderated, less frequently asserted and more often ironic rather than cutting (although there was something of a resurgence in his final novel, *La Dragonne*, perhaps due to the special circumstances of its composition). One may speculate that this moderation coincides with Jarry's relationship with Claudius-Jacquet, since it is he who was at least partially portrayed as Valens, the ambiguous love object in *Days and Nights*, written just at this time. Or perhaps this new mood signaled the ending of their relationship, which presumably dated from 1893 when they were at school, since in the novel Valens is depicted as far away and inaccessible. One chapter, entitled "Adelphism and Nostalgia," outlines an almost wistful erotic doctrine of narcissism and celibacy ("adelph" is Greek for brother):

> In my immense grief-stricken solitude
> I sense my brother has forgotten me.
> His dear face pales, his features all elude
> My grasp—and falsehood clouds my memory.
>
> His portrait lies before me as I write.
> It's handsome maybe ugly—who can tell?
> This Double vain and empty like a shell.
> His voice, once loved, no more rings clear and bright. […][9]

The word Adelphism, according to Sengle (the Jarry character in the novel), is "less medical" than Uranism. It designates for Sengle a most individual theory of "love," a love that does not concern the communion of two beings, but rather the communion of Sengle with his own past. He wishes to live "two different moments of time simultaneously; because this experience allows you to live out authentically one moment of eternity, or rather, all eternity, since it has no moments." But "Sengle, in love with the Memory of Self, was in need of a living, visible friend, since he had no recollection of his Self, being wholly devoid of memory." Thus Sengle's past is transferred on to, and embodied in, Valens, his "brother," his adelph, his double in fact, but a double of his past self. And this past is associated by Jarry with the landscape of his childhood. They go swimming in an open-air pool, identifiable as being just outside Saint-Brieuc.[10]

> [Valens] stooped down, and amid his dense-packed muscles his back smiled with nine delicate vertebrae. His tawny gold chest clicked gently against the flat water and for a brief glimpse his hips had a bronzer tinge about them on the sides, like a faun not midway between man and beast, an athletic ephebe rather, worthy of casting in metal. Then two narrow feet spread apart, divergent flight of two nacreous fish, and Sengle saw the water through his fingernails.[11]

The eroticism of such descriptions is self-evident. So what are we to make of this doctrine, except that its celibate cerebralism smacks of sublimation, and that it prolongs Jarry's dialog with the works of Bergson? Duration comprises exactly such an indivisible and endless moment, and for Bergson the fusion of past and present in duration is accomplished by memory, which is capable of actualizing the virtual past into the present, as was outlined in chapter 3 on Pataphysics.

Pataphysics, too, has the subsidiary function of reconnecting Jarry with his childhood past. The world seen anew, with its virtuality intact, resembles a child's perspective in which all sorts of imaginary solutions suffice to explain the world's complexities, and in particular the more incomprehensible preoccupations of adulthood. Thus if, at Rennes, Hébert represented adulthood and its stupidities, he also, strangely enough, represented its central mystery: that of sexuality. All those daughters … Jarry's idyllic childhood, overseen by an indulgent mother, is reminiscent of those of two other homosexual contemporaries: Marcel Proust and Raymond Roussel. Comparisons between their literary works, apparently so different from one another, could indeed be easily constructed from this perspective.

Jarry's valuation of childhood was perfectly knowing, however. In the same way as Bergson describes the past being brought into the present, Jarry described, in a brief essay on children's books, how childhood may be preserved and brought into adulthood, and specifically in the context of sexuality:

> If an adult male, as the saying goes, "is no more than a child who has grown up," is it not almost certain that he grew up as a child, and that this tends only to exaggerate his childish tendencies? His imagination becomes attenuated in a more capacious skull. His nervous system shrinks in

proportion to his body's growth. The "sexual parasite," according to the ingenious expression of Le Dantec, takes over. A new mood prevails: the world of grown-ups. […]

A sensible young man, no more intelligent than he should be, may reflect, and say to himself: "Here I am grown up, a man. Time to put away childish games."

Another *understands*: "Now everything is just a game. What big people call games are simply occupations different from their own, which do not interfere with their own; different games from their games, which is why they are permitted. Toys are nothing but decoys, so that we do not disembowel larger prey. […] So they gave us a green gauze butterfly net and tiny cages so we could only ensnare the smallest of creatures. But now we'll play for real."

Don Juan is only a little botanist who has grown up. Underneath he remains a bug collector.[12]

Collecting and record-breaking are common enough male sublimations, but what becomes clear here is that Jarry aimed to negotiate a compromise with adulthood *on his own terms*.

Days and Nights was followed by *Faustroll*, in which the erotic makes a purely academic appearance, and then, immediately afterward, by *Absolute Love*, in which Jarry plunged wholeheartedly into an Oedipal investigation of his childhood sexuality. This is described at length later on; here we simply note that it constituted his deepest, and thus final, exploration of this theme.

His last two novels, *Messalina* and *The Supermale*, are rather different again: they are far more sexually explicit, and almost entirely heterosexual. It is perhaps possible to attribute commercial motives to this realignment, although it would be uncharacteristic for Jarry to alter such a major aspect of his work for these motives alone.

Yet there are a few contrary indications that perhaps these novels were not so distant from Jarry's life after all. Rachilde, for example, assumed on more than one occasion that Jarry had recourse to "easy women" or visited brothels. Chauveau relates a particularly bizarre exchange, which he specifically states he got from Rachilde. The press was preoccupied with the murder of a prostitute, and several newspapers had reported that Jarry's card had been found in her possession. Rachilde told him that he might be considered a suspect. She mistook his angry reaction for one of maligned innocence, but Jarry corrected her: "It is not a question of whether we have killed someone or not. A man of the world does not give his card to whores, Ma-da-me. …" It has to be said that no such newspaper reports have ever been discovered.[13]

In Jarry's last finished novel, *The Supermale*, a certain amount of its detail, at least, is recognizably taken from Jarry's own experience. The great Sadeian château in which much of it takes place, for example, is identifiable as the spectacular Château de Courances, twelve miles from Le Coudray, where Jarry was then living. What else is taken from experience? In this novel, the much-abused Helen from "The Other Alcestis" reappears in a chapter entitled "The Discovery of Woman." It seems almost impossible to reconcile that earlier outburst with these lyrical and poignant evocations of the hero's love, and sexual passion, for his mistress.

The Supermale perceived that he was engaged in discovering Woman, an exploration for which he had not before had the leisure.

Assiduous love-making leaves no time to experience love.

He kissed all his discoveries like rare gems from which he would soon be obliged to part forever.

He kissed them—a thing he had not previously thought of doing, imagining that it would be evidence of a momentary impotence where more virile caresses were concerned—he kissed them to thank them for allowing him to discover them; he nearly thought: for allowing him to invent them.

And he began to sink softly down beside his companion, who was asleep in the absolute, just as the first man had awoken near Eve and thought that she had come out of his side because she was beside him, in his very natural surprise at finding the first woman, whom love had made to blossom, in the place where some still anthropoid female had slept before.

He murmured her name, the meaning of which he now understood for the first time:

"Helen, Helen!"[14]

Even if this were a homosexual scene transposed into a heterosexual one, such sexual tenderness is almost unique in Jarry's writing, and arouses the slight suspicion that there may be something unknown in Jarry's personal life around this time, in 1902. If so, he concealed it very successfully.

Despite such passages, elsewhere in *The Supermale* it has to be acknowledged that the sexual act is considered solely as a physical activity equivalent to any other sport, and one in which records may therefore be broken, Don Juan-wise. Both the Indian, the heroic sexual athlete of *The Supermale*, and the eponymous Messalina are celebrated for how often they make love in a single day. Both of them die of love, in a way. In the end, the Indian proves himself more machine than human, and the Machine-to-Inspire-Love falls in love with him. But machines do not really love. To make oneself a machine is to become immune to love. Invulnerable, and free … but also bereft.

8

1896

At the beginning of 1896, everything lay before him. With pockets comfortably plump, Jarry returned to Paris in January with two projects in mind: to create a new magazine to rival *L'Ymagier*, and to engineer the appearance of Père Ubu on an actual stage. There was only one serious candidate for this honor: the Œuvre.

8.1
Aurélien Lugné-Poe, around 1893.

During the previous year, he had rewritten, or at least re-edited, *Les Polonais*, and published it as the "Terrestrial Act" of *Caesar-Antichrist*. He had also written a new version of what eventually would become *Ubu cocu*, now called *Ubu intime ou les Polyèdres*. He had, therefore, brought two Ubu plays into a potentially performable state. Which one to stage? It seems he inclined toward *Les Polyèdres*; for one thing, it was entirely his own work.[1]

The lack of Lugné-Poe's early letters to Jarry means one must largely rely on inference to describe their negotiations. It was probably late in 1895 that Jarry had sent to Lugné-Poe what he referred to as an "unfinished version" of *Ubu Roi*. Lugné-Poe must have responded equivocally to this, and in his memoirs recalls that he could not envisage how to realize it on stage, a problem that was to persist even after he had accepted it. Undeterred, Jarry wrote to him again on January 8, 1896, to say that he would finish a new version of *Les Polyèdres* in a couple of weeks, and that this "may interest him." As for *Ubu Roi*, Lugné-Poe must have told him it was too long and that there were various practical difficulties in the staging. Jarry suggests he might simplify it a little, and proposes various innovations to overcome Lugné-Poe's objections which, furthermore, he is certain would "produce a guaranteed comic effect." Jarry's letter is carefully offhand; he implies that the play is a commercial proposition, since it would be cheap to put on, and potentially popular because accessible to a general public. Neither proved to be the case—as a direct consequence of the innovatory staging proposed by Jarry, and these innovations just happened to relate to Lugné-Poe's own preoccupations at the time. He had, for example, recently been studying the methods of the Elizabethan stage, such as its use of a single stage setting. Jarry listed his ideas:[2]

1. A mask for the principal, Ubu, which I can obtain for you if need be. I think the question of masks is one in which you have also been interested.

2. A cardboard horse's head which he would hang about his neck, as in the English medieval theater, for the two equestrian scenes, all details in the spirit of the piece, since I wanted to produce a "puppet play."

3. Making use of just one set, or better still, a plain backdrop, so as to avoid having to raise or lower the curtain during the single act. A person in evening dress would come on and hang up a sign indicating the location of the scene, like they do in puppet plays. (I'm sure anyway that a written sign is far more "suggestive" than a set. Neither set, nor extras, could adequately portray "The Polish army marching through the Ukraine.")

4. Do away with crowd scenes, which clutter the action and insult the audience's intelligence. Thus, in the parade ground scene, a single soldier, and the same for the battle scene when Ubu says "What a rabble, what a rout, etc."

5. Adoption of an "accent," or better, a special "voice" by the principal.

6. Costumes as unspecific as regards place or period as possible (to better suggest the idea of something eternal), preferably modern, because satire is modern; and wretched, so the play appears all the more squalid and horrible.

It seems unnecessary to stress just how radical these proposals were for a theatrical culture dominated by "realistic" melodramas and drawing-room farces. Such stage practices, although commonplace now, were still considered inflammatory half a century later. Yet Jarry's ideas also have a continuity with Symbolist theater practice: the single set, suggestions of eternity, and so forth. In the event, these continuities were to make the play all the more provocative, because sacrilegious. The general theater audience was bound to be appalled by Ubu; but many of Jarry's Symbolist colleagues were equally dismayed at the sight of Ubu trampling underfoot the theater of exquisite reverie that they had fought so hard to create.

Lugné-Poe, however, was concerned with the practical problems. According to his own account, he remained obdurate. He convinced Jarry it was impossible, that the stumbling block in both plays was the number of scene changes (addressed by Jarry in his letter). Jarry, he wrote, "pretended to abandon the project."[3]

In February 1896, Lugné-Poe put on Oscar Wilde's *Salomé* as part of the French campaign of solidarity with the imprisoned poet. The production attracted some of his remaining friends from London to see it. Ernest Dowson came with Aubrey Beardsley, and this may be when Jarry and the latter first met. The performance was fraught with problems, not least the possibility of an injunction being served by the U.K. government. The theater was ramshackle, there was a fire backstage during one of the performances, and the front-of-house staff were edgy in expectation of demonstrations against the author. Lugné-Poe's memoirs also recount that this was when he first encountered Jarry in person, introduced by A.-F. Herold after one of the performances. He recalled being intrigued by Jarry's "owlish gaze, his emphatic speech, his inexhaustible learning."[4]

There seemed no reason why the two should not get on—they had similar tastes, common acquaintances and interests, and there was only a small age gap between them (Lugné-Poe was twenty-six, Jarry twenty-two). Like Jourdain, Lugné-Poe was one of a group of artistic friends who had met at the Condorcet. The highly streamed nature of French education tended to produce these creative groups of schoolchildren, groups which often proved highly influential in French culture for years afterward. Lugné-Poe had begun acting at school and subsequently progressed through amateur companies to Antoine's Théâtre-Libre, but having no independent financial means, he had struggled both as an actor and a producer. After his military service, he returned to Paris in 1891 to share a minute studio with three other ex-pupils of the Condorcet: Édouard Vuillard, Pierre Bonnard, and Maurice Denis. This trio, along with Sérusier, formed the nucleus of the Nabis, and Lugné-Poe was thereby involved with this group from its beginnings, and was soon to incorporate many of their artistic theories into his stage productions. All four artists designed and painted backdrops for productions, and also drew many of the lithographed programs for which the Œuvre was to become famous, and which are avidly collected to this day.[5]

...

It was perhaps through Lugné-Poe that Jarry had resumed contact with Thadée Natanson, one of the Nabis' earliest patrons and another ex-pupil of the Condorcet. He was also the co-owner with his brother of the *Revue Blanche*, now effectively edited by Félix Fénéon. Jarry became a part of the coterie around that magazine as well as the *Mercure*.

Fénéon has already made a few enigmatic appearances in this narrative. Such was his preference; he was liable to show up as if from nowhere in the most disparate contexts. Although he was one of the most influential figures of the period, he was little known to the public, preferring to work behind the scenes as an unseen influence on events. This was understandable with regard to his anarchist activities—until his arrest he had been a clerk in the Ministry of War—but he also assumed the role of *éminence grise* in the fields of literature and painting. Here his intellect and opinions were widely felt: Fénéon edited or contributed criticism to dozens of literary, as well as anarchist, magazines, mostly anonymously. He also edited for their first publication Rimbaud's *Illuminations*, Mallarmé's *Divagations*, and the posthumous papers of Jules Laforgue. Fénéon wrote the first defense of the Post-Impressionists, at a time when even the cognoscenti were struggling to appreciate Impressionism: it was his only book, and a slim one at that. Gourmont explained: "Never to write, to disdain that; but to have written, to have proven an evident talent in the exposition of new ideas, and abruptly to have fallen silent? I believe there are spirits who are satisfied once they know their worth; a single attempt sets their mind at rest."[6]

8.2
Félix Vallotton, Félix Fénéon, 1895.

When Fénéon took over the editorial functions of the *Revue Blanche* it became a comple-
mentary rival to the *Mercure*. It differed by devoting more of its pages to leftish politics, and
had wider literary attachments: all the various schools were welcome in its pages (thus the name,
white signifying the mixing of all hues). Also, unlike Vallette at the *Mercure*, the Natansons realized
the value of publicity, and posters designed by Lautrec and Bonnard, often featuring Thadée's
wife Misia, projected a glamorous aura around the enterprise that contributed to its success.
Fénéon's free hand now allowed him to seek contributions from authors the magazine had not yet
published, including the new generation. On March 7 he wrote to Jarry:[7]

> **My dear Alfred Jarry**
>
> Please would you send me by return the plates and text of your announcement for *Perhinderion*?
> Thank you for the first number which I received a few days ago, and also for *Caesar-Antichrist*.
> Why don't you send me some copy for the *Revue Blanche*, perhaps choosing something that you
> like a lot and yet would not be too abstruse (the first time! …).
>
> **Most cordially,**
> **Félix Fénéon**

Jarry finished his short drama "The Old Man of the Mountain*s*" on March 13, and it appeared in
the *Revue Blanche* on May 1, 1896, along with the advertisement for Jarry's new publishing venture, *Perhinderion*. It may be that it was Jarry's keenness to appear in such an important journal
that caused him to return to the moribund conventions of Symbolist theater that *Ubu Roi* would
shortly make definitively redundant, but this rapidly written short play was a step backward in
formal terms. It suffered a fault common to Symbolist dramas, which were often meant to be
read rather than performed. Characters explain the action rather than acting it, a trait for which
Ibsen's plays were the initial purgative. Nevertheless, it was enlivened by Jarry's erudition, and
by certain lines such as this observation by Marco Polo, on being offered a draft that will open
the doors of the earthly paradise: "This potion has the garlicky flavor of a hanged man's semen."[8]

…

In February, Jarry had toyed briefly with the idea of using his inheritance "sensibly." Arnaud cites
a letter to him from a solicitor which probably concerns his buying an apartment. But the sixth
issue of *L'Ymagier* had appeared the previous month, with no contributions at all by Jarry, and his
newfound finances now allowed him the luxury of demonstrating the irrelevance of Gourmont
by producing a more extravagant and impractical art review even than *L'Ymagier*. Such a gesture
would lose whatever savor it might have had by being too long delayed, especially beyond the
next issue of its rival. Consequently, the first number of *Perhinderion*, which came out in March,
appeared a little rushed.[9]

Perhinderion—edited, designed, and distributed by Jarry alone—had a larger format than *L'Ymagier*, measuring an unwieldy 17 by 12½ inches. There was no text apart from a single, short editorial. Here Jarry explained that "*Perhinderion* is a Breton word meaning Pardon, in the sense of a Pilgrimage," and that it was at the end of these pilgrimages that hawkers sold devotional prints to the pious. He also outlined its ambitions: the careful reproduction of medieval cuts, Épinal prints, and "the presentation of the whole *œuvre* of Albrecht Dürer, plate by plate, in particular the *Great Passion*, beginning here with *Christ Presented to the People*."[10]

Similar to *L'Ymagier* in intent, then, but the lack of any contemporary artists, and the rather thin selection of plates, were only partially compensated for by the increased format. The format must in fact have caused problems, being difficult to shelve and therefore an impediment to booksellers. The lack of contemporaries may be explained by the fact that Jarry put this first issue together at short notice, or that artists were reluctant to offend Gourmont. There were other differences. Jarry promised six issues per year, not four, and while *L'Ymagier* was printed on four different papers, *Perhinderion* was on six—always the most expensive option, and Jarry's fortune was being eaten into. Paper and printing costs alone must have been considerable, and on March 31 Jarry signed the receipt from Renaudie just for casting the special fifteenth-century type: 259.85 francs.[11]

···

On March 12, Lugné-Poe received a copy of the first issue of *Perhinderion,* accompanied by a letter from Jarry asking for seats at the Œuvre so he might review its productions in the new magazine (he never did, although even this first issue carried the theater's standard advert). The letter continued with some deprecatory remarks about *Les Polyèdres*: it wasn't such a good piece after all, wasn't wholly unpublished, and bore signs of its rapid composition. The postscript makes it apparent that Jarry had effectively given up on the idea of Lugné-Poe producing either play, because he proposed to him something else entirely: a translation of a play by "a drunken author celebrated in Germany," Christian-Dietrich Grabbe.[12]

Jarry's disappointment can be easily imagined, but almost immediately a new avenue of attack opened up, that of publication. According to two separate accounts, however, he now needed persuading that *Ubu Roi* merited any more exposure than its previous appearance in the small, limited edition that had been *Caesar-Antichrist*. Such a loss of confidence is rather at odds with the usual portrayal of Jarry/Ubu carrying all before them.

Paul Fort had recently founded a magazine *Le Livre d'Art* and was keen to serialize *Ubu Roi*. According to his memoirs (written fifty years later, it should be noted), Jarry had now set his sights on poetry and was so little interested in this old work that he was tempted to burn it. In fact Fort tells us he had physically to remove the manuscript from Jarry's grasp and publish it against the author's inclinations. He also recalled that it was in chaos and that he, the poet Charles Guérin, and the artist Raoul Ulmann, but without Jarry, spent an entire night reordering it for publication. This seems improbable—or, to use Fort's expression, "miraculous"—because the

8.3
The woodblock for Jarry's portrait of Père Ubu.

8.4
Alfred Jarry, *Veritable Portrait of Monsieur Ubu*, 1896.

Véritable portrait de Monſieur Ubu.

scenes in this new version of *Ubu Roi* follow exactly the same order as those in *Caesar-Antichrist*, though it is possible new scenes were simply added in from other manuscripts into the existing version. Such uncertainties have meant that Fort's account has previously been dismissed, despite its relevance to the question of the authorship of *Ubu Roi*. There is, however, another brief description of the same incident. Charles-Henry Hirsch maintained that it was he, not Charles Guérin, who was present the evening Jarry read his play to Fort and Ulmann. After Jarry had explained its collaborative origins at the *lycée* in Rennes, Hirsch wrote: "that evening Jarry refused to entrust his manuscript to Paul Fort, who was then publishing a review called *Le Livre d'Art*, because he [Jarry] wondered whether a work with these particular origins possessed any literary value. He made extensive changes before allowing it to be printed; and I seem to remember that he only decided to do so after consulting Marcel Schwob." In fact, Jarry took the still incomplete play to Schwob's and performed it at his bedside; Marguerite Moreno and Willy (Colette's husband) were also present. Schwob laughed until tears ran down his face, and this despite the discomfort of an unspecified intestinal complaint which would soon require surgery.[13]

Jarry may have had other reasons for his reluctance to publish *Ubu Roi* separately. Up until then he had attempted to incorporate the monster from Rennes within his other literary and philosophical preoccupations. He envisaged a pataphysical reconciliation of his various enthusiasms, in particular Symbolism and the Ubuesque: hence Ubu's appearance in Jarry's first two books, and in his essay "Visions of the Present and Future." The publication of the play on its own confirmed an apparent rupture in Jarry's *œuvre*, one that allowed Père Ubu an unsettling independence.

The appearance of *Ubu Roi* in *Le Livre d'Art* (nos. 2 and 3, April/May and May/June) not only established the definitive text, but Jarry also carved for it the woodcut that finally fixed and immortalized the physiognomy of Père Ubu. He incurred further expenses, though, since according to Michel Arrivé, Jarry contributed toward the printing costs.[14]

…

In early May Jarry was disposing of yet more of his inheritance on the second issue of *Perhinderion*; he wrote to the printer Pellerin requesting him to edition Épinal prints for it. The magazine was losing money at a fearful rate. A few weeks after the issue of no. 2, Jarry revealed to an unknown correspondent, probably a bookseller, that it was recouping only between a fifth and sixth of its costs.[15]

Fascicle II appeared in June. It was similar to the first—a large Dürer, two large Épinal prints—but it also contained a print by Émile Bernard, and, typeset in the font Jarry had commissioned from Renaudie, was a short text attributed to Fénéon, on the futility of representation in art (reprinted from an old article of 1888), and a commentary by Jarry on Dürer's *Martyrdom of Saint Catherine*. This was one of the strangest bits of exegesis ever penned by Jarry. He attempted in this brief essay to reveal to the reader a hidden image of the Saint in Dürer's engraving by means of a description whose wordplays portray it in terms of the processes employed to make it. This voluntary hallucination offers an insight into Jarry's accelerated mental processes at this time, and his ability to extract multiple meanings from the form of language itself is here mirrored in the way he conjures a secondary image from the primary one by simply describing the carving of a woodcut.

...

It turned out that Jarry's postscript to his letter to Lugné-Poe of March 12, 1896 had done the trick after all. Lugné-Poe later acknowledged that Jarry's appeal to his enthusiasm for obscure foreign playwrights convinced him they could work together, which was convenient since he was about to lose his only employee. Adolph Van Bever had been acting as his general factotum since the founding of the theater, but the miserable income from this post fell so far short of a living wage that his health had been affected. Unable to afford a room, he had been reduced to sleeping on a straw mattress perched on orange crates in an unlit storeroom off the company offices. Jarry, newly of independent means, was the perfect replacement, even if his ulterior motive was utterly transparent. It was to be Jarry's only "proper job" in the whole of his life.[16]

However, when Jarry joined the Œuvre, probably early in June 1896, the company was coming toward the end of its least successful season to date. There had been too many second-rate French plays. The only notable productions had been *Salomé* and, at the season's end, Ibsen's *Pillars of Society*. Such was the situation when Jarry was attempting to persuade Lugné-Poe to devote an evening to yet another French playwright: himself. A letter to Lugné-Poe of June 11 reveals Jarry already hard at work. His job description seemed to be to attend to everything that Lugné-Poe couldn't deal with, and, when he was away, to take care of the rest too. Essentially, he managed Lugné-Poe's correspondence, the theater's relations with the press, and audience subscriptions (by visiting those who had lapsed at their homes by bicycle). He showed the door to importuning creditors, and handled the Œuvre's publicity and printing. He also helped Lugné-Poe write magazine articles, since the latter was uncertain of his grammar and spelling.[17]

...

June 11, 1896 had a further significance, since it was the official printing date for the book version of *Ubu Roi*. This was its fourth appearance in print in the space of only ten months, since the first in *Caesar-Antichrist*. It would have been in bookshops a couple of weeks later. This first edition of *Ubu Roi*, subtitled *A Play in Five Acts in Prose, Restored in Its Entirety as It Was Performed by the Marionettes of the Théâtre des Phynances in 1888*, was unusually attractive for a trade edition published by the Mercure. The woodcut of Ubu appeared in orange on the cover, and the whole book was very carefully and beautifully typeset by Renaudie to Jarry's specification, using the *Perhinderion* type and archaic spelling. Apart from the copies on special paper, it was printed on the usual execrable stock used by the Mercure, which means that nowadays copies are brown and crumbling. After the dedication it carried this epigraph: *Thereat Père Ubu shook his pear-head, and is afterwards yclept Shakespeare by the English, and you have from him under*

8.5
Ubu Roi, 1896.

that name many goodlie tragedies in his own hand. Prophetic in a way, since the authorship of Jarry's play was later to be as hotly contested as that of Shakespeare's. Jarry dedicated *Ubu Roi* to Marcel Schwob for several reasons: his role, with Mendès, in first publishing Jarry; his role in the publication of *Ubu Roi*; but also because he was one of Lugné-Poe's advisers for programming at the Œuvre.[18]

The Mercure's press list for *Ubu Roi* has survived, and this record of recipients of author's and reviewers' copies presents an interesting picture of the social group with which Jarry was associated; it is revealing in other ways too, since many were gifts for services rendered or in the hope of future favors. Although the list does not specify which copies are on special paper—there were five on *Japon* and fifteen on *Hollande*—a partial inventory can be cobbled together.[19]

On *Japon* paper: number one, being the author's own copy, bears his signature alone. Lugné-Poe received the next best copy, no. 2, with this dedication: "Intended to glorify Ubu-Lugné-Poe." Schwob's dedication reads: "Another copy for Marcel Schwob," because he had already received an ordinary copy with a more effusive inscription: "This copy of the book dedicated to him is for Marcel Schwob, because his works are among those we have admired the longest, Alfred Jarry."[20]

On *Hollande* paper: Rodolphe Salis, doubtless because at least a part of *Ubu cocu* was to have been played at the Chat Noir, although Salis's premature death put paid to that; Laurent Tailhade, "Monsieur Ubu glorifies Laurent Tailhade in all friendship"; Armand Silvestre; Christian Beck; Ernest La Jeunesse; Marguerite Moreno; Gustave Kahn: "with great admiration both ancient and recent, Knokke-sur-mer, 15 June 96"; and the critics Émile Faguet and Henry Bauer: "Another copy intended to particularly glorify Henry Bauer." Jarry used the same formula for the specially bound edition for Catulle Mendès which, like his copy of *Minutes*, had a drawing by Jarry on the cover, a portrait of Ubu this time, and a second inscription: "Monsieur Ubu offers his portrait in great veneration to Catulle Mendès."[21]

The press list itself is written out in a number of columns in Jarry's hand. The first column, given here in full, lists Jarry's friends along with a few Mercureists he presumably didn't want to offend by leaving them out (there is no evidence that Jarry was ever close to the likes of Albert Samain):

Rachilde is first, followed immediately by Jarry himself, and then Claudius-Jacquet, Vallette, Van Bever, (Édouard) Ducoté, (Paul) Fort, Bouillon (?), (Jean) Dayros, (Yvanhoé) Rambosson, (Théobald) Charly, Henri Albert, Gaston and Madame Danville, (Henry) Davray, (Louis) Dumur, (André) Fontainas, (André) Gide, A.-F. Herold, (Charles-Henry) Hirsch, (Tristan) Klingsor, (André) Lebey, (Pierre) Louÿs, St(uart) Merrill, (Pierre) Quillard, (Henri de) Régnier, (Jules) Renard, (Albert) Samain, Saint-Pol-Roux, (Marcel) Schwob, (Marguerite) Moreno, (Robert de) Souza, (Laurent) Tailhade, (Hugues) Rebell, (Francis Vielé-) Griffin, (Léon) Bloy, Fanny (Zaessinger), (Ernest) La Jeunesse, (Robert) Scheffer, (Claude) Terrasse, Morin (Henri, presumably, but not Charles), (de) Joly, (Firmin) Gémier (who eventually played Père Ubu), (Archag) Tchobanian, (Gabriel) Randon, Léon (Riotor?), (Edmond) Cousturier.

The second column contains the names of influential authors and editors, some of whom Jarry already knew well, such as Fénéon, the Natansons, Kahn, Lorrain, Huysmans, and theatricals

(Ginisty, Bauer). The third column has a further list of friends and literary acquaintances: C(amille) Mauclair (co-founder of the Œuvre), (Octave) Mirbeau, Mallarmé, Mendès, (Édouard) Rod, G(eorges) Rodenbach, J(ean) Richepin, followed by some critics, including the redoubtable Francisque Sarcey, who would have received this offering with little pleasure. Foreign periodicals and writers or critics follow, among them Maeterlinck, Elskamp, and Symons. The final column enumerates the publisher's review copies, including one for Edmund Gosse, and, tacked on at the end, a few more of Jarry's friends: Valéry, Dide, Tinan, Catrin.

The coincidence of two of these last names, in what appears to be an afterthought of Jarry's, is very suggestive. Dide, we know, was Jarry's fellow dissimulator in the army, and as for Catrin: the Julia copy of *Days and Nights* identifies a Doctor Catrin at the Hospital of Val-de-Grâce, from where Jarry made his escape from the military. For services rendered, perhaps.

Unlike Jarry's two previous books, *Ubu Roi* attracted a number of excellent reviews over the coming months. Jarry also received a modest flood of complimentary mail, including the letter from Tinan already cited, while the poet André Fontainas thought he had spotted Ubu in Brittany: "I think I've come across him here, unless some Englishman has assumed his delightful appearance: white trousers topped with a pullover in sickly dandelion-yellow and purple stripes, a peaked cap and a pipe clamped in his mouth, he strides erratically across the dunes [...] and pounds away at that idiotic game of GOFF. He strikes the ball confidently but automatically, his thoughts seem elsewhere, dwelling on past glories, campaigns against some chimerical Tsar, or Bougrelas." As Arnaud observed, Ubu was beginning to assume his generalized form, that of the despised "other." Mallarmé's response arrived some months later:[22]

> Tuesday 27 October [1896]
>
> My Dear Jarry
>
> Just a word of admiration for *Ubu Roi* and to squeeze your hand, because, as the saying goes, better late than … I genuinely believe that, here at the Natansons', apart from our Summer solicitudes and laziness in letter-writing, we have been too caught up with your remarkable work—with me declaiming it energetically at the top of my voice—to be able to write anything about it to you. From some rare and lasting clay your fingers, dear boy, have brought to life a prodigious character, or set of characters, with all the expertise and skill of a dramatic sculptor.
>
> He enters the repertoire of high taste and he haunts me; thank you.
>
> Best wishes,
> Stéphane Mallarmé

There were, naturally, enthusiastic notices in the *Mercure*. In August, Vielé-Griffin wrote: "Monsieur A. Jarry's astonishing *Ubu Roi* [...] is impossible to read without involuntary explosions of approving laughter," and in September, Louis Dumur:

> Ubu is a summary in caricature of everything wretched, cowardly, contemptible and disgusting
> that lurks in the human animal living in society. A cruel glutton, a mastodon of selfishness
> and vanity, a self-important swine inflated with stupidity and stuffed with presumption, this epic
> marionette, reigning over Poland by means of the all-powerful "phynance-stick," the "phynance-
> pistol" and the "schit-hook," wonderfully symbolizes the apotheosis of the belly and the triumph
> of the snout in universal history.

The *Revue Blanche* of July 1 featured it twice; Gustave Kahn gave the book a positive review and Cousturier, in an article devoted to an exhibition of modern book design, complimented its design and typography, within the constraints of the Mercure's format and paper. The longest notice, a full page in *L'Art Moderne*, a Brussels weekly, was by the poet Émile Verhaeren, who took his theme from the play's subtitle. He began:

> A particularly strange and droll little book which seems from its first lines to be no more than a
> hoax, the work of an extravagant and incoherent madman intent only on ridiculing his readers,
> a conglomeration of student buffoonery and bizarre associations, whose plot, effervescent,
> fragmentary, erratic, recounts the usurpation of the throne of Poland by PÈRE UBU, captain of
> dragoons, officer in the confidence of King Wenceslas, recipient of the Order of the Red Eagle
> of Poland and once king of Aragon, *cornegidouille*! But gradually the very special flavor of
> this drama, this play for marionettes, asserts itself and one begins to savor it.[23]

And Verhaeren concluded with a squall of exclamation marks: "Ah! the villain, ah! the cruel, ah! the despoiling, ah! the hilarious, ah! the idiotic, ah! the despicable, lovable rogue!" Evidently Ubu-speak was infectious, and if Dumur and Verhaeren were only mildly affected, the reviewer for *La Critique* went the whole hog in a short play that was later printed in the program for the Œuvre production.

The financial details of the Mercure's publishing operations at this time are unknown, with the exception of A.-F. Herold's *Livre de la Vierge* (1895), since Vallette's letter laying out arrangements with that author has survived. It describes what were probably the usual terms. The author was expected to contribute to the costs of publishing their work, or indeed bear the whole expense, and received half of the receipts in exchange. The book's retail price was calculated so that if the book sold out its print run, the author's return would equal the costs he had paid upfront. Reprinting would put the author in profit, provided the type had not been distributed. On this basis Jarry's contribution must then have been approximately 500 francs, since *Ubu Roi* was priced at 2 francs and the usual Mercure print run was 500. This call on his resources would have coincided with that for printing *Perhinderion* II, whose disappointing sales did little to offset its costs. Whether this was the whole reason for its demise is uncertain, but Jarry was certainly now busy working at the Œuvre, and the second issue of *Perhinderion* was the last.

The notices for *Ubu Roi* cannot have failed to impress Lugné-Poe, and there can be little doubt that Jarry made certain he saw them. Even better, the book probably turned a small profit as there were two further printings in 1896, meaning it sold better than anticipated. But amid all this activity, in mid-June, just a few days after the appearance of *Ubu Roi*, Jarry had traveled abroad, a rare occurrence.[24]

• • •

For the only time in his adult life, Jarry took a foreign holiday. He had been invited to stay with Gustave Kahn and his wife at their villa near the Belgian coast at Sint Anna ter Muiden on the border with Holland near Sluis. Kahn was one of the older generation of Symbolists, indeed he was credited as the inventor of free verse. He had been a prominent editor of little reviews, including *La Vogue*, a hugely influential small magazine in which Rimbaud's *Illuminations* first appeared. Also staying with Kahn—and Jarry may have traveled from Paris with them—were Fort, Hirsch, and Ulmann, the putative editors of *Ubu Roi*, and it was *Ubu Roi* that became the cause of a "misunderstanding." Lebois and Lot, not among Jarry's most reliable biographers, offer an explanation, but without any source (although Fort and his friends were still alive when they wrote). They relate that Jarry acted out the play to those present, and that it was such a success that it went to his head: he continued his personification of Ubu until the joke began to pall and an exasperated Madame Kahn asked him to leave. He returned via Bruges to Paris. Neither Fort nor Hirsch mentioned such an event in their brief memoirs of Jarry, though the latter subscribed to the idea that Jarry was "devoured by Ubu," which was perhaps something he had experienced firsthand.[25]

Jarry's inscription on Kahn's copy of *Ubu Roi* is dated June 15, 1896, a Monday, and the only other clue as to the nature of this incident is a hasty letter from Jarry which carries no date apart from "Tuesday evening 6 p.m.":

> My dear Paul Fort
>
> I must apologize to both you and Madame Fort, and to Messieurs Hirsch and Ulmann, and to Madame Kahn for leaving so suddenly, but the only possible train was at 6.30, and if I'd hung on till 7, misunderstandings of the type that are best avoided, or prevented altogether, would only have gone on and on. I am leaving these phynances (for Monday and Tuesday, yesterday and today) as agreed with Madame Fort and would be grateful if you'd hang on to various things of mine that I've left behind (my swimming costume and whatever else the laundry maid brings back).
>
> I made my farewells to Kahn but you can imagine I had more important things to say than asking him to forward on to me in Paris any letters that may turn up.
>
> Best wishes until we meet again in Paris.
>
> Alfred Jarry [26]

Soon afterward, in a letter to Lugné-Poe, with which he enclosed copies of *Perhinderion* II and *Ubu Roi*, Jarry mentioned that he had just returned from a trip to Holland. This appears to be the basis for the speculation that he traveled there with Léonard Sarluis at around this time, but Kahn's guests often visited the nearest town of Sluis in Holland, as did Jarry during his all-too-brief vacation. His letter to Lugné-Poe concludes: "Having returned yesterday, my services are at your disposal for future projects at the Œuvre."[27]

...

Around the time Jarry joined the company, it moved from no. 23 to no. 22, rue Turgot, and here Jarry ensconced himself, determined to become indispensable. Robichez, in his book on Lugné-Poe, described their makeshift premises:

> Beside the large doors to the courtyard was a dim vault containing the concierge, whom Lugné-Poe had managed to tame to such an extent that he spent his evenings manufacturing Scandinavian props and furniture for the theater. The rectangular courtyard was narrow, choked with the blackened growths of pipes and chimneys which framed the workshops and shops on the ground floor. To the left was a small door—later Lugné-Poe fixed a sign over it with Bonnard's workman wielding a pickaxe—which gave directly on to a dark staircase. The visitor had to clamber up this malodorous stairway straight out of some Naturalist novel in order to reach the Holy of Holies of Symbolist theater: two small rooms stuffed with old props, trophies from ancient battles, their walls covered with works by Lautrec, Bonnard, and Maurice Denis and its furniture painted in vivid reds and greens.[28]

One room served as a rehearsal room, and also as Lugné-Poe's sleeping quarters, the other as an office. During the daytime the screech of planks being sawn penetrated from the workshops below.

The last play of the season was Ibsen's *Pillars of Society*, which opened on June 23, after which Lugné-Poe departed for Quimperlé in Brittany and his summer vacation. He left Jarry in his stead: "installed in his new post, he takes his duties seriously. In his habitual cyclist's attire, Jarry helps me with everything, and removes all obstacles in my path. When I escape from the office at the end of the season so as to seek a little calm, it is he who continues to man it. He even went there with Lord Douglas, and some other young fellows, as I later discovered. I was not too pleased to hear of this, but after all wasn't he now a part of the company? He opens the mail and forwards it to me, avoids problems in a fraternal and sensible manner. Even better, he organizes the publicity for the forthcoming season. And with every move, he advances Ubu's pawn." As for this cyclist's outfit, it had been Jarry's habitual costume for some months, and from now on it would be so invariably: "black, all black, including the shirt and the tight calf-length cyclist's breeches, and by way of a tie pin, a silver skeleton the length of one's little finger." The tie pin was an all-too-temporary show of wealth.[29]

8.6
Gino Severini, *The Offices of the Œuvre*.

Either before he left Paris or soon afterward, but anyway by the end of July, Lugné-Poe succumbed. François Ubu, Master of Phynances, would tread the boards of the Œuvre. In truth, it had become an inevitability. Since January, Jarry had gradually increased the pressure on Lugné-Poe and orchestrated support in the pages of the various journals to which he had access. *Ubu Roi* had been several times published, publicized, written about, and in literary circles had become the most talked-about contemporary play in Paris. It must be put on, and who else could do it? There was only Lugné-Poe, whether he had intended to or not. The moment of decision had in fact arrived, since the next year's program had to be announced in August to secure sub-scribers to the fourth season. The list that appeared in the *Revue Blanche* on August 1 and 15, 1896 was far superior to the previous season: Ibsen's *Peer Gynt*, Maeterlinck's *Aglavaine and Selysette*, *Les Aubes* by Verhaeren, *Beyond Our Power* by Björnson, Marlowe's *Edward II* and, lastly, *Ubu Roi* by Alfred Jarry.[30]

Although *Ubu Roi* had been announced, Lugné-Poe still didn't really understand it. Despite all Jarry's letters and explanations, he had no conception of how to actually produce or direct the play, although initially he envisaged playing the main role himself, and producing it as a tragedy. He was aware of the play's origins, and that Jarry's private marionette productions had been popular with the Mercureists, yet "I was a million miles from suspecting the sort of thing Jarry had in mind." Fortunately it was a problem whose consideration could be postponed until after his holidays.[31]

If Lugné-Poe imagined that finally agreeing to put on *Ubu Roi* was going to silence his young employee, he was soon disappointed. Jarry immediately shifted from persuading Lugné-Poe to do the play, to persuading him to do it the way he wanted it done. The story of the pro-duction of *Ubu Roi* can be traced through a series of letters from Jarry to Lugné-Poe, a careful selection of which appeared in the latter's memoirs. Telephones were then rare, and the post was the main means of communication; a cross-Paris letter would be delivered the same day, in a matter of hours.

A letter of July 29 updates Lugné-Poe on administrative matters, and then turns to *Ubu Roi*. Jarry informs Lugné-Poe that Vallette is reserving space for him in the *Mercure* for an article on his ideas about actors and décor in the theater. This was to be Jarry's oft-reprinted "On the Futility of the Theatrical in the Theater," which built upon the ideas he had expressed in his letter of January 8, and took its title partly from an earlier, less radical manifesto by Pierre Quillard. Although Jarry had the tact not to mention Ubu in this text, which was cast as a more general study, he made Lugné-Poe aware that it was a manifesto for its production. This same letter had another, more specific suggestion. It was then traditional in the French theater for the parts of boys to be played by young actresses, but Jarry suggests that he knows a young boy who could play the part of Bougrelas. He gives Lugné-Poe no reason for this request, but when "On the Futility" was published it contained a typical piece of Jarryesque misogyny. After acknowledging that an adult actress may well have more experience than an adolescent boy, he opines that "this is small compensation for the ridiculous profile and unaesthetic walk, or for the way the outline of the muscles is muffled by adipose tissue, odious because functional. It produces *milk*."[32]

. . .

The young man in question seems to have been lusted after by a number of homosexual writer friends of Jarry, and Jarry certainly knew him well enough. There is an unusually warm letter to Claudius-Jacquet from some time in the autumn of 1896 in which Jarry is arranging a rendezvous between himself, "Bougrelas," and Fanny Zaessinger. The precise nature of Jarry's relationship with any of these three is impossible to ascertain. To complicate matters further, there is a fourth protagonist, Claudius-Jacquet's mother, whose first name, Valentine, more closely resembles "Valens," the name Jarry gave his "adelph" in *Days and Nights*, than does that of her son, François.[33]

Jarry seems to have been the subject of amorous reveries on the part of several women rather older than he was. Since March, he and Valentine had exchanged a number of letters. Most of hers (Jarry's replies have not survived) concern his assisting her in publishing symbolico-mystical texts she had written (shades of Berthe), and helping her get theater tickets through his position at the Œuvre. But according to Arnaud, Valentine conceived a passion for Jarry. She invited him to her Sunday "at homes," and then "one day she wished to enter Claudius's bedroom, the door was stuck, Jarry was standing behind it, and fearing some sort of assault, remained silent. When Valentine realized she had missed such an opportunity, she delectably expressed her regret at 'not having guessed.'" An intriguing extract that makes it all the more unfortunate that this letter is missing from the published correspondence.[34]

· · ·

Meanwhile, letters were passing rapidly back and forth between Paris and Quimperlé, though only a few of Lugné-Poe's survive. Jarry wrote again on August 1. After theater business, he passed on to encouragement. A couple of lapsed subscriptions had evidently put the wind up Lugné-Poe. Jarry wrote to reassure him that everyone thought the next season's program was "incomparably superior" to the previous one. On paper he was right, but things did not proceed as planned. Only *Peer Gynt*, *Ubu Roi*, and the Björnson survived from the original program. He then returned to the subject of the boy actor for Bougrelas, and enthused about his astonishing eyes and long brown curly hair: "he would perhaps provide a foil for Ubu, he would excite the old dears and certainly cause a scandal." The Œuvre, moreover, must retain its monopoly of theatrical innovations. These justifications do not quite convince, but Jarry's easy reference to a scandal rather implies that he and Lugné-Poe had already agreed that this would be desirable.[35]

Next, there was the problem of *Peer Gynt*, planned as the first production of the new season. Lugné-Poe's reply to Jarry's letter asked him to retrieve the manuscript of the translation from Octave Mirbeau. Lugné-Poe had sought Mirbeau's opinion of the practicality of staging such an ambitious project. A letter of Jarry's from August 17 makes it apparent that Mirbeau was proving tardy with his response, and Jarry proposes dropping in on him as if passing by on a cycling excursion, since he lived outside the city. The eventual verdict was negative; Mirbeau thought the Œuvre lacked sufficient resources. This left Lugné-Poe's plans in ruins before the season had even commenced. Jarry received a short letter bewailing the lot of the actor-manager, but in another he at last entered into the spirit of Ubu, suggesting that Jarry should acquire some mannequins to be used as stand-ins for the army, the nobles, etc. Lugné-Poe obviously envisaged these life-size marionettes being beaten about during the performance. He suggested soldiers positioned in aggressive postures "with breakable skulls." Jarry responded to the idea enthusiastically, but found it impossible to borrow anything suitable. Eventually he ordered forty mannequins made of wickerwork. In his memoirs, Lugné-Poe instances this as one of Jarry's extravagances that helped plunge the theater into debt, and complained that they cluttered the backstage for months afterward, but he neglects to mention that it had been his own idea, although he probably did not expect Jarry to order quite so many.[36]

Jarry replied to Lugné-Poe's despairing letter by disagreeing with Mirbeau: "we should still put on *Peer Gynt*," he wrote, since like the plays of Shakespeare it would benefit from being presented in a simple, even "squalid" fashion. Once again he was emphasizing practicality, and his essay for the *Mercure*, which would establish him as a published theoretician of the stage, was intended further to embolden Lugné-Poe in his forthcoming battle against the traditionalists. Jarry sent him proofs of it. Although Jarry's ideas may well have been practical, one wonders what Lugné-Poe must have made of this polemic whose vision of the theater seemed to exclude almost everything then considered essential. "What follows is a list of various outstandingly horrifying and incomprehensible things [...] which clutter the stage to no useful purpose, first of all *scenery* and *actors*." Bad enough, but Jarry's apparent contempt for the audience would have been little appreciated by a theatrical producer dependent on it for income: "I think that the question of whether the theater should adapt itself to the public, or the public to the theater, has been settled once and for all." Jarry then proceeds with constructive suggestions, but the initial demolition was alarming.[37]

Jarry's essay appeared in the *Mercure* on September 1. Soon afterward Lugné-Poe ended his vacation and traveled to London to make contact with the Elizabethan Stage Society. This theatrical company had been founded by William Poel two years earlier, although Lugné-Poe's main contact with them on this trip seems to have been Arthur Dillon, its financial backer. Poel's company had aims similar in some ways to those of Jarry and Lugné-Poe: to return Elizabethan productions to a semblance of how they were originally performed, which meant respecting the actual script, performing without complicated scenery, and instituting a comprehensive de-Irvingification of the role of the actor. As a side effect of this, Poel revolutionized the speaking of stage verse, aiming for comprehensibility over melodrama, essentially the present-day approach to acting Shakespeare. All of these aims received effusive praise in an article Lugné-Poe wrote for a London magazine, which he ended by approving the parts of Jarry's essay that related to his ideas on stage scenery. He also referred to *Ubu Roi* as "a sort of masterpiece," a verdict which he was soon to doubt.[38]

A further article by Lugné-Poe devoted to the work of the Elizabethan Stage Society appeared in the October issue of the *Mercure*. Although its title obviously referred to Jarry's essay of the previous month, in "Concerning 'On the Futility of the Theater in the Theater'" Lugné-Poe did not come to entirely the same conclusions as his secretary (who no doubt had helped him write it). In fact he used this essay to distance himself from some of Jarry's more *outré* suggestions, and to lay down some boundaries for the realization of *Ubu Roi*. He did not, in the event, get his own way; for example, he dismissed Jarry's idea of using written signs to indicate scene changes, an innovation that was retained. There were other not very subtle digs at Jarry's polemic; he compares a distaste for the audience with that of disgruntled taxpayers who nevertheless require the services of a justice system and an army to protect them. More surprising than these small signs of disagreement was the fact that Lugné-Poe, in order to see an actual production by the Elizabethan Stage Society, returned to London in late November for the performance of *Two Gentlemen of Verona*, thus absenting himself from rehearsals for *Ubu Roi* less than two weeks before it went on stage. One is constantly surprised by the brief rehearsal periods and technical amateurism of Parisian stage production at this time outside of the large official theaters, yet Poel's company was no different. It just seems to have been the way things were done, but as a method it was to be tested to its limits by the opening plays of the new season. *Peer Gynt* was far more demanding than *Ubu Roi*, and many suspected it was actually unstageable; even its author had had his doubts.[39]

However, Lugné-Poe maintained his resolve and took his secretary's advice.

…

Meanwhile, the publication of *Ubu Roi* had brought Jarry to the notice of a wider group than the coteries surrounding the *Mercure* and the *Revue Blanche*. The bizarre heterogeneity of his works began to arouse curiosity about his person, and elaborate anecdotes began to be passed around in bohemian circles. It was the beginning of his "legend."

Jarry's ex-sergeant Gaston Roig had become friendly with a group of young artists and *littérateurs* headed by Carle Dauriac (who wrote under the name of Armory) and the artist Paul Grollier. Their bohemian salon went distinctly up-market when Grollier acquired a rich mistress, Maggie Boehmer-Clark, herself a painter and an enthusiastic disciple of the Sâr Péladan and his Rose+Croix movement. This mysterious and chic divorcée led a life dedicated to art, spirituality, and romantic adventure. She held sumptuous receptions, balls, and dinners in an extensive apartment on the right bank and Armory, four years Jarry's junior, was keen to attract this rising star to one of their soirées:[40]

> For a while now Alfred Jarry had seemed to us to be some sort of fantastic, mythical and extravagant being. Some even asserted that his name was in fact a collaborative fiction and that, like Homer, Jarry had never existed. Others that he did indeed live and breathe, and that within him had been reborn the complicated soul of Gilles de Retz. Strange stories were told of happenings in the gloom of his apartment, which was situated down an ancient track beneath the walls of the Val-de-Grâce. Bloody handprints decorated the corridors, and grimacing death's-heads confronted those who dared cross the author's threshold where visitors were faced with obscure torments resurrected from the early days of Freemasonry.[41]

The habitués of Chez Ernest, victims of Jarry's "initiation," had spread word of their ordeal. Jarry was beginning to be lionized in artistic social circles, and the price demanded of him was the usual: a performance. He seldom disappointed.

Boehmer-Clark's salon was rather more genteel than most, a matter of petits-fours and tea rather than alcohol and cigarette smoke. She too wanted to meet this person who had infected the conversation of her guests, since Ubuesque expressions had become habitual even here, far from bohemia. Despite his reservations, Roig eventually persuaded Jarry to attend: once. He turned up at midnight, and although rain had lashed the streets all evening Jarry had, of course, made the trip across Paris by bicycle. Despite being soaked from head to foot, his hair plastered to his scalp, he made the rounds of the elegantly attired company, shaking hands and murmuring compliments, apparently entirely at ease, even as his sodden, mud-spattered (no mudguards) person was leaving a trail across the floor. Nevertheless, he was a great success, "the king of the soirée," according to Roig, though he rather spoilt the effect when Colette asked him why he was fidgeting in his chair: "Madame, I've got the squits!" he replied with deliberate audibility. He never reappeared at Boehmer-Clark's salon, but she conducted her followers to the Œuvre a few months later to support Jarry's play.[42]

Another salon Jarry is reputed to have attended was that of the Norwegian composer William Molard. Less formal than Boehmer-Clark's, it was frequented by the likes of Ravel and Delius, but most famously Gauguin, who lived in the same building, at 6, rue Vercingétorix. A number of accounts record Jarry there, but none gives firsthand sources. He could have been introduced by Gauguin, but also by Rousseau, and later on by Apollinaire; they were all regulars. Many Scandinavians attended this salon, including Strindberg and the artist Edvard Munch, both of whom knew Lugné-Poe through the Œuvre's tours of Ibsen's homeland.[43]

Munch had arrived in Paris at the end of February 1896 and was quickly established within avant-garde circles. Jarry and he must have met in late 1896, when Jarry was handling the Œuvre's publicity and Munch drew the program for *Peer Gynt*. However, there is only one source that describes any sort of social relations between them, by the German writer Oscar Schmitz:[44]

At this time I found myself in a large circle of friends, initially in connection with the Tuesdays at Madame Vallette's. A "gang" of around twelve young people, some still students while also active writers, accepted me as one of their own. […] Sometimes Hermann-Paul brought along the Norwegian painter Edvard Munch, who would sit the whole night long vacantly in our midst. The most illustrious member of this circle was the young writer Alfred Jarry, who had also attended the high school in Rennes at the same time as several of this group. At his school there had been a teacher, called Père Hébert, who was so infectiously comical that whole generations of schoolboys spoke like him. And this manner of speaking also gained ground in the group, so that even those who had never seen the old pedant became accustomed to speaking in this manner. Jarry, an outstanding Greek and Latin scholar who reveled in erotic Byzantine texts, was certainly the most perverse creature I ever encountered.[45]

The beginnings of Jarry's celebrity thus preceded the actual production of *Ubu Roi*, and not only in France. The English journalist and general man of letters Charles Whibley, who somehow reconciled his High-Toryism with a love of modern French literature, was often in Paris in the 1890s. He was a friend of Mallarmé, Valéry, and particularly of Schwob. It was probably the latter who directed Whibley toward Jarry when he came to write an article for *Macmillan's Magazine* on the "reckless squandering of adjectives" among the new young poets. After dismissing a number of the youthful writers associated with the *Mercure*, it was Jarry, and *Ubu*, he picked out for particular notice: "if Monsieur Alfred Jarry alone comes forth from the beardless mob, the beer of the boulevard Saint-Michel has not been spilled in vain." As for *Ubu Roi*, after a long description of the version in *Caesar-Antichrist*, he concluded primly that although "it is manifestly unfit for publication on our side of the Channel, it has a style and savour all its own, and it is Monsieur Alfred Jarry who, alone of all the youth, has cultivated a personal and distinguishable style." Jarry and Whibley remained friends: there are signed copies from Jarry to Whibley of nearly all the subsequent editions of *Ubu*. For another English reviewer, however, Jarry represented everything that was wrong with French poetry. Edmund Gosse despaired of it: "One had grown resigned: one had come to take for granted that French poetry was in future to be a negation of sense and light and nature, a Rosicrucian mystery inexplicable to everybody except the elect, a mixture of absinthe and anarchism and Monsieur Alfred Jarry."[46]

. . .

On October 6, 1896, as part of the ceremonials attending the state visit of Tsar Nicholas II, he, along with the Tsarina and dozens of dignitaries from the Russian court, processed down the boulevard Saint-Germain. Jarry invited Rachilde and Vallette to view the parade from his second-floor apartment. The Franco-Russian pact was celebrated across France with an orgy of flag-waving and patriotic fervor. Unintentionally, since the pact dated only from 1891, the passion for all things Russian lent an unintended political dimension to *Ubu Roi, ou les Polonais* (or *The Poles*), to give it its full title. Poland had not existed as an independent country since 1772, being partitioned between Austria, Prussia, and Russia, and this last had brutally suppressed a half-dozen insurrections since. The Tsar was offered various indignities in the play, including being pounced upon by Père Ubu and belabored by the physick-stick, the shittensword, etc.[47]

October also saw Jarry's only other literary publication for 1896. His commitments at the Œuvre, and *Ubu Roi* and *Perhinderion*, had left him little time for other activities. "The Other Alcestis," mentioned above, was an intense series of *récits* that collaged together the story of King Solomon and Queen Bilkis with a number of traditional accounts of after-death experiences culled from esoteric sources and popular magazines. Like "The Old Man of the Mountains," it appeared in the *Revue Blanche*; the *Mercure* was already becoming off-limits for Jarry's creative work. Otherwise it is likely that Jarry was working on his first novel, *Days and Nights*, which was to appear early the following year.

. . .

The Œuvre's season for 1896–1897 was played in the Nouveau-Théâtre in the rue Blanche below Montmartre. It was an elegant and spacious auditorium, now called the Théâtre de Paris, and in those days it seated just under 900 spectators.

The season was to open with *Peer Gynt* on November 12, 1896, with a public dress rehearsal the previous evening. The sheer scale of the play was daunting, and the meagerness of the Œuvre's budget called for some bold decisions. Even though it was abridged, the French translation was still too long, and Jarry and Lugné-Poe decided that further cuts and improvements were required. Despite these modifications, the performance still lasted more than four hours.[48]

The original production of *Peer Gynt* had been accompanied by music especially composed by Edvard Grieg. This was scored for a full orchestra, and Lugné-Poe eventually agreed to an ensemble of sixty musicians overseen by a French conductor chosen by the composer. One imagines the expense was rather greater than that for Jarry's mannequins which Lugné-Poe so bitterly resented. The poster and program were by Edvard Munch, who advised on the scenery, itself a complicated matter since the settings throughout the play switch from realism to fantasy. Jarry's name was clearly visible on Munch's poster, which assigned the role of the Troll-King to the clown Kobold. In fact Jarry played this part because of last-minute cast changes. Appropriate enough, for are not trolls a little Ubuesque anyway, and their king even more so?[49]

The production was a huge risk. The most detailed report came from an unexpected source: George Bernard Shaw. His long notice for *The Saturday Review* lamented the extensive cuts to the script but acknowledged that practicalities made some curtailment inevitable. Lugné-Poe's directorial interpretations did not entirely convince him either, on a point of which he comments: "I regret to say that Monsieur Lugné-Poe so completely missed Ibsen's intention here that he ought to be gently led away and guillotined." But Shaw praised the central portion of the drama, including Jarry's big scene when, as the Troll-King, he tells Peer that despite his "frantic attempts to prove that he has always been pre-eminently himself, and his calling as a witness the old beggared Troll king, who testifies, on the contrary, that Peer is a mere troll, shrunk into nothing by the troll principle of being sufficient to himself." Shaw, however, was unconvinced by the staging, which is where we can particularly detect Jarry's influence: "Many thousand pounds might be lavished on the scenery and mounting of *Peer Gynt*. Monsieur Lugné-Poe can hardly have lavished twenty pounds on it. Peer Gynt's costume as the Prophet was of the Dumb Crambo order: his caftan was an old dressing-gown, and his turban, though authentic, hardly new. There was no horse and—to my bitter disappointment—no pig. A few pantomime masks, with allfours and tails, furnished forth the trolls in the Dovre scene; and the explosion of the yacht was represented by somebody upsetting a chair in the wing."[50]

Despite his carping, Shaw's review was positive overall, even intermittently eulogistic. *Peer Gynt* was generally well received, and even the most reactionary French critics reluctantly acknowledged its power. Lugné-Poe and, presumably, his secretary Jarry were well satisfied with the result. As for Jarry's performance, according to Lugné-Poe "It was enooormous!"[51]

The production of *Peer Gynt* coincided with the Œuvre's annual manifesto for the new season. In 1896 this had a more iconoclastic tone than previously, or afterward, and Jarry's

8.7
Edvard Munch, poster for the Œuvre production
of *Peer Gynt*, lithograph, 1896. Jarry's name
is in the cast list.

influence has been suspected. The manifesto, published in *L'Éclair* on November 17, called for a theater where ideas would be preeminent almost to the point of its destruction: "If our vocabulary contained a word other than 'theater,' we would use it." The tract ended with an appeal for the authentic, the primitive even, in a statement that appeared eminently applicable to the next production, *Ubu Roi*:[52]

> Should we be sent a work that is rough and unpolished, one which is written with no concern for the rules of the theater, or in complete ignorance of what is called dramatic art, but a work that nevertheless discusses or resolves some serious social problem, and which by virtue of its inexperience, or even its faults, provides a new interpretation of a philosophical question, then we will accept it with joy […]

And now the moment had come. Lugné-Poe recalled in his memoirs: "*Peer Gynt* had triumphed, so I must keep my promise to Alfred Jarry […] and put on *Ubu*." With barely concealed reluctance.[53]

...

Jarry, as we know, was in charge of publicity at the Œuvre, and even his detractors were to grant that he excelled himself when it came to his own play. Sarcey's review recalled "an incredible fanfare of publicity." Jarry's campaign for *Ubu Roi* had effectively commenced the moment Lugné-Poe had agreed to produce it four months earlier. Articles in the press were appearing almost until the first night itself. Jarry's own article in the *Mercure* was intended to prepare his audience for the technical novelties they were about to encounter. He had then begun contacting critics and theatrical celebrities, making sure they had seen his essay, sending them copies of it. He also sent a number of them (Faguet, Bauer, Mendès, Silvestre, perhaps Sarcey) fine-paper copies of the text. Several of them wrote notices of the play before the production. Jarry also spoke to Fénéon, who kept a space in the *Revue Blanche* for a less theoretical text to appear just before the first night. He was leaving nothing to chance. The Œuvre always attracted an important audience because of its uniqueness within the theatrical establishment, but Jarry was determined that no one of significance would be absent.[54]

    As for the combined program and poster, Jarry drew this himself, but when exactly? The cast list looks as though it was added at the last moment down one side, and unlike other Œuvre programs, the roles are not assigned to specific actors. Ubu and Bordure were still not cast three weeks before the opening, as we know from Jarry's letter of November 17 to the playwright Armand Silvestre, so the poster must have been drawn after that date. It was not only the casting that was still undecided. The same letter affirms that the orchestra would cover any uproar in the auditorium, Jarry once again assuming this would be the case; but this is not exactly how things would turn out. In the end a single piano and some cymbals had to suffice. The music was composed by Claude Terrasse, then a church organist and private music teacher, but also Pierre Bonnard's brother-in-law and thus known to Lugné-Poe. According to Herold it was Terrasse himself who

8.8
Alfred Jarry, poster for *Ubu Roi*,
lithograph, 1896.

suggested to Jarry that the play should have an accompaniment. It was to be his first composition for the theater and thus the start both of his successful career, and of a long-term friendship and collaboration with Jarry.[55]

The production of *Ubu Roi* was rushed even by the Œuvre's standards. In fact all the evidence indicates that Lugné-Poe turned his attention to Jarry's play only after *Peer Gynt* had been staged, leaving everything to be accomplished, even the casting, in a period of less than one month. It is no wonder he was suddenly riven with doubts, and doubts of such substance they surely confirm that he had not given any real thought to this production. Now, too, he began to mistrust Jarry, who had never hidden his motives for working at the Œuvre. After all his efforts for *Peer Gynt* and for the Œuvre in general, Jarry was no longer considered the reliable collaborator. Lugné-Poe suddenly found him exasperating, even somewhat dubious. He complained of "all the stories attached to his person," and that his demands as an author were "irksome." Not to mention the play itself: Lugné-Poe was apprehensive. How would it be received? But then again, perhaps his doubts were unfounded after all? He unburdened himself to Rachilde, hardly an impartial observer, and on November 15 she wrote him a letter which makes it quite clear that he had been on the verge of canceling the play altogether.[56]

> Well! If you did not think that this play would be a success, you, a theater director who is well aware that success can sometimes be just causing a terrific *uproar*, then why agree to do it?
>
> Personally, I am not very up to the minute in these matters because I go out very little, and especially not in those lofty circles frequented by journalists. Nevertheless I continue to hear over and over again at the Tuesdays that all the younger generation, including a few characters who like a joke, are eagerly awaiting this production.
>
> So what is the problem?
>
> [A barely legible paragraph follows that is omitted from Lugné-Poe's memoirs, in which Rachilde notes that Silvestre is ready to lead the *claque*, the traditional group of supporters who cheered on new plays.][57]
>
> And after the success of *Peer Gynt*, it seems quite a clever move to put on such an extravagant piece, especially if it is as overdone as a puppet play. My poor Lugné, don't do anything shabby, like in that *Florentine Masque*, in order to protect the reputation of the Œuvre. And I think it would be a shabby act indeed not to keep your promise to an author who has every reason to count on you.
>
> Perhaps it is not so much a question of achieving an *ideal* success, but rather of a piece of buffoonery which will perfectly show off your eclecticism; better that than putting on some well-crafted mediocrity like some I've seen.

Emphasize the *puppet* aspect as much as possible, and if need be, and if it's possible (I've had this idea in mind as long as I've known the play), attach your actors to the theater borders with strings or ropes, since they are meant to be even bigger buffoons than everyone else.

Do without the lecture! Between ourselves, I think it could be risky, and good plays have no need of it, especially comedies. There's no point in explaining what we should laugh at … we know perfectly well.

So, drop a few lines to my husband, he has more influence on the author and will be able to pressure him tactfully into doing what you want.

Yes, the Œuvre must get better …

… but there is only one Ibsen …, and one could almost die of grief that there can only ever be one!

Your friend
Rachilde.[58]

Rachilde saved the day, though we don't know which of her arguments swayed Lugné-Poe. He and Jarry certainly ignored her practical suggestions: there were to be no strings attached to the actors, and the introductory lecture was given by the author. All in all, her letter shows little comprehension of *Ubu Roi*. The various reviews, by Dumur, Bauer, Kahn, and Verhaeren among others, offered elaborate interpretations, but for Rachilde it was a bit of drollery, an amusement, nothing more.

As well as his letter to Silvestre, Jarry wrote two others on November 17, both to Lugné-Poe and posted from different districts of Paris. It had fallen to the author to help cast his own play, and he was rushing about the city trying to put one together. Not only that: he was also running errands for Lugné-Poe at the *Mercure*, arranging publicity and props, and somehow trying to attend what rehearsals there were, which had to be fitted in whenever the various actors could manage them between other commitments. There was irritation on Jarry's part too, more justifiable than Lugné-Poe's, whose ill-preparedness was surely infuriating. One of Jarry's letters indicates the pressure he was under: "Don't worry if I am not able to make it [to the theater] until just before midnight, I have been rushing about since early this morning and I'd better get some sleep if I have to start all over again tomorrow until rehearsals." Jarry had good reason to be disgruntled, but Lugné-Poe merely recalls that he "was driven by some sort of tormented genius and a thousand difficulties, each more irritating than the last, dog our steps."[59]

The casting was quickly resolved, of necessity, and the two main parts were taken by actors of great experience. Mère Ubu was to be played by Louise France, whom Jarry may well have met at the Chat Noir, where she was disposed toward too much absinthe with Francis Jourdain and friends. It was to be her downfall. Not long afterward she was often to be seen staggering drunk in the less salubrious streets around Pigalle. Firmin Gémier took the part of Père Ubu. Gémier went on to become one of the most celebrated actor-directors of his generation, and in 1912 he directed another uniquely bizarre work of theatrical legend, Raymond Roussel's *Impressions of Africa*. Much of the rest of the cast was comprised of professional comic actors, and Lugné-Poe played two very minor parts. Some of Jarry's friends were also involved. Herold took charge of lighting, and according to the program Tinan was to take a part, although in the event he played a more important role in the audience. Cremnitz was to appear as the bear, and La Jeunesse as a palotin who would explode when pierced by a sword. He was still the butt of Jarry's pleasantries. At a production meeting Jarry told him he intended secretly to remove the safety button from the tip of the foil.[60]

8.9
Père Ubu: Firmin Gémier, photograph for Félix Potin, 1902.

8.10
Mère Ubu: Louise France, drypoint by Edgar Chahine, 1902.

Some good news arrived in the form of an exultant preview in *L'Écho de Paris* by Henry Bauer:

> [*Ubu Roi*] is a farce of extraordinary power, excessively expressed with extreme vulgarity, a truculent fantasy whose corrosive and aggressive animation overflows with a haughty disregard for humanity and its concerns; it is a pugnacious philosophico-political tract that spits in the face of the illusions of tradition and its great reputations based upon the opinions of a fawning public. [...] But it is something even rarer still, an original and discordant cry of dissent in the concert of everyday habituations.[61]

Quite a lot to live up to, and preparations were not proceeding smoothly. The first rehearsal with music took place on the evening of November 27, at 9 p.m., despite Gémier later recalling: "we had no time to rehearse." Exaggeration, of course, but Gémier was only on loan from Ginisty's company, where he was still performing in the evenings, and was therefore often unavailable. Time was so short that rehearsals continued on Sundays, according to Jarry's letter of November 29. Nevertheless, that weekend Lugné-Poe went to London to see the Elizabethan Stage Society's production of *Two Gentlemen of Verona*.[62]

Amid all the confusion Jarry found time to write the piece for the *Revue Blanche* that appeared on December 1, "The Paralipomena of Ubu." "Paralipomena" are things omitted or neglected, hence this article concluded with extracts from some of the Rennes manuscripts. The earlier part of it purported to be an explanation of the character of Ubu, except that Jarry approached this task in a typically oblique manner, and intimated somewhat prophetically that he thought Ubu was already receiving rather too much attention. (Adolphe Thiers, mentioned in the second paragraph, was the effective president during the Commune, and took charge of its suppression.)

> Because Ubu needs repeatedly to be paraded before the crowd, who will never understand him, and also for the benefit of a few friends who know him well, it may be useful perhaps, especially for the latter, to explain something of his past, so as to finally have done with the fellow once and for all.
>
> *He is not exactly* Monsieur Thiers, nor the bourgeois, nor the boor: he is more the perfect anarchist, except that he possesses all those eminently human qualities that prevent *all of us* from becoming the perfect anarchist, namely cowardice, filth, ugliness, etc.
>
> Of the three souls described by Plato: the head, the heart, and the *gidouille*, in him only the last is less than embryonic.
>
> In one of the ancient plays devoted to his glorification (*Les Cornes du P. U.*, during which Mère Ubu gives birth to an archaeopteryx), which was originally performed by shadow puppets, the scene is set inside his *gidouille*. There the Epithumia of Ubu wandered like the soul within this brain.

I do not know what the name Ubu means; it is a more eternal deformation of his still-living accidental prototype: *Ybex*, perhaps, or Vulture. But this is only one of his various incarnations.

If he calls to mind any animal—with his porcine face, his nose resembling the upper jaw of a crocodile, and the whole effect of his cardboard caparison—he appears to be a close relative of that most aesthetically disgusting of sea creatures, the King crab.

Given that the play was written by a child, it is worth pointing out, in case anyone is paying attention, the ingredients for synthesis a creative child can find in his teachers.[63]

And now it was Gémier who got cold feet. At Ginisty's he took major roles, and he had become concerned that playing Ubu might compromise his growing reputation. No one knew how this play was going to be received, after all. A letter of Jarry's of Sunday December 6 to Lugné-Poe, just three days before the public dress rehearsal to which all of literary Paris had been invited, reveals that the lead actor had suddenly decided he could not go on.[64]

This crisis of Gémier's was presumably the one which Lugné-Poe describes in his memoirs. Apparently, even at this late stage, Gémier still had not found a way into Ubu's character, an approach to its interpretation. Lugné-Poe suggested he assume Jarry's voice, a mode of speaking that the director described as "a machine for crushing humanities." Gémier was struck by the phrase, and it gave him the key to his characterization. Thus it was that Jarry's diction became Père Ubu's (but how had Jarry spoken the part of Ubu during the marionette performances?).[65]

The crisis thus averted, Gémier soldiered on, but rehearsal time was now so short that the actors demanded huge cuts in the text at the last moment. Most of the final two acts were discarded, and while some scenes that Jarry considered extraneous were retained on the actors' insistence, others he thought essential to the plot were cut. The scene with the bear, always a highlight of Jarry's readings, was among those excised, and Cremnitz was demoted to Palotin. Jarry later complained to Bauer that these cuts were caused by lack of preparation (and were thus Lugné-Poe's responsibility), but by now he was ready to agree to whatever was necessary, just so long as the performance would actually take place.[66]

The last few days were devoted to practical tasks, all apparently undertaken at breakneck speed. On the Monday Jarry, according to his last letter to Lugné-Poe before the actual performance, arranged for a wicker and papier-mâché construction to be delivered to the theater: it was Ubu's strap-on belly. There were also a couple of masks for Gémier to rehearse with, since the actual mask would not be ready until the last moment (but it never arrived in time). Jarry had also ordered a "Phynance Charger" which was scheduled to turn up at the theater that evening. This was a full-size wickerwork horse that Gémier had requested instead of the horse's-head-on-a-string that Jarry had originally proposed for the equestrian scenes. It was expensive, and Jarry suggested that should Lugné-Poe deem it too costly, then he could cancel the order when the belly was delivered in the afternoon; this would surely have been too late, and what could replace it at such short notice? On this occasion at least, Lugné-Poe was backed into a financial commitment he could not avoid. He paid for the horse.[67]

Shortly before the public dress rehearsal, Jarry and some of Lugné-Poe's artist friends painted the single backdrop for the play. It was an illustrious group: Bonnard, Toulouse-Lautrec, Paul Ranson, Sérusier, and Vuillard. The backdrop was most likely a theatrical flat (canvas mounted on a wooden frame), since it is described as having central doors, and it would have been laid on the floor and weighted or nailed down, and painted with powder pigments mixed with animal glue. The fact that so many artists worked on it simultaneously indicates that it had to be executed in a hurry, probably on stage over the course of a single night, so as not to interfere with rehearsals and to avoid having to use the Œuvre's usual paint shop, which was open to the elements. The horse too was painted—the night before the opening, according to Jarry.[68]

The overall design of the backdrop was Jarry's, although it allowed the individual artists to paint its various components according to their own inclination. In place of the plain backdrop Jarry had proposed at the beginning of the year, he had come up with a scheme which was shockingly original and yet succeeded in incorporating many of the ideas current among his contemporaries. Nothing like this had ever been seen in a European theater, and nothing would be for several decades. It was composed of realistic elements by turns banal (window, bed, fireplace, tree), incongruous (skeleton, elephant), or farcical (chamber pot). Each was perfectly plausible on its own, but all were here arranged in a completely illogical synthesis so that it was simultaneously day and night (bright blue sky and red setting sun), summer and winter, tropical and arctic, inside and outside, rational and absurd. This contradictory pictorial equation conveyed the same pataphysical resolution of opposites as the setting of the play described by Jarry in his opening address to the audience; its conglomeration of elements added up to Everywhere, but their illogical juxtaposition produced a canceling-out effect that signified Nowhere ... or (the then nonexistent) Poland. Thus Jarry contrived to combine Symbolist ideas of the universal, the Nabis' conceptions of spatial deformation and synthesis, his own ideas of nonrealist stage production, and the actual country where *Les Polonais*, a schoolboy skit at the expense of a physics teacher, was set. From the various descriptions of the backcloth it is possible to offer this reconstruction:[69]

8.11
Alastair Brotchie, reconstruction of the backdrop for the 1896 production of *Ubu Roi*, 2010.

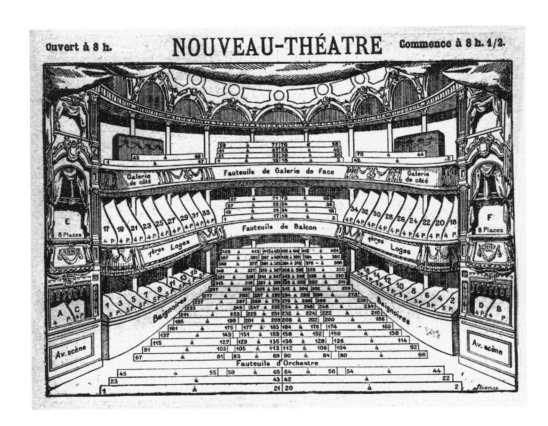

8.12
Seating plan of the Nouveau Théâtre, from the
Almanach Hachette.

8.13
Charles Léandre, Alfred Jarry reading before
the première of *Ubu Roi*, 1896.

The Œuvre attracted a rather special audience. Although made up of a real mixture of classes and occupations, it was dominated by a strong bohemian contingent, for whom these evenings were an important occasion, and for which they assumed a particular mode of dress. Performances at the Œuvre, in Bauer's words, "were unique events attended by an audience that differed from all others both by virtue of its intellectual capacities, and by the multifarious cuts assumed by its members' hair, beards and clothes."[70]

The four hundred seats in the upper tiers were free, and these were taken mainly by students, friends of the theater, the petite bourgeoisie, workers and shopkeepers, and by the less reputable part of the local population. The stalls accommodated another five hundred, but these too included nonpaying artists, critics, etc. There could be as few as one hundred subscribers at the Œuvre's performances, which goes a long way to explaining the precarious state of the company's finances. Subscription was not cheap, however: a box for the season was 500 francs, a seat in the stalls 100. Among the subscribers were famous writers, artists, politicians, even scientists, as well as a scattering of aristocrats. Thus, all in all, a comprehensive cross-section of society.[71]

The bohemian portion of this audience was especially renowned, even infamous. Secret police reports initiated after *An Enemy of the People*, three years earlier, described them with relish: "Decadent poets and writers, long-haired and eccentrically turned-out aesthetes, ladies of the night who have graduated to the 'old guard,' in other words the whole bohemian population of Montmartre and the area round the rue Blanche," not to mention "dabblers in anarchism and theoreticians of revolution." They went to great lengths with their costumes. The men, hirsute, with ornately sculpted mustachios and beards, sported lace cuffs and brilliantly colored velvet doublets or boleros, satin capes or floor-length overcoats, elaborate cravats, beribboned monocles, hussar-style riding breeches, and flamboyant medievalist headgear. The women had their hair plaited into elaborate braids parted in the center which fell over the sides of the face and were then gathered over the ears in two swirls, the center of the forehead being usually decorated with a *ferronière*, a large jewel on a chain (this look was so common at the Œuvre that it was remarked upon in the press). They draped themselves in richly decorated flowing velvets *à la* Botticelli, and were festooned with chains and semiprecious stones.[72]

...

Description of the performances of *Ubu Roi* is complicated by the fact that the audience reactions on the two nights were not the same, and it is impossible always to be sure which performance is being referred to in reviews or memoirs. Furthermore, some of Jarry's supporters went to both performances—Gide for one. Most of the accounts seem to refer to the second performance, the night of the première on the 10th. All the reviews are dated December 11 or afterward, and where diary entries exist, such as Renard's, or reminiscences are specific, such as Régnier's, they usually mention the 10th. The first performance, the public dress rehearsal, effectively served as a sort of prelude to the main event, and rumors of the play's reception the evening before would have alerted the audience at the première as to what was likely to occur, especially when more partisan spectators, including all the critics, were present. Thus the première is usually presumed to have been rowdier than the dress rehearsal, although even this must remain provisional, not least because a few, including Gémier, maintained the opposite, albeit in an interview twenty-five years after the fact.[73]

Tickets were impossible to come by; Colette had been promised tickets for the public dress rehearsal by Jarry, who had forgotten to send them, and she was reduced to a desperate appeal by telegram to Vallette at the last moment. On the night of the première all of the principal journals and newspapers were represented. As for Jarry's literary friends (and enemies), all were present, more or less, with the exception of Mallarmé, with the younger avant-garde represented by serried ranks of writers from the *Mercure* and the *Revue Blanche*. More venerable *littérateurs* came too: Catulle Mendès, Jean Richepin, Jean Lorrain, José-Maria de Heredia (who had written to Jarry personally to secure a seat near the stage so "I do not miss a single word"), and Willy, then far more celebrated than his young wife Colette. Willy was familiar with both the play and its author, and eagerly anticipated a riotous evening. Valéry came with Marguerite Moreno and Schwob (despite his illness), Fanny Zaessinger with the artist Charles Léandre, her lover. Antoine was there, and more traditional theatricals too, headed by the critics Sarcey and Henry Fouquier, and including Courteline and Rostand. Other reactionaries were present, notably Arthur Meyer, editor of *Le Gaulois*. Madame Boehmer-Clark led in her salon, right-bank aristocratic aesthetes along with Armory, Roig, and their friends. Henri Morin came, but not his brother, and there was an English-speaking contingent which included Arthur Symons and W. B. Yeats.[74]

Jarry had made certain preparations for the event that he had probably kept to himself. Some months earlier he had returned to the tables of Chez Ernest to discover that he had been forgiven his initiatory practices. Jarry had decided that he needed a faction in the audience that was independent of his known friends, and the patrons of this establishment were charged with forming the main body of his "counter-*claque*." Planning was careful. Jarry told them: "The scandal must be greater even than that of *Phèdre* or *Hernani*. The performance must not be allowed to reach its conclusion, the theater must explode." If the play was being well received they must unleash cries of protest, and shouts of ecstatic admiration if the audience booed it. They should provoke fights with their neighbors and, being situated in the circle, bombard the stalls with projectiles. On the night, Rémond, Sior Carlo, Don Beppi, Fluchaire, and most of the rest of the clientele of Chez Ernest took their seats, accompanied by Père Ernest himself, attired in an unintentionally Ubuesque outfit topped by a Cronstadt hat. He surveyed the packed theater, and the exuberant and noisy crowd below, with some amazement: "All of this because of my customer Jarry?" Henceforth his customer Jarry was to get credit at Chez Ernest.[75]

•••

On December 9, 1896, for those of a theatrical bent, the great event of the morning was a lunch-time banquet in honor of Sarah Bernhardt at the Grand Hôtel. Five hundred attended before proceeding to the Théâtre de la Renaissance for a matinée in which she played scenes from Racine's *Phèdre* and Voltaire's *Rome Saved*. But the evening was Jarry's: the public dress rehearsal of *Ubu Roi*.[76]

After three raps on the stage, the house lights dimmed, and two workmen, very appropriate to the Œuvre, backed on to the stage in front of the curtain carrying a small wooden table covered in a coal sack, and a cane-bottomed chair. Jarry—with white-powdered face, hair plastered down, dressed in an "improbably" large black habit, and a collarless white shirt with a large white Pierrot's cravat—followed, and sat down. It was the "introductory lecture" that Rachilde had urged Lugné-Poe to omit. The latter cannot have failed to notice that Jarry's speech was less an explanation of the play than an apologia for its practical shortcomings. Jarry spoke quietly, deliberately, as tonelessly as ever, and not all of the audience could hear. His presentation ended with an explanation of the *mise en scène*:[77]

> Our stage setting, however, is perfectly exact, for just as it is a simple matter to set a play
> in Eternity by, say, having the players fire revolvers in the year one thousand or thereabouts,
> so you will see doors opening from snow-covered plains under blue skies, mantelpieces
> adorned with clocks splitting apart to serve as doorways, and palm trees flourishing at the
> foot of beds so that the little elephants perched on bookshelves can graze on them.
>
> As for our nonexistent orchestra, we shall miss its brilliance and its fury, although various kettle
> drums and pianos will execute Ubu's themes from the wings.
>
> The action, which is about to begin, takes place in Poland, in other words: Nowhere.[78]

When he finished: nothing. No applause, no boos—silence. Rémond and his fellow conspirators were uneasy. According to Moreno, however, there were disturbances even during the lecture, but these could have been on different evenings.[79]

The performance comprised three acts of around twenty minutes each according to one critic's account, though others make it much longer owing to the interruptions. The original play was five acts, but Jarry's opening speech had announced that the first three would be played in full, followed by extracts from the last two, so it is likely the intervals did not conform to the play as written. It is therefore hard to estimate how long the first performance had run before it all became too much. Gémier himself described the moment:[80]

> You know what the first word of the play is: it was well received. The dinner scene amused the
> public. Everyone laughed. Some of the laughter was guarded, others laughed with approval,
> but at least they laughed. The scenes of the messenger, in Ubu's house, the King's palace, the
> parade ground, in the cave with the shades of the ancestors, the massacre of nobles and
> phynanciers in the great hall of the palace, all went very well, that is to say, as well as could be

expected. But hostility erupted suddenly and completely during the scene in the casemate of Thorn. You will remember that Père Ubu, who has been king for five days, goes to see Captain Bordure, whom he holds prisoner. In place of the door of his cell, an actor stood on stage with his left arm outstretched. I placed the key in his hand as if it were the lock. Then I made the creaking sound of a lock turning and I moved his arm as if opening the door. At this point the public, no doubt thinking that the joke had gone on long enough, began to howl, a tempest broke out on all sides, with shouts, yells, insults, accompanied by a broadside of whistles and a thousand other sorts of noise, a racket the like of which I have never heard. It exceeded everything I had ever experienced, and even though I have played other avant-garde parts that have been poorly received, I have never had such a feeling that the public had plainly just had enough.[81]

Gémier danced a jig in an attempt to restore order, and the production struggled on, but the fact that such a simple piece of theatrical business, which nowadays would pass as something of a cliché, should cause such an extreme reaction only underlines the innovatory nature of the staging. It is recognizably Jarry's creation, derived from the pantomimes in which he was so keenly interested. The play continued to be interrupted by catcalls, whistling, and fist fights, according to Moreno: "I do not know how many punches were exchanged between the spectators during the three hours the show lasted, but it is certain that no boxing match could ever compete with the public dress rehearsal of *Ubu Roi*." At one point Gémier, stifling in his mask and costume, gave up and sat on the stage apron with his feet in the stalls; the theater director Alphonse Franck, who was in the first row, gesticulated at him: "The exit's over there!"[82]

It was not quite the explosion Jarry had hoped for, but the following evening would not disappoint.

. . .

The première commenced in the same manner as the dress rehearsal. Following his speech, Jarry hung his Pierrot's robe on a coat rack, and disappeared through the curtain. Terrasse's brief overture on the piano accompanied the dimming of the house lights. The curtain opened to reveal the everywhere/nowhere that was at some remove from Ibsen's vague Nordic forests or the dream settings of Maeterlinck. A robed gentleman with the attributes of Father Time, excessively long white beard and hair, shuffled to the front of the stage and hung up a sign on the coat rack, indicating the scene, "The Home of Monsieur and Madame Ubu." Then Gémier, bulked out with his enormous belly and his face masked, crashed through the fireplace and uttered the famous first word of the play: "*Merdre!*" ("shit," but with a second "r" to make it all the more resonant).[83]

This time there was an immediate uproar. "From all sides a tumult of protest quickly arose, a chaos of shouts, whistles, mewling, hooting and barking, which found new pretexts to be constantly renewed due to the shameful coarseness of nearly every sentence," reported one of the critics. Quite a few walked out, and such violent invective was exchanged between supporters and detractors that the play came to a complete halt for some fifteen minutes. Baroque variants of the word passed back and forth. Willy whipped up the fracas: "On with the show!" he cried, waving his hat—the action was now in the hall, and the actors were watching motionless from the stage. Half the audience was wildly enthusiastic, he recalled, the other possessed with fury. Jean de Tinan encouraged both factions with simultaneous raucous applause and piercing whistles. Gémier had armed himself with a tram horn to try and quell the audience, and eventually managed to divert the protest into laughter. A modicum of quiet was restored, but each time the word was uttered, as it frequently was, the din resumed and reached new heights. Yet another "*Merdre*" from Gémier, "*Mangre!*" came the retort ("eat it," *mange* with an extra "r"), to general hilarity. Sarcey left during the first act, in part because of the loud applause from the woman behind him, but then because she leant across and whispered: "You old bastard!" The critic Jules Lemaître was unsure: "It's just a joke, surely?" Jarry's friends from Chez Ernest threw themselves into their task, Morand insulted everyone within earshot in an attempt to provoke fist fights, the rest whistled and shouted at the tops of their voices, but Ernest himself was bemused: "Why all this racket? What are they all so worked up about?"[84]

A good question, but the various playgoers present that night found themselves confronted with something inexplicable, a sort of nightmare, which one critic described as "five acts of shrieking and gesticulating by utterly grotesque puppets that created the impression of some sort of hallucinatory vision." Jarry had outlined his own ideas about setting a play in eternity, but this spectacle presented another degree of anachronism altogether. It was as though a modernist play from the middle of the next century had been dropped on the stage without all the intervening theatrical developments that might have acclimatized the audience to its conventions. Courteline boiled over during the prison scene and, standing on his seat, shouted: "Can't you see they're making bloody fools of us!" Apart from the prison door, we know of other similar bits of stage business, and there must have been many more. At one point the Palotins exited in single file, their bodies concealed from the waist down by a low screen. By successively bending their knees they gradually disappeared behind it as if descending an incline, presumably to crawl off into the wings. Such apparent idiocies were bad enough, but nothing compared to the main character, an inhuman monster in mustachioed mask and false belly devoid of any saving graces whatsoever, a so-called king waving a toilet brush as his scepter. He and the rest of the cast cavorted about the stage in puppet-like staggers for no apparent reason: "these jerking and hopping, these filthy, fighting, swearing *gamins* of wood," as Symons described them. Actual dummies representing nobles, lawyers, financiers, were gleefully consigned to the pit, battles were fought between armies of one, the Tsar (so recently fêted in the streets of Paris) and Ubu, perched on his preposterous painted horse. The set made no sense; the costumes were not only wretched but were likewise a hopeless mishmash from different eras, different places; and the actors' lines, when not muffled by their masks, were enunciated in a plethora of foreign accents—Mère Ubu a bizarre patois, Bordure English, Rosamund some sort of Auvergnat, etc. All this, of course, was part of Jarry's "universal" staging, but to much of the audience it appeared at best gratuitous and unfathomable, at worst either plain mad, or a deliberate affront. As for the plot, it was merely schematic, the lighting blue and unearthly, Ubu's jokes feeble, and then the language …[85]

At the end of the first act, Gémier came to the front of the stage and uttered another, more menacing "*Merdre!*", and such was his presence that the audience, stunned, were silenced, then burst into applause; but the upheavals resumed when the curtain rose again. Throughout the rest of the evening, Herold often had to raise the house lights to try and restore order, but on each occasion a new outrage on stage unleashed further protest. Shouts of "Long live Scribe!" (Sarcey's favorite playwright), or more obscurely "Dung beetle!" (to Ubu?), were interposed with more commonplace cries: "Bravo!"—"Shameful!"—"Superb!"—"Idiotic!" The director was ennobled; more than one wit came up with "*Lugné-Poe de Chambre*" ("Lugné chamber pot"), to wide-spread approval, but Louise France's puppet-like gesticulations prompted outright personal abuse: "You're drunk, you slut!" Jarry's supporters responded with extravagant acclamations. "It's sublime!"—"Better than Aeschylus!"—or attacks on the opposition: "You'd have booed Wagner too!" The poet Fernand Gregh shouted: "It's as beautiful as Shakespeare," to which his own brother shot back from the balcony: "You've never even read Shakespeare, you imbecile!" Jean Lorrain's column in *Le Journal* reported that by ten o'clock seats were flying through the air, accompanied by the animal cries and the protestations of cravated aesthetes and their pale-faced companions in braided plaits. Meanwhile, in the darkness behind the set, Claude Terrasse stood at his piano surrounded by kettledrums and cymbals. According to Lugné-Poe the uproar was so loud he was unable to follow the action and was reduced to striking the cymbals now and again more or less at random, "like a dog catching flies." The result: "zing, zing, bada-zing, boom, boom," said the critic for *La Patrie*.[86]

Finally it was over. Gémier came to the front of the stage, relieved himself of a final "*Merrrrrdrrrrre*," took off his mask and announced: "The play which we have just performed was by Monsieur Alfred Jarry!" A new uproar. The curtain fell, no curtain calls, the house lights went up, then off and on in an attempt to quell the crowd. Altercations continued, with occasional blows and much repetition of "the word." The police were summoned to help usher the audience from the theater. Rémond and his gang, exultant, returned on foot to Chez Ernest for a nightcap, the *patron* repeating over and over: "All that, all those society people turned out for my customer, Monsieur Alfred!"[87]

...

Jarry, enchanted by the evening's events, according to several of the critics, went to a café with friends. Paul Léautaud's diary has this entry written after Jarry's funeral:[88]

> Vallette said some very true words about Jarry. Nothing of the ambitious careerist about him. Thus, after the evening of the first performance of *Ubu Roi*, Vallette, he, and Rachilde were in a café with Mendès, who was sitting at a separate table writing his review. Not quite knowing what to say, and without wanting to seem publicly anxious for explanations from Jarry, he asked Rachilde to arrange for him to come and sit beside him. Then they could chat openly, and Mendès would get what he wanted. Jarry refused absolutely, saying to Rachilde, "No, no, no,"

with that special intonation of voice he had, and laughing, "let him struggle and flounder in his quagmire. Then it'll be all the funnier." Which was typical of Jarry's character.[89]

The Œuvre was accustomed to poor reviews from conservative critics, who were in the majority. Only Henry Bauer had consistently supported their program over the past few years, and it was fortunate that his column was prominent. Mendès's review was among the partly favorable, and there were few enough of these: [90]

Whistles? Yes! Screams of rage and ill-tempered laughter? Yes. Torn-up seats about to fly on stage? Yes. The boxes vociferous and shaking their fists? Yes, in a word, a crowd enraged at being tricked, leaping to its feet and surging toward the stage where a man with a long white beard, dressed in a long black habit, and who undoubtedly represented Time, walks slowly forward to hang a symbolic sign on Harlequin's mantle so as to give the illusion of a setting? Yes, and allusions to the eternal imbecility of humanity, its eternal lust, its eternal greed, misunderstood? Yes, and the symbol of its base instincts which erect a tyranny, unnoticed? Yes, and from those who had recently dined well, such splutterings about decency, virtue, patriotism, idealism that they managed to work themselves up into an orgy of remorse, virtue, patriotism and ideals? Yes, and more: unfunny jokes, offensive absurdities, braying laughter that ends up resembling the macabre rictus of a corpse? Yes, and in fact, the whole piece tedious and lacking any explosion of joy, despite it being so keenly awaited? Yes, yes, yes, I tell you. [...] But, nevertheless, make no mistake, there was nothing indifferent about these performances over the last two nights at the Œuvre, nor were they devoid of significance. From out of the ruckus came a shout: "You would not have understood Shakespeare!" He was right. Let me make myself clear. I am not saying at all that Alfred Jarry is Shakespeare; in him everything Aristophanic has been turned into a repulsive puppet show or a squalid fairground attraction, but believe it or not, despite the nonsensical action and its mediocre structure, a new type has emerged, created by an extravagant and brutal imagination that is more that of a child than a man.

Père Ubu *exists.*

[...] As for the abundantly ignominious vocabulary employed by the protagonists of this inept and astonishing play: moments arise in every century when the pavements split and the sewers, like volcanoes, must explode and ejaculate.[91]

Not exactly unalloyed praise.

The *Mercure* did not review the play, it would have been seen as hopelessly partisan in any case. Instead, it simply published Jarry's speech and his program notes. Bauer defended it twice in *L'Écho de Paris*. The first notice was celebratory and fully in the spirit of the piece: "How was it that some of the audience were not able to understand that Alfred Jarry was making fun both of himself and of us, that he offered a canvas where everyone might embroider his joy, where everyone could come together in madness?" [92]

Following the assaults of the other critics, Bauer changed tack and a second article attempted to represent the play as an anarchist allegory, wondering why Ubu's mask was not that of a specific historical character, since this would have "clarified its meaning." His defense missed the point. For Jarry, Père Ubu was Everyman; but Bauer's misinterpretation has been often imitated, especially in modern productions. Ubu has represented Idi Amin, Ceauşescu, Mugabe, any number of tyrants in recent years. Jarry wrote Bauer a letter of thanks nevertheless.[93]

The Œuvre used a press-cutting agency, and Jarry collected together the wholly hostile reviews and saved them in a scrapbook; he did not bother to keep the few that were in any way complimentary.

Sarcey did not disappoint. His brevity was intended to express displeasure, and he was very cross indeed:

Should I even mention *Ubu Roi*, given at the Œuvre after such an incredible fanfare of publicity? It is a filthy hoax which deserves only contemptuous silence. I saw with pleasure that the public (even that very particular public to be found at the Œuvre) has finally revolted against these excesses of ineptitude and rudeness. Despite the indulgent and skeptical bias that it brings to these productions they heckled it sharply. This is the beginning of the end. For too long now these pranksters have laughed at us. Enough is enough. (*Le Temps*, December 14, 1896)[94]

8.14
Félix Vallotton, Francisque
Sarcey, 1896.

There were plenty of others in similar vein, but they do not merit extensive citation. The vocabulary of their indignation was limited: coarse, vulgar, Charentonesque (after the lunatic asylum), Cambronne (where the French refused to surrender at Waterloo with a single word: shit), etc. Some distinguished themselves, however:

> In spite of the late hour, I have just taken a shower. An essential purgative measure after such a spectacle. O my head! My head! Nothing to say about this "dramatic comedy"—which is how the program designated this Cambronnesque madness by Monsieur Alfred Jarry—except that the audience is drowned in the two syllables of Waterloo, as was the European coalition. A detail, though. The word of Cambronne used to have five letters: for Monsieur Jarry it has six, but he has added an extra "r" in vain, because it still smells the same. (Anon., *L'Événement*, December 11, 1896)[95]

"Criticus," one of the Fouquier/Sarcey camp, even exceeded the poor taste he supposed himself to be condemning:

> Stupidity has its limits, the indecency of these jokes cannot go unchecked, and all of these more or less Ibsenist symbols lead directly to just such scatological and coarse allusions against which the public has at last erected a dam of common sense. [...] Ah! Appeal to the heart, it is there that genius resides. But how many of this current generation possesses a heart along with their genius. They have not suffered enough, they do not understand enough. Lulled by the sensuality promoted by Péladan, fired up with the blood of the anarchists, spoiled children and underhand butchers, their empty brains full of dreams, acclaimed by hypocrites and cowards, they have nothing in their guts except what Oscar Wilde might have left there ... (*La Critique*, December 20, 1896)[96]

An exclamation seems appropriate: !

Not all the reviews were so intemperate. Some thought it merely a joke and "refused to believe in the author's sincerity," others accepted the honesty of his intentions but felt it was buried beneath the coarseness of expression, and when critics discerned a real power in the character of Père Ubu, they tended to attribute it to Gémier's superb performance, rather than the author's text.[97]

The most sustained assault, however, was launched by Henry Fouquier in the *Figaro*, an attack whose ferocity can be partly explained by his personal and political dislike for Bauer, who had been a frontline fighter during the Commune, and suffered deportation to New Caledonia. For Fouquier, the play was a call to arms, which he was prepared to conduct at length in the *Figaro* (December 11 and 13, 1896), although a couple of extracts will suffice here. After dismissing any claims to originality, he used the case of *Ubu Roi* to attack "the hoax" of Symbolism in general, but inadvertently contradicted himself by invoking Ubu, whom he had just dismissed as meaningless, to perform his traditional role. (9 Thermidor was the date in the Revolutionary calendar when Robespierre was overthrown and the excesses of the French Revolution were brought to an end.)[98]

Notwithstanding the tedium of this tiresome, feeble and nauseating farce, I repeat, that for myself
[…] this performance resembled more a sort of deliverance, a literary ninth of Thermidor.
At the very least, it is the beginning of the end for this Terror which has reigned over our literature.
The time has now come to depose this symbolic tyrant many of whose traits are present in the
person of King Ubu, and who resembles it in so many respects. […] Empty of ideas, but bloated
as Ubu's belly, this despotism of the mind at least had the stroke of genius to realize that one
can easily found an empire by relying upon human credulity. It is enough to persuade a herd of
imbeciles that everything new, or promoted as new, is superior, that tastelessness is strength,
that all obscurities are profound, and that anyone who does not agree is stupid and backward,
for this herd to obey and follow, cheering all the while. And really, for the past few years, this
abstract and impersonal tyrant, this literary Ubu, terrorist of snobs, has become a dictator who has
subsequently turned on the public. But he overestimated its complaisance and counted too much
on its docility. The public became angry, and I am delighted to have been present at its revolt.

Fouquier thought the audience's reaction boded well for the future of theater, and this prompted
him toward a premature conclusion: "The performance of *Ubu Roi* […] seems to constitute a
splendid victory: that of enlightened and progressive good sense over coarse stupidity, and of
true art over its caricature."

On December 16, Jarry addressed a polite appeal to Fouquier asking if he might be allowed
a response in the *Figaro*—not so much as regards *Ubu Roi*, "which would be of limited interest,"
but rather to address his more general comments upon the state of the theater, its public, questions
of art and anarchy, etc. "I rely upon your kindness and courtesy regarding the insertion of this
reply," but Jarry's request was either ignored or refused, and no article by him appeared.[99]

···

Not all the press was negative, but the favorable responses tended to come from friends or par-
tisans. The *Revue Blanche* spoke for the younger generation, reviewing not only the play, but the
polemic that followed it:

Ah! What a marvelous evening, the première of *Ubu Roi*, and historic too! Since then, literature,
art and politics, all are impregnated with Ubu, Ubu pervades everything, they fight over Ubu,
they tear each other apart over Ubu. […] It is truly an exquisite moment, which it will be difficult
to improve upon. We should savor it by thanking Providence, who rarely lavishes upon us such
entertainment, but which, on this occasion, has managed things so well.[100]

Coolus was also the only one to notice that the production itself was of technical interest:

[…] certain details of the staging were especially interesting. The unchanging décor meant that
the various scenes of the action had to be evoked rather than represented, by recourse to a

number of signs that suggested what it was impossible to show; and various parts of the action used schematic and synthetic methods that were very expressive—the race, climbing the hill, the battle—and constituted a sort of new theatrical language which deserves further exploration.[101]

Ubu Roi is nowadays cited as the first "modern" play, its place in history partly assured by the splenetic incomprehension of its contemporary critics. Yet even among its supporters there were many who were not prepared for what this modernism would necessitate. Rachilde's book on Jarry, written three decades after the critical attacks on *Ubu Roi*, blamed him for the excesses of the avant-garde just as bitterly as did Fouquier. Others found the performance a dispiriting failure. Renard recorded in his diary that the evening had been a total disaster. Bauer's judgment had been proved false, they were all wrong in fact, and "If Jarry doesn't admit tomorrow that he was having us on, then he's done for." But he recorded Vallette as being amused and Rachilde trying to silence the dissenters. Régnier's verdict was delayed until the following May, "Ubu, Piranesi of the urinals." Mauclair, among the founders of the Œuvre, later wrote that this performance had "interred" Jarry, had finished him. Jourdain was likewise disappointed, feeling obliged to cheer the performance of a play he and his friends knew word for word, but which he thought lost its humor and subtlety on stage. Paul Valéry also knew the play by heart, but wrote to his brother: "A truly extraordinary evening [...] Gémier was magnificent." For Rachilde, Tailhade, Terrasse, and many others, it was remembered as the Symbolists' battle of *Hernani*, a pivotal struggle between youth and the older generation. "A sign of the times," said Schwob, a little more prophetically—a presentiment shared by many, and expressed with solemnity by W. B. Yeats:[102]

Feeling bound to support the most spirited party, we have shouted for the play, but that night at the Hôtel Corneille I am very sad, for comedy, objectivity, has displayed its growing power once more. I say: "After Stéphane Mallarmé, after Paul Verlaine, after Puvis de Chavannes, after our own verse, after all our subtle rhythms, after the faint mixed tints of Conder, what more is possible? After us the Savage God."[103]

One of the undoubted achievements of *Ubu Roi* was that it upset almost everyone who saw it, no matter what their allegiances. Symbolist theater was essentially concerned with mental states and intellectual conflicts. But the protagonist of *Ubu Roi* had no intellect, Ubu was pure appetite. The intellectual conflicts in this play are situated at one remove, embodied in the action, and in the audience's response, rather than in the play's apparent narrative, or in those explanatory monologues that Symbolist dramas were so endlessly prone to. Père Ubu is a character who offers nothing apart from a personification of some of the less comforting aspects of the human condition. No explanation is tendered, no solace is offered, and no solutions envisaged. All that remains for the audience—who have agreed to "become Poles for a few hours," as Jarry wrote in the program notes—is laughter, which, moreover, it cannot help suspecting is at its own expense.

Apollinaire, a great admirer of this play, was sensitive to the significance of its humor for modernism. In a lecture in 1917 he stated: "It is thanks to Alfred Jarry that humor has arisen from the lower regions in which previously it had been mired, and now furnishes the poet with an entirely original lyricism." At once bleak and celebratory, *Ubu Roi* was the first eruption on the stage of black comedy in the modern sense of the term—what André Breton referred to as "objective humor" (an eminently pataphysical concept). Jarry had considered every element of theater production as then practiced, and revitalized it in some fundamental manner: by turning it on its head, or allying it with something incongruous. A few years later the Dadaists recognized a true precursor in this approach.[104]

Ubu is obviously in part a caricature, which *is* a sort of symbol—and Arthur Symons perceptively titled his thoughtful review "A Symbolist Farce"—but a caricature extracts only base elements, rather than the sublime called for by Rachilde's "Gentlemen of the Symbol." Thus the dismay of many among them. Nor do the exaggerations of caricature have anything in common with notions of realism, especially in the theater. Antoine, its chief practitioner from the Théâtre Libre, thought the performance "completely idiotic," and jeered it as loudly as he was able. Jarry's staging was emphatically intended to underline its distance from every "serious" theatrical convention to date. Jarry called it a comedy in the program, but it is far from certain that this was his intention. Transforming actors into puppets meant the removal of all humanity from the proceedings, leaving only a grim masque of stupidity and cruelty. Renard found the evening's performance distinctly sinister; and Lugné-Poe's initial idea of playing it as a tragedy was not at all far-fetched.[105]

All of this controversy doubtless delighted Jarry, but there is an inexplicable contradiction at work here too. His theoretical writings on the theater were undeniably sincere, and many of the innovations he introduced into the production of *Ubu Roi* were genuinely liberating and became increasingly influential in the century to come. And yet he sabotaged his own play, urging his followers from Chez Ernest to do all they could to prevent it from being played to its end. Perhaps he thought the compromises caused by Lugné-Poe's ill-preparedness had fatally damaged the production, or that since it would be misunderstood anyway, he might as well exchange sheep for lambs? The undeniable result of the scandal was that he was to be forever associated with Ubu, in his own life and afterward. It was a typecasting he sometimes relished, sometimes endured, and occasionally resented.

9

WHO WROTE *UBU ROI*, AND WHY?

"More ink has been spilled over whether *Ubu Roi* is or is not the work of Alfred Jarry than in discovering whether Naundorff was really the son of Louis XVI and Marie-Antoinette." Such was one journalist's comment in January 1922, after the "Ubu Affair" had erupted in the press the previous year. In 1921, Charles Chassé had published a short book, *Les Sources d'Ubu-Roi*, which was intended to destroy the reputation of both Jarry and *Ubu Roi*, by revealing that Jarry was not the play's author, and that the play was anyway only a worthless skit written by schoolchildren.[1]

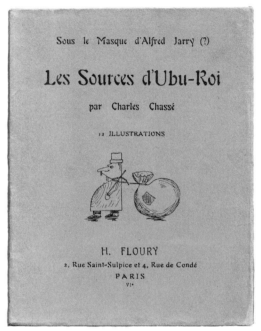

Sous le Masque d'Alfred Jarry (?)

Les Sources d'Ubu-Roi

par Charles Chassé

12 ILLUSTRATIONS

H. FLOURY
2, Rue Saint-Sulpice et 4, Rue de Condé
PARIS
VI•

9.1
The cover of the first edition of Chassé's book
featured a drawing of P. H. by Charles Morin.

9.2
Georges Jauneau, Charles Morin, 1921, from the
second edition.

The origins of *Ubu Roi* have been broadly outlined in earlier chapters, but Chassé's accusations require specific answers. They also give rise to other questions that are of rather more interest. Did Jarry attempt to conceal the fact that the play was a collaboration? Does the controversy surrounding its authorship undermine its validity as drama; and if so, then why did Jarry promote it so assiduously? This chapter looks briefly at the so-called "Ubu Affair," and at what is more important in the context of a biography, namely Jarry's motives in all of this.

That the Morin brothers wrote *Les Polonais* is not in dispute. Soon after the premiere of *Ubu Roi* at the Œuvre, Henry Bauer received an unexpected letter from Charles Morin:

17 December 1896

Dear Sir,

Since you are amused by the activities of Monsieur Ubu, please allow me to offer some further details concerning this character. Monsieur Ubu is an actual person, but in real life he is a large, inoffensive and harmless fellow. It took the shameless imagination of two *potaches*, my brother and I, who are now both artillery officers, to make him into the bloodthirsty monster depicted in *Ubu Roi*. But this play, if it is a play, was written by us, and Jarry, a friend of my brother, published it after simply changing the names of some of the characters. We do not think badly of him for this, as you might have thought, but I am writing to inform you that I have other manuscripts concerning Ubu, in verse this time, but written in the same sinister and grotesque manner. Will you allow me to send you these incoherent scribblings? Besides, the longest is only thirty verses and so they may be read very quickly. If you judge them worthy of publication, the glory of Père Ubu will certainly be augmented, but we, my brother and I, naturally wish to maintain in this matter the most comprehensive anonymity.

Please accept, Sir, my sincere consideration.

Charles Morin
Lieutenant in the 15th Artillery, Douai [2]

Charles Morin's letter is curious. He appears unaware that his brother had given his permission to publish or produce the play, yet maintains that he is unconcerned at Jarry's use of it. Rather, he wishes to partake of Ubu's glory … but anonymously. Some twenty-five years later, egged on by Chassé, he would have become rather more bellicose, judging by the portrait of him in the second edition of Chassé's book. Charles Morin's ill-humor was but one of several motivations behind this attack on Jarry.

Chassé was a great admirer of Symbolist art, notably of Gauguin and the Nabis, to whom he devoted several books, but he held an altogether contrary opinion of Symbolist writing, and like Fouquier, he considered *Ubu Roi* symptomatic of the degeneracy of a literary generation. "*Ubu Roi* was characteristic of an era, this book was its witness," he explained. Thus, if the admiration in which it was held by the Symbolist writers could be shown to be uninformed, then "the dangers of admitting obscurity as an element of literary beauty will clearly emerge. Because, sometimes one may believe something to be obscure and admire it as such only—alas!—to discover it is no such thing, that it is perfectly obvious, ludicrously obvious in fact, once one has been given the key. By pure chance I have been able to strip away from *Ubu Roi* all the symbolic interpretations put upon it by readers. Who is the real author of this minor work? This question is unimportant. […] The important thing is, now that the leather bottle has been emptied of the wind that inflated it, whether it will remain upstanding."[3]

Chassé therefore aimed to "strip away" the interpretations of *Ubu Roi* by revealing its origins. This was an impossible task, since they were not dependent on these origins. It was also complicated by hidden motives, not only his own, but those of his various collaborators. Chassé, at least, did not conceal his own agenda: the discrediting of literary Symbolism. The idea for the book had been put in his mind, "by pure chance," as he said, by an aggrieved ex-pupil of the Rennes *lycée*, Gustave Jarrier. This individual had become obsessed by the Ubu "hoax" after his acting career in Paris had petered out, which necessitated a humiliating return to his hometown of Rennes. One of the rare high points in his career had been playing the role of Bordure in the 1908 revival of *Ubu Roi*. It was Jarrier who persuaded Chassé to denounce the play, and who also tracked down Charles Morin. Even so, he felt obliged to warn Chassé that Morin's reliability was compromised by his fondness for the local cider and his "extreme vanity, which causes him to

9.3
Henri Morin, around 1896.

claim the paternity for things upon which he only collaborated." Still only a captain after some thirty years' service, Charles Morin by then had his own well-nurtured grudges; and he was to be highly selective in what he passed on to Chassé. He failed, for example, to mention the letter to Bauer cited above.[4]

Chassé and Charles Morin then composed their denunciation in partnership, seeking further testimony from any other ex-pupils they could contact. These did not include Henri, however, and only when the book was essentially complete did they think to show it to him, or to ask his opinion of it. So that was probably the moment when Henri had to confess what he had hitherto concealed: that he had given Jarry permission to use the Rennais material, including *Les Polonais*. Finally, although the Morin brothers had retained various other manuscripts featuring P. H., including that of *La Chasse aux polyèdres*, Chassé's book uses only the illustrations from this text. Thus these key pieces of evidence, in particular a Morin play predating *Ubu Roi*, were either withheld from Chassé by the Morins, or they agreed collectively to omit them from Chassé's book. The reason is obvious; *La Chasse* was a very poor piece which bears little resemblance to *Ubu Roi*, either in its content, language, or style, and especially not in its punctuation: !!!!![5]

The questions raised by Chassé's book may, in the main, be quickly disposed of, not least because previous authors (such as Beaumont) have dealt perfectly sufficiently with most of them. Thus the text of *Ubu Roi* occupies around 100 pages in print. Charles Morin's own description of the Rennes manuscript has it consisting of a school exercise book of 30 pages, which had already been partly employed to describe some fossils, and further space was taken up by illustrations. This manuscript cannot have contained the whole text of *Ubu Roi*. The manuscript could have settled this argument for good, but it was irretrievably lost. It was perhaps inadvertently destroyed by Franc-Nohain, although he maintained that his was a simple acting copy with no corrections.[6]

Then there is the testimony of various writers, after the appearance of Chassé's book. Many took up Jarry's cause in the press, and their recollections were essentially similar. They saw an incomplete manuscript with corrections and erasures that was very different from the published version. Fontainas, Fort, Franc-Nohain, Hirsch, Tinan, Lugné-Poe, Moreno, and Schwob were all in agreement. At the very least Jarry had recast and rewritten the play, and more than once, since the versions in *Caesar-Antichrist* and the later *Ubu sur la Butte* are substantially dissimilar.[7]

There were other questions that Chassé did not think to pose. Could the Morins themselves legitimately claim paternity of this work, when it was the result of the inventiveness of generations of schoolboys? They were not even the first to write a play featuring P. H.: they acknowledged this to have been a certain Lemaux. Jarry, then, was simply following this tradition by modifying previous students' work in accord with his own imagination. The ineffectual Hébert had been transformed by his pupils into P. H., who came to represent the idiotic tyrannies inflicted upon them by adults. When Jarry transposed this allegory into adulthood, he added a crucial extra layer to its symbolism. It became an allegory of the tyranny of adulthood directed upon itself, of society as the representation, or sum, of the inner drives of *all* of its constituents. Thus Jarry's transposition was in part contextual; this Chassé failed to understand. Even if Jarry had changed nothing, this play, when published, or acted on a stage in a major theater in Paris, would have meant something altogether different from the same text residing in the memory of ex-pupils from the *lycée* in Rennes. At the very least, it is hard not to agree with the words of Lugné-Poe: "Whether or not Jarry was the principal creator of *Ubu Roi* is irrelevant: the passion and the genius were his, and no one else's."[8]

The question of whether Jarry concealed the facts around the play's origins may be answered unequivocally. Jarry introduced Henri Morin to his friends at the Mercure, and all of them were aware of his role in the play's creation. Nor did they consider this a secret: Vallette, for example, refers to Jarry's collaborators in his obituary of Jarry. Likewise Léautaud, never close to Jarry, recalls the facts in his diary a few days after Jarry's death; it was obviously common knowledge at the Mercure, and therefore throughout literary circles in Paris.[9]

Henri Morin appears to bear much of the blame for the whole affair. He may have allowed Jarry to believe he was the principal author of the play. Only one of the Morin brothers was on the press list for *Ubu Roi* when it was published, almost certainly Henri, and Jarry asked Henri alone for permission to use the text. Henri admitted in a letter to a friend that his part in the writing of *Ubu Roi*, although real, had not been extensive, and that it was primarily his brother's work. It was therefore his responsibility to ask his brother's permission on Jarry's behalf.[10]

Chassé, however, makes it plain that the principal aim of his book was not to prove that Jarry did not write *Ubu Roi*, but to show that the circumstances of its composition invalidated it as a serious work of art. Since *Ubu Roi* was the work of schoolchildren with no literary talent or ambitions, it must be worthless. Even in Chassé's day, however, critical theory did not view the intentionality of authors in quite such a naïve manner. Jarry was certainly the first to see that this play had a mythical quality precisely because it was collectively composed, and he was not alone in this opinion. Chassé would have been infuriated by certain of the reviews, which employed the evidence he thought so damning to exactly reverse his argument:

> these interesting details help to explain the literary phenomenon with which we are presented. We are in fact witnessing, in the midst of modern life, the formation of a burlesque epic, the work of a tiny nation which has its own manners and customs, its own language, its own inner life and profound impulses. But this little nation is suffering under the yoke of authority: every hour of every day, parents and teachers are intent on curbing its taste for freedom, on thwarting its will and curtailing its powerful urge for independence! [...] That is why, beneath its apparent puerility, this work supposedly by Jarry possesses a human value, an originality and a primitive verve that fired the enthusiasm of reviewers at a time when literature consisted of artificial and ornate works that reeked of decadence.[11]

On leaving Rennes, Charles Morin had played the "sensible young man" in Jarry's text cited on p. 121, when he announced that he had "better things to do than concern myself with such stupidities." Jarry, however, saw that as well as preserving this product of childhood, *Ubu Roi* could assume more universal meanings that made it perfectly appropriate to serious theater.[12]

When Emmanuel Peillet visited Fargue to discuss the first performance of *Ubu cocu* in the mid-1940s, he found that Fargue was still able to recite long passages from it by heart, using the various voices Jarry gave to each character. Jarry "had literally saturated him with it in the early days of their friendship." Thus Jarry had been performing *Ubu* to his friends from his earliest days at Henri IV, at the time he was attending Bergson's lectures. He later recalled that Bergson, "in our presence—we adolescents just awakening to the serious—improvised his theory of humor." However, Bergson's theory of humor, later written up as *Le Rire*, does not feature in Jarry's lecture notes. This may mean that these "improvisations" lay outside of the syllabus and did not merit recording, or that they occurred in early 1892, when some of Jarry's notebooks are missing. But if Bergson did what Jarry said he did, and improvised the arguments of *Le Rire* before his class, it may be that this was when Jarry realized that the contents of the little green exercise book might have a greater significance than he had imagined heretofore, because it appeared thoroughly to contradict Bergson's ideas of the function of humor.[13]

Bergson's analysis of the *techniques*, particularly of stage humor, and of why something strikes us as funny, has interesting features that are directly relevant to *Ubu Roi*, as would have been obvious to Jarry. He would also have noticed that Bergson's conclusions as to the *aims* of humor could be comprehensively disproved by *Ubu Roi*, especially in the interpretation Jarry was to give to it.

For Bergson, the techniques of humor (the means devised to make us laugh) allow the discovery of something mechanical in a living being, and it is this mechanical element that constitutes the essence of the comic. "The attitudes, gestures and movements of the human body are laughable in exact proportion as the body reminds us of a mere machine." This mechanical element can manifest itself as repetitive or habitual gestures, pratfalls, absentmindedness, etc., and Bergson instances marionettes in this context. Furthermore, he says, comedy is concerned with the *general* and with the creation of *types*, rather than individuals. "Comedy depicts characters we have already come across and shall meet with again. It takes note of similarities. It aims at placing types before our eyes. It even creates new types, if necessary." His list of the general attributes of comic types is easily applicable to Père Ubu, and ideas of the mechanical were intrinsic to the staging of *Ubu Roi*. Thus these theories may well have informed several of Jarry's dramatic innovations.[14]

However, *Ubu Roi* does not at all support Bergson's conceptions of the *function* of the comic. For Bergson, comical characters or types are "models of impertinence to society." The function of comedy is this: "Laughter is, above all, a corrective. Being intended to humiliate, it must make a painful impression on the person against whom it is directed. By laughter, society avenges itself for the liberties taken with it." Jarry's Père Ubu, on the contrary, typifies the individuals who collectively make up this society, not its social outcasts, and thus attacks this society by inviting it to laugh at what it most fears, or in Jarry's words: "its own ignoble self." The play does not at all avenge society, but it is Jarry's revenge *upon it*: an exact reversal of Bergson's thesis. If Bergson's ideas accurately represented the comic theater of the time, then this inversion would go a long way to explaining the reception accorded to *Ubu Roi*, as Jarry himself was to note in his article "Theatre Questions" in the *Revue Blanche* in January 1897.[15]

Above all, Chassé could not comprehend that a hoax might also be a work of art, even though the logical conclusion of Jarry's play was all around him. Chassé was writing at the height of the most public scandals of the Paris Dada movement in 1921. The Dadaists had turned upon the more reactionary of the old fellow travelers of Symbolism. After attacks on Rachilde and the ultra-patriot Binet-Valmer, who will appear in Jarry's story later on, they accused Maurice Barrès of betraying the ideas of his youth, in a public trial that caused prolonged outrage in the press. Charles Chassé's attack on Jarry prompted a riposte from the editors of the principal Dada review, *Littérature*, which concluded:

> Jarry is one of those men whose attitude we admire unreservedly, and we challenge anyone to tarnish his character by contesting one of his works. We are delighted that *UBU ROI* should be taken to be "b..locks" by imbeciles.[16]
>
> André Breton & Philippe Soupault

10

1897–1899

Over the next few years, during a period of remarkable productivity, Jarry would write most of his best work. Ubu was ever at his side, however. The shadow of the "Savage God" fell across his daily life, just as the Ubuesque portion of his writings continued to eclipse the other parts of his literary output, as it arguably still does. Among his contemporaries the scandalous events at the Œuvre had made him famous, or at least infamous, and Jarry came to be identified with the protagonist of his creation. This was a further irony, since Ubu was intended to personify everything Jarry found repellent and idiotic. Not only was he confused with his creation, but in some circles he was expected to *be* Ubu, an obligation that was often onerous. It could be simpler to submit than to disappoint, however, and the Franco-American poet Stuart Merrill related just such an occasion. The meaning of the word missing from his manuscript may be easily surmised:[1]

10.1
"Naval Maneuvers," a page from the photo album made by Gabrielle Vallette and her mother Rachilde in 1898 (see p. 220). Jarry, Quillard (bearded), and Alfred Vallette (with hat) attend to the boats.

Jarry was, by nature, an exquisitely courteous person. His friends alone understood his great simplicity, the nicety of his social relations and the noble pride that underlay them. But the public insisted on seeing in him only the traits of Ubu, and Jarry played along with this game a little too often. One might surmise that he [*word missing*] donning Ubu's tunic.

One day he was lunching in good bourgeois company when, at the end of the meal, the lady of the house leaned over to him. "But Monsieur Jarry, you are just like everybody else, not at all the extraordinary and extremely ill-mannered person described to me, indeed it is obvious that you have been very well brought up." "*Merdre*," Jarry replied, knowing what was expected of him. "Bring back that roast, or by my *gidouille*, I'll have you all disembrained." When the leg of lamb reappeared, Jarry grasped it with both hands and proceeded to devour it as lustily as a savage in a freak show. His hostess was in heaven, but the unfortunate Père Ubu departed with indigestion.[2]

The split between Jarry's public and private personas became very evident to his friends. Those who were close to him were generally in accord with Merrill's opinion cited above, and remembered him for his humor, generosity, solicitude, and for the general sensitivity of his friendship. He was as much in demand among his contemporaries as in the salons: "He was popular among us, this sensitive and spiritual young man, pale and well-muscled," according to Paul Fort's recollection. Yet Jarry's wholesale adoption of nonconformity, especially as regards the common requirements of *politesse*, could be quite a test for these friendships, and no doubt a deliberate one. One regular at the Tuesdays, the monocled Henri de Régnier, an extremely upright and particular individual who for that reason was not close to Jarry, recalled the loyalty of his intimates: "Those who knew him said that his nauseating appearance hid a youth who was stubborn yet shy, proud and a little full of himself, but good-natured and ingenuous behind his cynicism, one who was fiercely independent and rigorously honest."[3]

However much Jarry came to resent his identification with Ubu, there is little doubt it was willfully self-inflicted, although he may not have anticipated the popularity of the performance. Jarry's Ubu-speak became ingrained and even more elaborate, and his conversation was further obscured by the habitual use of the phrase "*celui qui*," meaning "he/she who" or "that which," which was intended to impart a mock-Homeric cast to his pronouncements. Rachilde recalled that this did not exactly simplify comprehension: "Alfred Jarry had a very particular way of speaking that was disconcerting to those who heard it for the first time. He said 'we,' when referring to himself, and substituted verbs for nouns, in imitation of ancient Greek. Example: '*celui qui souffle*' (that which blows) for the wind, and '*celui qui se traîne*' (that which crawls along) for a train, even if it was an express! This made conversation somewhat complicated, not least because of the rapidity of his delivery."[4]

The furore around *Ubu Roi* showed no sign of dying away and articles in support, but mostly against, would continue to appear in the press for months to come. According to Rachilde, Jarry shrugged it off, "as unconcerned with this business as about a game of ninepins." Ubu, however, had taken on a life of his own, and quickly became an abusive adjective in the political press.[5]

Since Fouquier had suppressed any debate in the *Figaro*, Jarry replied to his critics in the *Revue Blanche* on January 1, 1897. In his essay "Theater Questions," he purported to be perfectly resigned to the public's misapprehension—after all, they had not understood Baudelaire and Mallarmé, and had not even heard of Rimbaud. Eventually they would come round, but by then "we too shall have turned into a solemn and fat Ubu and, after publishing some very classical books, will probably have become the mayor of some small town where the local scribblers will present us with a Sèvres vase on the occasion of our election to the Academy." No such fate was in store. He did object, however, to the public claiming that it had not understood: "it was not surprising that the public should have been aghast at the sight of its ignoble other self, which it had never before been confronted with in its entirety."[6]

· · ·

On November 30 the previous year, Jarry had ordered a bicycle from the substantial premises of Jules Trochon on the quai Jehan-Fouquet in Laval, just a few yards from the house in which he had been born. The bicycle was delivered to him in Paris, and the presumption is that he purchased it in Laval because he was known there, having bought his previous bicycle from the same establishment, and because his credit was still deemed good. Jarry treated himself to a professional racetrack model, a Clément Luxe 1896, which cost a stupefying 525 francs, the special racing wheels being an additional 20 francs.[7]

Jarry's bicycle was expensive, but then again he had not actually paid for it. In fact, he was broke; somehow he had squandered the whole of his inheritance in just one year, the expenses of *Perhinderion* and *Ubu Roi* being the only obvious explanation for this hemorrhage. Monsieur Trochon had the unlucky privilege of becoming the first, and one of the most determined, of his many future creditors; but being first in the queue was to be no guarantee of payment.[8]

Jarry signed an order agreeing to pay Trochon the bulk of the price by the end of 1896, and a second order, due at the end of February 1897, for the wheels. Neither was honored, so legal fees of 11.35 francs were added. He signed a second agreement to pay the sum now owing by May 31, and it is thanks to the address on this document that we know that he had surrendered his apartment on the boulevard Saint-Germain and moved back to the Calvary. When this deadline passed, a new agreement was drawn up for 567.70, payable on July 10. Two days afterward, a bailiff named Marquet paid Jarry a visit, and reported back that he was "unable to pay the said amount, being short of funds." His description of Jarry's unusual residence must have alarmed Monsieur Trochon. Suppose his creditor was not the wealthy owner of property in the rue de Bootz that he had assumed him to be, following his parents' demise? Jarry's debt was now 568.35 francs, and the bailiff's suspicions were confirmed by consulting the Jarry family's solicitor: the property in Laval was owned by Charlotte, and her brother had no known assets. Yet on July 19, Jarry bought a small rowing boat from a Monsieur Debray in Alfort for 60 francs, which he must have paid for in cash.[9]

Trochon then appointed a new bailiff, Maître Breux, who would have recalled previous dealings with the Jarrys: the matter of a "vague" overcoat. Letters passed to and fro for some months, with no concrete outcome. The fourth from Breux, in November, finally produced a result—Jarry's reply enclosed some money to show goodwill: 5 francs. He promised more substantial payments at an unspecified date, and reassured Maître Breux that he "was not mocking him." At the end of the year's skirmishes, Jarry owed only 23.35 francs more than he had at its beginning. It was a saga that would continue.[10]

…

In April, the artist Aubrey Beardsley made his final trip to Paris. Jarry was an admirer of his work, but it was not previously known whether they ever met. This mystery can be resolved: they were introduced by André Raffalovich.

Raffalovich was eight years Jarry's senior, an overtly "adelphic" dandy, and although not judged to be favored with particularly good looks, he was at least handsomely well off. This, and his slim volumes of decadent poesy, gained him entry to the Mercure. Born in Paris, his father a wealthy Russian-Jewish banker, he had lived in London from the age of eighteen, but since the beginning of the Wilde affair he had spent rather more of his time abroad, for obvious reasons. Even so, discretion was not part of his nature, and his historical study of homosexuality,

10.2, 10.3, 10.4
Three Englishmen with Uranian tendencies. 10.2: Alfred Douglas in 1893, from the French edition of his memoirs; 10.3: André Raffalovich, the only known portrait (from Brocard Sewell's *Footnote to the Nineties*); 10.4: Aubrey Beardsley, undated photograph by Frederick Hollyer (mid-1890s).

Uranisme et unisexualité, had been published in Paris the previous year, in 1896. Uranism was acknowledged code for homosexuality even on this side of the Channel, although an attraction for Uranus forms a less obvious pun in French than it does in English. Raffalovich's notion of homosexual practice was close to Jarry's; he too favored abstinence, in part because of his recent conversion to Catholicism. Beardsley was also a recent convert, and Raffalovich had supported him financially since he had lost his position as art editor of *The Yellow Book* because of his perceived proximity to Wilde. Raffalovich also organized Beardsley's last trip to Paris.[11]

Beardsley stayed at the Hôtel Voltaire on the Seine opposite the Louvre, but there was no lift, and he was so weak from tuberculosis that he had to be carried up and down to his room by the hotel staff. Despite his illness, Beardsley was looking forward to meeting Raffalovich's friends. On April 15, he wrote: "I'm sure Rachilde's Tuesdays are charming, I hope I shall make my bow in her Salon e'er long." Raffalovich arrived in Paris soon after and arranged a lunch one Sunday at the Lapérouse, a luxurious restaurant in an eighteenth-century building famed for its gilt and plush interiors and its small private dining rooms. According to Raffalovich, it was an intimate affair: "It is like a dream that we lunched with Rachilde and her husband, and Mademoiselle Fanny and Alfred Jarry!" Jarry can rarely have dined in such a place, its prices being as sumptuous as its décor. When Beardsley described it in a letter to his sister (April 26), the occasion appeared more populous, presumably an attempt to impress: "Yesterday we had a charming lunch at Lapérouse. Rachilde and some long-haired monsters of the Quarter with us. They all presented me with their books (which are quite unreadable)." Beardsley and Jarry would have made an unlikely pair: the former languid, attenuated, and rather sentimental, and Jarry with his squat intensity. He greatly admired Beardsley's drawings, and dedicated a chapter of *Faustroll* to their evocation. It has been often asserted that Beardsley drew Jarry's portrait, but there is no known evidence for this, the fictional portrait of Faustroll by Beardsley in Jarry's novel being the apparent source of the confusion.[12]

Beardsley did make it at least once to a Tuesday, on May 4, but it is unlikely that he found the smoke-filled room quite as "charming" as he had anticipated, given the condition of his lungs. Fargue described him there as looking so pale and doll-like that he "seemed made of soft paste."[13]

···

In July 1897, Alfred Douglas wrote to thank Rachilde for her latest book and to explain that his absence from the Mercure's Tuesdays was because she was "surrounded by persons who seem hostile toward me, and who anyway I find of little interest … the Raffalovichs and Jarrys, who inspire in me a physical repulsion, which although involuntary is no less unpleasant for that." The reason for this repulsion may perhaps be found in the French edition of Douglas's autobiography. Its additional chapter contains the following paragraph:[14]

> As for Alfred Jarry, he was a dangerous man, very dangerous. One evening we were in a restaurant, La Jeunesse, Jarry and some other friends. Suddenly Jarry withdrew an

enormous pistol from his pocket and fired four or five shots into the ceiling. The owner of the restaurant threw himself on him, followed by several waiters; and after being thoroughly knocked about, he was thrown out, and the rest of us with him.[15]

Jarry's exploits with his "enormous" pistol are the subject of numerous anecdotes. The most lurid have been worked up from a brief passage in an article by André Salmon. He described Jarry venturing out at night, "and should a passerby ask directions, Père Ubu indicated the way, his upraised arm augmented by his pistol. And if someone should ask for *du feu* [a 'light,' but also a gunshot], then Jarry's joy was boundless!"[16]

He must have acquired the weapon early in 1897 at the latest. Douglas's tale cannot date from much after then, and he exaggerated its size. Jarry's pistol was a small English snub-nosed revolver known, for these reasons, as a "bulldog." Its most infamous deployment occurred on the evening of March 2, 1897, during a dinner for the Mercure salon at the Taverne du Panthéon, the target being Christian Beck. The Taverne, situated at the corner of the boulevard Saint-Michel and the rue Soufflot, had opened in October the previous year and almost immediately took over from the Harcourt as the favored meeting place for the writers of the quarter, along with the usual mix of students, anarchists, and simple drinkers. It was also known for the convivial, not to say obliging nature of its female clientele, which made it especially attractive to the more predatory of the *littérateurs*, such as Louÿs, Tinan, Willy.

Beck merits a brief digression. He had arrived from his native Belgium a few months before, probably in the summer of 1896, and quickly became a part of the Mercure circle, taking on its Social Sciences column. He was still only sixteen—intelligent, precocious, although somewhat shy and hesitant, which was hardly surprising given his youth. Jarry and he must quickly have found each other congenial company since Jarry gave him a dedicated copy of *Ubu Roi*, dated October 14, 1896, one of the last remaining copies on fine paper. The letter it contained, now lost, might have shed some light on their relationship, although it is easy to imagine that Jarry saw aspects of his earlier self in the young and provincial newcomer to the Mercure. "Christian Beck was one of Alfred Jarry's closest friends, and one with whom he did not perhaps play too excessively the role of Père Ubu. Jarry sought out his company, a rare thing," recalled André Salmon. He goes on to wonder why Jarry ridiculed Beck in *Faustroll*, where he appears as the baboon Bosse-de-Nage, condemned repeatedly to utter a single phrase, "Ha ha," which "proclaimed in him effort, servile and obligatory labor, and the consciousness of his inferiority."[17]

Beck's literary ambitions seem to lie behind the rapid cooling of relations between him and Jarry. Almost as soon as Beck arrived in Paris he decided that he must have a review of his own, one that would combine the best of both the *Mercure* and *L'Ymagier/Perhinderion*. To put it simply, he intended to supersede the efforts of those who had shown him only hospitality and friendship. We know of his plans through a long—very long—letter to the writer Paul Gérardy (whose wife gave birth to Beck's child a year or so later). Dated August 25, 1896, just after he had arrived in Paris, this extraordinary communication reveals Beck as a supreme fantasist rather in the mode of Fargue. He tells Gérardy that he is gathering various of his new literary

10.5
The Taverne du Panthéon.

10.6
A bulldog revolver.

10.7
Félix Vallotton, Christian Beck, 1897.

acquaintances to be *actionnaires*, meaning they would stump up the money for the new publication (the list included Jarry); and that cash was going to flood in from the sale of posters, prints, paintings, and drawings done for the review, books published at the expense of authors, from rich subscribers, such as wealthy German princes, etc., and Gérardy himself would of course be sending two thousand francs. Jarry was further assigned a specific role:[18]

> One thing already settled is that *Perhinderion* will merge with us; all the costs will be borne by Jarry, we will send free prints to our subscribers, and in addition, Jarry, through his long-standing friendship with Gourmont, and the hard work he did at *L'Ymagier*, has many connections in the world of collectors, so should not find it difficult to get us subscribers for the *de luxe* copies of the review.[19]

Perhinderion had been defunct since the second issue in June, and Jarry might have seen a way of assisting Beck and simultaneously disposing of back issues and prints, but that is not the same as agreeing to an effective takeover at his own expense. Beck's ambitions had run well ahead of reality. No review appeared, and this episode was almost certainly at the root of the ill will that developed between them. It has been suggested that there may have been a homosexual element to their relationship, but the possibility of Beck being homosexual (or, rather, bisexual) appears to be based on a misreading of a book dedication from Gide.[20]

Were it not for this letter to Gérardy, one would feel only sympathy for Jarry's prey. He was an easy victim: "his speech, like his gestures, was extremely slow; he seemed to chew his sentences; and he was so anxious not to say anything until it was wholly thought out, that he hesitated a little between each word and only let go of all of it with great deliberation. [...] His extreme slowness of speech was the joy of some at the *Mercure*, of Jarry in particular." It was, of course, Beck's laborious and hesitant manner of speaking, punctuated by a nervous "hem, hem," that Jarry mocked throughout *Faustroll*, in a joke with a sinister conclusion:[21]

> Faustroll crouched over the baboon, spreading his four limbs out on the ground and strangling him from behind. Bosse-de-Nage made a sign that he wished to speak, and, when the doctor had relaxed the grip of his fingers, said in two words: "Ha ha!" and these were the last two words he uttered.[22]

There are various accounts of the evening of March 2, 1897 (and Douglas's anecdote may be one of them). Following the usual Tuesday soirée, around twenty-five of the Mercure regulars went on to eat at the Taverne. Come 2 a.m., at the end of the meal, Fanny Zaessinger, slightly the worse for kümmel and engrossed in a sobbing recitation of Rimbaud's "Drunken Boat," was interrupted by a commotion at the end of the table. Beck had thrown chestnuts at Jarry, or vice versa, or several glasses of crushed ice. According to Léon Paschal, a Belgian author passing through Paris, they came to blows and were separated, but his account becomes a little vague and he must have left before the dénouement. Jarry, refreshed by a full glass of neat absinthe, pulled his revolver from his pocket and carefully announced: "And now we are go-ing to kill the lit-tle Beck." In a show of bravado, Beck climbed on his chair, assumed a Napoleonic pose, and offered his chest as a target. Jarry too stood on his chair and took aim, at which point Vallette called for someone to extinguish the lights. The switch was flipped and the gun exploded, its flash visible in the darkness, and there was a cry of pain, but when the lights came back on Beck was still stand-ing, "as if turned to stone." The gun was loaded with blanks and the shot had anyway gone wide, but the wadding had struck another guest in the eye. General confusion. Rachilde fainted, and Jarry dabbed her temples with a handkerchief soaked in brandy. According to Fort, Jarry then ejected Beck from the window; they were on the first floor, and he was only slightly bruised. The shock precipitated Fort's heavily pregnant wife into labor and she was urgently conveyed home, where she gave birth to their daughter. In the meantime Tinan and La Jeunesse had entered the room. Mauclair, the frequent butt of La Jeunesse's sarcasms, remarked that, given the fracas, this was no place for a coward. Amid raised voices from all sides, La Jeunesse challenged him to a duel, which he refused with an insult. Someone else took offense at this slight to La Jeunesse and threw a punch at Mauclair. The arguments spilled out into the street, where cards were exchanged all round.[23]

A few days later, Beck wrote to Tinan asking him to pass a message to Jarry. A duel was necessary. Tinan dissuaded him from pursuing the matter, which was wise given Jarry's experi-ence with both pistol and foil. Still smarting, La Jeunesse spent the next two days seeking out Mauclair so as to provoke him into a duel by striking him in public. He finally tracked him down at a dress rehearsal at the Œuvre, and delivered his slap. Mauclair hit him back, and they ended up brawling on the floor.[24]

...

During March and April 1897 Jarry was finishing his first novel, *Days and Nights*, and then cor-recting the proofs. Coincidentally, or perhaps not, this labor saw the return of the skin complaint he had acquired in order to escape the army: a letter from Tinan to Louÿs contained news of a large boil on Jarry's nose.[25]

The novel was printed at the end of May, and published by the Mercure. Copies of the "second" and "third" editions bear the same printing date, May 25, according to the eccentricities of French publishing, which probably signifies a print run of 1,500 copies. This was large for the Mercure, so Vallette must have been hoping for increased sales following the publicity generated by *Ubu Roi*. As a "trade" edition, its production costs were probably borne entirely by the Mercure, and in any case Jarry could hardly have contributed, given his impoverishment.[26]

The autobiographical parts of *Days and Nights* have been covered earlier and need no further description. Following so soon after the furore of *Ubu Roi*, this densely poetic novel disoriented its early readers. Jarry's military service constitutes the surface events of a book in which he ex-plores the various modes of perception that define human consciousness—waking life, reverie, dream, memory, and hallucination—and then evokes, or describes, these states in a poetic prose by turns intensely subjective and rigorously analytical. This collision of subjectivity and analysis aims at a comprehensive representation of consciousness and the self.

The few reviews tended to compare the novel to *Ubu Roi*, which inevitably led to misunderstandings. Several criticized its apparently chaotic structure, but its style was at least considered original. Émile Straus in *La Critique* compared it to Japanese art: its artificiality was at once crude and subtle. "Even the descriptions of Breton landscapes are Japanized by Monsieur Alfred Jarry; he depicts them in precise, brief, dry phrases like the schematic strokes of a paintbrush." Most avoided discussion of the central themes of the book, or were baffled by the attempt. Léon Blum, the future leader of the Popular Front government, was then the books reviewer for the *Revue Blanche*. His presumption that a work by Jarry was bound to be comic inevitably led him astray, but his final evaluation was probably widely shared:[27]

> I have to admit that I did not know what to make of this book by Alfred Jarry: *Days and Nights.*
> I am one of those who appreciate and enjoy the beauty of Ubu. And I do appreciate this novel's
> specific approach to comedy, that is to say its precise and scientific madness, its hallucinatory
> dogmatism, the astronomical and philosophical import granted to the smallest actions, and
> especially its severe and deadpan tone. But I cannot say anything more about this novel of a
> deserter. Only brief glimmers of comprehension illuminated its story for me. I don't say this
> to be pedantic, because Monsieur Jarry certainly has talent, he may even be a great genius, but
> I have to say that he really seems to have overstepped the mark on this occasion, even for
> his friends and contemporaries.[28]

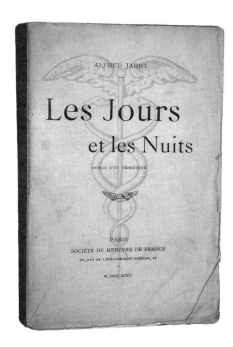

10.8
Les Jours et les nuits, 1897.

Despite the fact that Rachilde's review in the *Mercure* was mostly devoted to rehashing *Ubu Roi*, she did acknowledge the beauty of the ideas in *Days and Nights*, but she was unhappy with the vulgarity of Jarry's language, especially in the chapter titles. For an author specializing in works that tended toward the *risqué* she could be surprisingly prim, and on this occasion her conclusion was unjustifiable: "I wonder whether it was helpful to conceal so many beautiful things beneath such a sumptuosity of putrefaction." Maternal advice, presumably.[29]

As before, there was a friendly and complimentary letter from Mallarmé: "My surprise at this wonderful and accurate imagery was complete: it is set out in sharp and vivid tones, but then transposed into the infinity of the dream. A geometry of phrases, straight or curved, but always lucid, that creates a strictly definitive and literary language which charmed me."[30]

Whatever else it was, *Days and Nights* was not a realist novel, despite the naturalistic descriptions of army life, but it was not a Symbolist one either. In fact it marks Jarry's break with the tics and archaisms of Symbolism, and the end of the obvious influence of *Maldoror*. The nineteenth century was nearing its end, and the increasing pace of industrial and scientific progress promised a very different century ahead. In such a context, Symbolism itself was beginning to look its age, and the Symbolist theater was about to be the first casualty of the modernist sensibility then in the process of formation.

...

What had happened between Jarry and Lugné-Poe after the production of *Ubu Roi*? Jarry left his post at the theater, but under what circumstances is not known. Lugné-Poe's memoirs are rather bitter at this point. The company, still with six productions scheduled before the season's end in June, was in serious difficulties, and he blamed both Jarry and his play. He listed his woes: *Ubu Roi* had bankrupted the company (despite the sellout performances); Bauer's sidelining at *L'Écho de Paris* had cost the theater its principal supporter; his audience had deserted him, the avant-garde was fickle, and so on. These protestations were perhaps intended to excuse the fact that, at the time, he had not comprehended what he had achieved. When his memoirs appeared in the 1930s it was already clear that *Ubu Roi* would be seen as one of its most significant productions, a judgment posterity has confirmed. His beloved Ibsen would have been played anyway, but *Ubu Roi*?[31]

However, when Lugné-Poe came to write these memoirs, he had forgotten that less than a week after the production he had written an article in enthusiastic support of the play and what it presaged: "The revolution now in preparation, which is almost ready in fact, attracts youth by the thousand because it is adorned by a new Art that is both affecting and ennobling." He soon lost his nerve, not to mention his sense of humor. Fouquier's tirades had aligned all the "serious" critics against Jarry's play, and more importantly, against what it represented. Most held Lugné-Poe responsible, and he opted to back down against such opposition. He declared *Ubu Roi* an "artistic disaster" in his memoirs, the turning point, the moment when he had gone too far. The play would indeed be Fouquier's "victory of good sense" over the modernizers. In the short term.[32]

Thus the causes of the rupture between Symbolism and the Œuvre lay, to a great extent, with the wholesale destruction of theatrical conventions by *Ubu Roi*; and even though the production offered ways toward a dramatic renewal, Lugné-Poe would not risk taking this path. Just before the last play of the season, subscribers to the Œuvre received the manifesto for the new season, a polemic quite unlike the one from the year before, which had been written under Jarry's influence. Lugné-Poe had it published in, of all places, the *Figaro*, bastion of Fouquier. In a survey of the past year's activities, he noted that foreign works had been the most successful, "whereas little attention was paid to the works written in French and they attracted only brief notices in the press [...] our country lacks the ability to produce original dramatic works, especially since no great national masterpiece has yet appeared." It is hardly necessary to point out the inaccuracy of this statement, particularly with respect to *Ubu Roi*. He continued:[33]

> Born after seven years of Naturalist theater, at a time when the younger authors called themselves Symbolists, the Œuvre therefore found itself incorporated into this movement, despite the obvious contradiction that exists between the theater of Ibsen and the theories of Symbolism. A misunderstanding thereby came into being which we wish to correct.

This *volte-face* was nothing less than a betrayal of the Œuvre's most loyal supporters to date, of both its authors and its audience, and the terms in which it was expressed came close to insulting personally the French playwrights whose works had been staged. Pierre Quillard drafted their reply, which appeared in the *Mercure* and was signed by most of the authors who had collaborated with Lugné-Poe, the majority of whom had considered themselves his friends up until this moment. Fort, Herold, Jarry, Kahn, Rachilde, and Régnier were among the signatories. After disputing whether most of the French works Lugné-Poe had presented were Symbolist at all, it concluded:

> Symbolism, if Symbolism exists, therefore has nothing to do with Monsieur Lugné-Poe, organizer of theatrical performances.
>
> On the contrary the Œuvre has profited, in its presentation of both French and foreign plays, from this movement of ideas which attracted to it writers that Monsieur Lugné-Poe is not qualified to pronounce upon. They were able to support him when his efforts were of interest, just as they felt able politely to withhold their appreciation on the occasions when he presented these works to the public in a somewhat eccentric manner.
>
> It is not up to him to break off relations that are purely fictitious, if that is how he wishes to characterize the too-generous condescension that was shown him.[34]

The argument occupied the press for several weeks, and burst into new life following an article by Mendès in July in which he referred to Lugné-Poe as a "mediocre comedian." The latter's response was a personal attack on Mendès in *La Presse*, in which he described him as a disorderly old soak. A farcical duel took place during which Lugné-Poe, an inexperienced swordsman outside of a theater, backed away so continuously from his opponent that Mendès threw down his blade in fury and accused him of cowardice. In the confusion it was noticed that Mendès's thumb had been scratched, probably by himself, but it was first blood and he was therefore declared the loser.[35]

Lugné-Poe was then free to pursue his career unencumbered by difficult French writers, but the establishment he courted failed to come to his rescue. He had alienated both collaborators and supporters, and the Œuvre effectively closed at the end of the following season. The Symbolists may well have felt vindicated, but they should also have felt a certain premonitory unease.

...

The trolls in *Peer Gynt* are differentiated from humans by virtue of being "sufficient unto themselves," a conception of personal independence with which Jarry came increasingly to identify. For him and his friends it had also a more cordial significance: trolldom singled out those among them devoted to various country pursuits, particularly boating and fishing on the Seine outside Paris. Vallette and Jarry formed the core of this group of enthusiasts. Jarry's purchase of a small scull was confirmed by a letter from Vallette to Herold of July 28 in which, for the first time, we see that Jarry and Père Ubu have become synonymous:

> Trollism is a marvelous thing: Père Ubu has bought a boat, and I have too. We are hoping to house them at Villeneuve Saint-Georges or nearby. You are familiar with this part of the country, do you know of a boathouse at Ablon, Athis, or Villeneuve?[36]

A boathouse was soon discovered in Athis-Mons, nowadays beside Orly airport south of Paris, and then easily accessible by train or bicycle. Although he was an experienced fisherman, Jarry was a novice with the oars, and Vallette initiated him into the joys of boating. Reckless as ever, Jarry nearly drowned on several occasions, since he swam "like a lead weight." In return, Jarry taught Vallette to ride a bicycle. The copy of *Days and Nights* Jarry presented to him was inscribed to the "Father of the Trolls," and if Vallette was the Father troll, then Jarry was to be the Faust-troll.[37]

Jarry's letter of August 23, 1897 had informed Trochon that he had been expelled from the Calvary. He was taken in by Henri Rousseau who lived, and painted, in a single room not far away, near Montparnasse railway station. The two of them shared this room for several months, a perfectly amicable arrangement by all accounts. Jarry particularly enjoyed Rousseau's descriptions of a foul-smelling ghost that used to haunt him when he was a duty collector at the gates of Paris. Both were broke. Rousseau lived on a minuscule pension and was running up large debts with his paint supplier.[38]

Given the cramped conditions at Rousseau's—there was only one bed—Jarry probably spent days at a time at the boathouse in Athis, between fishing excursions with Vallette, since it was possible to stay there overnight. It would have been his first taste of living by the Seine, and from now on he would try and spend most of the summer months by the river. He may well have rowed upriver as far as Corbeil, where the trolls would soon establish their summer residence.[39]

...

Money was pressing, and Jarry's only income was from his writing. *Days and Nights* appears to have disappointed in this respect, and something more commercial must be attempted. At about this time Jarry was putting together his novel *Visits of Love*. "Putting together" because much of it consisted of earlier writings roughly fitted into an overall schema that might well appeal to a publisher of libidinous literature, provided he did not look at it too carefully. Fortunately Rachilde had found just such a person, Pierre Fort (who was unrelated to Paul Fort). On September 18 she received a letter which was at once unctuous and semiliterate, agreeing to look at the manuscript she had proposed to him. Presumably Rachilde had taken upon herself the task of finding a publisher for *Visits* because the Mercure could not contemplate a work that included Jarry's account of his visit to the Old Lady.[40]

In the meantime, *Ubu Roi* appeared yet again so as to capitalize on the recent production. Perhaps to compensate for turning down *Visits*, the Mercure produced a "facsimile" version of the play, with the text in Jarry's handwriting and the music in Terrasse's. It was a small edition: 300 copies, including 20 on fine paper.[41]

It must surely have been while preparing this edition that Jarry and Terrasse came up with the idea of a puppet theater for adults that would present a range of Symbolist-inspired theatrical productions and fill the void left by the Œuvre. Terrasse, as it happened, had suitable premises, the *Mercure* and the *Revue Blanche* would supply the authors, Lugné-Poe's ex-friends, especially Bonnard, would design the productions, and Jarry was a skilled puppeteer. The venture might even turn a profit.

In November Jarry found himself somewhere to live.

...

His new apartment was both sparsely appointed and gratifyingly unusual. It would be Jarry's permanent, if uncomfortable, residence in Paris, and within a matter of months he managed to ensure that he lived there as seldom as possible. The second-floor rooms in the building at 7, rue Cassette had, and still have, exceptionally high ceilings. Its enterprising landlord had taken advantage of these unnecessarily generous proportions by dividing them in two horizontally. The upper part of this division, the "second-and-a-half floor," thereby contained a number of small rooms which were only five foot four inches in height in places. Most were presumably let as workshops or storerooms. Jarry, however, was a perfect tenant since he could stand upright, with an inch or so to spare. Henceforth he would often appear to suffer from dandruff, because his hair brushed the flaking whitewash that coated the ceiling.[42]

One entered this abode from the courtyard by means of a stairway that was narrow and tortuous even by Parisian standards, and would have been particularly difficult to negotiate with a bicycle. Off the staircase was a low door, and even here it was necessary to crouch in order to approach it. The door opened into a corridor at right angles. Immediately to the right, where the corridor was narrow (three feet), a window opened at an angle onto the courtyard. To the left was a longer stretch of passage, six foot four inches wide at the far end, where there was another small window beneath which there would eventually be a toilet and a small hand basin. Most such buildings would then have had a communal toilet and basin on the stairs, so there is unlikely to have been any plumbing at all in Jarry's flat when he first moved in. Opposite the entrance was a second door opening into his single room. Irregularly shaped, from the entrance it was 15 feet at its deepest where there was an alcove, and 12 feet 4 inches at its widest. It was lit by a small double window in the right-hand wall on entering. The alcove in the far wall was large enough to contain a bed, while a diagonal partition between the corridor and the room cut off the left-hand corner of the room beside the door so as to allow for the widening of the passage behind it. There was no electricity or gas, and since the top half of the bisected room did not contain the fireplace, no means of cooking. On the second floor of the building a manufacturer of ecclesiastical garments plied his trade, sufficient reason for Jarry to refer to his new dwelling as "Our Grand Chasublery."[43]

10.9, 10.10
Jarry's "Chasublery" was photographed in the 1950s by Jean Weber for the Collège de 'Pataphysique.
10.9: The courtyard. The small half-shuttered window is Jarry's, also visible in the second photograph.
10.10: Interior. Looking from the main room, across the small vestibule to the back of the main door.

The infrequent glimpses we will be granted into the interior of Jarry's final Paris residence will constitute a sort of barometer of his circumstances. Only a few of Jarry's intimates were invited there. Jarry guarded his privacy, it was his refuge and here, according to Tailhade, he enjoyed "a seclusion in the center of Paris achieved by few." He even avoided conversation with his concierge by employing a system of baskets lowered from his window to receive his post. Rachilde confirmed these reclusive tendencies, although it may be that Jarry never invited her there so as to avoid her disapproval of his domestic arrangements. The first to leave an account was Marguerite Moreno, who called on him with Schwob, although her comments about the fireplace must be mistaken:[44]

> A person of average height could only enter by bending their knees or by lowering their head, and only remain inside by adopting a seated position. Everything was strange and rare in this home: a huge sofa and armchairs in white lacquered wood, draped with red velvet, a bed barely visible in the half-light permitted by the half-window, horrific and terrifying woodcuts, and in the fireplace, so close to the ceiling that one could only place a half-candlestick topped with half a candle on its mantelpiece, in the fireplace I say, owls regarded the visitors with their lovely blind eyes, tearing with beak and claws at large pieces of raw meat. Jarry moved easily among the furniture, birds, masks of Ubu made from painted cardboard, the tattered books, and when he saw our attention had fixed upon a bicycle leaning against the bed, he said, simply:
>
> "That's so I can take a turn around my room!" And to prove his point, he did.[45]

The last person to visit this room would be the previously mentioned Doctor Saltas, as it fell to him to empty the place when he became Jarry's executor. They first met at the salon held by Gaston and Berthe Danville, both of whom were contributors to the *Mercure*; their salon was something of an offshoot of Rachilde's. Berthe wrote under the name Karl Rosenval; she later coauthored a libretto with Jarry, and was thus another female friend of the heinous misogynist. The Danvilles were later bankrupted by a fantasy that should have remained firmly within the realms of literature: Gaston's scheme to establish a dirigible service between London and Paris. Saltas's memoir of their salon was put into literary shape by Paul Léautaud, who failed to correct Saltas's miscalculation of Jarry's age:[46]

> I first came across Alfred Jarry during the winter of 1897, in a small hotel on the rue Bara, where, every Monday evening, a small group of the younger writers and artists used to meet. Among them were Madame Rachilde, Henri de Régnier, Pierre Louÿs, Alfred Vallette, Ferdinand Herold, Gustave Kahn, Charles-Henry Hirsch, Franc-Nohain, Maurice Ravel, Claude Terrasse, and others. We talked, we smoked, we ate something. The hours passed quickly and it was often dawn before we parted. On one of these Mondays a young man of eighteen or nineteen years turned up very late in the evening. Muscular, dressed in cycling gear, and certainly the youngest at the gathering. It was Alfred Jarry. He greeted the ladies with great correctitude, shook hands with

the men, took a seat and immediately began to recount, with extraordinary verve, one of those wonderful stories of which he had the secret. And which were, moreover, not always entirely improbable. I remember on that evening he described a city where the pavements walked instead of the people, and houses had their entrances on the top floor. In those days there was no question of moving walkways or aeroplanes, but Jarry, as you can see, had already imagined both.[47]

The Chasublery meant that Jarry once again had a permanent place to work. *Visits* was under way, but he had also begun *Faustroll*. When the chapter concerning Henri Rousseau was published in *La Plume* three years later, it bore the date November 1897. Likewise, a letter from Pierre Louÿs to Tinan in December 1897 refers to the final chapter of the book, which suggests that Jarry had already "measured the surface of God." The same month, the *Mercure* published the answers to its questionnaire about the situation of Alsace-Lorraine and the Treaty of Frankfurt that ended the Franco-Prussian War in 1871, thus eliciting from Jarry a rare political pronouncement:[48]

Having been born in 1873, my recollections of the war of 1870 are three years previous to absolute nothingness. It seems likely to me that this event never took place, but was simply a pedagogical invention to encourage recruits into the cadet corps.[49]

• • •

December 1897 was otherwise devoted to realizing Terrasse's and Jarry's plans for a marionette theater, an enthusiasm that was shared by many of their contemporaries. There was, of course, the famous shadow-puppet theater at the Chat Noir, but a number of their immediate acquaintances had mounted amateur marionette productions too. Several of the Nabis, including Ranson and Denis, performed a repertoire in 1892 that included Maeterlinck, the Symbolist playwright *par excellence*. Likewise, Ranson, Vuillard, and Ker-Xavier Roussel had presented a puppet version of Herold's translation of *Paphnutius* by Roswitha of Gandersheim in May 1894, which had been well received by an audience comprising most of the Mercureists. Despite the illustrious names involved, these had been strictly amateur productions for private audiences. Jarry and Terrasse had more professional ambitions, although nearly all of the artists involved with these earlier productions would be a part of the new project.[50]

In the garden behind Claude Terrasse's house at 6, rue Ballu, just south of Montmartre, there was a spacious pentagonal atelier capable of seating an audience of about 100, and it was here that the Théâtre des Pantins held its performances (both the house and the atelier are long gone). Its principal collaborators were five in number: Jarry, Terrasse, the poet Franc-Nohain, who was almost exactly the same age as Jarry, and from the Œuvre, A.-F. Herold and Pierre Bonnard. They had also recruited an administrator, Georges Roussel, brother of the painter Ker-Xavier Roussel.[51]

Work had begun in earnest at the beginning of December. Arnaud quotes a letter from Terrasse of the 8th, in which he invites Jarry to a meeting with Herold's brother, "Alphonse, decorator" (he being an artist), to discuss the project. The remainder of the month was spent in preparation. Jarry designed the heading for the notepaper; he also built the stage machinery for the actual puppet theater, and decorated its interior. Vallotton painted a sign to hang outside, and the auditorium featured murals of marionettes in gray and black silhouette by Bonnard, and exploding fireworks by Vuillard; Ranson and K.-X. Roussel also contributed to the décor. Although Natanson, in the *Revue Blanche*, suggested it was worth going to the theater to see these decorations alone, no trace or record of them has survived apart from an indistinct painting by Bonnard depicting the proscenium. No trace, either, of the dozens of puppets constructed by Bonnard, or the many scenic backdrops he painted for individual productions.[52]

The *Mercure* and *La Critique* announced the theater's formation in December and its first three productions: *Paphnutius*, *Ubu Roi*, and Franc-Nohain's *Vive la France!* Seats cost 3 or 5 francs. *Paphnutius* was first, a revival of the play put on by Herold et al., presumably because it was simpler to mount than a new production. It was submitted to the state censor at the end of December and passed, except that the word "brothel" had to be replaced with "an immoral place." At first sight a work by a tenth-century nun, in which the prostitute Thaïs is converted to the path of true religion, would make an unlikely evening's entertainment, but a review noted that it evoked "her voluptuous life and her ascetic life," which might have allowed for interesting comparisons. It was first performed in public on December 28, although there may have been a private show for friends on Christmas Eve. The evening opened with a poem composed by Franc-Nohain and included various other short pieces along with the main event. The number of performances is unknown, but by January 10 the theater was being prepared for the production of *Ubu Roi*.[53]

The play had to be submitted for censorship since, unlike the Œuvre, this was not a subscription theater. The "word" was judged unacceptable, and after other alternatives were rejected, "*merdre*" was replaced with "*—dre*" throughout, an entirely transparent substitution. Rehearsals followed. The voices for *Ubu Roi* were spoken by actors: Jarry himself played Père Ubu, Louise France reprised her role as Mère Ubu, Jacotot played the King of Poland, and Fanny Zaessinger the Queen and Captain Bordure. Terrasse and his wife accompanied the action on piano and percussion. Everyone received a fee, and Jarry, according to Bordillon, earned a more than respectable 90 francs in January 1898.[54]

The whole enterprise appears to have been a most congenial affair, undertaken in an atmosphere of friendly cooperation that owed much to the irrepressibly ebullient personality of Terrasse. Family ties made this a close-knit group of friends, with the two Bonnard brothers and their sister, married to Terrasse, and the brothers Roussel and Herold. There were pets and children, and one of the few firsthand memories of the Théâtre des Pantins was later recorded in an interview with Terrasse's son, who was three and a half years old at the time. It presents such a novel portrait of Jarry that it is worth quoting extensively, even though it covers the years up until Jarry's death, by which time Charles Terrasse was fourteen:

> I can still hear my mother telling me sadly: "You know, my little one, he is dead, the poor man." And we really felt the hurt of it, it was my first real grief. For he was a most charming companion to us children.

10.11
Jarry's letterhead for the Théâtre des Pantins.

10.12
Claude Terrasse, late 1890s.

10.13
Jarry and Charles Terrasse at his father's house in
Noisy-le-Grand, circa 1900.

I know nothing of Jarry the man of letters, whom so many others knew. But the simple, kind, and childlike Jarry, the friend to children, deserves to be remembered. This was the Jarry I knew, the one who spoke to children with the heart of a child.

First of all, there was the Théâtre des Pantins, at 6, rue Ballu, near the Place Blanche. To the small children we then were, my brother Jean and I, this theater was a place full of enchantment, a forbidden paradise. It was there, at the table, that I so often picked up and played with those puppets which represented Père Ubu, Mère Ubu, the Palotins, and especially, the Bear.

I often saw them sitting around this table, sorting out the puppets, or repairing them, or just talking. Firstly there was Uncle Pierre, Pierre Bonnard, here the puppet maker but otherwise, because he was of course a painter, it was he who had decorated the theater. Then my father, and Franc-Nohain, Ferdinand Herold, and finally, he who I never heard called anything except Père Ubu, but whom I called, using the familiar "*tu*," just plain Alfred: Alfred Jarry.

One night he provoked my father into a duel. A duel with gruyère and red wine. Who could finish first, eating three or four ounces of gruyère cut into tiny pieces, or drinking a glass of wine, both with a tea spoon? Neither one of them managed it, they both laughed so much, the one at the sight of the other swallowing, the other because he could no longer swallow at all.

He taught me many things. He remembered so much from his school days. And it was he who taught me my first word of Latin, and, by repeating it the way he said it, I can still remember it: *T-A ta B-E-R taber N-A taberna C-U cu nacu bernacu tabernacu L-O lo culo naculo bernaculo tabernaculo R-U-M rum, lorum, culorum naculorum bernaculorum tabernaculorum*. It has to be said all in one breath.

He always seemed the same, a kindly man who rarely laughed, but who was never morose either, although he was sometimes a little sarcastic, but he always regarded me with a beautiful smile, and whenever I approached him he would always deposit on my forehead his little mechanical kiss.[55]

Duels by cheese were not the only entertainments. Franc-Nohain's son gave Arnaud an anecdote he had from his father, which probably dates from this period:

Alfred Jarry, one evening, decided to paint himself entirely green—face, neck, hands, wrists— so as to enjoy the stupefaction on the boozers' faces when he entered the café. My father got wind of the joke. He hastily told all his friends, all the customers, all the staff. And Jarry walked in, green, green, green: green as Vert-Vert, the parrot in Gresset's poem. Nobody batted an eyelid. They carried on talking, drinking, reading their newspapers, all perfectly naturally. After a while, Jarry, on the verge of exploding, asked my father: "D'you not notice anything unusual this evening?" "No, nothing special. Why?" It took Jarry many hours to remove the paint, and traces of green were visible behind his ears for some time afterward.[56]

The only puppet not made by Bonnard was that of Père Ubu, which Jarry made himself. There are two early photographs of a marionette of Père Ubu. The first appeared in Apollinaire's review *Les Soirées de Paris* in May 1914, with the caption: "Two views of the original marionette for *Ubu Roi*, belonging to Madame R." Madame R is undoubtedly Rachilde, and this puppet, which still exists, was later depicted in Chauveau's biography before being given by Rachilde to Sacha Guitry in 1944, and then making its way into a private collection. The second photograph belonged to Tristan Tzara and is the only surviving documentation of Bonnard's puppets: it shows Bougrelas and the Tsar along with Jarry's Ubu. Are the two Ubus one and the same? Difficult to be certain, but probably not. The head of Rachilde's puppet appears far less expertly modeled than the one in the Tzara photo. Furthermore, the head of the existing puppet is today essentially the same as when it was photographed in 1914, which suggests that the difference between the two was not due to simple deterioration and shrinkage. If they are not the same, then this "original marionette" may well be the first puppet sculpted by Charlotte in 1889 in Rennes, and subsequently pressed into service for the private performances prior to the Œuvre production. The letter from Rachilde to Guitry that accompanied her gift appears to confirm this supposition, and both Paul Chauveau and Michel Georges-Michel identified it very specifically as the puppet made by Charlotte, as did Léautaud in his not very reliable journal.[57]

10.14
Two views of "the original marionette for *Ubu Roi*," as depicted in Apollinaire's magazine *Les Soirées de Paris*, May 15, 1914.

10.15
Marionettes from the Théâtre des Pantins:
Ubu by Jarry, Bougrelas and the Tsar by
Pierre Bonnard (photographer unknown).

10.16
Alfred Jarry, poster for *Ubu Roi*, lithograph, 1898.

Ubu Roi opened in mid-January 1898, probably on the 15th. Valéry, in a letter to Gide, reported Quillard and Herold engrossed in an intense discussion, during the interval, of the Dreyfus case, which had just dramatically reignited. The program also included the "Song of Disembraining," and ended with Terrasse's setting of poems by Franc-Nohain. There are very few accounts of the show. An anonymous reviewer in the *Revue Blanche* mentioned the gourdlike figure of the king of Poland, exploding Palotins, and Captain Bordure zigzagging around the stage like a streak of red lightning, and also that "the applause was unanimous." Terrasse's settings of the songs were a huge success, and Vallette recalled the audience joining in the choruses of the "Song of Disembraining" and their "loud enthusiasm" for the "March of the Poles." In fact Franc-Nohain's and Jarry's lyrics were so well received that the Mercure decided to publish them as a series of scores. Thus the *Répertoire de Pantins* came into being: a series of nine publications, three with lithographic covers by Jarry and the remainder by Bonnard, for poems by Franc-Nohain.[58]

The actual puppetry for all the performances was undertaken by Jarry, assisted by Franc-Nohain when necessary. They strove for a stylized simplicity of movement. Characterization was conveyed by specific gestures, and superfluous movements were avoided. Franc-Nohain greatly admired Jarry's abilities, as he made clear in a letter to Terrasse of February 1: "Finally, I put to you, since it particularly concerns you, an idea I have for a set piece to end the second act. 'In the 2nd act, a grand ballet overseen by Monsieur Alfred Jarry.' […] It seems to me that six dancers in tutus, performing five minutes of clowning under the agile fingers of Jarry, and accompanied by some ingenious music, would bring this act to a triumphant end!" Léautaud too rated Jarry as a performer, especially of *Ubu Roi*; he later wrote that only Jarry could bring this play to life, he alone had the voice and intonations capable of bringing out its full savor. The revival provoked no riots.[59]

…

Work was continuing on *Faustroll*, and reached a significant moment on February 8, 1898, unless this date was chosen at random. *Faustroll* begins with a series of bailiff's summonses addressed to the principal character. The first of these, indeed the first line of the book, bears this date. It probably indicates the day on which Jarry began the final draft of his novel, in which many of his collaborators at the Théâtre des Pantins were later to find themselves portrayed. There are chapters dedicated to Bonnard and Franc-Nohain, while the immense good humor of Terrasse, photographs of whom invariably feature a beaming grin drowned in beard, is conveyed by the opening words of the chapter dedicated to him, "Concerning the Ringing Isle":

> "Happy the sage," says the *Shi Jing*, "in the valley where he resides, a recluse, who delights in the sound of cymbals; awakening alone in his bed, he exclaims: 'Never, I swear, shall I forget the happiness that I feel!'"[60]

10.17
Jarry as puppeteer, drawing by Émile Couturier for
La Critique, 1898.

10.18
One of the three issues of the *Répertoire des Pantins*
with a lithographic cover by Jarry, 1898.

To Herold, Jarry dedicated his sentimental tale of the romance between a lobster and a can of corned beef, two creatures whose external skeletons ensured that they were *Boneless and Economical.*

The *Mercure* for February 1898 announced that the first series of performances of *Ubu Roi* had been interrupted to allow rehearsals to take place for the next two presentations, *Vive la France!* and *Les Silènes*. This latter was Jarry's adaptation of Christian Dietrich Grabbe's *Comedy, Satire, Irony & Deeper Meaning*, the play he had proposed to Lugné-Poe in March 1896. Jarry and Terrasse completed the adaptation and music for this production, but it was never to make it onto the stage. Nor was *Ubu Roi* to have a second season, and this was because *Vive la France!* fell victim to political events.

On January 13, 1898, Émile Zola's "J'accuse!" was published. This must still be the most famous letter ever to appear in a newspaper. Addressed to the President of the Republic, it occupied the whole front page of the newspaper *L'Aurore*, and accused the government of anti-Semitism and of the illegal imprisonment of Alfred Dreyfus. The "Affair" was finally unleashed. Its immediate consequence was the trial of Zola for libel, which itself generated enormous polemics and disturbances. He was found guilty and escaped into exile to avoid imprisonment. Its general effect was more far-reaching: the splitting into two factions of the whole of French society, either supporters or opponents of Dreyfus. Even such close associations as those of the Mercure and the *Revue Blanche* were riven in two. The editors of the *Revue* were galvanized by this event, Thadée Natanson especially. Henceforth it would ally itself with the most progressive political factions; anti-Dreyfusards were barred from its pages, and he and Quillard were quickly active on the committee founded to defend Dreyfus.[61]

Various public manifestos or open letters appeared for both sides. Most of the Mercure signed those in support of Zola and Dreyfus, including Fénéon, Fort, Herold, Mirbeau, Tailhade, and Vallette; but some supported the opposition, among them Louÿs and Valéry. Jarry signed nothing, neither did Schwob or Rachilde, although she was already moving toward a more conservative stance and appears to have been an anti, although not an especially vocal one. Even for the pro-Dreyfusards, though, Dreyfus himself presented an inconvenient cause for political radicals. He remained a stubborn patriot and a reactionary militarist despite the injustices heaped upon him by both country and army. Tailhade later pointed out: "had he not been the 'hero' of the Affair, he would have been an anti-Dreyfusard!" The closest Jarry came to pronouncing on the case was in a book review of 1901: "As for Dreyfus, everyone knows that he is innocent, and this is also our personal opinion: one needs only to realize that he is the very model of a good soldier and a junior officer, all discipline and loyalty. Treason implies a freer mind, office work and the higher ranks."[62]

In the increasingly tense atmosphere, state censorship was swiftly and rigorously intensified, and *Vive la France!* was banned in its totality. The reason? The edition published by the Collège de 'Pataphysique explained: "When it is a matter of Monsieur God, accompanied by the Exterminating Angel, and at the height of the Affair, coming to France in order to improve its 'moral state' so that it might be made fit for his Son—who is obviously Jewish—to live there, this was not exactly anodyne subject matter."[63]

Vive la France! was by far the most ambitious of the Théâtre's projects. As an entirely original and full-length production with a large cast, it had entailed considerable effort and, presumably, expense to prepare. It was banned on the very night of the première, March 29, and was consequently performed behind closed doors to a private audience, where it was very well received. Next day the police arrived and arrested the cast of puppets. Allies of the theater in the press attempted to have the ban overturned, but to no avail, and the run was canceled. It may have been the financial loss, or simple discouragement, but this was the last of the Théâtre des Pantins as originally conceived. Jarry and Terrasse hoped for a new season the following year, 1899. It is unclear why the works they wrote for it were not performed. There were some very occasional amateur performances, and Jarry took a few of the puppets (which the police must therefore have returned) to a lecture he gave in Brussels in 1902, so as to give extracts from the Pantins' repertoire. Even then he implied that the Théâtre would soon be resurrected, but Terrasse had already moved from the rue Ballu. In the end, it did have a brief rebirth, a single private performance on March 10, 1900 of a *Revue des Pantins*. The cast list in the program includes characters from *Ubu Roi*, *Paphnutius*, and *Vive la France!* all together (and Gémier read some of the parts), but Jarry's script for this revue has never surfaced.[64]

…

Simultaneously with his activities at the Théâtre des Pantins, Jarry had been putting the finishing touches to *Visits of Love*. His original plan, proposed to Fort in September 1897, had listed twelve chapters, or "visits," but the book as published comprised only nine of these, with two other chapters substituted.

The book's first few chapters appear to be out-takes from *Days and Nights*. Two of the planned chapters were never written, although one of these was later expanded to become Jarry's next novel, *Absolute Love*. The final version of *Visits*, which Jarry presented to Fort early in January or February, substituted for these a scene from "Guignol," previously published in *Minutes*, as the last of eleven chapters. However, all of Fort's books had the same format and pagination, and at the last minute Jarry received a barely comprehensible letter from his publisher requesting that Jarry shorten his book to fit the series format. For once Jarry agreed to change something he had written, and "Alcestis" was removed from the final version, perhaps because it was the only chapter not written as a dialog or play.[65]

This shuffling of content and last-minute alterations, so untypical of Jarry, allows the conclusion that this book was primarily a commercial venture, and not something to which he was particularly attached. The result is somewhat chaotic, both structurally and conceptually. The first seven chapters recount what appear at first to be mildly titillating narratives of bourgeois sexual initiation. Lucien, the hero, who resembles Jarry in many particulars, visits the standard venereal Stations of the Cross before his final syphilitic fall, confirmed in chapter 7, "Visiting the Doctor." Despite the conventional nature of his material, or perhaps because of his impatience with it, Jarry's narrative mode becomes increasingly bizarre. By the time of his "visit" to the doctor, he has assumed a sardonic affectation of Symbolist expression which verges on the ludicrous.

The visit to the doctor commences with Lucien's flirtation with a lily. This flower usually symbolized virginal purity, but here it also represents veniality, owing to its phallic appearance; and its association with Oscar Wilde added homosexual overtones. The chapter culminates in Lucien's explanation of how he contracted his illness:

> LUCIEN: [...] The lily, a trifle obtuse, sought to prove to me that nevertheless its perfume outmatched that of my armpits. It turned in every direction (it's astonishing, my dear fellow, the directions there are to a lily), turned and twisted in seventy different ways (there are, at the lowest estimate, *thirty-six*), and ended up ripping itself from its stem; scattered itself, petals upon petals, dewdrops upon dewdrops, to die of languor like an ordinary narcissus, right by the fountain's brim, and remain blighted: like a young prince of the Orient who might too greatly have loved hashish!
>
> Well now, my dear doctor, I have my doubts about the purity of lilies ... And if, like me, you had contemplated them, writhing in the most intemperate spasms, while in the distance the nuns were chanting the *De profundis* of their amours, I am quite convinced you would have expressed the same doubts. (One expresses what one can—is that not the case?)
>
> THE DOCTOR: ! ...
>
> LUCIEN, *still smiling:* It is not entirely in that way, Monsieur, that I lost it. ... But I have every reason to believe that it is probably in that way that I must have caught it!
>
> THE DOCTOR: ! ...[66]

It was not only lilies that could be "a trifle obtuse." This progressively obscure style and content must surely have been intended to get a rise out of his illiterate publisher? And, contrariwise, to have a detumescent effect on Fort's loyal readership who would have been expecting his usual fare, a "one-handed" novel. After this chapter, the seventh of eleven, the main character is cast aside, never to be referred to again. All pretense of conventional narrative is then discarded, not least because most of the remainder of the book consisted of texts that had been previously published, or in one case, not even written by Jarry at all.

One of the chapters, "Fear Visits Love," appeared in the *Revue Blanche* on March 15, 1898, just before the novel as a whole was published. It was almost certainly the work of Rachilde, written after a wager with Jarry that she could imitate his style. Whether he paid up or not we do not know, but the text does not really succeed in replicating Jarry beyond its surface characteristics. As for content, we may well suppose that Rachilde allegorizes Jarry's own romantic inclinations:[67]

> FEAR: Your clock has three hands. Why is that?
>
> LOVE: That is customary here.

FEAR: Why those three hands, for God's sake? It makes me uneasy …

LOVE: Nothing could be more natural, nothing simpler. Calm down. The first marks the hour, the second urges on the minutes, and the third, forever motionless, eternalizes my indifference.[68]

Rachilde had not only found this book a publisher, and written a section of it, but she also attempted to persuade Jarry to suppress the chapter concerning the Old Lady. This business was now beyond a joke, if it ever had been one. The prospect of the whole thing blowing up again when Jarry's book appeared appalled her, and Vallette too, since Gourmont was vital to the Mercure. Only a part of the letter she wrote to Jarry on February 16 is known, but she mustered a good many arguments aimed at deflecting his resolve.

> The story of the Old Lady saddens me, my little Ubu … There's no getting away from it, it's slander, and if she should be less crazy than usual, she will take you to court, and then … well, that might amuse you but I don't at all understand why. It is perhaps unfortunate that mad people are not locked up for good, but if we allow them their liberty it is not so they may be betrayed by people who are more rational and … reasonable, than they are. I find it revolting when you pick on the stupid or defenseless. The fact that you find it amusing is not at all sufficient reason to do so … There's no revenge to be had from an act committed in anger, don't you see![69]

Furthermore: Berthe was ludicrous, but only because she was mad. She had done Jarry a service (presumably helping him out of the army). The whole thing was likely to lead to bailiffs, or even attacks with vitriol. Mud sticks, and may sully "your future as a little man of genius." This last appeal succeeded in being uncomprehending and condescending both at once: Jarry dug in his heels, he would change nothing. And when Fort wanted cuts a month later, he chose "Alcestis." Even so, his refusal to cut the "visit" to the Old Lady seems not to have affected his friendship with Rachilde. Her knowledge that the affair was her fault must have played a part in that, and Jarry may have felt able to refuse her request because he suspected her involvement. Speculations which lead only to further questions: is the whole story even known? Jarry's anger seems extreme in the circumstances, as does Rachilde's tacit acknowledgment that some sort of revenge was justifiable. In the event, there was to be no trial, no bailiffs, and no vitriol was thrown.

The press list for *Visits of Love*, like that for *Ubu Roi*, presents a snapshot of Jarry's immediate circle. Ten copies went to F.-A. Cazals, who illustrated the book and drew its cover, which, somewhat incongruously, appeared to depict Jarry in the role of Cupid. Others went to critics, and the remainder to his immediate friends: Vallette and Rachilde appear first, then Fénéon, Danville, Herold, Kahn (and Madame Kahn, perhaps as a peace offering), Mallarmé, Quillard, Régnier, Schwob and Moreno, Tinan, Tailhade, Valéry, La Jeunesse, Lorrain, Terrasse, Mendès, Bauer,

10.19
L'Amour en visites, 1898.

Ranson, and around a dozen others. Claudius-Jacquet, long gone from Paris, is listed, and there is only one name signified by a single initial: "F." Fanny Zaessinger, presumably.[70]

The name "Melmoth" occurs near the end of the list. This was the pseudonym assumed by Oscar Wilde on his arrival in Paris after his release from prison in May 1897. The *Mercure* published his "Ballad of Reading Gaol" a year later, in a translation by Henry Davray (also on Jarry's press list). Davray had been the English literature correspondent for the magazine for the past two years; he was well known to Jarry, and they were exact contemporaries. Davray was to become a crucial intellectual bridge between England and France, spending much of his time in London, where he was close to most of the younger literary figures, including the Rhymers Club (Dowson, Yeats, etc.). He translated a large number of works by various authors, especially the novels of H. G. Wells, and directed the English publishing program for the Mercure. His relative obscurity nowadays is partially explained by the loss of all his papers in 1944 during the London Blitz. Evidently he knew both Jarry and Wilde, and it may have been his idea that they should meet, although he makes it sound like Wilde's. Jarry was at least interested enough to keep the letter from Davray arranging the rendezvous:

> 19 May 1898
>
> My dear Ubu Nautilus,
> O. Wilde assures me that tomorrow evening at nine thirty he will be at the café de Rohan Place du Théâtre Français in the hope that you will be there—I will be—so as to make formal introductions.
>
> Yours with devotion
> Henry D. Davray [71]

Jarry had not been active in the campaign in support of Wilde, but the two appear to have got on well enough to meet again, when Jarry brought Wilde a selection of his works, as the latter reported in a letter to Reginald Turner on May 25.

> Alfred Jarry has sent me a complete collection of his works. He is a most extraordinary young man, very corrupt, and his writings have sometimes the obscenity of Rabelais, sometimes the wit of Molière, and always something curious of his own. He made his début by producing a play called *Ubu Roi* at the Théâtre de l'Œuvre. The point of the play was that everyone said merde to each other, all through the five acts, apparently for no reason. The play was so hooted that Jarry became famous, and the Mercure de France has published *Ubu Roi* in an edition de luxe. Jarry is now the rising light of the Quartier Latin. In person he is most attractive. He looks just like a very nice renter. [72]

"Renter" was London slang for a homosexual prostitute.

Visits was another disappointment financially, and Jarry did send copies to at least some of those on his press list (Wilde's copy is known, for example, as is his copy of *Ubu Roi*). Pierre Fort, seeking an explanation for the poor sales, called on him repeatedly, but could never find him at home. He therefore wrote him another of his inimitable letters, from which it is obvious that he suspected, probably correctly, that Jarry had not bothered sending review copies to the press.[73]

Jarry, in fact, had removed to the country for the summer some weeks earlier, as he casually informed Trochon's bailiff, whose entreaties had resumed:

> Corbeil, 15 June 1898
>
> Monsieur,
>
> If Monsieur Trochon has not forgone any of his measures, I for my part have not given up on paying him. At the moment, though, I am in Corbeil, with friends, on holiday, which is why your letter has reached me somewhat late, and I cannot consider a further payment until I am back in Paris at the end of the month.
>
> Monsieur Trochon has been paid altogether too promptly as regards my first purchases from him for him to doubt my fidelity to my obligations. Moreover, it is easy for me to demonstrate that, of the many accounts I have been able to settle with various tradesmen, his is the first I have not been in a position to meet. It is for him, then, to spare me threats which are more risky for himself than for me.
>
> I am holding on to the letter addressed by him to a third party, but I am benevolent enough not to bear the matter unduly in mind and to continue, as regularly as I can, to send payments.
>
> Yours faithfully,
> Alfred Jarry
>
> To my Paris address, or until the end of the month and perhaps for part of the summer, Quai de l'Apport, Corbeil, Seine-et-Oise.[74]

The "Paris address" was left conveniently unspecific.

• • •

A "Phalanstery," in the erotico-socialist utopia envisaged by Charles Fourier, was a perfect community in which all the needs of its members would be matched to their desires. Fourier had a mania for taxonomy, and had devised a system in which all human personalities could be classified using a combination of twelve "passions." Should the most important combinations of these passions be represented by a member of the community, then every task would fall to someone whose desire it was to do it. To put it crudely, the person who happened to delight in foul smells would undertake waste disposal, and so on. Thus would the Phalanstery be "sufficient unto itself." Ideal for trolls, in other words.

In the spring of 1898, Jarry and five other writers from the Mercure (Marcel Collière, Pierre Quillard, A.-Ferdinand Herold, Vallette, and Rachilde) rented a holiday home on the banks of the Seine at Corbeil. It was probably Jarry who named it the Phalanstery, and on the boat shed constructed in the extensive back garden he wrote its name in *faux*-ancient French: "Falanstère de Corbeye." Corbeil was, and is, a small town straddling the Seine some fifteen miles south of Paris. Although in parts picturesque, its center, next to the town square, and the small car park that is nowadays the Square Alfred Jarry, is dominated by enormous mills which stretch back from the river toward the railway station. In the 1890s they provided Paris with flour and paper, transported via Corbeil by the large barges which docked directly outside the house on the quai de l'Apport rented by Jarry and his friends.

The prospects in the other directions were a little less industrial: a towpath replete with anglers where pleasure boats were moored, and directly across the river on the edge of the opposite bank of the Seine was the large white Château du Castel-Joli which the Minister of the Interior, Waldeck-Rousseau, made his summer home the following year.

Jarry, alone among the Phalansterians, had no particular commitments in Paris, and so settled in more or less permanently. The others could generally visit only at the weekends and during the vacation of high summer, along with spouses and children. Or rather, with one particular child: Gabrielle, the eight-year-old daughter of Rachilde and Vallette, whose contribution would turn out to be significant. It is thanks to her that there is a record of Jarry's life by the river, which at Corbeil lasted for around ten months. Gabrielle took many of the photographs for an album that she and Rachilde assembled to record their summer holidays, all spent on the banks of the Seine. They are the only unposed photographs of Jarry, and include a famous image of him, outside the Phalanstery on his bicycle.

The Phalanstery was to be the headquarters of trollism. Here Jarry, Quillard, and Vallette especially could devote themselves to important tasks and occupations, principally boating, fishing, cycling, walking, drinking, and, certainly in Jarry's case, writing. Jarry moved in some time in April or early May. He took the smallest, most inconvenient room, presumably because his contribution to the rental was the least. His bedroom was at the top of the house in the attic, its mansard window in the center of the roof. It could be reached only by passing through the room of either Herold or Collière. So as to preserve his independence, Jarry cut a trapdoor into its floor and ascended by means of a knotted rope.[75]

Because of this behavior and other uncivilized habits supposedly typical of savages, the maid nicknamed him "The Indian." It was not intended as a compliment. This formidable giantess, a "maid of all tasks," was known locally as La Briquette, since she was often to be seen blackened with coal dust, her other occupation being to assist with loading the tugs with briquettes of fuel. Her real name was Marie, and she and Jarry did not hit it off. She came to the conclusion that he was a foreigner, some sort of Asiatic, with his sallow complexion and oriental-looking moustache. Unamused by either his eccentricities or his character, she told Rachilde: "So far as I am concerned, Madame, such persons are insufferable!" She found it incomprehensible that such an *outre-mer* ("overseas" person) should be so politely treated by people who otherwise

10.20, 10.21, 10.22, 10.23
The Phalanstery in Corbeil. This page: 10.20: From the album of Gabrielle Vallette. Jarry's room was behind the central mansard window. 10.21: The Phalanstery (visible on the extreme right) seen from the opposite bank of the Seine. Following page: 10.22: Looking south along the *quai*, this view shows the proximity of the mills. The Phalanstery is again extreme right. 10.23: The Phalanstery's roof is visible at the bottom of this photograph, taken from the tower of the largest mill.

557 — *CORBEIL. Vue sur les Grands Moulins.* ND Phot.

1897–1899

72. - CORBEIL. - Quai de l'Apport Paris - *A. R.*

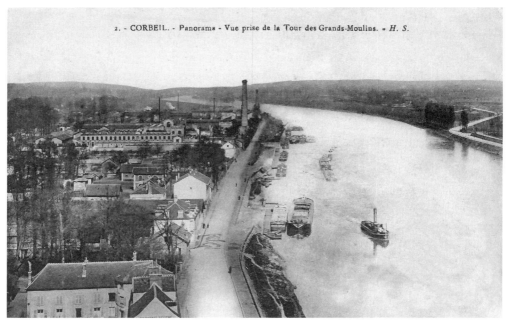

2. - CORBEIL. - Panorama - Vue prise de la Tour des Grands-Moulins. - *H. S.*

appeared to be respectable. Worst of all, it was Jarry, as the principal resident, from whom she most often had to take instructions.[76]

Vallette and he must have rowed their boats from Athis to Corbeil, and it was Jarry who was to maintain them and look after line and rod whenever necessary. This ensured that the most important activity of the trolls could be undertaken at the shortest possible notice: fishing. The fishing season did not start until June 17, but Jarry's familiarity with angling law was detailed, and in a book review in 1899 he carefully pointed out the various exclusions that allowed certain forms of fishing out of season. This knowledge may well have proved vital to his survival later on, when fish from the Seine constituted the major part of his sustenance whatever the time of year, but even now the fish he caught were an important part of his diet. They were free.[77]

Early in 1898, Jarry was concerned to finish a clean copy of the manuscript of *Faustroll*, since chapters of it (VI, and X to XXV) were to appear in the *Mercure* at the beginning of May 1898. Completing this section of *Faustroll* may well have been a matter of urgency, since *Visits* was also to be published that month, and Jarry cannot have been in much doubt as to Gourmont's reaction to it. At the same time, on May 2, Jarry wrote to Rachilde. It was only a few weeks since her letter to him urging him to remove the Old Lady episode from *Visits*, but there appeared to be no ill will between them:[78]

> We write to you today, Madame, the second of May, to inform you that we have well and truly killed all those nasty brutes of nightingales which were preventing us sleeping in our phalanstery, at last cleared out of its trolls and trollesses (to be pronounced, if you would be so kind, with a German accent). It could not go on. The nightingale [...] had a snide way of smuggling into our ears the beginning of a music-box waltz in a minor key which we had no desire to remember.
>
> The nightingale, grilled on a skewer, suitably basted in alcohol, is not at all bad. The ancients, whose appetites were as refined as they were stupid, preferred to consume only their tongues, and so as to follow this practice we have tried in vain to extract them.[79]

Later in this letter, Jarry mentions a fishing trip with Eugène Demolder, another contributor to the *Mercure*. He was one of a number of local artistic exiles eager to escape the city during the hotter months of summer. Demolder lived only a mile or so upriver in an enormous house belonging to his father-in-law, the magnificent "Pornocrates," the artist Félicien Rops. Mallarmé, another boating enthusiast, was further upstream at Valvins, near Fontainebleau, about fifteen miles as the crow flies, or by bicycle. Here too, until very recently, the Natansons had had their summerhouse, the scene of many house parties attended by Bonnard, Lautrec, Vuillard, and other artists and writers associated with the *Revue Blanche*. These occasions continued there, since it was now occupied by Thadée Natanson's brother-in-law.[80]

Jarry was in his element at the Phalanstery. He plunged himself into the daily practicalities of the house, seeming to enjoy the manual work, and happily applying himself to domestic chores at table, which was set up in the garden when the weather permitted. Sometimes he would concoct

10.24
Jarry arriving at the Phalanstery, from the album
of Gabrielle Vallette.

a meal, although Jarry's notions of sustenance were another cause of irritation for La Briquette. When he prepared a meal in honor of Rachilde, she arrived to find it consisted of cakes, sweets, and jam, until some fried fish inexplicably appeared at the end. Jarry refrained on this occasion from his habitual absinthe, aware that its odor was disagreeable to his guest. Instead "he apologized for not being able to swallow the water," and launched into a discourse on the virtues of alcohol. Rachilde was, in fact, endangering her health by virtue of her preposterous insistence on drinking water:[81]

> "You are poisoning yourself Ma-da-me," he explained, as seriously as could be. "Water contains, in suspension, all the microbes of the earth and sky, and the sugary things which constitute your principal sustenance are alcohols in a rudimentary state which intoxicate one quite differently from spirits, whose noxious components have been prudently destroyed by distillation."[82]

It appears impossible to underestimate the importance of fishing to Jarry and Vallette. "It was a passion, and one does not argue with a passion," wrote Rachilde. Much of Jarry's correspondence with Vallette concerns angling, the purchase of bait and tackle, or reports of marvelous halieutic exploits: "Taken today (by line, as always) twenty-nine fish between noon and two o'clock, all affecting the form of plump gudgeons. Caught from the skiff with Collière, with a spoon bait, with a short, sharp strike, *celui qui broche* [a pike], fishhook snapped off, water taken in, skiff overturned full of emotions and glory, all too heavy for the cart." It was fishing with Quillard that Père Ubu decided to celebrate in his *Almanac* at the end of the year, and Jarry's agricultural commentary for February relates a hunt for barbel they had undertaken that month. They followed the spawning fish for three days up the Yonne to Vinneuf, a distance of some forty miles. Bonnard depicted barbel and Quillard side by side owing to the similarity of their beards, as Jarry explained in a letter.[83]

Every morning, often at dawn, Jarry, with Vallette if he was in residence, would row to "Les Îles." This group of wooded islands downstream was particularly propitious for fishing, since the trees overhung the river. Here they would remain until lunchtime, when they would return to the Phalanstery and rehouse the skiffs in the back garden. This was not entirely simple because of the narrowness both of the gateway at the front of the house and of the passage beside it. The page of Rachilde's album devoted to the "Naval Maneuvers" required to squeeze them through for maintenance and storage is illustrated at the start of this chapter.[84]

Another page of the album, now lost, although some of its photographs were published, was entitled "Phalansterian games and exercises," and depicted Rachilde costumed as a "Javanese," others playing shuttlecock, and Jarry and Quillard jumping over a rope.

...

Rachilde's account of the Phalanstery in her book on Jarry is frequently little more than a collection of anecdotes, two of which may be swiftly summarized. The first, elliptically, concerns exploits with the rod.

One day Jarry came back from Les Îles earlier than usual, and interrupted Rachilde's writing with a dramatic announcement. Her husband had fallen in the water, and she must rush to his rescue. Why had Jarry not done so? Because he can't swim! Why hasn't he called for help? That's why he's here. Eventually she decides she must go and see for herself, and naturally discovers her husband absorbed in his fishing. On her return she finds Jarry apparently engrossed in repairing his bicycle in the garden. Revenge. She tells him it's true, he's not there, and his boat has gone too. Jarry does not believe her at first, but then jumps on his bicycle. When he comes back, he tells her: "Naturally we had to make sure, one can never trust a woman: *they are capable of anything!*"[85]

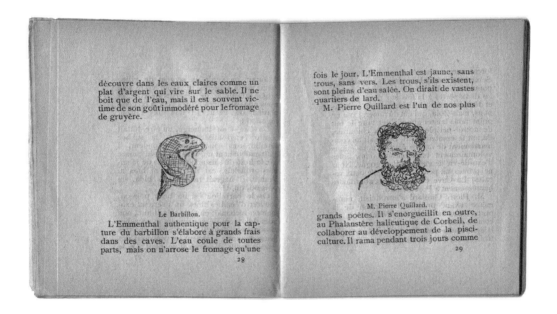

10.25
Bearded creatures: Quillard and a barbel, as
depicted by Pierre Bonnard in *Ubu's Almanac*.

10.26
Vallette and Jarry carrying the skiff.

10.27, 10.28, 10.29
Phalansterian games and exercises. 10.27: Jarry and
Rachilde. 10.28: This photograph of Jarry, Rachilde,
and Marie-Thérèse Collière was titled "The Three
Graces," perhaps because Jarry is wearing Rachilde's
shoes. 10.29: Jarry jumping a rope.

The second is one of the most oft-repeated anecdotes of Jarry's life. The landlord and the owner of the Phalanstery, Monsieur Béglet, lived in Paris, but his family occupied the next-door building during the summer. His wife became concerned at the gunshots emanating from their new neighbors' garden, at Jarry's habit of firing his revolver at all and everything, nightingales, frogs, cockchafers, spiders. She called on Rachilde to complain, since her children played behind the wall that separated the two gardens. Rachilde asked her inside, hoping to persuade her that "their games were harmless"; and also hoping that "the guilty party would not appear and join the conversation." As Madame Béglet's supplication reached its climax, Jarry came up behind Rachilde, gun in hand.[86]

> "Suppose, Madame," lamented the poor woman, "he was to kill one of my children?"

> "Ah, Ma-da-me," Jarry replied thoughtfully, "should such a misfortune occur, we would make you some more!"

Madame Béglet turned on her heel and was never seen again, and it was probably this witticism that cost the Phalansterians their summer residence: *celui qui bégle* (which sounds like *beugle*, "he who howls") would refuse to renew their lease.

...

It goes without saying that Rachilde and Jarry already knew each other well, but encountering him frequently at the Tuesdays, and in literary contexts in Paris, was quite different from sharing a house with him. She was afforded new insights into Jarry's daily life, and they were not at all reassuring. Her book was written in considerable hindsight, and from the viewpoint of a thoroughly conventional morality, but it is clear that Rachilde was beginning to understand that Jarry was an exceptional being, and not necessarily in a good way. They were overwhelmed by his conversation; Jarry lingered at table, and inveigled his fellow Phalansterians into "interminable discussions." The effect was disquieting rather than amusing, because it seemed to her that it was his endless absinthes that brought about this "terrifying incontinence of language." He seemed, she says, "to quiver in a state of permanent inebriation," and it was well understood by his friends that "excess was his discipline." Rachilde deplored the fact that they encouraged his drinking by joining in, before returning to their thoroughly comfortable lives elsewhere. She does not name the culprits, but Demolder, Quillard, and Herold were all friends of the bottle. Jarry kept this telegram from Herold:[87]

1 AUGUST 3PM I HAVE JUST DRUNK AN EXCELLENT MARC BRANDY HEROLD [88]

Jarry and Quillard became good friends while at the Phalanstery, although not all of their interests coincided. Quillard began as a Symbolist, the author of *La Fille aux mains coupées*, one of the most experimental of the productions at Fort's Théâtre d'Art. In 1898 he took over the poetry

10.30
Phalansterians at table. Marcel and Marie-Thérèse
Collière, Vallette, Jarry, Herold, Quillard, Rachilde.
The photographer is presumably Gabrielle, occupant of
the empty seat.

column for the *Mercure*, and was a notable classics scholar, the translator of Iamblichus among others. Such activities were certainly to Jarry's taste, but Quillard was also deeply involved in politics, and had only recently returned from Constantinople as part of the campaign against the Armenian genocide unleashed by the Ottoman sultan, Abdul Hamid. Author of a passionate defense of Ravachol, he contributed to the main anarchist newspapers, and was a tireless activist in support of Dreyfus. He was the first general secretary of the League for the Rights of Man, founded as Dreyfus's defense committee. Later he was a supporter of the revolutionary movement in Russia, but died in 1912, "his life prematurely used up, having been given to political activism when it had seemed destined for the dream," in Mauclair's words. Despite such earnestness he was far from po-faced, and his trollish proclivities for fishing and alcohol were sufficient to cement his friendship with Jarry—and earn Rachilde's disapproval.[89]

It is striking how rooted the *Mercure* was in its close friendships, and even though the review was widely read across Europe it did not refrain from gentle self-satire and publishing items for its contributors' own amusement, which contained private references that must have puzzled many of its readers. It often included poems by "Quasi," a collective pseudonym that is usually thought to have concealed the identities of Fort and Herold, although one may suspect the hand of Jarry too, since Quasi was the diminutive of his nickname at Rennes. A (rhymed) verse from one of them, published in March 1897, reads:[90]

> Quillard complains to all, that grim
> Abdul Hamid's sword does widows make;
> "*Merdre*" pronounces Jarry haughtily;
> And Vallette reads more proofs. [91]

The *Mercure* also helped its contributors in more concrete ways. When Jarry had interrupted Rachilde to inform her that her husband was drowning, she had been writing book reviews for the magazine. She had Jarry read and comment upon the books she was supposed to review. Not only did she trust his opinion on such matters, but she frequently expressed admiration for his erudition, his wide reading and feats of memory. "I remember a discussion about fashion between two literary ladies neither of whom could recollect the nickname given to an ornament pinned to the back of the waistband or worn on a ribbon at the back of the neck: it was known as a 'follow-me-young-man.' Much to our stupefaction, Jarry provided the date and title of the magazine that had launched this frippery. And this from someone who was totally neglectful of his dress, who would happily sit in a muddy puddle to repair his bicycle." Jarry was an acknowledged classical scholar, had already worked as a reviewer of art and drama, had edited two art magazines, was up to date with modern scientific theory, especially physics, read widely in mathematics and psychology, and had an extensive basic knowledge of philosophy. Both Rachilde and Vallette respected his abilities and his opinions, and yet Jarry was never given a column in the *Mercure*, despite his needs being more urgent than most. The likes of Beck were granted this favor within weeks of turning up at a Tuesday. One can only presume it was another consequence of Rachilde's "joke."[92]

Meanwhile, it now fell to Rachilde to review *Visits* for the June issue. A minefield. Not to offend Gourmont, what to say about the Old Lady, the question of what Tinan would think, and of course Jarry, who had refused to tone down his book. In the end it was a carefully coded reproach of its author whom, in the final paragraph, she admonishes for taking the advice she herself had proffered after reading *Caesar-Antichrist*: that he should try "writing like everybody else." ("You can show me how," had been the icy response.)[93]

> I have left this spicy morsel until last, although I am a little nervous about serving up to my readers something that it is my professional duty … to respect. In this one, there is no cooing of amorous doves, and despite the old-fashioned title, these visits are not exactly … formal. What it is: my God, I have no idea! It is an absurd book, both brutal and charming. Marcel Schwob, who knows about such things, calls it: *delicious!* The author, having already had the audacity to launch that monstrous farce, however brilliant, *Ubu Roi,* seems to delight in such pranks as this, and in plunging us, still alive, into dark realities with which we would prefer not to come into contact until after death. Endowed with a very unusual scientific talent which has enabled him to acquire, long before his youth would justify it, a technical experience of certain things and deeds, and to tackle any subject with the clear vision of maturity, and with all the cynicism of the jaded, Alfred Jarry also has a tendency toward that unnecessary nastiness, deceitfulness, and malice which is common to precocious brats that are supposed to die young from a surfeit of spirit. […] The unbiased reader will be dismayed to see an original writer being tempted by his diabolical facility to simply amuse himself and others. Alfred Jarry should apply his talents to better things than this.[94]

Jarry did not spend all of his time in Corbeil; he had been working on an adaptation of Rabelais's *Pantagruel* with Terrasse since the previous year, and this necessitated trips to Terrasse's house to the east of Paris at Noisy-le-Grand, or to the rue Ballu in the city.

In July 1898, Gaston Danville conveyed his fealty to Père Ubu in a letter requesting information about Le Pouldu, where he was going on holiday (the Isle of Bara is a reference to the rue Bara, the Danvilles' address in Paris):

> Milord Ubu
>
> Should it please your lordship to give us some information concerning the village of Le Pouldu of which you have spoken, regarding habitable places, hostelries, lanes, roads and communications by means of which one may reach the same, no one would be more grateful than
>
> Your devoted vassal,
> Gaston Danville
>
> Shall we have the pleasure of seeing you one of these days, directing the tip of your canvas skiff in metal (Faustroll model), or the wheel of your bicycle toward the Isle of Bara, an island of dry land which you know well and whose inhabitants once more send you respectful salutations.[95]

The reference to *Faustroll* means it is finally time to consider this work, which Jarry completed in Corbeil in the summer of 1898, although it was not published in his lifetime. *Faustroll* is one of Jarry's greatest books, and it is certainly one of his most unusual; moreover, despite all appearances to the contrary, it was also deeply autobiographical.

...

The Exploits and Opinions of Doctor Faustroll, Pataphysician was assembled from various components, some of which dated from four years earlier. As outlined earlier, in chapter 3, Jarry had originally envisaged a straightforward exposition of Pataphysics: an "*Elements of Pataphysics*." Although fragments of the *Elements* do appear in it, they constitute only a small part of *Faustroll*; this is doubtless because Jarry became the first to discover that Pataphysics was easier to demonstrate than to explain.

It appears to have been Henri Bouché, of the Collège de 'Pataphysique, who originally proposed what now seems obvious: that while the "public" identified Jarry with Ubu, Jarry identified himself with Faustroll. This being the case, the name of Faustroll, a sort of self-portrait, becomes significant. He is a double being: Faust, the scholarly magus, evidently derived from Goethe, is combined with the troll, a self-sufficient creature (the only connection with Ibsen's trolls), who needs only the freedom to exercise his trollish pursuits of cycling, fishing, and drinking, activities which are all represented in the novel. The character of Faustroll himself is strangely vague, especially in comparison with that of Ubu. This is because, being a personification of Jarry himself, he is not so much a character in this novel as the novel itself, and this is why his name may serve as the key both to Jarry's intentions and to the novel's unusual structure.[96]

Although Book II of *Faustroll*, which consists of three brief chapters, has the title "*Elements of Pataphysics*," it cannot be the original version of this long-announced work, since the second chapter of it is based upon an article by William Crookes that appeared only in May 1897, and the third introduces Bosse-de-Nage, the caricature of Beck, whom Jarry had first met later the same year. Its first chapter, which carefully defines and elucidates the basic principles of the Science, is probably all that remains of the original. Pataphysics, we have already discovered, has no truck with dualities, including that between the "imaginary" and the "real." Jarry likewise made no distinction between the life of the imagination and that of the everyday, being equally Faust and troll, philosopher and drunkard. It was therefore perfectly logical that Jarry's self-apotheosis should be distilled from the circumstances of his recent existence.

After the brief elucidation of Pataphysics in Book II, the most substantial part of the book describes Faustroll's allegorical journey in the company of the bisyllabic Bosse-de-Nage and the ex-bailiff René-Isidore Panmuphle, the fictional recorder of the events in the novel. Like Sherlock Holmes, the exceptional hero of Jarry's novel must have his Watson as an everyman narrator; and as with Faustroll, his name may be decoded into contradictions that cancel each other out like the Polish Everywhere and Nowhere of *Ubu Roi*. Thus René signifies order and rationality, from René Descartes; Isidore, disorder and delirium, after Isidore Ducasse; Pan, the pagan god of music and sexuality, signifies poetry; and *mufle*, philistinism. In Faustroll's skiff (what else?), the trio navigate a succession of islands which represent the imaginary worlds created by artists and writers associated with the Symbolists, and hence with Jarry's life in Paris. These miraculous lands, to be found amid the streets of the capital, are rendered in beautiful and complex prose poems which constitute a high point of the Symbolist movement, even as they intimated a future poetry that was to be taken up in the following century.[97]

By representing his colleagues through evocations of their creations rather than by the more usual descriptive biography or critical exegesis as undertaken, for instance, by Gourmont in *The Book of Masks*, Jarry lays claim to the superior, or rather the equivalent, reality of the imagination. He chose only those artists and writers he knew personally, or had at least communicated with, and presents their imagined portraits or dedicates chapters to them. They include, from *L'Ymagier*, Bernard and Gauguin; from the Mercure, Bloy, Dumur, Fort, Kahn, Rachilde, Régnier, Schwob, Tailhade, Valéry, and Vallette; from the Revue Blanche, Bonnard, Fénéon, Mallarmé, and Thadée Natanson; from the Théâtre des Pantins, Terrasse and friends, as already mentioned; from the Phalanstery, Quillard and Herold; and then a number of recent acquaintances such as Beardsley and even a few who had aroused his ire: Beck, Lormel, Loti, and Trochon. He actually showed some restraint with respect to his foes, since there is no mention of Fargue or Gourmont, for example. After this series of evocative poem-portraits, both Faustroll and Bosse-de-Nage die, yet continue their adventures, since neither is restricted to the confines of normal physical laws. These laws are among the topics explored in the final chapters, which are mostly dedicated to contemporary Scottish physicists, in particular Lord Kelvin, and reveal Jarry's enthusiasm for the more imaginative scientific speculations of his time. He demonstrates that even such apparently dry material may be transformed, by *his* science, into literature.

So much for Faust, the intellectual and imaginative aspect of the book's creator, but what of his trollism, and his life in Corbeil? *Faustroll* certainly baffled Jarry's contemporaries. Even recently, for example in Michel Arrivé's notes to the Pléiade edition of Jarry's works, its structure has been criticized for its incomprehensibility: even more chaotic than *Days and Nights* in fact. Indeed, it was as disorderly and haphazard as Jarry's existence since the production of *Ubu Roi*, as evidenced by the meandering nature of this chapter.[98]

However, it is precisely this existence, symbolized by the name of "Faustroll," that may provide the key to the structure of this book. *Faustroll* should be seen as a representation of Jarry's present life *in its totality*. Just as *Days and Nights* was structured around the opposition between a soldier's moments of freedom (the nights, representing escape and imagination) and the days in which every waking moment is dominated by army discipline, so *Faustroll*, in order to represent the integration of the imagination into the everyday, must incorporate Jarry's trollism too, his debts, his friendships, his life in the country … and his indulgence in alcohol. Rachilde maintained that Jarry was permanently inebriated, even resembling an "enraged monkey locked in a cage." Although philosophy was as vital to his existence as sharing a bock with the bargees in the local taverns, the combination was even more seductive: sobriety passing unnoticed into drunkenness, and the two states imperceptibly merging together. In *Faustroll* such distinctions are dissolved in an exuberant and luscious prose whose narrative appears thrown together like a splendid evening's drinking. It has a structure and inevitability that would appear entirely logical to a particularly lucid inebriate, a structure that exactly mirrored its author's existence and thus forms a representation supplementary to the book's actual narrative.[99]

Jarry held his own creative process in particular reverence, and he would often, as a mark of this respect, preserve aspects of a work's beginnings in the finished version. *Ubu Roi*, for example, contains references that would have been meaningless to any but an ex-pupil of Hébert. He often cited his own books, and this self-referentiality is symptomatic of the extent of his literary ambitions. They were limitless, or in the parlance of the time, absolute: it was quite simply a matter of creating one's own universe, a "bootstrap theory" of literary creation. Thus the apparently chaotic structure of *Faustroll* may simply be a structure that he preserved from another state of consciousness (just like those in *Days and Nights*), one carefully conserved during the periods of sobriety necessary to set down a work imagined and organized in a state of semi-hallucination induced by absinthe.

This is simple conjecture, admittedly, but nothing expresses more clearly the seamless alogical continuum that connects the everyday with the most outlandish speculation, via a sort of Symbolist shaggy-dog story, than the book's beginning and end. It commences most precisely with a date on a bailiff's writ, concrete and immediate, on that official paper costing exactly 0.60 francs with which Jarry was so familiar thanks to Maître Breux and his colleagues. It ends with Faustroll's rumination upon something ultimately inestimable, in which he literally has the measure of God. This is an extravagantly grandiose scheme, bordering on megalomania, and confirmed by some of Faustroll's pronouncements ("I am God," "the universe is that which is the exception to oneself"), which Arnaud and Bordillon tactfully categorize as "Promethean." No wonder this pudding appeared a bit rich even for the avant-garde publishers of the day, and only appeared posthumously.[100]

...

There are two manuscripts of *Faustroll*, known as the "Lormel," because it was later purchased by Louis Lormel, and the "Fasquelle," which was the manuscript used to produce the first French edition published by Eugène Fasquelle. The Lormel is almost certainly the earliest, from the spring of 1898. A measure of Jarry's lack of resources can be gathered from the fact that part of this manuscript is written on the backs of large lithographs by Jarry of Ubu and the Palotins, torn into quarters. He could not even afford new paper. The Fasquelle manuscript was probably copied out later the same year. This manuscript ended up in the collection of Tristan Tzara, who had it bound in vellum into which Picasso drew a portrait of Jarry using a soldering iron.[101]

The Fasquelle manuscript includes typeset versions of the chapters published in the *Mercure*, and dedicated to various Mercureists, including Rachilde and Vallette. Certainly Jarry had hopes that Vallette might publish the whole of it, but it was not to happen. The fallout from the business of the Old Lady was not the only reason, since Vallette later confessed to Léautaud that he found it "unreadable owing to its obscurity." It was presumably following Vallette's declining the manuscript as a whole that Jarry appended a brief coda to the Lormel: "This book will not be published in its entirety until the author has acquired experience sufficient to savor all its beauties in full." Schwob and Mallarmé wrote to Jarry to express their appreciation of the extracts in the *Mercure*, both having chapters dedicated to them. So too did Valéry who, in a letter to Louÿs in February 1899, informed him that he "was writing the life of Doctor Faustroll." This reference is presumed to equate the doctor with Monsieur Teste—the protagonist of Valéry's own ongoing "sort-of" novel—whose life is devoted to the exploration of his own mind.[102]

A letter from Thadée Natanson in January 1899 reveals that Jarry had sent him the Fasquelle manuscript. It had an additional dedication to Natanson that is missing from the Lormel version. Natanson thanked him, but asked him what he wanted: publication of extracts in the *Revue Blanche* or of the whole book by the publishing house? Neither occurred, but Natanson became a good friend to Jarry, especially in his final years. *Faustroll* finally appeared in 1911, four years after Jarry's death, in an edition edited by Saltas and Gaston Danville. It is significant that, of only three reviews of this first edition, two were by Apollinaire, the harbinger of modernism in France. Otherwise *Faustroll* was passed over in silence by Jarry's contemporaries; they had already consigned him to the past—an eccentric whose work was in the process of being forgotten.[103]

One of the final touches to the Fasquelle manuscript was a footnote to the chapter devoted to Mallarmé: "Since the writing of this book, the river around the island has become a funeral wreath."[104]

...

A blow had befallen the literary world, and especially the circles of which Jarry was a part. It was a loss he felt personally and deeply: the sudden death of Stéphane Mallarmé on September 9, 1898 (the day after Jarry's twenty-fifth birthday), at the age of fifty-six. The widespread grief of his many friends was a testament to Mallarmé's gracious personality. His literary influence was equally indisputable, and the loss of Symbolism's figurehead was another setback to the movement which was keenly felt at the time, and in retrospect appeared to mark its terminal decline.

The funeral took place only two days later at the small church in Samoreau, just across the river from Valvins. Despite the short notice, a distinguished group of some fifty mourners assembled on a bright afternoon in the autumnal countryside. Most of the Revue Blanche and the Mercure were there, including Rodin, Renoir, Lautrec, Vuillard, the Natansons, Maeterlinck, Bonnard, Terrasse. Jarry cycled the twenty miles from Corbeil; his shoes were in tatters, so he had helped himself to a pair of Rachilde's for the ceremony. Unfortunately they were bright yellow, and particularly prominent since his trousers were, as ever, tucked into his socks at the knees. The trousers too were filthy, and Mirbeau gently chided him for them. "We have much dirtier ones," replied Jarry.[105]

Jarry's *Ubu's Almanac*, published three months afterward, carried a couple of pages completely at odds with the buffoonery of the rest of its contents. The chapter devoted to Mallarmé from *Faustroll* was followed by this evocation of the funeral, the whole bordered in black:

> In autumn Faustroll disembarked again, leaving the nave of the forest, and walked barefoot alongside the tapering ferns—tappiced and tapestry—their scythes hanging, pustules of Atropos, on the road to the arches at Valvins.
>
> The funeral swelled on the road to Samoreau, and ebbed away at the sea wall of many cemeteries.
>
> The church was small, sober and absolute; the two choristers, more saddening for singing out of tune; the poor stained-glass windows were reconciled in the shining light, just as a crowd elects a plurality of personal beliefs when they all kneel together before a glory that is catholic— for the word does sometimes mean universal.
>
> Two very noble women were the caryatids of all this grief.
>
> As Faustroll hurried back through the forest of blighted palm trees, following the current of the road that was white like the borders of church hangings, he feared he would hear the dreadful voice informing Thamous three times of the death of one also written about— for those who understand what they read—by Herodotus, and Cicero in his third book of *On the Nature of the Gods*.
>
> The river has laid its funeral wreath, a circular mirror of glory, for all eternity, around the tomb and as far as the penultimate horizons.[106]

The two caryatids here represent the poet's wife and daughter, and in Rabelais (Bk. IV, ch. XXVII) Thamous, the pilot of a ship rounding the Isle of Paxos, is commanded by a "dreadful voice" to announce to the world that the great god Pan was dead. In the church, Valéry attempted an address, but was too overcome to complete it. Afterward, the cortege followed the coffin down to the cemetery beside the river. There Mallarmé was buried beside his son Anatole, who had died aged nine, nearly two decades earlier. Jarry walked beside the poet Dujardin, observed by Thadée Natanson:[107]

> Of all those in distress, none appeared to feel the blow more than Jarry. He seemed overwhelmed. The only clothes he could find, or had, were sports or summer wear, but this was not going to prevent him from attending. I had to turn away so as not to laugh. In 1898, that would have been shocking at a funeral. No one else realized at the time that he was wearing straw-yellow cycling pumps because Madame Rachilde had lent him them at the last moment. Jarry's expression was lifeless, his face somewhat crumpled and his black eyes dry. No face stained with tears could have expressed more affliction.[108]

Another funeral must have taken place around the same time: that of Maggie Boehmer-Clark. It is hard to date precisely but Rachilde, in her account of it, in a novel rather than her memoir, tells us that Jarry cycled twenty-five miles to the cemetery from their summer home the following year at La Frette; however, the cemetery at Billancourt is only ten miles from La Frette, although twenty-five from Corbeil, so on that basis it is more likely the funeral occurred late in 1898.[109]

It had been a tragic end. Maggie Clark, her fortune depleted, had emulated the recent suicide of her lover Paul Grollier by taking chloroform. Despite her social standing, her funeral was attended only by Armory and Grollier's friends, although a single representative of the wealthy set who had enjoyed her entertaining followed at a distance in his coupé. Jarry's outfit was all the more noticeable because of the sparse turnout. "Lamentably dressed," Armory recalled. Jarry followed the coffin pushing his bicycle, and when pressed by Rachilde as to why he had come, since he rarely attended funerals, he reminded her: "But Ma-da-me, we drank some excellent alcohols at the residence of this person of a different sex." And besides, while making the sign of the cross, "It is always agreeable to bury a woman." Rachilde excused his comment as a means of protecting an overly nervous and sensitive disposition, a sort of "armor." Rather too generous of her on this occasion.[110]

…

Vallette's letters to Herold allow us partially to track the residents of the Phalanstery during the late summer of 1898. Jarry stayed there more or less continuously, on his own for much of August until Vallette and Rachilde joined him. They spent the weekends there until the end of September. Quillard returned from his travels in October and joined Jarry and the Collières in Corbeil, after which Jarry spent the winter in the house alone. It was during this period that he resumed work on his adaptation of *Pantagruel*, a task which had already occupied him periodically since early in the previous year, when it had been intended for the Théâtre des Pantins.[111]

The works of Rabelais, usually translated in English as *Gargantua and Pantagruel*, must be the most often cited in all of Jarry's writing, and had been his favorite reading since his schooldays. His fondness for verse drama can be dated back to the same period. What could be more natural than to adapt *Pantagruel* in this manner, for his favorite medium, the puppet theater? Such a simple notion, but it was to have far-reaching consequences.

Most of Jarry's manuscripts for *Pantagruel* were first organized and commented upon by Jean-Hugues Sainmont in the 1950s. Sainmont's biographical and critical articles for the Collège de 'Pataphysique have rarely been surpassed, but even he baulked at the task of disentangling *Pantagruel*. The manuscripts consisted of some two thousand sheets of paper, an inextricable jumble of rough drafts, legible (in ink) and illegible (in pencil), copies, second copies, nth copies of several completely different versions, unpaginated and in no discernible order. Subsequently, Arnaud discovered at least three further complete manuscripts. Yet the published version of *Pantagruel*, when it was finally ushered into print in 1911 with the assistance of a collaborator, Eugène Demolder, numbered a mere 91 pages: and the manuscript of this version was not among either cache of papers.[112]

So why did Jarry devote so much time and effort to this enterprise? His motives were various, and changed over the too-many years devoured by this task. What began as an attempt to translate his beloved Rabelais into the dramatic medium he most admired, was gradually transformed into a project whose principal aim became financial. The battle to preserve his original vision was progressively lost, and Jarry's interest was eventually worn down to almost nothing.

The envisaged puppet production of late 1898 required a deal of hard work in itself, and Terrasse and Jarry met many times during the months of August and September of that year, in Paris, Noisy-le-Grand, or Corbeil. Even at the start, Terrasse's impatience with some of his librettist's working practices is apparent in his letters, but by the end of October the first version was effectively finished. Jarry was summoned to stay at the rue Ballu to make copies of the manuscript and to go through the role of Panurge with the actor cast to play him—but this production never took place. According to Arnaud, Bonnard proposed to Natanson that he publish it, but despite Fénéon's support, he remained unpersuaded.[113]

When it became apparent that there was to be no new season at the rue Ballu, the two collaborators decided to convert *Pantagruel* from a puppet play into a stage play, and later into a full-scale comic opera. This was difficult enough simply in terms of staging. Puppets have abilities that actors, let alone singing actors, do not. But changing it from an entertainment destined for the Théâtre des Pantins, whose small audience was drawn primarily from avant-garde artistic circles, to one destined for a larger and more diverse public meant making the work accessible, which was not something for which Jarry was then renowned. Rabelais's book is large and unwieldy; it might not have been too difficult to adapt it for an audience already familiar with its eccentricities, but popularizing it, abridging and simplifying it, while somehow retaining its marvelous and extravagant prolixity … this was to prove nigh impossible.

Pantagruel and *Par la taille* were the first of many libretti Jarry was to undertake, often at Terrasse's suggestion and frequently with collaborators, over the next eight years or so. Some critics treat these as serious works, and there is little doubt that Jarry did not entirely dismiss them as potboilers intended to raise some much-needed phynance. Nevertheless, he christened them his "Théâtre mirlitonesque" (a *mirliton* is a kazoo, an instrument that turns meaningful speech into a buzz, and *vers de mirliton* is "doggerel"), which indicates an unusual modesty of ambition on his part. Further consideration of these plays is peripheral to a biography; only *Pantagruel* remains relevant, not so much for its content, but for the labor its composition entailed.

In contrast, *Père Ubu's Illustrated Almanac* appeared quite effortlessly at the end of 1898. Beneath the optimistic heading "Prophecies: To Be Presented at the 1900 Exposition" was the program of the first version of *Pantagruel*. The audience was in for a long night: prologue, five acts, six tableaux, seventeen scenes, a ballet.[114]

…

Meanwhile, in November, since Jarry was on his own in the Phalanstery, he wrote a number of letters to Vallette and Rachilde in Paris. They concern fishing, provisions (of alcohol in the main), and the payment of bills, which Jarry seemed to presume was Vallette's responsibility. This alone must have been mildly irritating, but Jarry's sole occupancy of the Phalanstery was also creating some tension. A letter from Rachilde on the 12th lets Jarry know she is coming to the Phalanstery the following weekend, and reveals her surprise that she feels obliged to inform him that she is visiting her own residence.[115]

There were other irritations. At the beginning of November Béglet informed his tenants that part of the back garden had been sold off to make a new road to the nearby mill. It meant the end of the boathouse as well as the demolition of the house next door. And then at the end of the month, according to Jarry at least, there was a burglary, although nothing was stolen, since he thought the culprits might have been disturbed by his return. The lock was damaged, and then broken by the locksmith called to repair it. Vallette suspected Jarry of forcing the lock, and that the burglary was fictional. Rachilde informed him that her husband was furious, having trusted him completely, and he'd better turn up at the next Tuesday and explain himself (he did). Either way, Jarry had broken some of the rules that the Phalansterians had agreed upon, as he admitted in one of several letters of self-justification and remorse sent to Vallette. He also wrote a rather more apologetic letter to Rachilde, in the first person for once: the Ubuesque "we" was discarded at this moment when he might lose his closest friends. Its postscript contained a final admission of guilt.[116]

These two letters were written on Sunday 20 and Monday 21 November 1898; the second coincided with the funeral of Jean de Tinan, which Jarry missed, probably because this disagreement with Vallette was still unresolved. After the Tuesday they were reconciled, but this episode, along with Vallette's refusal of *Faustroll*, contributed to a certain cooling of the friendship between himself and Jarry. On the surface, though, relations between these three continued as before, and Jarry and Vallette would continue to fish together.[117]

On December 5, Jarry finished his libretto, *Par la taille*, and the following day wrote to Quillard to "inform you that you are granted, as much out of pure generosity, as in consideration of our debts, an in-no-way-limited credit upon the WINE, and that the password to the cellar, in the event of your having the leisure to explore it, is none other than QQQQ." Not only Quillard's initial, but the letter Q in French sounds like *cul,* which means "arse" in English.[118]

The same month, Jarry returned to Paris to supervise Renaudie's printing of the *Almanac*. This was perhaps an attempt on his part to capitalize financially on the notoriety of Père Ubu, but he ended up publishing it himself, though with financial assistance from Charles Bonnard. His brother, Pierre, had approached Natanson in the hope that the Revue Blanche would take it on, but had received the same verdict as for *Pantagruel*. This first *Almanac* was a simple stapled booklet printed on cheap paper, measuring only 4 by 4¾ inches—a long way from the luxurious editions Renaudie had first produced for Jarry. The texts were Jarry's but it was illustrated by Pierre Bonnard, who henceforth became Ubu's official portraitist. They had put it together mostly at the rue Ballu when Jarry had been visiting Terrasse in connection with *Pantagruel*. Bonnard became particularly fond of Ubu; he had a succession of basset hounds throughout his life, and each was named after him.[119]

10.31
Almanach du Père Ubu illustré, 1899.

In the *Almanac* Jarry adapted a traditional literary form, one related to the popular culture of the Épinal print and the devotional texts whose woodcuts had been celebrated in *L'Ymagier*. The almanacs of the period were small, cheaply printed and cheaply sold. They usually contained a calendar listing saints' days, holidays, sunrise and sunset, high tides, phases of the moon, and so forth. The main text consisted of moral and practical advice ("useful tips"), entertainments, songs and ballads.[120]

Père Ubu's Almanac covered the first three months of 1899. Jarry evidently hoped it would become a quarterly publication, and the cover suggested one might take out an annual subscription, but yet again commercial success proved fugitive and there was only one issue. Its anonymity may not have helped. Neither Jarry nor Bonnard was credited, but in this it conformed with the tradition of the popular almanacs, as did its contents, after a fashion. First came a calendar, then "Useful Knowledge" (How to dye your hair green, How to refine gold using salamanders), and monthly agricultural advice. This was followed by a play featuring Père Ubu, in which one may perhaps detect Quillard's influence, since it is an adaptation of the scene from *Ubu Roi* in which Bordure's prison has been transposed to Devil's Island. The main butt of this satire are the anti-Dreyfusards, who include two particular Generals, Mercier and Zurlinden, who had happened to preside over Jarry's own military career: a belated revenge. Another short play features Ubu's opinions on art and literature, and then promulgates a long list of definitions of various of Jarry's contemporaries based on his Homeric formula of "*celui qui.*" The obituary for Mallarmé precedes the summary of *Pantagruel*. Advertisements follow, placed by Charles Bonnard (a product for clarifying wine), Vollard (albums of lithographs by Bonnard, Denis, and Vuillard), the Revue Blanche and the Mercure. This last reveals that the 197 copies of Jarry's first book, *Minutes*, had finally been sold, but that *Caesar-Antichrist* was still available for three francs.

It was a curious assembly all in all, and aimed at what audience? In place of the customary caricatures or decorations it had modern pen sketches from Bonnard, and its content demanded familiarity with a wide range of contemporary artists and poets. It was an in-joke, poorly distributed and with a limited shelf life; its print run is unknown, but three years later Jarry still had nearly 800 copies left. This first *Almanac* cost only 50 centimes, although nowadays it is one of his rarest publications and a copy would fetch four figures in euros, dollars, or sterling.[121]

There was, however, the odd subscriber, according to Ambroise Vollard: "Alfred Jarry! There was never a nobler figure in the world of letters. [...] And so scrupulous! I remember meeting him one day on his way to see a subscriber to a little review that he edited, so as to restore the sum of one franc fifty that he had overpaid. To do this he had come all the way from Corbeil on his bicycle."[122]

...

The Phalanstery was dissolved early in 1899, when Monsieur Béglet declined to extend his troublesome tenants' lease. Since Jarry's novel *Absolute Love* was written there, it does not seem fanciful to suppose that its unusual character may have been influenced by the circumstances in which he was then living. The Phalanstery in the oncoming winter, devoid of its other inhabitants, must have assumed a progressively more somber aspect. With the summer residents departed and their houses shuttered, Corbeil reverted to industry, inhabited mainly by bargees and mill workers, and the sluggish river, gray and rain-swept, was emptied of pleasure boats and anglers.

Absolute Love, once envisaged as the final chapter of *Visits*, is an intense and labyrinthine book despite its brevity (the current French edition totals 50 pages). There is nothing quite like it in Jarry's work; it is an exception in an *œuvre* made up of exceptions. It appears to have held a deeply personal meaning for its author, to have been written primarily for his own benefit; and mostly during the three months he spent alone in the house at Corbeil between November 1898 and February 1899. A "confession made to Silence," to cite chapter 2, *Absolute Love* appears as the concluding statement in the series of semiautobiographical explorations of consciousness and "the intersection of mind and matter" that began with *Days and Nights*. As a conclusion it presents a circular movement, mirrored in the structure of its own plot, since the autobiographical elements of *Absolute Love* constitute a return to Jarry's childhood in Laval and Brittany. Yet it has to be admitted that this book presents a highly inconvenient culmination of this important aspect of Jarry's writing; it is such a personal work, and has so little regard for the reader, that it is almost impossible to comprehend except in momentary glimpses. Even the essential events of its narrative remain obscure, to the extent that the various summaries of it to be found in critical works on Jarry disagree about its most essential elements.

In 1894 the *Mercure* began serializing Georges Polti's theoretical text outlining *The Thirty-Six Dramatic Situations*, a listing of all the possible theatrical plotlines that was intended to be definitive. The epigraph to chapter 3 of *Absolute Love* points out an omission by Polti: "Realizing that one's mother is a virgin." This is one of the inconveniences of being God, and Jarry's novel is a further manifestation of his God complex as previously revealed in *Faustroll*. The hero, unmistakably a transposition of the author, is called Emmanuel Dieu, and scenes from his childhood in Brittany are superimposed upon those of the Holy Family. Thus his mother and father are here named Varia and Joseb, the Breton forms of Mary and Joseph, although the father is given the attributes of Jarry's grandfather, the notary at Saint-Brieuc.

The principal "events" in the plot are the hero's incestuous affair with his mother, only partially extenuated by the fact that he is adopted, and so she is not his biological parent (and is only ten years his senior), and her attempted murder of her husband under the suggestion of Emmanuel Dieu after he has put her in a hypnotic trance. The circular plot begins with Emmanuel Dieu in prison, or imagining he is in prison, condemned to death for this murder, or possibly for the murder either of his mother, or of her somnambulist alter ego. Even such an extremely reductive summary reveals a complex variant of the Oedipal situation. Jarry has already committed a symbolic parricide by replacing his father with his grandfather in the novel, and is therefore also urging his mother to murder her own father by proxy. The sexual scenes are narrated with passion and tenderness, without irony and also with an apparent lack of guilt. Freud's Oedipal theories were at their earliest stage of formation at this time, and as yet unpublished, but Jarry's accounts of extreme mental states in *Absolute Love* are based upon his extensive readings of the same French psychologists, such as Pierre Janet and Charcot, who significantly influenced Freud. Ironically, the text has resisted Freudian interpretation precisely because it is so overt and exhibits little in the way of inhibition or sublimation. And God, by definition, cannot really suffer from an Oedipus complex.[123]

...

Absolute Love marks Jarry's deepest and final exploration of his childhood; it was completed, according to the manuscript, on February 20, 1899. Soon afterward, Jarry was evicted from the Phalanstery, since it must have been let on an annual lease that ran until the end of February or March. He gave the manuscript to Vallette with few expectations. He had found *Faustroll* too obscure for publication, so there was little chance that this would be any more to his taste. The day after he sent Vallette a defiant letter warning him he would not change anything in the book, and hoped for publication within three months.[124]

Jarry was not mistaken: the Mercure turned it down. He therefore decided to print it himself, which again indicates the particular significance it held for him, since he had not resorted to this for *Faustroll*. *Absolute Love* appeared in a facsimile edition, so as to save the cost of typesetting, and resembled a school exercise book in format, bound in a blank white paper cover. Such restraint, after the careful design of so many of his previous publications, is almost certainly due to his lack of resources. It was published in May 1899, as he had wished, having been announced in the March issue of the *Mercure*. Vallette had agreed to stock and sell the book, but not to it bearing the imprint of the Mercure. It may be no coincidence that soon afterward Charlotte Jarry borrowed 3,000 francs against her remaining property in the rue de Bootz in Laval, which was nearly half its value. She may have helped her brother with the printing costs.[125]

The edition purported to consist of fifty numbered copies, but there were at least twenty-five or so copies for friends and reviewers, at most a print run of a hundred. Jarry's press list is a little more confused than those for previous books, no doubt because he could ill afford to give away copies when there were so few. His hesitation is signaled by erasures, although some of these probably indicate that the person has received his copy:[126]

1. Vallette, crossed out and replaced with Cazals. 2. Rachilde and Vallette. 3. Herold. 4. Quillard. 5. A. Natanson, crossed out and replaced with Fénéon. 6. T. Natanson. 7. Dujardin. 8. Dumur. 9. Elskamp. 10. Schwob, crossed out and replaced by Émery (Rachilde's real name). 11. Moreno and Schwob. 12. Danville. 13. Régnier. 14. Mallarmé (despite his death?) 15. Kahn, crossed out and replaced with Terrasse. 16. E. Kahn and G. 17. Bauer, crossed out. 18. Mirbeau, crossed out. 19. Straus, crossed out. 20. Fazy, crossed out.

He gave around twelve of the extra, unnumbered copies to various friends, including Valéry and Wilde (it is not known if they met again on this occasion). The list also records approximately fourteen sales. A little over six years later, in October 1905, he decided to dispose of the remaining copies to a bookseller in order to raise some cash. There were, he wrote, thirty-two or thirty-three copies remaining, which means the Mercure can have sold no more than thirty copies in the meantime.[127]

Jarry was never happy with the deal he had done with Vallette. It was obvious to him that he could no longer work with the Mercure, and must seek a new publisher. The inscription in Quillard's copy signaled his discontent:

> Sold in the most abject manner
> in order to get something to drink
> *to Pierre Quillard* [128]

The extremely limited distribution of this book meant that it went unnoticed in literary circles. There was a single review, and this was by Rachilde in the *Mercure*, an aside while reviewing Jarry's next book, *Messalina*. Having described it as "completely closed to humble mortals," she concluded:

> Reading these pages plunges one into some sort of nightmare, since beneath the bitterness of its sentences, and its elegantly correct expression of wickedness, one is aware of the boiling current beneath, a hot blood of voluptuousness. [129]

. . .

Earlier, in February 1899, the *Mercure* had published its last text of any substance by Jarry, under the pseudonym of Dr. Faustroll. It was Jarry's response to the first of Henry Davray's numerous translations of the works of H. G. Wells: *The Time Machine*, serialized in the *Mercure* over the previous two months. Almost immediately on reading Wells's text Jarry had the idea of writing a paper which would explore the physics of such a machine, and show that it was theoretically possible. Or at least, he had the idea of writing a text that appeared to do this, since there is no reason to believe that Jarry saw his "Commentary and Instructions for the Practical Construction of the Time Machine" as anything but a work of fiction, albeit one disguised as a scientific paper. A letter from Vallette of January 9 agreed to Jarry's proposal, but with certain conditions: "Père Ubu must agree to express himself with clarity." According to Vallette, Jarry was perfectly capable of explaining such matters in person, but his written expositions tended toward opacity. [130]

Jarry's text was composed in haste, and a large part of it was added at the proof stage. After a brief disquisition on the nature of time, in which Jarry refers to the difference between physical time and duration, he describes the actual construction of the machine in precise detail. Its appearance is based upon that in Wells's novel. The final section, "Time as Seen from the Machine," concludes with a new definition of duration, which Jarry then paraphrases as "The Becoming of a Memory." This connects what is an apparently theoretical text with the notions of nostalgia and the erotic in *Days and Nights*. As ever, his writings link together when one least expects it. [131]

Paul Edwards has demonstrated how most of the physics employed by Jarry/Faustroll in the "Commentary" is taken from the French translation of Lord Kelvin's *Popular Lectures and Addresses: The Constitution of Matter*, published in 1893, with Jarry even quoting an English footnote to give his text extra verisimilitude. Lautréamont had employed technical terms too, but for strictly literary effect, as fixed points of precision that served to highlight the general frenzy of the narrative. In his "Commentary" Jarry did something quite different: he wrote a piece of fiction employing *only* the nonliterary means of the scientific paper. The use of specialist and technical languages would became something of a literary commonplace some decades later, but Jarry was perhaps the first to employ them in this way.[132]

In his memoirs, the Baron Mollet claimed that Jarry was in regular contact with contemporary mathematicians. No trace of this correspondence has ever been found, but it could explain a small mystery connected to his article on the Time Machine. The archives of the Society of Psychical Research in Cambridge contain this letter:[133]

> 7 Kensington Park Gardens
> London W
> July 7th, 1899
>
> My dear Lodge,
>
> I send herewith a number of the *Mercure de France* containing an article "On the construction of a Time-exploring Machine" by Dr. Faustroll. Langley drew my attention to it and is rather inclined to think it is a real attempted suggestion of something hypothetically possible.
>
> I see two possible fallacies. One is that a system of gyroscopes will not resist motion in a direct line, but only angular motion, and the other is that even could we fix a machine rigidly in space it does not follow that it is also fixed in time.
>
> But I may not have followed the writer's meaning very well. I think you will be interested in reading it, and I should much like to hear how it strikes you. Please return the book, and with kind regards to Mrs Lodge and yourself, in which my wife joins,
>
> Believe me,
> Very sincerely yours,
> William Crookes

The three scientists involved, Samuel Pierpont Langley, Sir William Crookes, and Sir Oliver Lodge, were indeed eminent in their respective fields, and two of them at least were partially convinced that Jarry's "Commentary" was a scientific paper rather than a work of fiction (Lodge's response is unknown). Langley, then the secretary of the Smithsonian Institution, was a celebrated astronomer and aviation pioneer: his "Aerodrome" was the first heavier-than-air machine to make a sustained flight, which is why the Langley Air Force Base is named after him. Crookes was a fellow, then the President, of the Royal Society and President of the Society of Psychical Research from 1896 to 1899 (his address to the society of 1897 was published in French the same year and formed the basis for chapter IX of *Faustroll*). Lodge was likewise an FRS; he was both a theoretical physicist and a practical one specializing in wireless telegraphy. He is chiefly remembered nowadays for his work in psychical research, and was twice President of the Society.

How did Langley come across this text, buried in a French literary magazine? It would be surprising if Jarry had not asked his friend Davray to show it to Wells, since Wells was one of the few authors he actually admired, but there is no surviving evidence that he actually did so. Wells, too, certainly knew Langley, and had corresponded with him since at least 1896. Thus it seems plausible that either Wells or Davray sent Langley the text of Jarry's essay. It would be interesting to discover which person in this possible chain of transmission, Jarry-Davray-Wells-Langley, decided not to mention that the text in question was a work of fiction.[134]

…

Monsieur Béglet must have made it plain that the Phalansterians' tenancy would not be renewed as early as January 1899, since it was then that Rachilde wrote to Terrasse to inquire whether there were any suitable houses for rent by the river near Noisy-le-Grand. They had been unable to find any near Corbeil. It seems to have been Jarry who discovered their new summer residence, after a number of exploratory trips by bicycle. The new Phalanstery was on the other side of Paris in La Frette, a small town in a valley leading down to the Seine. The owner wrote to Jarry on May 18 to confirm that arrangements were complete, and he could collect the keys the following Sunday.[135]

The Phalansterians reinstalled themselves, with the possible exception of Quillard. The house was new, and its garden rudimentary, but it was built into a lilac-covered hill; consequently it could be entered through the attic at the back, or the basement at the front, something "which delighted Père Ubu." The Seine flowed past the end of the garden, summer would soon be upon them, and Rachilde looked forward to bathing in the river. Then she noticed something odd about the neighboring houses. All the windows facing the water were tightly shut. The skiffs were launched, lines cast over, not a single bite. When Jarry plunged his hand in the river, it disappeared from view, the water was so murky. "The Styx!" he muttered.[136]

All was explained with the onset of the summer heat in July, when a foul odor blanketed the town. On the opposite bank of the river, but concealed by the bend of the oxbow, was the huge sewage works of Achères. Henceforth fishing was undertaken by rowing up the Oise to Eragny, otherwise cycling became their chief occupation. Anything to escape the deceptively idyllic landscape of La Frette. Most of Rachilde's account of this summer is devoted to a single cycling anecdote which she thought illustrative of Jarry's character.

At that time, she recalls, it was considered the height of style for gentlewomen to ride behind a bicycle pedaled by someone "gifted with a good pair of thighs" while reclining in a small two-wheeled wickerwork cart attached to the cycle by a leather strap.

On such a trip one summer's day on the heights above the town, they found they needed to descend the steep valley spanned by the viaducts visible in the postcard (figure 10.33). From the summit, Jarry and Rachilde looked down at the road which twisted steeply into the abyss.

Vallette had fallen behind. "Careful, Père Ubu," he called out, "better go down on foot!"

Seconde année   (1899)

Phalanstère de La Frette - Montigny.

Ces photographies
sont dues à la
gracieuseté scientifique
de Marie Thérèse
et de Collière

Nouveau phalanstère.
(L'astre blanc indique les fenêtres de Rachilde)

Jardin du phalanstère.
(Les arbres sont à l'état d'espoir ...)

10.32
The second Phalanstery. The house at La Frette,
from the album of Gabrielle Vallette.

1 — **La Frette** - Vue des Ponts

LA FRETTE (S.-et-O) — Le Viaduc.

"In this heat?" came Jarry's reply. "Besides, bear in mind that we are already thirsty."

Jarry plunged down the hill, but soon realized the hairpin bends were difficult to negotiate at speed because Rachilde's trailer tended to overtake his bicycle. Their speed mounted, the contortions of the road became more severe, and when they came to a sharper bend near the base of the viaduct, Rachilde cried out: "Not so fast, Père Ubu!" "Not so fast yourself, Ma-da-me," came Jarry's growl, "it's you who are driving us now, our roles are reversed!" The cart was forcing the cycle toward one of the enormous pillars supporting the viaduct. A collision was imminent. Then, writes Rachilde, her blood froze in her veins. Jarry took out a knife and attempted to cut the strap attaching the cart to the bicycle. She clamped shut her eyes in terror and awaited catastrophe; then, hearing a hollow laugh, she saw Jarry cast the knife aside and throw himself from the bicycle, still grasping the handlebars. Dragged down the road on his rapidly shredded knees, he eventually brought the whole contraption to a halt a few yards before the pillar. "Well, Ma-da-me," he said, "we think we were a little afraid for a moment." Jarry recovered his knife before making a final observation: "Never before have we wanted so much to take leave of a woman!" Rachilde interpreted this as a gallantry intended to forestall her thanks. All of which, she concluded, was entirely typical of him: half criminal, half noble. When Vallette turned up, expecting to find them in bits, Jarry's thoughts were already elsewhere:

"Oof, Sire, our throat is parched, let's go for a drink."

Rachilde continued to ride in her wickerwork cart, but in future it would be fixed to the bicycle with a rigid metal bar, and the cyclist was more often her famously reliable husband.

...

10.33
The second Phalanstery. La Frette with its viaducts visible in the distance.

10.34
Scene of the accident. The road down into the valley, where it passes beneath the railway viaduct.

In the summer of 1899, following the publication of *Absolute Love*, Jarry was seeking a new direction for his future writing. He looked over his unpublished manuscripts. This was probably the moment when he assembled and recopied the texts he named *Onotogeny*, his collection of juvenilia and later works "that it is more honorable not to publish." He considered writing a book of poetry to be called *Navigations in the Mirror*, and although a few fragments of these neo-Symbolist verses survive, they must have seemed too *passé* to continue with. Finally he decided on a sequel to *Ubu Roi*, which was not exactly striking out into unknown territory, especially as parts at least of this new play derive from Rennais sources. Its original title announced in the *Mercure* was *Ubu esclave* (*Ubu Slave*), later altered to *Ubu enchaîné*. Just as the name of *Ubu Roi* was modeled on the French title of Sophocles' *Oedipus Rex*, so that of *Ubu enchaîné* was based upon Aeschylus' *Prometheus Bound*.[137]

Ubu enchaîné was written at La Frette, in September according to the manuscript, at the exact moment when Félix-Frédéric Hébert was working himself into a patriotic frenzy over the retrial of Dreyfus in Rennes. No reference to either can be found in the play, but perhaps the pungent breeze from Achères may be detected in its first two lines:[138]

> Mère Ubu: What! Nothing to say, Père Ubu? Have you forgotten the word?

> Père Ubu: Ssshhhi…an't say it, Mère Ubu! It got me into too much trouble before.[139]

In his defense of *Ubu Roi*, "Theatre Questions," Jarry had dismissed the simple changes that would have made it a hit with the public. Altering "the word" had been one of them. *Ubu enchaîné* was perhaps his attempt to write such a play, and it is a poor performance compared to the Ubus *Roi* or *cocu*. In a rather too rare moment of verbal felicity, Père Ubu remarks: "I'm afraid, my dear friend, that your singular idea of liberty will never make a good snail fork, which is a bifurcated instrument." This could be applied to the play itself; it is too much of a one-joke farce in which Ubu declares his intention of becoming a slave and of course finds it harder than he imagines, and in which an army composed of "free men," obliged to disobey orders, are simply ordered to do the opposite by their officers.

Ubu enchaîné was published by the Revue Blanche the following year, 1900. The original plan had been to publish the trilogy of Ubus: *Roi*, *cocu*, and *enchaîné*. Jarry had been rewriting *cocu*, and a page of calculations survives in which he computed the number of pages such a volume would require: 350. Too many, presumably, so *enchaîné* was published along with *Ubu Roi*, whose "counterpart" Jarry thought it to be. This sixth printing of *Ubu Roi* must have meant the Mercure edition had sold out, and it is doubtful Vallette can have been delighted to lose the only book by his friend that actually made money.[140]

The second Phalanstery had been a disappointment compared to the first, as Rachilde admitted, and the "dismemberment of their frivolous association" can be dated to November 20, when they handed back the keys. Winter in Paris.[141]

11

THE WRITING MACHINE

Jarry's magnificent Clément Luxe, being a racetrack model, was stripped of nonessentials. No luxuries such as mud or chain guards, and no brakes either. The complicated mechanisms required to brake the rear wheel were yet to be perfected, and front brakes simply sent the rider over the handlebars. Instead it had a fixed wheel, and braking was accomplished either by standing on the pedals or by holding one's foot against one of the tires. Not particularly effective, as Jarry had discovered at La Frette. Variable gears likewise remained clumsy and inefficient, and were shunned by professionals. Thus Jarry's bicycle had only a single gear. Rather more than a simple vehicle, the writing machine was powered by human musculature and fueled by alcohols. Once launched into duration—Jarry informs us that "Space around us is fixed, and to explore it we travel in the vehicle of Duration"—it functioned very much like the stomach of an ostrich.[1]

Technical specifications: the gearing of a professional bicycle would be stipulated by the customer on ordering. The gearing of Jarry's may be calculated using two pieces of evidence. First, the photograph of him posed outside the Phalanstery (figure 10.24), in which Jarry is doing a "track stand," standing motionless on the pedals, as can be seen by the rigidity of the lower part of the chain; and second, Rachilde's assertion that his machine had a "development" of 9 meters. This was the distance traveled with each complete revolution of the pedals.[2]

Given that Jarry's height is known (5 foot 3 inches), we can estimate the diameter of the wheels on his bicycle: 28 inches. The chain wheel appears to have 36 teeth, which allows us to calculate the number of teeth on the back hub, since the formula $\frac{N_2}{N_1}\pi d$ equals the distance traveled for each revolution of the pedals, where N_1 = the teeth on the chain wheel, N_2 = the teeth on the hub, and d is the diameter of the driving wheel. Thus,

if $\frac{36}{x} \times 3.14 \times 28 = 354$ inches (the equivalent in inches of Rachilde's 9 meters),

then x (the number of teeth on the hub) = 9 (approximately),

which gives a gearing of 36/9.

The normal gearing for a touring cycle at the time would have been between 16/9 and 20/9. Such an extreme ratio as that of Jarry's bicycle appears unlikely—and Jarry may well have exaggerated his machine's development—but the diminutive size of the back hub on Jarry's bicycle is visible in the photograph. Although this gearing is comparable to the top gears of modern racing bikes, it would require a formidable effort to ride it in everyday circumstances, particularly when pulling off. It says much for Jarry's physique that he was able to ride it at all.[3]

Jarry, as we have seen, had been a keen and constant cyclist since his late childhood. At the Phalanstery, he would race the Paris train for the seven miles between Corbeil and Juvisy, where the track ran close enough to the road for this to be possible. Gabrielle Vallette recalled his announcing on his arrival at the Phalanstery, with great solemnity: "We have broken a record."

11.1
The chain wheel of Jarry's bicycle.

11.2
Carrie Nation.

Racing the train was subsequently transposed into his fiction. The centerpiece of *The Supermale* is a contest between a locomotive and a five-man bicycle over a distance of ten thousand miles. A member of the cycling team dies *en route*, but continues to pedal—in fact pedals all the harder, because the team is fuelled by "Perpetual Motion Food," a substance with an alcohol base. This novel of Jarry's is set in the future of 1920, and the Edison-like inventor of Perpetual Motion Food is named William Elson. His researches proceed in accordance with the then-prevailing opinion that "the only hygienic beverage is pure alcohol." Elson, in this golden age, is thus responsible for "the philanthropic invention of denaturing the water piped into our houses so as to render it undrinkable, while leaving it fit for washing and toiletry." The inventor's opinions regarding both alcohol and water were of course perfectly contingent with Jarry's own.[4]

Jarry's dislike for the one, and enthusiastic advocacy of the other, made him an inevitable opponent in his journalism of the temperance movement, then at its most active throughout Europe and the United States. A report of the activities of Carrie Nation—an alarming matron who stormed into saloons in Kansas and wrecked them with an ax—prompted this response from Jarry in the *Revue Blanche*: "We thought we had dealt once and for all with the question of alcoholism, and that all sensible persons now acknowledged that the use of, and thus *a fortiori*, the abuse of, fermented beverages is what distinguishes man from the beasts." He challenged another campaigner to "admit that anti-alcoholics are victims of that poison, water, a solvent so corrosive that out of all possible substances it is the one chosen for scouring our bodies and our clothes, and a single drop of which, added to a pure liquid such as absinthe, muddies it?" Jarry's genuine dislike of water may have originated in his childhood. Charlotte Jarry's *Notes* record her brother's first experience of alcohol. At the age of three, he was left alone with a four-year-old friend, collecting frogs in a bucket. Their mothers returned to find the two infants totally inebriated: they had gorged themselves on cake and emptied most of a bottle of wine. Large quantities of water were immediately administered as an antidote.[5]

In Corbeil and La Frette Jarry lived a vigorous open-air existence. He had fished with Vallette and Quillard, cycled with Herold, Demolder, Rachilde, and Vallette, and taken walks in the surrounding countryside. Such activities would normally promote ruddy good health in their participants. For Jarry, though, they were always immeasurably enhanced by a slug from a bottle. Thus his account of the three-day barbel hunt with Quillard records it as punctuated with swigs of Marc de Bourgogne, a fine French brandy aged in oak barrels. Jarry's enthusiasm for alcohol in general, and absinthe in particular, was undoubtedly vast. Excess was his discipline, as Rachilde had noted, and she famously described his regimen:[6]

> Jarry began his day by sinking two liters of white wine. Three absinthes marked the hours between ten o'clock and midday, and then at lunchtime he washed down his fish, or his steak, with red or white wine alternating with further absinthes. In the afternoon, a few cups of coffee laced with brandy or other spirits whose names I have forgotten. With his dinner, and of course afterward, further apéritifs, and he could still consume at least two bottles of some vintage or other, good or bad. Now, I never saw him really drunk, except on one occasion when I took aim at him with his own revolver, which sobered him up instantly.[7]

This predilection for alcohol appears, at first sight, to be at complete odds with his athletic prowess and physique, of which Jarry was fiercely proud. His prodigious consumption of alcohol was partly a matter of pure bravado, another instance of "record-breaking," but it was also systematic, almost scientific, and deemed by him highly purposeful. He seems indeed to have viewed alcohol as an almost magical substance. He informed his friends that it constituted a complete and ideal form of nutrition, and his alter ego in *The Supermale* described it as a superfood and called for "alcoholizing the alcoholics," in other words cure by excess. According to Chauveau, and thus probably Rachilde, Jarry elevated the use of alcohol to a principle. Its benefits could be demonstrated scientifically, and it was the source of all power. Judiciously employed, he claimed, it was capable of infinitely augmenting human capabilities. Extremes meet, and thus enough alcohol, an excess of alcohol, would surely give rise, eventually, to perfect sobriety, to a supreme lucidity. But how much was enough? Many of Jarry's pronouncements on this subject were, of course, witticisms, but Jarry could be entirely serious when making a joke. Rachilde remembered his arrival at Maggie Clark's funeral:[8]

> [He had] timed himself on the road, having received the summons to the funeral only an hour before. "Ma-da-me. We have done forty! We are not tired because yesterday we ate a large steak, and drank almost four liters of white wine, followed by our most pure absinthe!" In any situation, he whom we called Père Ubu [...] was the equal of himself, if not of his sinister puppet. He drank and ate, disdainful of emotion, as if he were a one-horsepower motor which must absorb so many liters of fuel per ten kilometers and imperturbably pounded the dusty or muddy roads, covered in dust or mud according to the season, equally indifferent to both.[9]

Mechanization, progress … the bicycle was a step toward the technological perfectibility of man, in accord with an unfolding modern sensibility, the fusion of humanity and mechanics. Sufficient fuel and physical effort were all that was required to set this perfect creature, this perfect machine, into operation. It might then generate a rapid and fleeting succession of images and sensations, a mental state approaching those described in *Days and Nights*. Alcohol, especially absinthe, could only intensify this experience, which was all a part of the writing process:

> If man has been inspired enough [...] to perceive that his muscles can move, by pressure rather than traction, a skeleton exterior to himself—a preferable locomotor indeed since it does not need centuries of evolution to convert itself according to the line of maximum functional force— being the mineral prolongation of his bone structure, and almost infinitely perfectible because based on geometric principles; he should use this machine with gears to whisk up forms and colors as fast as possible with a rapid suction as he whirls along roads and bicycle tracks; for by serving the mind pulverized and scrambled scraps of food one is spared working through memory's destructive oubliettes, and after this ingestion the mind can far more easily re-create its own new forms and colors. We do not know how to create out of nothingness, yet we can do so out of chaos.[10]

And this chaotic *materia prima* must then be refined:

> A truly original brain works exactly like the stomach of the ostrich: everything is good for it,
> it pulverizes rocks and twists bits of iron. This phenomenon should not be mistaken for the
> ability to assimilate, which is of another nature altogether. A real personality does not assimilate
> anything, it deforms; better, it transmutes in the ascending direction of the hierarchy of metals.
> When it is placed in conjunction with the unsurpassable—with the masterpiece—what occurs is
> not imitation, but transposition: the whole mechanism of the association of ideas is triggered
> in parallel with associations of ideas in the work which, to use a sporting expression that is here
> quite appropriate, then serve as a trainer or "coach."[11]

The cyclist, a modern centaur, conformed to a new notion of beauty. Jarry defined it as the "combination of inexorable mathematics and human action," a symbiotic representation that significantly predated similar pronouncements from Marinetti's Futurists, and a combination which was "probably the only means men have for pickling the absolute." When Rachilde asked him if he had hurt himself after their accident at La Frette, he replied: "Nothing damaged, apart from the left pedal," referring to his injured leg. This comic mechanization of his persona, already implicit in his mode of speaking, could also be a means of distancing himself from others; and it found a literal counterpart in his domestic arrangements. Over the next few years Jarry would, to a great extent, withdraw from the literary society of Paris. He soon would establish himself permanently on the Seine outside the capital, not far from Corbeil, and live there for extended periods, an existence not entirely unlike his Breton childhood.[12]

This alteration in his daily life would also coincide with a change of emphasis in the meaning Jarry accorded to Pataphysics. If his early formulation of it may be interpreted as a call for the intensification of reality, henceforth he would interpret it rather as an analytical method, an approach that would characterize his later journalism. Whereas the more dandified of the Symbolists delighted in elitism—nothing suited a *fin-de-siècle* poet better than imagining himself the last of a line of Usher-like aesthetes—Jarry "modernized" this attitude in anticipation of the coming century. Pataphysics allowed the adoption of an *hauteur* equivalent to aristocratic disdain, but associated instead with the scientists' objectivity. The powerful scientist-hero, the all-conquering Edison or Nemo, was a common enough conceit at the time, but Jarry's science was far from common. Unconcerned with the average—that grubby herd of facts—it would privilege only the exceptional, and thus put scientific objectivity at the service of a radical individualism, in other words of pure subjectivity. This formed a satisfying pataphysical conjunction; but it was one which again implied a certain distancing from the everyday, a distancing similar to his self-mechanization—which was likewise bound to be further exacerbated by taking on too much "fuel."

12

1900–1904

Jarry must have noticed that the returns for his past three years' productivity, both critical and financial, had been distinctly poor—none more so than the reception accorded to *Absolute Love*. Not a single one of his books in which commercial considerations had played a part had earned him any significant income. The same held for his wholly noncommercial works, and yet Jarry never considered earning a living by other means. His known income had indeed been small these previous years: an advance from *Visits*, royalties from the various editions of *Ubu Roi*, a brief wage from the Théâtre des Pantins, these are all that can be identified with any certainty.

12.1
The Barrage at Le Coudray, a general view from the road up to the village. This photograph dates from about 1910, and already there are more buildings than when Jarry lived here. Key: A. the lockkeeper's house; B. the inn; C. Jarry's shack (these first three concealed by trees); D. La Demi-Lune, Demolder's house (approximate site); E. Mère Fontaine's; F. the limekiln; G. the Tripod; H. the Villa Vallette.

There would now be a change of direction in Jarry's literary output, although this was not necessarily the result of practical considerations. His next two novels would lack the obvious autobiographical elements that had been so prominent up to now. Henceforth, Jarry would take another course, less personal and more "technical," as Rachilde noted in her review of *Visits*, by which we take her to mean, at least in part, more conventionally heterosexual. At La Frette he had begun work on his next novel, *Messalina*. This necessitated a certain amount of historical research in Parisian libraries, which occupied him during the winter of 1899 and for the first half of 1900. There are few other events that can be confidently assigned to these months, and even fewer letters to offer clues. Cafés were patronized, no doubt, and Tuesdays attended, but otherwise there is little that can be said about Jarry's everyday existence until the summer. So far as his writing was concerned, Jarry spent the first six months of 1900 on a number of projects, many of which did not come to much; in July, however, there would be a positive change in his fortunes.

The Mercure now appeared closed to him; the obvious alternative was the Revue Blanche, similarly both a literary review and a publishing house. *Ubu enchaîné* might be seen to have some commercial potential, and it is likely that he used it to approach either Natanson or Fénéon in the hope of finding a regular outlet for his writing. In January their review published extracts from his translation from Grabbe, originally completed for the Théâtre des Pantins, which he had probably turned up when looking through his old manuscripts the previous year. In January too, Terrasse was trying to tempt theater managements with *Pantagruel*, and Gémier was called in to use his influence: without success.[1]

In early February, Jarry and Terrasse had opened up the box containing the old puppets from the Théâtre des Pantins. Finding them in good condition, they decided on a final performance, Jarry's *Revue des Pantins*, which took place on March 10. The script has not survived, but the evening was a success; according to Terrasse's diary, they finally finished supper at 5.30 a.m. *Ubu enchaîné* appeared in book form also in March, published by the Revue Blanche and prefaced by a slightly revised *Ubu Roi*. The print run was small, only 1,000 copies.[2]

Pantagruel resurfaced. In the early months of 1900, Terrasse invited Willy and Gémier to help him remake the play so that it might be easier to stage. Jarry appears to have taken only a small part in the butchery, but must have given his permission since a letter of May 24 from Terrasse informed him of what they were up to. This version, jointly attributed to Jarry and Willy, whose principal contribution was to update the language, was then passed around various theater managements, but again elicited little interest. Willy once more suggested publication, once more with no result. In the meantime, Terrasse's personal career was booming, and he was soon much in demand as a composer of operettas. He plunged himself into this work, and *Pantagruel* was again set aside.[3]

Jarry's absence from the work sessions for *Pantagruel* is explained by the fact that he was writing the *Revue des Pantins*; and in March and April he collaborated with Berthe Danville on yet another operetta scored by Terrasse: *Leda*. Like *Pantagruel* it was fated not to be performed, despite being scheduled for mid-May, nor to appear in print (at least not until 1981).[4]

Trochon's bailiff put pen to paper on June 5, 1900. The sum of 553 francs and 75 centimes was still owing, and Jarry was "advised *for the last time* that Monsieur Trochon is absolutely determined to use extreme measures to obtain payment. Your bad faith in this matter is beyond all toleration." However, Trochon thought him still at the boulevard Saint-Germain, and Jarry never read this letter. It was sent and returned on five different occasions, each time stamped "addressee unknown."[5]

...

On June 22, Jarry, along with Rachilde and Stuart Merrill, paid a visit to Demolder in his great house near the Seine at Le Plessis-Chenet, a couple of miles upstream from Corbeil. Both Merrill and Franc-Nohain had recently rented properties in Corbeil, but here, around the bend in the river, its banks were as yet undeveloped, although the new railway line would soon lead to houses being built on this side of the Seine. For now, though, a single residence was to be found round the curve from Corbeil, and in the early summer of 1900 Vallette and Rachilde rented this house, situated in a locale known as Les Bas-Vignons, before eventually buying it in 1904. Jarry was not only visiting Demolder and Rachilde, he too was in search of a riverside bolt-hole, since the Vallettes had made it clear that they were not intent on founding a new Phalanstery.[6]

Visible upstream from the house was the weir, or "Barrage," at Le Coudray. This was one of many built in the 1880s to rationalize the commercial river and canal systems of France. They were navigated by means of large locks of uniform dimensions. Between the Barrage and the "Villa Vallette," a distance of half a mile or so, only a couple of buildings were to be found on the west bank of the river: an abandoned limekiln and a small ramshackle bar and café. At the Barrage too there was only a scattering of buildings: the lockkeeper's house, a shop for the bargees, and a small inn where they ate and drank as the boats passed through the lock, or queued up to do so, and beside it a small one-story shack made of wood and plaster and divided in two. The left-hand side of it had been a stable, according to the sign above its large doors; the right-hand side was probably a general storeroom, although it had recently been used for breeding rabbits. It belonged to the inn, and Jarry persuaded its owners to rent him this half of the building, a single room, which did at least benefit from a window.

This was not some quiet spot beside the river conducive to creative reverie. Immediately outside the stable was the lock, with its constant procession of large barges. Individual barges might be pulled through by mules or horses from the towpath, and there are photographs of these animals in Rachilde's album. Mostly, however, great trains of barges were towed up and down the river by large steam-driven tugs belching smoke from tall funnels. Diesel engines and efficient propellers lay in the future, and these tugs pulled themselves along the river by grinding along a tow chain hauled up from the riverbed: the chain on this part of the river stretched to Montereau upstream and Paris down, a distance of some sixty miles. Apart from the racket of the barges, the water passing over the weir provided a constant and thunderous background. Just visible from Jarry's window, the Villa Vallette was serene and calm.[7]

...

PLESSIS — COUDRAY-MONTCEAUX — Ecluse

Collection Guillaume

12.2
The lockkeeper's house; the inn is just visible behind
the trees, Jarry's shack at the extreme right.

Coudray-Montceaux (S.-et-O.) — Le quai de Halage au Barrage

Edit. Mignon

12.3
Further along the towpath, the inn, then Jarry's shack.
The embankment behind the figure was built for the
railway, and the tunnel to Demolder's emerged just to
the right of his head.

Jarry's shack was not a building that many would have considered strictly habitable. There were no amenities except, judging from the chimney, a stove. No power, no water, and no toilet. It had a simple barn door and a floor of beaten earth. When Rachilde proposed a visit with a female friend, Jarry washed the floor. It promptly turned to mud, and his visitors had to hold their skirts aloft for the duration of their call. Yet it was in this ramshackle hut that Jarry applied himself industriously to journalism over the coming four years, producing the 600-odd pages that were later collected together as *La Chandelle verte* (*The Green Candle*), as well as his last completed novel, *The Supermale*.[8]

This stretch of the Seine was then fairly isolated. The villages of Le Coudray and Le Plessis-Chenet were over the line of hills that here run parallel to the river, and were further separated from its bank by the new railway line. The riverbank opposite was principally occupied by the forest of Rougeau, and there were no visible habitations at all from Le Coudray all the way round to Corbeil, apart from a couple of buildings for the use of the Barrage workers. The local population was therefore very small, but the bar at the Barrage, the Rendez-vous, had a large and regular clientele of nomads: the bargees. Jarry was soon on good terms with them, which presents something of a problem for his biographers, since they left no recollections of their drinking companion. A large portion of Jarry's daily life is henceforth partially obscured, and this problem is compounded by the fact that although Jarry kept most of his correspondence, and this was saved after his death, for unknown reasons almost nothing between 1900 and 1904 has survived.[9]

The crews on the barges, often with their families, lived most of their lives on board, in an endless journey punctuated by regular stopping places where they met to eat and drink. It was a closed and separate existence, with its own customs and slang, as distant from the rest of society as Jarry seemed to have determined to be. He became accepted into this world and a feature at the inn, with his own regular seat, the first table on the left through the entrance. The nature of his new companions is evoked by the list of their nicknames at the head of a short piece of Jarry's fiction, later a part of his last unfinished novel, *La Dragonne*. It is a bizarre mixture of the poetic and the abusive: Baked-Apple, Goat-Butter, Egg-Yellow, Slacker, Smashed, Gingerbread, The Bandage, The Eye, Yelper, Skinflint, Rat's-Arse, Yellow-Foot, The Snake, Cat's-Nose, Love-*en-route*, The Beard, also known as Bigtache, The Fly, The Owl, Look-Below, Bellyache, The Bleak (a type of fish), Oil-Stone. Life on the barges was hard and interminable, moments of recreation were relished, and Jarry delighted in these characters whose forthright good humor and blunt but poetic conversation, littered with expletives, was a never-ending novelty.[10]

He began collecting material for a new book, and much of his research found its way into *La Dragonne*. He noted down the bargees' slang along with data regarding their work, recording that there were 112 bridges between Paris and Lille, and 192 locks. He kept a journal devoted to the barges passing through the Barrage, with their names, destinations, and cargoes. It is another list that appears fanciful, but was in fact entirely documentary: *The Dice, The Desired, The Littré* (after the famous French dictionary?), *The Cyrano, The Julius Caesar, The Bottom, Another-One-Caught, The Pay-Up, The Holy Family, The Mocker of the Jealous, The Atlas, The Protector,*

The Blunderer, Souvenir of a Friend, The Parthenope, The Bosphorus, The Golgotha, The Hoar Frost, The Returning Swallows, The Cayman, The Noah's Ark, The Twentieth Century, The Fin-de-siècle, The Go-See, etc. This self-sufficient world even had its own mysterious siren. When the tow chain on the riverbed broke, they sent for the *chaînier* in his special craft, piled high with rusting metal used to make patch repairs. The *chaînier* sported a scarlet jacket, and sang operatic arias as he passed up and down the river. His exquisite voice, magnified by the water and surrounding hills, was audible for miles; but he was hare-lipped, and the words were unintelligible. One of Jarry's last poems, published in 1903, was devoted to this enigmatic personage.[11]

12.4
Monsieur and Madame Dunou (left and right)
outside their establishment. The lady in the
center is a Madame Charles.

12.5
The view across the lock from the
Rendez-vous.

The inn by the weir, Au Rendez-vous du Barrage, was run by Madame and Monsieur Dunou. The *patron* was also a municipal councilor, and captain of the local brigade of voluntary firemen. Although primarily a drinking establishment, it provided basic food and supplies to the barge families, and to Jarry too. Monsieur Dunou soon took to his new tenant. They often fished together, and he lent Jarry his boat on those occasions when he could not accompany him. Jarry's skiff must have been sold off. Apart from Dunou, Jarry's most constant companion was his close neighbor, Demolder. Jules Renard left a sketch in his diary of this Rabelaisian *bon-vivant*:[12]

> Demolder, a little tobacco pot. An inflated Leander, a charming smile though, and that delicious Belgian way of speaking which graces so many men of talent.
>
> He claims to be more timid than anyone else in the world.
>
> A great belly, a large face, two small eyes bursting from his head, fine hair, a small mustache, carefully curled, no collar, just a black silk scarf around his neck.
>
> His laugh brief, an immediately extinguished flame. Sometimes the unexpected gestures of an actor, a bit of a ham.
>
> He travels a lot. He speaks of Italy, Naples. The Neapolitans are wonderful (here an explosive gesture), but so dirty! He saw a maid, too lazy to fetch water, piss on the floor and then use it to mop up with.[13]

12.6, 12.7
Two immediate neighbors. 12.6: Eugène Demolder and
his dog Mastoc; they are in front of the left-hand
building in the previous picture, on the opposite bank
of the Seine to the inn. 12.7: The witch of Le Coudray,
Mère Fontaine.

Within days of Jarry taking up residence, in July 1900, Demolder and he had embarked on fishing and cycling expeditions, and, no doubt, drinking, since Demolder shared Jarry's proclivities in this regard. Otherwise their situations were very different: Jarry alone in his shack, Demolder and his wife in the huge mansion of La Demi-Lune on the other side of the railway, hung with the works of Rops, and set in extensive grounds filled with rosebushes. Demolder was now master of this pile, Rops having died in 1898. When the railway was laid between this house and the riverbank, the company had built Rops a private tunnel beneath the tracks, just wide enough for a single person. Thus Demolder had direct access to the river, and the tunnel's entrance was only twenty yards from Jarry's shack. Demolder and Jarry were very different writers too. Although Demolder had been involved with the important avant-garde review *La Jeune Belgique*, his writing was a little dull. His most famous book, *The Emerald Way*, was a conventional biographical novel based upon the life of Rembrandt. Nevertheless, he was a convivial character with an acute critical eye, who had arranged Ensor's first show in Paris at the end of 1898, and maintained a massive correspondence with any number of Belgian artists and writers—a sign, perhaps, of his comparative isolation in his mansion. He and Jarry became almost constant companions, and Jarry's visits to La Demi-Lune were frequent.[14]

Despite the cramped modesty of the stable, Jarry was delighted to be able to resume his preferred existence on the banks of the Seine. Here he followed a simple daily routine. Fishing in the morning, essential since it furnished the principal part of his diet, followed by several absinthes at the Rendez-vous around midday. More absinthe was taken home, or consumed in cafés elsewhere. At other times he would provision himself for several days at a stretch and disappear into his lodging to write for extended periods. In the summer, the living was entirely to his taste, idyllic in fact, and for the next five years Jarry would stay here as late in the year as he was able. He was also frequently in Paris, since he regarded the forty-mile bicycle ride as inconsequential, frequently making the return journey on the same day. Thus he was able to pursue his literary activities in the capital, and he lived there when the weather made his country retreat intolerable.[15]

Jarry also frequented the other bar on the river. This was a more rudimentary establishment of distinctly ill repute whose clientele was less select even than that of the Rendez-vous. Originally patronized by the tunnelers working on the railway, in Jarry's day its habitués were mostly poachers and other rural reprobates intent on achieving inebriation somewhere remote from surveillance. Rachilde recalled its *patronne*, an eccentric old crone known as Mère Fontaine: "I have never come across a more startling character than this old sorceress who, simpering like some ancient hetaera, [...] called all her male customers, be they some well-known bourgeois or a dead-drunk sailor: 'my sweet little ducky.' This amazing creature conceived a great affection for Père Ubu, and made him propositions of such indecency as to make him blush." Mère Fontaine's was situated between Jarry's residence and that of the Vallettes, and thus convenient for an apéritif before lunch on Sundays.[16]

...

Also in July 1900, the *Revue Blanche* began the serialization of Jarry's first "genre" novel, *Messalina*: "A Novel of Ancient Rome." This had proved a popular subject with novelists ever since Flaubert's *Salammbô*, partly because comparisons were assumed between the morality of Rome and that of *fin-de-siècle* Paris. More often it was simply a pretext to smuggle a little prurience into "serious literature" under the guise of historical scholarship. Such works had proved remarkably lucrative. The finances of the Mercure de France had been transformed by the success of Louÿs's more Grecian novel *Aphrodite*, published in 1896, which sold 10,000 copies in its first year alone. This was an unheard-of amount for a publisher accustomed to editions of 500. While Jarry was correcting the proofs of *Messalina*, the Revue Blanche put out a translation of a more stodgy effort with a similar setting. Henryk Sienkiewicz's *Quo Vadis* appeared in June 1900, and was reprinted more than one hundred times before the end of the year.[17]

Jarry's novel, like those of some of his predecessors, certainly had its salacious moments— and on this occasion they were mostly heterosexual in nature—but its scholarship and erudition were more thorough than most. And although he may well have set out with the intention of replicating the commercial success of Louÿs, Jarry was unable to bend himself to such a task, not least because more than once he had expressed his indifference to such historical reconstructions. Something more intriguing was certain to occur, for Jarry's novels are not really "about" what they seem to be about, even when, as here, the work is saturated with sexuality and death.[18]

In this novel, Jarry refined the mode of writing that he had gradually created since *Days and Nights*—and which had seen its purest expression in *Absolute Love*—in which sentences, or even phrases, propel the narrative with brief bursts of meaning that gradually reveal an argument. Parts of *Messalina* resemble a series of statements in formal logic, each sentence the inevitable outcome of the one preceding it. From numerous Classical sources, diligently cited, Jarry extrapolates a narrative with such precision that it seems as if each of these sentences, these propositions, might be replaced by an equation. The final demonstration, achieved by means of a narrative of considerable poetic power, lies at some remove from its original premises in the historical record. In fact, with *Messalina*, one of Jarry's most apparently conventional novels, he assayed a grand paradox: he wrote an entirely fictional account of the events in the life of the Roman Empress Messalina—a wholly fantastical account, in fact, but one in which every element, almost every detail, was based on specific sources and careful research (along with a few deliberate anachronisms to "eternalize" it). The sum of Jarry's Rome would be unrecognizable to its inhabitants, despite the familiarity of its parts.

Thus history is revealed at its most pataphysical, as an imaginary solution. The past is a universe "supplementary to this one," as malleable as the future, which may be actualized in the present by an act of imaginative representation. The conflict between the rigorous precision of the exposition, and the extravagant obscenity and cruelty of the content, creates a very modern sort of dislocation that alerts the reader to the existence of a different underlying narrative, like the hidden figure Jarry discovered in Dürer's woodcut of St. Catherine. Even as readers are drawn into the novel's events by their luxuriance, they are made aware that this is only the pretext of the book. Jarry's real interests lie elsewhere: in a formal manipulation of symbols, in generating a flux of related signifiers which the reader may clump together into a meaning. Such attributes are more often associated with poetry, and although previous works of Jarry's such as *Absolute Love* were more obviously "poetic" than *Messalina*, with its apparently conventional novelistic form, here Jarry succeeded in combining both novelistic and poetic modes, neither being sacrificed for the other.

Despite which … he still hoped for a financial and popular success. His own blurb did not refrain from puffing the book by stressing its more lurid details (along with its historical authenticity), and he told Rachilde that he expected sales of twenty thousand. In the event, it sold three thousand, which, although disappointing compared to *Aphrodite*, let alone *Quo Vadis*, meant it was still his best-selling work since *Ubu Roi*. More importantly, the publication of *Messalina*, apparently so different from his earlier works, seems to have finally silenced certain of Jarry's detractors, or at least to have brought round many of his contemporaries who had been unconvinced by his literary works to date.[19]

Messalina would go a long way to reviving Jarry's literary reputation among his contemporaries. Rachilde was so startled by it that when it appeared in book form in January 1901, she undertook a reevaluation of Jarry's earlier works:

> Just as curiosity impels one to follow the always fatal descent of a meteorite through the darkness of the sky until it falls to earth, it likewise seems interesting to me to seek within the already published works of Alfred Jarry the generation of his latest novel, a work that marks a new development, perhaps a permanent revolution, in the earlier obscurities of his style.[20]

Her review for the *Mercure* then looked back at Jarry's writings to date (which explains the presence within it of her comments about *Absolute Love* cited previously). She discovered that the seeming diversity of Jarry's works concealed a surprising thematic unity that could be traced to "Lintel," the preface to *Minutes*. There were other reviews. Kahn in *La Plume* was not entirely convinced (he praised it rather half-heartedly); Arnauld in the *Revue Blanche* was keener, especially as regards its stylistic felicities. But the really positive reaction occurred among Jarry's friends and acquaintances, universally impressed by this new direction. He received fulsome letters from unexpected correspondents, writers he barely knew such as Francis Jammes and Albert Mockel. Toulouse-Lautrec cut the pages of *Messalina* from the *Revue* and saved them. Fagus was not alone when he later concluded that *Messalina* was Jarry's "masterpiece, a book which crystallized all that was best in him."[21]

···

A third and more important alteration in Jarry's circumstances occurred that same July: the publication of the first of his regular book reviews for the *Revue Blanche*. It was the beginning of a regular income, a novelty indeed, and happened to be on a subject much to his taste: the early volumes of Mardrus's translation of *The Thousand and One Nights*. He reviewed many other books in 1900, and they were indeed "other," a peculiar selection of titles on all sorts of topics. Jarry seems to have been the reviewer of last resort at the magazine, and here a charitable motive may be attributed to Fénéon: that of putting some cash Jarry's way. Even so, it remains a little mysterious why a periodical whose main preoccupation was literary should review books concerning fishing and hunting legislation, human evolution, naval medicine, a means of inhumation designed to avoid premature burials, the Gnostic catechism, the superiority of animals to humans, the situation of women in Arab societies, and a guidebook to the golf clubs of England and France. These are only some of the subjects Jarry pronounced upon, and his famous erudition was being put to the test. Golf, he explained to his readers, is a game in which "a small ball is knocked by a sort of mallet, using the smallest number of blows, into a series of holes drilled at irregular and often extended distances into a terrain strewn with obstacles."[22]

Jarry's position as a reviewer necessitated numerous visits to Fénéon at the magazine's offices, cluttered with books, papers, and passing contributors. They were then situated at 23, boulevard des Italiens, but until recently they had been a few yards further along the boulevard on the corner with the rue Laffitte. Close to the main auction house in Paris, this street was then dominated by art galleries, including the famous Durand-Ruel where Gauguin had shown, and in 1900 the gallery of Ambroise Vollard was at number 6, having gradually migrated down the street since it opened in September 1893 at number 41, when Jarry and Fargue had first visited it.[23]

...

For more than a decade Vollard would be the most influential modern art dealer in Paris—which meant anywhere, given the city's cultural prominence. His courage would fail him in the face of full-blown modernism, however, and his support of Picasso and Matisse waned as their works outgrew their Symbolist or Post-Impressionist origins. Originally from the French colony of La Réunion in the Indian Ocean, he was half-Creole on his mother's side; his father was a French attorney. Aged thirty-six when his gallery opened, he was a small and distinctly pugnacious character, whose irascibility with clients was legendary. The profession of picture dealer requires a certain amount of cunning and guile as well as a thick skin, and Vollard was judged to be blessed with these qualities in rather too much abundance. He managed to remain on good terms with most of those he exhibited, although Gauguin was a notable exception. Vollard mounted the first one-man shows of Cézanne, Picasso, and Matisse, to name only the most celebrated, and soon began issuing portfolios of artists' prints; the first, by Gauguin, in 1894. A few years later he expanded into publishing "livres d'artiste," which joined classic texts to works by the most famous artists of the day, essentially inventing the genre as practiced in the first part of the twentieth century. It would be surprising if Jarry and Vollard were not in contact during this period, not only because of their joint interest in artistic publishing, but also through Jarry's close friendship with Bonnard, Vollard's most consistent collaborator, and later the illustrator of many

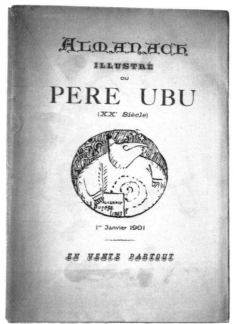

12.8
Félix Vallotton, Ambroise Vollard, pencil drawing, 1902.

12.9
Almanach illustré du Père Ubu, 1901.

of Vollard's own Ubu plays. There is indirect evidence of their relations. Vollard contributed to the financing of the first *Almanac* by advertising in the back pages, and Jarry was presumed to be behind Vollard's decision to exhibit Rousseau, from whom he accepted a batch of paintings on commission in 1895.[24]

Vollard's famously unreliable memoirs recall his meeting Jarry when he lived at Corbeil, although he seems to mean Le Coudray and to be referring to the time soon after the first *Almanac* appeared. Vollard was still in his first flush of enthusiasm for publishing, and since 1901 was imminent, the start of a new century, why not do a second *Almanac*? Jarry, meanwhile, had become a regular guest at the dinners Vollard hosted in the basement of rue Laffitte. These continued nearly until the First World War, and Jarry probably came often whenever he was in Paris. Apollinaire wrote an evocation of these evenings in the white-walled cellar where a group of unnamed "pretty women" and artists and writers associated with the gallery or the Revue Blanche, or expatriates from La Réunion, would gather to sample Vollard's Réunionnaise cuisine: chicken curry. Among the regulars he listed Dierx, Forain, Redon, Denis,Vuillard, Bonnard, Bernard, Terrasse, and … Picasso. Vollard's memoirs recall that the idea for the second or "Great" *Almanac* was born at one of these dinners, and that he and Jarry had the idea for a "colonial issue" after Jarry heard Vollard recount tales of his native island and its inhabitants. Apollinaire had the same story:[25]

> It was in the basement of the rue Laffitte that the Great Almanac was written. Everyone knows that the authors were Alfred Jarry for the text, Bonnard for the illustrations, and Claude Terrasse for the music. As for the song, that was by Ambroise Vollard. Everyone knows this and yet nobody seems to have noticed that the *Great Almanac* was published without the names of authors or publisher. The evening he came up with almost everything in this book worthy of Rabelais, Jarry startled those who did not know him by asking, when dinner was over, for the bottle of pickles, which he then greedily devoured.[26]

Apollinaire was always fascinated with Jarry's passion for the *cornichon* (gherkin). He is here writing at second hand, since it would be a little over a year before he and Jarry met, and he described the *Great Almanac* being composed in a single evening. Vollard says it took three days, including Bonnard doing the illustrations, and this is almost confirmed by Terrasse's diary. He records that their first meeting was at Noisy-le-Grand on Monday, December 10, with Bonnard, although Vollard had already agreed to finance it. The remainder of the work was mostly done at Vollard's and it was finished that same week, perhaps with contributions from two others, Paul Ranson and Odilon Redon, who joined them for dinner at the end of work sessions. There was also one further collaborator, Félicien Fagus, art critic for the *Revue Blanche*, and an anarchist poet with a day job at the local town hall in Montmartre. French law then decreed that children could be baptized only with the name of a saint, and Fagus's position meant he had access to the complete list, which yielded some bizarre yet "true" names for the *Almanac*'s calendar (where they are marked with an asterisk): Saint Alopecia, Saint Ghoul, Saint Profit, Saint Carp, Saint Viol (which could also mean Saint Rape), Saint Specious, Saint Bosom, Saint Wench, etc. Apart from the calendar, the *Almanac* contained two plays. The first, by Jarry, was described as Ubu's "commentary on recent events," and was followed by Père Ubu's description of his most recent inventions, and then satirical nominations to his "Order of the Grande Gidouille." The second play, *Ubu Colonialist*, was probably mostly the work of Vollard. Finally there was a *chanson* set to music by Terrasse: "Tatane."[27]

One experiences a distinct feeling of discomfort on reading parts of the *Almanac* today, and it would indeed be convenient to be able to follow Apollinaire and blame Vollard for vulgarities such as "Tatane," a song which is supposed to "make Negroes blush." *Tatane* was a Creole word that signified tiredness feigned to avoid work, that habitual imperialist lament about "malingering natives." Not all such references may be attributed to Vollard, however, and the manuscripts of "Tatane" are in Jarry's hand. Parts of the *Almanac* that are definitively Jarry's work are marred by casual racism, albeit of the tamest variety, especially considering the date it was written. And yet, although the *Almanac* was promoted as the "colonial" issue, neither Jarry nor Vollard were writing in its support. The latter made this plain in his own *La politique coloniale du Père Ubu* in which, for example, Ubu informs a parliamentary commission that only fools imagine that colonies exist because of colonials. On the contrary, it is obvious that colonials are simply the product of a colony, its parasite in fact. (The pun on "colon," more obvious in the French, is never far away.)[28]

Colonialism was in fact the topic of the moment because of the Exposition Universelle of 1900. When the Thai Prince Iukanthor had visited, as his country's ambassador, he had scandalized his hosts by denouncing its French administration. Two weeks after the appearance of the *Almanac*, Jarry reviewed a book on this affair for the *Revue Blanche*. It demonstrated, he wrote, the absurdity of "a culture, that is so immature as to be capable of admiring the plaster monuments of the Great Fair of 1900, asserting its right to impose itself upon a civilization that dates back several thousands years … and which does indeed impose itself upon it." There is a pun in Jarry's text, too: *foire* means a "fair," but is also slang for diarrhea.[29]

Vollard did the *Almanac* proud. It appeared on January 1, 1901, in a large format (11 by 7½ inches) of 56 pages, on good paper, and was printed in three colors throughout. At the last moment he feared it might run into legal problems because of its sexual content. Thus, like the first *Almanac*, it was published without crediting its authors, but also without an address, a printer's name, or that of a *gérant*, the publisher's representative who would take the consequences should the law be invoked, an omission that was of course illegal. This was something of a pointless precaution. It would have taken minimal investigation to discover the perpetrators, since the last three pages consisted of advertisements for Vollard's and Jarry's publications. Pointless, too, because Vollard found it impossible to sell. He had 1,000 copies printed at a cost of 1,000 francs. He tried placing them in bookshops for a franc apiece, but with little success, and he quickly realized it was a commercial failure. Much later a collector asked for copies and offered him eight francs each. Vollard had left the bulk of the run with the printer, but on going to retrieve it he found that the printer had died, and his stock had been destroyed. Probably only 200 copies survived, most of them given away by the contributors.[30]

One of the most successful parts of the *Almanac* was Ubu's description of his inventions, the umbrella, gloves, and carpet slippers:

> We have often deplored the fact that the state of our phynances does not permit us to bestrew the entire floor surface of our abode with soft, yielding carpets. We do indeed have one in our banqueting hall, but there is none in our French-style lavatory, nor in our kitchen. We thought originally of having the carpet transported, when necessary, from the banqueting hall to the adjoining rooms; but then the aforementioned banqueting hall would have been bereft of carpet, and in any case, the carpet would have been too large for the exiguous dimensions of these other chambers. The idea then occurred to us of trimming it, but then it would have become too narrow for its original situation. Such narrowness, however, would not present an entirely prohibitive imperfection were it possible to keep the trimmed portion of the carpet underfoot at all times, no matter which room we might decide to grace with our person. Fortified by these considerations, and being no longer reluctant to sacrifice the object itself, having found a better use for it, we stood squarely upon its gorgeous center and cut out that section situated beneath the soles of our feet which, in geometry, is known as the sustentatory pedal polygon. We then fastidiously adjusted the contours of these two fragments to the exact size of our footprints, while simultaneously improving our comfort, by folding the edges of the material firmly and cosily around our basal extremities. We considered christening this dual apparatus the *portable universal insulators* but decided eventually upon the more euphonious appellation of *carpet slippers*.[31]

The vocabulary of François, Père Ubu, was certainly much improved; so too the precision of his thought, despite its somewhat unconventional logic. Jarry announced the appearance of the *Almanac* in the *Revue Blanche* for January 1, 1901, and pointed out that a feature of Ubu, "not so apparent in *Ubu Roi* or in its counterpart *Ubu enchaîné*, is highlighted here: we are referring to the 'pataphysics' of this personage, more simply his confident holding forth on *omni re scibili* [anything that can be known], sometimes competently, sometimes with intentional absurdity, but in the latter case following a logic every bit as irrefutable as that of the mad or the senile." Ubu was no longer the entirely idiotic buffoon of yore, but was beginning to share the mental processes of his creator, a blurring of identity neither appeared to have noticed. This fact would become implicit in the new column Jarry was to write for the *Revue Blanche*, beginning in the next issue. His "Speculations" would subject recent events and "anything that can be known" to the same unsettling coherence. The first of these columns—and there were to be some one hundred and sixty of them over the next three years—was devoted to "The New Stamps," and could just as easily have been another of Ubu's inventions. Pataphysics was assuming its new objective tone, resembling that of an anthropologist exploring some newly discovered civilization.

But should this scientist/explorer be named Ubu, Faustroll, or Jarry? Or have the distinctions between these three now all but disappeared?[32]

> It is a superstition common among humans, who wish to converse with near relations from whom they are temporarily separated, for them to toss the written expression of their affection into some convenient orifice, such as the opening of a drain, after first having charitably encouraged the otherwise sinister trade in tobacco, by acquiring in exchange a few small images, doubtless blessed, which they then devoutly kiss on the backside. It is not our intention here to criticize the coherence of such practices, since it is undeniable that long-distance communication is made possible by their means.[33]

(In France, postage stamps were, and still are, sold by tobacconists.) Even this extract from Jarry's first speculation shows him employing a method he was to use often, logically extrapolating an absurd conclusion from a false premise—a procedure analogous to that of theology, which perhaps explains Jarry's interest in it. The starting points of these articles were recent events, which required Jarry to read the daily press. Over the next three years he cites some thirteen journals and newspapers, which he probably consulted in libraries. The topics covered appear as random as the books he had reviewed, but this was a deliberate choice on Jarry's part: a demonstration of pataphysical equivalence. High and low culture, farce and tragedy, major scandals, such as the Dreyfus Affair, or apparently insignificant events were all of equal interest: Pataphysics implied it, and he devoted one of his articles to explaining this necessity. So far as Jarry's "Speculations" disclose aspects of their author's character and opinions, the most general impression given was that they revealed someone for whom no topic was off-limits for mockery. All was grist.[34]

12.10
Félix Vallotton, Alfred Jarry, ink drawing, 1901.

These mini-essays seemed a better outlet for his talents than random book reviewing (but he continued with this too), and gained Jarry a new audience, since the *Revue Blanche* was widely distributed and had a print run of 10,000. In February 1901, to coincide with the book publication of *Messalina*, the *Revue* contained Arnauld's review of it and Vallotton's "mask" of Jarry, drawn for this occasion (rather than for Gourmont's *Book of Masks*). Jarry's "journalism" and the royalties from *Messalina* and *Ubu Roi/enchaîné* meant he was earning an income, but how much? The *Revue Blanche* paid him fifty francs a month. Royalties might have bolstered this figure, and selling review copies helped subsidize his drinking. There were further sources of income: between February and May Gustave Kahn's faltering magazine *La Vogue* serialized Jarry's extremely odd, or very poor, translation (depending on whether the errors are judged to be deliberate or not) of a novella by Robert Louis Stevenson, *Olalla*.[35]

...

Jarry's earnings from journalism were not exactly bountiful, and the commercial theater still looked attractive, especially since Claude Terrasse was on the verge of becoming one of the most celebrated composers of his day. His first popular success had been his operetta *La Petite Femme de Loth* in October 1900. His next triumph was *Les Travaux d'Hercule*, which opened at the Bouffes-Parisiens on March 7, 1901. The theater had been founded by Offenbach, and was not a bohemian establishment in the manner of the Œuvre. Evening dress was expected. So it was with both amusement and trepidation that Guitry accompanied Jarry and Demolder to the public dress rehearsal for *Les Travaux*. They were armed with a letter from Terrasse requesting that the management give them the best seats. An usher looked them up and down and, Guitry recalled, "hesitated to put them in the front stalls":

> Demolder was wearing an outfit of beige corduroy topped by a fur cap, and was carrying a shepherd's crook. Jarry was dressed entirely in white linen, which was far from white, and had fashioned himself a shirt out of paper. The tie was painted on with Indian ink. The usher and the house manager whispered in each other's ear, and obsequiously assigned Jarry and Demolder to the first gallery. They took their seats without a word, but Jarry was preparing his revenge. The conductor took his place on the podium, raised his arms, and eventually achieved the requisite silence ... into which Jarry dropped his Punchinello voice, speaking slowly and distinctly: "I do not understand why the theater management allows the first three rows of the audience to bring in musical instruments."[36]

Jarry and Terrasse's collaborations had continued, even while they were working on the *Almanac*. In December the previous year Jarry had rewritten *Par la taille*, which Terrasse set to music. This too he was unable to get staged, probably because in this work Jarry had attempted to write a piece of pure mime with universal characters; it was rather too close to his actual dramatic preoccupations to be commercial. Terrasse, Willy, and Jarry now thought *Pantagruel* finished, after the latter's final modifications, but it suffered the same fate as previously. Jarry was now cycling back and forth between Paris and Le Coudray with remarkable frequency. A letter to Terrasse apologizes for not being at the première of another of his operettas on Thursday April 18, 1901, because he had that minute returned to Le Coudray, but would have to race back to town to deliver his copy to the *Revue* on Saturday, at the last possible moment, as was his invariable practice.[37]

The summer appears to have passed in such occupations: his life by the river, journalistic research in Paris, and he had also begun writing his next novel, *The Supermale*. Also that summer, Picasso had his first exhibition at the Vollard gallery, between June 24 and July 14, which Jarry could easily have seen. Although he was doubtless in Le Coudray for most of this period, trips to the offices of the Revue Blanche would still have been necessary, and their paths could easily have crossed. The July issue of the *Revue* carried the first critical appreciation of Picasso to appear in France, written by Fagus.[38]

…

The regular salons attached to the Mercure, and the social life around the Revue Blanche, meant the authors associated with them met each other with great regularity. This tended to make other forms of communication unnecessary between regulars, and certain of Jarry's friendships might have gone unremarked but for the existence of a few letters. The warmth of those from Octave Mirbeau appear surprising, so infrequently has he previously appeared in this narrative, yet he and Jarry had no doubt met on an almost weekly basis for some years. Mirbeau was an *actionnaire* of the *Mercure* and the *Revue Blanche*, and contributed to both.

> 6 August 1901
>
> Dear [Jarry]
> I am told that we are almost neighbors, but nobody could give me your exact address. I only know that it is near Corbeil. The *Revue Blanche*, which you make illustrious with such admirable things, will forward you my letter.
>
> All this to tell you that I live in Veneux-Nadon, near Moret, beside the Seine, in a venerable and delicious situation, that I have a boat and around the boat are shoals of barbel and bream, and that I like you very well … and I hope you might stay a few days at my home with your friend Quillard.
>
> Would you? It would make me very happy. When would suit you? Would you write to Quillard on this matter as I will also, but let it be soon.
>
> I am leaving tomorrow for somewhere absurd, but I'll be back here Sunday night.
>
> Best wishes, my dear Jarry, with all my heart,
>
> Octave Mirbeau[39]

Jarry accepted, and a second letter from Mirbeau, known only from an extract in an auction cata-log, urged him to provision himself for a substantial stay, and to bring all the "engines" necessary to wage "patriotic massacres" against the barbel and bream.[40]

Octave Mirbeau, Jarry's elder by twenty-five years, was a formidable and highly influential anarchist journalist who wrote both for the mainstream press and for more overtly radical publi-cations. His polemic "The Voter's Strike," first printed in Jean Grave's journal *La Révolte*, became the most widely distributed anarchist text in France—100,000 copies in four years—and remains in print to this day. He was also a successful playwright and novelist, and most of his novels are still available, even in English, perhaps the most famous being *The Diary of a Chambermaid*, which Luis Buñuel made into a memorable feature film. His only radical blind spot was feminism, to which he was vociferously opposed. Supporters attribute this to his miserable marriage to Alice Regnault, an ex-actress and only partly reformed "courtesan." Their marriage was difficult, to say the least. She drove away many of his friends, and, on his death in 1917, notoriously forged a document purporting to be his political testament, in which he declared himself a patriotic supporter of the war.[41]

Mirbeau's country house was around thirty miles from Le Coudray, on the other side of Fontainebleau. Jarry presumably cycled there, arriving on August 26. Quillard came the day after, and almost immediately they decided to invite Fénéon, too: a regular hotbed of piscophile anar-chists on holiday. Details of their activities are lacking, except that Jarry's prowess with the rod was much admired. He caught a barbel in a stretch of the river where no one had ever caught one before, nor ever would again, according to Mirbeau: "and God knows we tried everything."[42]

Mirbeau did not mention whether Madame was in residence, but a number of Jarry's run-ins with her are recorded. She was socially ambitious, which seems a little odd given the political affiliations of her husband, and she profoundly disapproved of improper behavior. She found little to admire in this new friend. One day Jarry was to join them and some other guests for din-ner. He strode in late, his head held up, but drunk, very drunk, his chest clattering with military medals he had acquired in a junk shop. At table Madame Mirbeau asked him (and a variant of this conversation turns up in *The Supermale*, then under way): why did he drink so much?[43]

"To make me strong, Madame!" Jarry replied.

"To make you strong? But bulls are strong and they don't drink absinthe …"

Jarry gave Madame Mirbeau a long look, at once ingenuous and mocking.

"You are certain that bulls do not ever drink absinthe?" he asked.

"I swear it!" she affirmed.

Jarry appeared lost in contemplation, then replied:

"In that case, Madame, I feel profoundly sorry for them."[44]

Nearby were the houses where the Natansons and the artists of the Revue Blanche congregated in the summer, either at Thadée's or at his brother-in-law's. Mirbeau's house party paid them a call. Thadée, according to the many accounts of his friends, appears to have been a gentle, generous man and a real enthusiast for the most authentic efforts of the artists and writers who surrounded him. He helped many of them on the occasions when they most needed it. But the social center of the Revue Blanche's sojourns in the country was inevitably Misia, Natanson's reputedly beautiful wife, although not many photographs of her are as flattering as the portraits left by Vuillard, Bonnard, and Lautrec. There is a brief passage in her autobiography concerning Jarry in which one can recognize a number of anecdotes from different sources, all mixed together with various obvious inaccuracies. It is impossible to date very exactly, not least because Misia's memoirs become deliberately obfuscatory when relating these years at the turn of the century, so as to conceal her ill treatment of her husband:

> Mirbeau, who lived near Fontainebleau, brought Alfred Jarry to see me, as did Vallette, the editor of the *Mercure de France*. Jarry had a cottage somewhere on the banks of the Seine. I was very fond of the charming little clown who fished for his food and wore Madame Vallette's boots, usually tied on with a black velvet ribbon. […] I introduced Jarry to Madame Mirbeau, a great social climber, who asked him to lunch the next day. He arrived on a bicycle, filthy enough to frighten anybody. When Madame Mirbeau gazed with distress at his shoes, their large bows covered with mud, he said: "Don't worry, Madame, I have a much dirtier pair." There was roast beef for lunch. Jarry disdained the carvings and seized the joint. A dead silence fell, dominated by an angry glare from the hostess, a strange wink from Père Ubu, then the guests collapsed with stifled laughter.[45]

Misia's memoirs do her no favors; she appears vain and shallow, with flirtation her principal means of discourse. She must nevertheless have possessed great personal magnetism, judging by the number of her amorous conquests among the artists and writers associated with the *Revue Blanche*: all were firmly unconsummated, and she made a show of carelessness with their gifts. Mallarmé presented her with a manuscript poem every New Year's Day, but she kept only one of them, and that by accident. She mutilated the paintings Bonnard made for her sitting room because she thought the bottom edges would be improved by being scallop-shaped, and so simply hacked away the canvas; and various of Lautrec's paintings were ruined when she lacquered them with motorcar varnish.[46]

She and Thadée, surrounded by all their artistic friends, appeared to lead an idyllic existence, but matters were not quite as they seemed. It is not necessary to adjudicate between the different accounts of their separation, the reasons for the financial troubles of Thadée, or why Misia abandoned him in favor of a millionaire newspaper magnate by the name of Alfred Edwards. After much maneuvering, which did little credit to the future Mr. and Mrs. Edwards, the outcome by the end of 1903 was that Thadée was ruined and Misia rich, although the discovery that her husband's sexual tastes ran to coprophilia may have dulled the shine of his lucre. This outcome was not only a personal and financial disaster for Thadée, but had serious consequences for many others, especially perhaps Jarry: it meant the end of the Revue Blanche. Misia went on to become a famous society hostess with a salon patronized by the likes of Cocteau, and she was later cruelly immortalized as Madame Verdurin by Proust.[47]

Misia had been introduced to Edwards by Mirbeau, who was among the besotted. Edwards was immediately captivated, and henceforth openly pursued her with great persistence under the very nose of her husband. At some point during this lengthy courtship Edwards passed through the lock at Le Coudray on his yacht and moored outside Jarry's lowly hovel. To amuse his guests, he had decided to invite the penurious author aboard for cocktails. After a while he objected to Jarry's habit of clinking glasses with his guests. "Come now, my dear Jarry, one only clinks glasses with the vulgar!" "That is our opinion too," replied Jarry. Followed by a clink and a glacial: "Here's to you."[48]

...

Montmartre is nowadays remembered for its cabarets (pallid versions of which persist) and its artists, depicted as cheery bohemians in Hollywood musicals. But at the turn of the last century the immediate history of the *butte* (the hill) had been rather more desperate. The insurrection leading to the establishment of the Commune had been ignited on its summit in 1871, when the Vigilance Committee of Montmartre prevented the regular army from seizing the cannons that commanded the city. When the revolutionary administration was overthrown two months later, Montmartre was almost the last to hold out. Those who escaped fled eastward and were cut down in the cemetery of Père-Lachaise, or were captured there and shot by firing squad. Only two years after these massacres, the government voted to construct the Basilica of Sacré-Cœur on top of the hill. There was never any doubt that this prominent wedding cake of a cathedral was intended as a symbol of the victory of Church and State, the two avowed enemies of the anarchist cause. The Basilica was still under construction in the 1890s, by which time the Communards who had escaped execution had been released from prison or deportation, and many returned to the district. They opened bars, or patronized them, and the cabarets were hotbeds of both radicalism and common criminality. Their entertainers, the *chansonniers*, sang satirical ballads of the dispossessed, or humorous celebrations of everyday hardships. It was a rich mixture of artists, radicals, and vagabonds.

Jehan Rictus and Frédéric-Auguste Cazals were two such entertainers, but they could not have been more different. Cazals, a flamboyant dandy whose verses tended toward literary satire, had nevertheless experienced the hardships of the Commune at first hand; when he was six his father, a jobbing tailor, had only just escaped being shot during the repression. As a youth he gravitated toward bohemian circles, within whose purlieus he seems to have been universally popular both as a performer and as an individual. He drew and painted portraits, wrote verse, and became a *chansonnier* at an early age. He was close to Verlaine in the poet's last absinthe-sodden days. Accounts differ as to whether this friendship was platonic or not, but otherwise Cazals seems not to have been homosexual. Jarry had known him at least since the end of 1897, when he drew two portraits of Jarry; one was a rapid sketch (figure 12.13), the other a more worked-up drawing that was eventually used as the frontispiece for the last of Jarry's publications to appear in his lifetime, *Le Moutardier du Pape* (figure 14.11). Earlier, in 1898, Cazals had drawn some of the illustrations for *Visits of Love*, including the cover.[49]

In September 1901, Cazals was finally persuaded to collect his verses into book form and the collection, *Le Jardin des ronces* (*The Garden of Brambles*), was published a few months later with a preface by Rachilde and a "Privilege," or license to print, from King Ubu, which parodied the royal permissions that prefaced Jarry's beloved Rabelais. Ubu's "Privilege" was first published in September in *La Plume*, another important periodical of the period, and although Jarry had published short pieces in it before, it seems likely that it was Cazals who introduced him into the social circle around this magazine. The soirées of *La Plume* were famous, and there Jarry would soon encounter a whole new generation of authors. He gave Cazals's book a very sympathetic review in the *Revue Blanche*, but could not resist noting that the poets he caricatured from the great days of the Decadents now seemed hopelessly remote, the twentieth century being now upon them.[50]

12.11
Rictus by Steinlen.

12.12
Cazals by Jossot.

Born two years after Cazals, in 1867, Gabriel Randon had something of the down-at-heel dandy about him too, but rather more cadaverous. Tall and forlorn, with a great black beard and lank hair, he was better known by the name Jehan Rictus, and his performances of his "Soliloquies of the Poor" were a long-standing fixture at the famous Montmartre cabaret, the Quat'z'Arts. In these lugubrious and passionate song-poems, Rictus gave a voice to the tramps, prostitutes, and petty criminals he had known all too well, having experienced several years of living rough on the streets around Les Halles in his late adolescence. Rictus was temperamental and volatile, and his relations with Jarry remain a little obscure, but it appears that each thought the other might be useful, and for this reason put aside a mutual antipathy. Rictus's *Soliloquies* were republished by the Mercure in 1897, but he was soon disillusioned with the whole coterie, whom he dismissed in his diary as literary jokers, dilettantes, and "eunuchs." Jarry for his part was interested in Rictus's contacts with the Quat'z'Arts, since it had a marionette theater, a guignol operated by the famous Anatole from Lyon.[51]

This cabaret on the boulevard Clichy was the nearest thing to a successor to the Chat Noir. Decorated in a similarly extravagant pseudo-Gothic-Renaissance style, it had a suitably stout impresario, François Trombert, and seated an audience of 150. Here Jarry hoped for a new production of *Ubu*, and in November 1901 it came to pass. Rictus, as protective of his misery as ever, described the opening night in his diary:[52]

12.13
F.-A. Cazals, undated sketch of
Alfred Jarry.

2056. - Paris. — Le Cabaret des Quat-z-arts (Boulevard de Clichy)

12.14
The Cabaret des Quat'z'Arts.

12.15
The puppet for *Ubu Roi* at the Quat'z'Arts.

The guests [illegible word] little by little. The coteries of the Mercure and the Revue Blanche. Vallette appeared peeved at my determination [to publish elsewhere]. I saw Charles-Henry Hirsch and his pregnant mistress—Monceau—etc.—Fénéon—All of them affecting the superiority and the skepticism of great artists. Only they may guard the Sacred Flame of Art— It is just a fashion for them to admire *Ubu Roi* since this fantasy really cannot possibly justify the sincere admiration they affect for it. I too admire it, but not for its outrageousness and its eccentricities—

Ubu was performed. Well, migrating up here to Montmartre did it no favors. It will be a flop— The Public here understands nothing—It was too messed about with, cut, emasculated, updated— now it is shapeless and terribly poorly performed—the play, the drama, has been lost. The hilarious scene in which Père Ubu is led to believe that Mère Ubu is an apparition of St. Michael [he meant Gabriel] has been cut. This is a shame. It will not succeed.[53]

The play had been rewritten so extensively it was effectively a new work, and when it was published five years later Jarry renamed it *Ubu sur la Butte*, although this version had also been revised in the meantime. The five acts of *Ubu Roi* occupy 45 pages in Jarry's *Œuvres complètes*; the two-act reduction of it contained in *Ubu sur la Butte* is only 16 pages long and has a number of new songs. It is preceded by a prologue (6 pages), a version of a one-act puppet play of Jarry's dating from December 1898, featuring Guignol and Trombert, from which it is obvious that he and Jarry had quickly hit it off.[54]

Some changes to the play were unwished for. The production was delayed by a dispute with the censor over "the word." The solution used at the Théâtre des Pantins, "—*dre*," was allowed only once, and the remainder were suppressed. The private performance described by Rictus took place on November 23, 1901, the official opening being four days later.[55]

The Lyonnais tradition of the guignol, like the English Punch and Judy, was performed with glove puppets, and there is no suggestion that Jarry had any part in this production as a performer, either voicing the parts, or operating the puppets. Indeed, he was disappointed by the actor playing Ubu, according to an unpublished letter to the critic Émile Straus, but delighted by Antoine, who played Lascy. There was a *chansonnier* to render the songs, and there were four sets, two more than Jarry had originally intended: The Ubus' House, The King's Palace, The Battlefield, whose windmill had rotating sails, and the final scene set on a galleon.[56]

Rictus's prediction proved incorrect. *Ubu Roi* received appreciative notices, some of them even by critics unacquainted with the author. It ran for sixty-four performances. Not only was this production a success, but it allowed a far larger audience to see the play than heretofore, even if it was "mutilated by the necessities of staging and the exigencies of the censor," according to Quillard's review. On December 18, Jarry finished writing *The Supermale*. It had been a productive year for him, but this novel would be his last significant book.[57]

...

For the past year, since the commencement of his "Speculations" in January 1901, Jarry's income from his journalism had been sufficient for his immediate needs, and he had ceased writing libretti for Terrasse. He may of course simply not have had the time, and yet he continued to attend performances of Terrasse's operettas. In January 1902, he went several times to see Terrasse's latest success, *La Fiancée du scaphandrier*, each time requesting complimentary tickets. Judging from his review for the *Revue Blanche*, he genuinely admired the piece. The libretto was by Franc-Nohain, and Jarry's visits to the theater were perhaps made so as to discover how his old collaborator had achieved what he had so arduously failed to do. Jarry ended his review with a plug: he noted that Terrasse's music was as good as that for *Les Travaux d'Hercule* and for *Pantagruel*, which no one had yet heard.

At this juncture, Jarry made a trip to Brussels. The previous October he had received an invitation to speak to the Salon de la Libre Esthétique, an annual series of lectures and exhibitions put on by the Association des XX, a group of the most modernist artists in Belgium. Demolder had suggested Jarry to Octave Maus, the founder of Les XX, and Jarry had accepted forthwith, without specifying the subject he would speak upon. The lecture was arranged for March 21, 1902. During February Jarry decided on his topic: Marionettes.[58]

Jarry's trip to Brussels was described in formidable detail by the art critic Sander Pierron (all the unattributed sources in this section are from his article). He had a particular interest in Jarry's lecture, being himself the author of a history of marionettes under the name Paul de Glines. A committed socialist (his father Évariste Pierron had been an activist in the Belgian section of the International), he was the lover of Georges Eekhoud who, eighteen months earlier, had been prosecuted for "promoting pederasty" in his novel *Escal-Vigor*. Jarry had signed the protest against the trial in the *Mercure*; Eekhoud was acquitted, in what had been something of a test case in Belgium.[59]

Jarry was met at the Brussels railway station by Demolder, probably on the 16th. He was booked into a far-from-luxurious hotel across the street, whose proximity to the station made it a popular venue for "assignations." The two of them spent some time visiting bars, the major art galleries, and a puppet theater. They mailed postcards to both Vallettes, and Jarry sent one to Claudius-Jacquet, more discreetly worded than usual, given the latter's newly married status. Their card to Rachilde, dated March 18, naturally had to feature the famous Mannekin-Pis, and Demolder assured her they were drinking plenty of beer so as to be able to imitate the statue.[60]

Pierron met him on the day of the lecture, and recorded a most singular first impression of Jarry:

> In my mind's eye I can easily picture Jarry in his unusual get-up. Despite being in his thirtieth year, he looked like an adolescent, even like a female adolescent. At first glance one might take him for a girl in disguise. A soft felt hat shaded the delicate skin of his clean-shaven and open face, his gaze at once nervous and mocking. He was wearing a very tired black jacket, over a waistcoat overhung by the crumpled ends of a wide black cravat, which was wound about a false

collar of dubious whiteness. Equally questionable was the whiteness of his overlarge cuffs, which continuously slid over his hands and down his long tapered fingers. No cufflinks; one cuff was tied with a piece of red wool, the other with blue. It must be said that although Jarry cared little for his clothes, he was himself meticulously clean. Over his shoulders, a very short schoolboy's hooded cape. His somewhat short trousers, buttoned high above the ankle, revealed small women's boots with a low Louis XV heel, and walking with short strides, Jarry tip-tapped along the pavement. [...] He was charming and funny, and his slightly shrill and crystalline voice contributed to the impression of transvestism. Passersby stared back at him in an attempt to work out what sort of androgynous ephebe this was. And Demolder, with his customary grin, told him: You walk like a tart!

The lecture hall was the grand colonnaded gallery of the Musée Moderne, with its skylighted barrel ceiling, brocaded walls, elegant chairs, and potted aspidistras. The walls were hung with paintings by the recently deceased Toulouse-Lautrec, in the first retrospective of his work.[61]

For the lecture Jarry had prepared an uncontroversial entertainment, a good-natured introduction to the work of the Théâtre des Pantins with extracts from several of its productions, to be performed by him with puppets retrieved from Terrasse. However, the lecture was in the afternoon, and he found himself pleasantly relaxed by an extensive repast accompanied by plenty of wine, and confronted by a large audience of indubitable respectability. Seated ladies in hats and furs disappeared into the distance, besuited gentlemen too. "Ladies and gentlemen," he therefore began, in a quiet and moderated tone, followed by a brief pause. Then: "*Merdre!*," enunciated with such assertiveness, says Pierron, that had the windows been open it might have been audible on the plains of Waterloo. The word was not ubiquitous outside Paris, and its effect was immediate. Octave Maus recalled that "the word rolled like an avalanche through the vastness of the gallery and battered the ears of the horrified ladies, echoing back from the walls. There were cries, stifled laughter, desperate flights for the door." Jarry waited patiently for quiet to be reestablished, and then explained: "Such was the signal employed by the hero of my play to launch his attack upon King Wenceslas." Honor satisfied, Jarry returned to his prepared text:[62]

Marionettes are a quite separate race of little people with whom I have had the occasion to make a number of journeys. Far from being hazardous, such voyages of exploration require neither sola topee nor a large military escort. These small wooden beings dwell in Paris with my good friend Claude Terrasse, the well-known musician, and seem to take great pleasure in his music. Terrasse and I, for the past one or two years, have been the Gullivers of these Lilliputians. We govern them by means of strings, which suits them very well.[63]

Extracts from *Ubu Roi*, *Paphnutius*, and plays by Franc-Nohain, Grabbe, and Ranson were incorporated. The Word was forgotten, the audience laughed and applauded, Jarry had triumphed and afterward had to be extracted from a towering mob of elegant ladies who threatened to suffocate him with their perfume. Propelled into the square outside, he seized the arms of his rescuers, Eekhoud and Demolder, and suggested they go and take some Lambic, a beer particular to Brussels, because Demolder had never ceased telling him how good it was. Drinks were consumed until it was time to cross the city and join a photographers' association for dinner. Here Jarry astonished his hosts by methodically working his way through numerous generous courses, while sinking an endless succession of glasses of Lambic, each time smacking his lips in appreciation and muttering variants of "*Cornegidouille*, it's delicious, this Lambic!" At 2 a.m. they found themselves outside on the pavement in the freezing cold, an hour's walk from the hotel.

> But there is a special god for drinkers. An empty fiacre appeared from the direction of Laeken. We barred the path of this Rocinante. By holding on to each other we managed to clamber into the cab, I was on the tip-up seat facing Jarry and Demolder, the latter to the right of the other. [...]
>
> The half-asleep old nag resumed its trot. The vehicle, following the edge of the pavement, inclined steeply on the convex slope of the road. Losing his balance, the formidable Demolder fell heavily on his puny companion, almost suffocating him. I succeeded with considerable difficulty in shoving Demolder back into his corner. But with each new jolt my rotund friend came crashing down again on the unfortunate author of *Ubu* who, by way of objection, endlessly repeated a certain word, the same word, according to the orthography he had given it and which has remained in common usage. This exercise, the ceaseless separating of two excellent comrades, the one not at all keen to grapple with the other, ceased only when we reached the asphalt of the central boulevards. Demolder began to snore and Jarry, through the open window, counted the street lamps which transmitted to us their ludicrously tiny blue gas flames, which the ingenuous Jarry, then far from the land of reality, doubtless mistook for little blue flowers.
>
> In front of the hotel, disembarkation was rather laborious. Luckily, Jarry was not heavy; once I had descended from the cab, which Demolder refused to get out of, it was easy to carry his skinny frame in my arms, and to cross the vestibule of the hotel of assignations. I rang the bell. A grumbling youth opened up. I gave him the traveler, who had booked the first morning train to Paris, and who still retained enough lucidity to thank me:
>
> "It's very kind of you, *cornegidouille*, very kind of you, what you're doing. ... When you visit Essonnes, I shall repay you!"

This experience must have agreed with Jarry, since he soon undertook another lecture. It was an established means of earning a living: Tailhade, for one, was forever on lecture tours. Thus, a couple of weeks later, Jarry discoursed to the Salon des Indépendants on the subject of "Time in Art." As in Brussels, it was very much intended to entertain a general audience, Jarry's experience of journalism having opened to him such a possibility. He nevertheless expounded on various aspects of his theme that were close to his concerns—the idea of an authentic artwork being outside of time, or eternal, and the function of anachronism, which was here discussed in relation to Breughel's *Massacre of the Innocents* which Jarry had seen in the Brussels Fine Art Museum. Such ideas connect it to *Messalina*, and once again the notion of art as depicting duration in the Bergsonian sense is briefly noted. Despite the simple exposition, the only witness who left an account of it, Doctor Saltas, afterward confessed his bafflement to Jarry. According to the good doctor, Jarry's response was a little po-faced:[64]

> "That is exactly what I was seeking to do," he replied; "discussing comprehensible matters only weighs down the mind and distorts the memory, while absurdities exercise the spirit and make the memory work all the harder."

…

It is not a contradiction that the more settled Jarry became at Le Coudray, the more disjointed his biography becomes. This is simply because the events of his everyday life went largely unrecorded. Its continuity may be conjectured, however, as an existence by the river, at once bucolic and alcoholic. The parts that were recorded, on the exceptional occasions when his literary friends were present, constitute a few unrepresentative anecdotes. Rachilde's book describes one of these "set pieces." She called it "A Gala at Le Coudray."[65]

This event was by way of a return invitation to the subprefect of Corbeil, a novel-writing policeman who used the pseudonym Jean Madeline. Some months previously, this admirer of Jarry had invited him to dine with his family at the Subprefecture. On his arrival by bicycle, Jarry was mistaken for a miscreant by a "white-gloved flunkey" because of his bare feet. He had hung his only pair of shoes about his neck so as to preserve them from the mud of the towpath. Nevertheless, by the end of the dinner he and Madeline had become firm friends, and Jarry had charmed the ladies present.

Preparations for the return banquet were extensive. Jarry's stable suffered the rare attentions of a broom. An enormous *gigot* was acquired from the local butcher, and a fish for each plate from the Seine. What most concerned Rachilde, however, was that Jarry was determined to cook this meal himself, she being one of the few to have sampled his skills in the kitchen. The prospect aroused much local curiosity, and a crowd of bargees, poachers, scullery and laundry maids assembled to watch him poach the fish, and to proffer advice:

> "Is it a *court-bouillon* you're after?"
>
> "You need to add red wine and spices … ," said the landlady of the inn.
>
> "And herbs to season it!" added the lockkeeper's daughter.
>
> Mère Fontaine arrived, fists on her hips, followed by her favorite goat, a horned animal, black as the devil and just as stinking:
>
> "My little sugar ducky, my little green dog, so we're dressed up as a cook's boy are we?

For a *court-bouillon* you must add a good measure of old Marc brandy ... and a pinch of gunpowder and sage!"

"Not sage, rosemary!" exclaimed the mattress-maker from Pressoir-Prompt, and a very old shepherd from Moulin-Galant grumbled into his beard that he knew nothing better than a handful of gray mint thrown into the sauce at the last minute.

My daughter and I crept away on tiptoe from this scene of pure witchcraft.

"It doesn't much appeal to me!" whispered Gabrielle.

"What can we eat," I asked myself, "if not the fish? Not the *gigot,* since it will be full of garlic! I have an idea: we will make a dessert, a huge chocolate mousse."

The evening of the great day arrived, and an impressive procession wound down to Jarry's shack: the subprefect's gig, writers on bicycles and someone, Rachilde could not recall who, on a great white horse. She lists the guests, "some accompanied by their wives": Terrasse, Franc-Nohain, Fénéon, Quillard, Herold, Collière, Demolder, and his wife, "the beautiful Claire with her golden-copper hair," finally Vallette, Gabrielle, and herself.

The fish was not a success, the wine had turned during the cooking, and Rachilde refused the meat, but much wine was consumed and the company became exuberant. Eventually the mousse, turned out of a great round bowl, was brought in. "This," announced their host, "is a representation of one of the breasts of the giant Negress of the carnival in the Place du Trône. Ma-da-me Rachilde copied it from life using chocolate, vanilla, and milk from Mère Fontaine, who, as everyone hereabouts well knows, sleeps with her billy-goat. ..."

The remainder of Jarry's speech was drowned by applause, and soon the more determined among them moved on to the *auberge*. The evening's drinking came to an end around five in the morning when they were interrupted by the local constabulary investigating reports of a drowned man washed up at the Barrage. Rachilde informs us that the ladies present took this opportunity for a change of air and went to view the corpse.

The following month, Jarry's speculation in the *Revue Blanche* concerned the habits of this newly discovered species, the river corpse, those "dead-drunks of aquatism." A sequel lamented the fact that, in Seine-et-Oise, rescuing a drowning person was rewarded with a payment of 15 francs, whereas the remuneration for fishing out a corpse was 25 francs: "and since even the most honest of men may be inspired by the proverb 'little fish become bigger fish,' this may well give rise to a very understandable temptation: that of throwing the former back into the water like fry, until their value has increased."[66]

...

The Revue Blanche published Jarry's novel *The Supermale* early in May 1902. Apparently his most conventional—and therefore most accessible—novel, it has been his most oft-reprinted work after *Ubu Roi*. Jarry subtitled it a "modern novel," and set it in 1920 (when its characters continue to discuss the Dreyfus case). Despite being set in the future it was not really science fiction, nor even an "anticipatory" novel, to use the French term, although it does bear comparison with Wells's fiction. Whereas Wells used the trappings of science fiction to comment on the social problems of the present (*The Time Machine* was essentially a critique of the class system), Jarry used these conventions to explore eternal themes of love and death (and record-breaking). However, its early chapters more closely resemble an entirely different genre of novel, that of bourgeois manners. The "polished insignificance of society conversation" is perfectly imitated, and then directed down distinctly unsettling paths. These parts of *The Supermale* in fact bear comparison with the comedies of Wilde; the opening sentence of the novel takes the form of a Wildean paradox: "The act of love is of no importance, since it may be performed indefinitely."[67]

Despite being a companion piece to *Messalina*, in which the courtship of love and death is transposed from past to future, it is executed in a tone new for Jarry: urbane, sophisticated, the prose pared away and with none of the baroque mathematics of his previous book. In *The Supermale* Jarry appropriates all the techniques of the realist novel, in particular that of the omniscient narrator, but Jarry's narrator is too much Jarry himself, and cannot resist undermining the conventions of realism by typically idiosyncratic devices, constantly switching emotional tones, now facetious, now sincere, and repeatedly inserting citations from his favorite authors (including himself) at the most inappropriate moments. The subjectivizing effect is similar to Lautréamont's undermining of Romanticism, but it is more slyly sprung. What is usually intended as a transparent mode of writing is constantly occluded by its obvious artifice, and one effect of this diverting game with the reader is to veil the fact that the incredible narrative is literally that: barely credible.

Jarry later told Apollinaire that the Catholic poet Francis Jammes, no doubt at one of Rachilde's Tuesdays, reproached him for the book because it "reeked of the city-dweller, of someone who needed to escape Paris to restore him to health and morality. 'What would he say,' observed Jarry, 'if he knew that I spent most of the year on the banks of a river fishing every day?'"[68]

The part played by cycling in the book's narrative has been noted in chapter 11. The description of the five-man bicycle race against a railway locomotive, from Paris to Paris via Siberia, was one of Jarry's greatest prose achievements and showed him in perfect control of his medium. He seemed on the verge of writing works that might embody his "polyhedra of ideas" while attaining a wider readership, yet this was to be his last finished work of any substance.

Despite its achievements, the sexual content of the novel did not go down well with reviewers, even the one for the *Revue Blanche* (which perhaps explains why, unlike *Messalina*, *The Supermale* was not first serialized in the magazine). Rachilde in the *Mercure* also adopted a prudish tone. She praised aspects of the book, but concluded with a wagging finger:

> But now he should gather a sprig of morality as a nosegay in this horrible garden whose
> blossoms consist only of scorching garlands of meshing gears, white-hot spikes of electricity,
> and a host of numbers as barbed as instruments of torture; but, rather than waste my time

searching here for this humble little flower I prefer to end with the ingenuous words of an honest woman of the last century, Princess Metternich. When a great explorer, returning from the Indies, showed her a bronze phallus of quite inappropriate proportions, she remarked, "Oh! What a nice trinket for the mantel!" We should give credit to the great explorers! Poets, and Alfred Jarry is one, are the great explorers of the impossible but what would be even more surprising would be for them to give an account of the possible; that is something we would find more difficult to believe in, since the truth is only rarely credible.

The Supermale, therefore, resembles just another nice little trinket, a poet's plaything.[69]

Over the past year and a half, Jarry's "Speculations" had become an important part of the *Revue Blanche*, and had delighted both its readers and its editors. Fénéon and Jarry became close over the months of this collaboration, and although Jarry's letters to him mostly concern his contributions, sent or delivered at the last minute, many refer in passing to evenings spent with Fénéon and his family, and with the painter and anarchist Paul Signac, who recorded in his diary a number of dinners with Jarry at Fénéon's flat in Montmartre.[70]

Thus the summer months appear to have passed uneventfully, but behind the scenes at the Revue Blanche its problems were becoming ever more grave. Alexandre Natanson, the main administrator, was suffering from some sort of nervous illness, Thadée was afflicted with financial problems, and Misia had, to all intents and purposes, deserted him, although she dragged the process out by not seeking a divorce until a year later. In October 1902, Thadée sent a letter to all those connected with the publishing house, announcing that due to his own ill health, it must close, and that Eugène Fasquelle had agreed to take over part of its list. Jarry and Fénéon realized that the *Revue* itself must surely follow.[71]

Jarry cast around for other outlets for his journalism, and somehow selected a wholly inappropriate periodical, *La Renaissance latine*, edited by Jean-Auguste-Gustave Binet. This confusing character, known as Binet-Valmer, was the author of novels in praise of homosexuality, and an extreme political reactionary who later founded an association for nationalist ex-soldiers. A letter from him to Jarry of October 1902 confirms his acceptance of Jarry's financial terms for his contributions. Two articles appeared in November and December under the rubric "The Journal of Alfred Jarry," which means his name was now a selling point in itself. However, his career at *La Renaissance latine* was short-lived. A very cantankerous group of French patriots was gathered around this magazine, and they were unlikely to be sympathetic to Jarry's brand of mocking irreverence. His third article supposedly revealed a plagiarism of Kipling by Georges d'Esparbès. Despite being tongue-in-cheek it aroused the anger of the magazine's backer, Prince Michel Constantin Bibesco Bassaraba de Brancovan. Rash words appear to have been exchanged in Binet-Valmer's office, because in a letter to Fénéon of January 6, 1903, Jarry wondered whether seconds might be dispatched to call on him. This was dangerous territory. The Bibesco-Brancovans were powerful aristocrats, and keen swordsmen.[72]

In the meantime Jarry offered the offending text to Karl Boès, the editor of *La Plume*, where it was published in January. Boès appeared willing to give Jarry a regular column, and Jarry's resources must already have been severely stretched for him to consider endangering such a promising relationship by touching its editor for an advance. Nevertheless he did just that, although he leavened it with the Ubuesque:

31 January [1903]

Dear Monsieur Boès,

I hereby submit to you an extraordinarily injudicious request, but one which your previous kindness has to some extent encouraged. I had promised myself not to squeeze *La Plume* before the fateful period of three months had come to pass, but the adventure with that rebel prince and unworthy slave of ours Bibescubum, also known as Brancovan, has caused a kind of earthquake in the phynances of the King of Poland. I could have greedily applied for the money due according to the treaty agreed with these persons, but then I would have lost the pleasure of inviting them to face an avenging blade. In a word, would it be reckless, immoral and excessive to implore from *La Plume* a capital amounting to approximately twenty francs in coin of legal tender, the which is necessary for us to meet the conditions of payment in respect of the mirific residence whose splendors and exorbitant cost I have previously expounded upon?

I will pass by *La Plume* on Monday morning, but it goes without saying that if this lust for cash happens to be, by some calamity, inappropriate, then you should have no scruples in pointing this out. Such an arrangement will ensure the tranquility conducive to the blossoming of our complete works … and then this has only happened this month because of Brancovan, and it is not a habit of ours.

I will certainly bring my copy on Monday so as to avoid any delays, as you requested.

Sincerely yours.
Alfred Jarry
7 rue Cassette[73]

It must have been in relation to this affair with Brancovan that Jarry encountered Marcel and Jacques Boulenger, members of the circle around the poet Anna de Noailles, the Prince's sister. These two brothers, authors of works celebrating the glory of the French aristocracy, were fanatical duelists, Marcel in particular. *The Pall Mall Gazette* for June 7, 1899 reported his advocacy, in practice sessions, of swords in which the point protruded beyond the button, so the flesh wound caused by first contact on the bare chest was unmistakable. Jarry was informed that they were to call upon him regarding a matter of honor. Something must be done, and Jarry consulted Fénéon, who agreed to represent him at the meeting and to devise a means of avoiding the duel.

At twelve o'clock on the day appointed, they awaited their visitors at the Chasublery. The brothers were well known for their formal elegance, and so it was that two frock-coated aristocrats in top hats and cream kid gloves became acquainted with the splendors of Jarry's mirific residence. Having hauled themselves up the narrow stairway, they duly made their appearance. Clutching their hats, they seemed inexplicably discomfited, and not only by a conversation conducted in a room in which they could not even stand up. Fénéon, polite and authoritative, explained to them a technicality that ruled the proposed contest out of the question: Jarry's opponent could be considered a professional duelist. The brothers appeared eager to leave, and readily granted the validity of Fénéon's objection. Their impatience may have been due to the fact that Jarry had previously smeared the staircase handrails with excrement.[74]

...

12.16
Félix Vallotton, Marcel Boulenger, 1899.

For Jarry, 1903 began with a bout of influenza. He sent a New Year's greeting to Claudius-Jacquet: "My affectionate good wishes," and he must then have turned his attention to his worsening financial situation. When Binet-Valmer had agreed to publish Jarry's speculative essays it was on condition that he was not publishing similar pieces elsewhere, and so Fénéon had offered Jarry something different at the *Revue Blanche*: the theater reviews. This was a curious decision given that Jarry lived outside of the capital for much of the time. His first column covered six plays in six different theaters, but devoted a significant part of it to a play by Karl Rosenval, the pseudonym of Berthe Danville, his collaborator on *Leda*. He explained in a postscript to a letter to Fénéon: "P.S. I have devoted so much space to *Les Nèfles* because: 1. It was the only one of the plays I went to see; 2. The author is a friend of mine and anyway the play is really amusing." It is not known whether this was to be his habitual methodology during the few months he wrote this column.[75]

The severance of Jarry's connection with *La Renaissance latine* also left him free to publish in *La Plume*, where Karl Boès gave him a regular column. Even so, his daily existence was becoming difficult. Thadée remembered him looking "funereal," perhaps because the situation at the *Revue Blanche* appeared terminal, and it had assumed a role in Jarry's life which was not simply financial. Although it did not have a regular salon like the Mercure, he was always welcome at its offices. They were a permanent literary meeting place, as Lucie Delarue-Mardrus, wife of the translator of the *Arabian Nights*, recalled. "We would often go to the Revue Blanche," she wrote, before describing its staff, the Natanson brothers and Fénéon, and[76]

> … one was also likely to come across Fagus, with his vaguely medieval profile, the painter Félix Vallotton and his half-ironic smile, Alfred Jarry, tiny, his poorly shaven face powdered and covered with spots beneath his long lank hair parted exactly in the middle. Short of linen, he was always dressed in grimy black clothes with espadrilles on his feet for preference. His staccato speech and his sorcerer's gaze frightened me a little, especially his sudden smile that reached from ear to ear and was then instantly extinguished as if with a click, and which never seemed to affect his eyes. Mirbeau was always there, talking, standing between two open doors, always on the verge of leaving but never actually going anywhere.[77]

The return of Jarry's skin problems was probably a symptom of his worsening situation. In February the *Revue Blanche* contained two poems by him, along with his theater reviews. Most unusually, the poems found approval with Rachilde:

> Since there are no more Tuesdays, I am not able to tell you what I think of your poems in the *Revue Blanche*, so I have to write instead. (All old ladies have foibles—scepters, specters, or quivering madness—mine is literature until the day I become young again, in other words until eternity.) […] So your "Madrigal" is something as wonderfully beautiful as a sonnet by Baudelaire, with the essential difference that it does not resemble anything except a work by Jarry. If you were to make a volume of verse like this […] Sire UBU, such a volume would represent how many liters of alcohol—absolute proof—and how many easy girls?[78]

The lack of Tuesdays is explained by the Mercure having moved from its cramped premises in the rue de l'Échaudé to a more elegant building near the Senate at 26, rue de Condé. Rachilde refers here to Jarry's patronage of "easy girls," which means exactly what one assumes it to mean. One of these poems, "Madrigal," is also reminiscent of certain passages in *The Supermale* already noted. It was a love poem addressed to an unnamed, or universal, woman.[79]

My girl—my, since you're part of everyone
Though no relationship has been so deep,
Let's draw the curtains—do your best to sleep:
We're home at last—our lives are almost done.

How high it is, this ending our world knows,
And all that's absolute's no more denied.
It's fine to be the last one to decide
Since Messalina's day has reached its close.

Alone you find yourself with ears and eyes.
A frequent fall forgets the way to crash.
Earth's distant rumblings float like dusty ash
Of inky incense filtered through dark skies.

As gaping, gobbling sounds from each carp's jaw
    In Fontainebleau this
    Voice is bruised by your
    Subaquatic kiss.

How may a double fate re-seal things torn?
As long as I stand by to let you pass
A virgin still, you still were not yet born
Like past times drowned behind a mirror's glass.

The mud has barely kissed the slippered tip
Of your infinitesimal small shoe,
And tasting evil through and through
Brought this purity to your pale lip.[80]

The final issue of the *Revue Blanche*, of April 15, 1903, included Jarry's poem about the "chaînier" of Le Coudray. The end of the review meant the end of Jarry's regular source of income.

    The penultimate issue of April 1 had included a self-standing extract from *La Dragonne*, Jarry's novel in progress. This text, "The Battle of Morsang" (the name of a village situated across the river from Le Coudray), describes its protagonist arranging the self-destruction of an army by inveigling it into a circular engagement at night so that it fires upon itself. In this text Jarry returned to a pseudo-autobiographical form, the hero's surname being Sacqueville, the supposed noble ancestor on Jarry's maternal side. He was further identifiable to anyone familiar with Jarry by his shoes: espadrilles so frayed they resembled "camel's feet." After *Messalina* and *The Supermale*, this text shows a distinct falling-off; the writing style is ill-disciplined and ill-formed, and—even more unusual for Jarry—it appears ill-considered, almost a self-parody, with none of the intimations of different degrees of meaning or intention that so distinguish most of his prose. The concision of his last two novels is absent too, and instead it resembles more a sprawling vehicle for simple self-aggrandizement, as if the boastful tendencies that Jarry normally suppressed with irony or self-deprecation were here erupting unhindered. That such traits should coincide with his worsening circumstances can be no accident. Even so, Fasquelle was interested enough to offer an advance for the completed novel. In retrospect, however, these problems can be seen to become ever more prominent in the remainder of this novel, which gradually became as bogged down in rewrites as was *Pantagruel*.[81]

...

On the evening of March 21, 1903, Jarry's prowess with marionettes was once again called upon when he was asked to perform Paul Ranson's *Abbé Prout* at the home of André Fontainas. He was thrown a financial lifeline the same day, with the launch of a new satirical magazine, *Le Canard sauvage*. Its editor was his old co-puppeteer Franc-Nohain, who would seek regular contributions from Jarry. Thus, for the moment, the disappearance of the *Revue Blanche* was cushioned by new outlets for his journalism, although it is unlikely that they paid as well as had the Natansons. *Le Canard sauvage* was belligerently libertarian, and Jarry was therefore free to aim at whatever establishment targets he cared to puncture. One of his most famous texts, "The Passion Considered as an Uphill Bicycle Race," appeared just in time for Easter. One would imagine that only exceedingly fervent cyclists could consider this as anything but a mockery of Christianity in particular, and religion in general, although one of Jarry's biographers thought "it might be construed as evidence of a hidden attachment to Christianity." *Le Canard sauvage* was slightly more expensive than its rivals; its visual aspect was carefully considered: well-known artists were employed as illustrators, and it was printed on fine paper. Among the artist contributors was Hermann-Paul, so this may be when he and Jarry met. He left a remarkable portrait of Jarry which probably dates from a year or so later.[82]

    Le Canard sauvage was a success and its proprietor launched a sister publication, *L'Œil*, which had a lower cover price and was aimed at a wider audience, and to which Jarry also contributed on a regular basis. In the six months between April and August, he produced more than fifty separate texts for these reviews; and his collaboration with *La Plume* had benefits that were not simply financial. It was through their famous soirées that Jarry came into contact with a new generation of authors, and, especially, with Guillaume Apollinaire.

...

Apollinaire's role as the great pioneer of modernist poetry is well known, but he was also the chronicler of the movement as a whole, and one of its most jovial social impresarios. His art criticism is now seen as rather eccentric, but it played a vital role when it first appeared, and his most important collection of poems, *Alcools* (1913, and a very Jarryesque title), was immediately recognized as the beginning of something entirely new, entirely of the moment, and of the future too. His close friend Picasso had accomplished the same task in painting, with his *Les Demoiselles d'Avignon* of 1907, and around these two revolved a group of friends who were to dominate the Parisian avant-garde until the First World War.

This all lay in the future, since according to his diary, Apollinaire first met Jarry on April 18, 1903. He left an appealing account of this encounter, and although he was often more interested in a good story than in strict adherence to facts, on this occasion his account appears fairly accurate: [83]

The first time I saw Alfred Jarry was at one of the evenings organized by *La Plume*, the second series, which they say was not as good as the first. The Café du Soleil had changed its name and was now called the Café du Départ. Such a melancholic title no doubt helped to bring gatherings to a rapid close and possibly even hinted at the demise of *La Plume*. Their invitation to the voyage sent us all off quickly in different directions! All the same we did have several delightful evenings in the basement at the Place Saint-Michel, and a few friendships were struck up there.

Alfred Jarry, on the evening in question, seemed to me the personification of a river, a rippling river without a beard, clad in the damp garments of a man recently drowned. His small downward-curving moustache, his frock-coat with symmetrically flapping tails, his floppy shirt, and his cycling pumps—the whole ensemble had something limp or shapeless about it, something sponge-like; the demi-god was still damp since it seemed that only a few hours previously he had leapt out of the current of his river-bed, soaking wet.

Drinking stout cemented our friendship. He reeled off some verses with metallic rhymes such as *-orde* and *-arde*. Then, after listening to a new song by Cazals, we left during a frenetic cakewalk danced by the combined efforts of René Puaux, Charles Doury, Robert Scheffer, and two women whose flowing hair became looser and looser.

We spent the best part of the night walking up and down the boulevard Saint-Germain and had a lengthy conversation about heraldry, heresy, and versification. He told me about the bargees among whom he lived for a large part of the year, and the puppets he had used to perform *Ubu* the very first time. Alfred Jarry's voice was sharply articulated, very rapid, low and often emphatic. He would suddenly stop speaking in order to grin, and then immediately become serious again. His forehead was in perpetual movement—but horizontally and not vertically, as is usually the case. About four in the morning a man came up to us and asked if we could tell him the way to Plaisance. Jarry immediately pulled out a revolver, ordered the man to take six paces back, and only then indicated the direction [with his gun]. We eventually left each other and he returned to his Grand Chasublery in the rue Cassette, asking me to go and visit him there.[84]

The Café du Départ is still situated on the first corner of the boulevard Saint-Michel on the left bank of the Seine, and the soirées in its basement, run by *La Plume* for invited guests, were indeed legendary. As Apollinaire mentions, the second series was not quite so famous as its predecessors, presided over by the likes of Verlaine, but these evenings provided an important opportunity for the new generation of poets to meet their forebears. The first soirée was on April 18, 1903; Apollinaire read at the second, on April 25. On this occasion he, and perhaps therefore Jarry, met André Salmon, also reading his poetry that evening, and Jean Mollet, a delightful character whose chief pleasure was collecting interesting personalities and introducing them to one another. He would famously arrange the meeting of Apollinaire and Picasso the following October.[85]

Jarry and Apollinaire quickly became close friends and drinking partners; they discovered numerous shared interests: not only heraldry and versification, but billiards, and practical jokes. Apollinaire was surely delighted that Jarry was able to recite from memory some lines of his: a poem that had appeared in the *Mercure* a whole two years earlier. On May 16, 1903, Boès invited Père Ubu to take the chair at the soirée. He presided first over the preliminary banquet at the Restaurant du Palais—the diners included Boès, Cazals, Dumur, Jean Grave, Charles-Louis Philippe, and Salmon—and then over the soirée itself. Salmon recalled that Jarry disguised his lack of a shirt with a piece of purple satin about his neck, secured with a safety pin, and dropped the role of Ubu only when he came to read his own poems during the course of the evening. Later, according to Richardson's biography of Picasso, Apollinaire and Jarry spent many of these evenings puncturing the pretensions of the more earnest Symbolists: they foisted spoof guests on the meetings, and Apollinaire once turned up in a pastiche of bohemian rags so extreme he resembled a tramp.[86]

One of Apollinaire's, and soon Jarry's, favorite watering holes was Austin's (also known as Fox's) English Bar on the corner of the Place de Budapest and the rue d'Amsterdam, a narrow inclined street beside the Gare Saint-Lazare. (Austin's Hotel is still there, but the bar is no longer English.) Here they shared another passion: beer, more specifically stout, and Bass's Pale Ale. It was to this bar that Mollet brought the newly discovered Picasso, and he too became a regular. Another oft-frequented café was the Rocher, on the Place de l'Odéon, where they could indulge in Jarry's latest passion for billiards. In July, a letter from Apollinaire informs a friend that he spent most of his evenings playing billiards with Paul Fort, Boès, and Jarry, who had therefore broken his habit of spending the summers in Le Coudray.[87]

The painter Michel Georges-Michel, twenty at the time, left memoirs of evenings on the boulevard Saint-Michel, some certainly dating from the previous year, others following the soirées at the Départ. After ascending the boulevard, calling in at many of the "zincs" along the way, the company would end up around two in the morning at a bar on the rue Saint-Jacques called the Académie, on account of its forty barrels of wine on tap, the same number as the Immortals of the Académie Française. Should further drinking be favored, and following an invitation from Jarry to the Chasublery, they would purchase bottles of red and climb the staircase to his room.

Here Jarry performed his party trick, a tour of the premises by bicycle, around his guests sitting in a circle on the floor. A candle thrust in a bottle in the center cast their shadows on the walls. The bottles, ranged about the candle, were seized by a lasso and passed around, glasses being dispensed with. Afterward, if thirst were still unquenched, the empty bottles were carried to Montmartre, where they could be exchanged for a final small glass of wine. Among the regular celebrants, Georges-Michel lists Apollinaire, Cazals, Cremnitz, and Mollet.[88]

The "incomparable disorder" of Jarry's apartment around this time was described by Salmon, who visited him in daylight shortly after their first encounter. He relates that there was an ordinary wooden table, stained with ink and piled high with manuscripts, its only decoration being two porcelain owls. The window was broken and mended with newspaper fixed over the hole. Toward the back of the room was Jarry's substitute for a wardrobe: a cheap suitcase from which spilled shirts of doubtful cleanliness, handkerchiefs, slippers, a ball of string, and a tin whistle. The most prominent feature, however, was Jarry's library. Against one wall a pyramid of books, magazines, newspapers, and bailiffs' summons was stacked up to the ceiling, in no discernible order whatsoever. Salmon noticed in the chaos copies of the *Mercure* and *L'Ymagier*, and was surprised to see copies of the Catholic paper *La Croix* (a source for Jarry's "Speculations"). There were books on philosophy, mathematics, theosophy, episodes of the serial about Colonel Ronchonot, a pastiche of military life, and catalogs from Le Barc de Boutteville. The tour concluded with Rousseau's portrait:[89]

> Whereupon, Jarry asked me to give my considered opinion on the magnificent portrait of him, done from life, a masterpiece by Henri Rousseau. I could see nothing apart from a background of drapery, in the manner of Stevens but executed with touching naïveté and, on a perch, the much-esteemed owl which, I repeat, was made of porcelain. Of Jarry one could only distinguish a silhouette, since the middle of the canvas had been cut out, leaving only a void. Père Ubu did not consent to confess that he had mutilated the picture of Rousseau because the presence of his own image got on his nerves. He preferred to recount that, after it had been holed by some clumsy oaf's umbrella, he had carefully cut it out, rolled it up and placed it in the "single and central drawer of our Colbert bureau in white wood."

Jarry's menagerie. Salmon insists, contrary to Georges-Michel and others, that there were no live owls, only porcelain ones, but this is easily explained. The live owl—or owls, according to Moreno—could come and go as they wished. Jarry must have brought one with him when he moved, and released it after it had become accustomed to his new home. The gardens of Val-de-Grâce were not far away. Vollard visited Jarry too, and recalled not only a live owl, but also two cats—a somewhat unlikely combination, but Lebois even tells us the (single) cat's name: Tatou, which, being French for "armadillo," has a Jarryesque anti-logic.[90]

...

Mollet and Apollinaire had a favorite restaurant, Au Père Jean in the rue de Seine. Not only was it remarkably cheap, but its *patron* was generous to a fault when it came to credit. At the end of their meal favored customers wrote out their own bill on a piece of paper and signed it, whereupon it joined a pile of others in the *patron*'s pocket. Should the customer wish at some future moment to exchange this for cash, he would not object. Such an establishment was bound to prove attractive to Jarry, and his appearances there were awaited with some anticipation. In fact, according to Mollet, they became "an important event," partly, he says, because Jarry took great pleasure in inventing new ways of irritating the customers, and of surprising its abnormally phlegmatic owner. It was here that Jarry is supposed to have acquired the habit of eating his meals in reverse order (but he probably did so only once). Thus, to the pleasing bewilderment of the staff, Jarry ordered a succession of items, each separated by a glass of the best absinthe: a cognac, a cup of coffee, a little gruyère, a fruit salad, half a roast chicken, some macaroni, an *entre-côte*, a few radishes, and finally a portion of vegetable soup. "Young man, you will give yourself a bellyache." This observation of Père Jean's must be refuted. Jarry called for some red ink in a glass, into which he dipped sugar cubes before consuming them at leisure. On another occasion he insisted on a "Pernod aux haricots," green beans immersed in absinthe, a beverage contrived simply to confuse the waitress, Marie.[91]

A regular group was in formation at Père Jean's, of which Jarry was a part, although this time he was the oldest, if only by some seven or eight years. Its other members included Salmon, Mollet, the poet Nicolas Deniker, whose search for Mallarméan perfection reduced his life's work to almost no verse whatsoever, the Norwegian author Arne Hammer, the Spanish sculptor Manolo, and the painters Henri Fricks and Edmond-Marie Poullain. Apollinaire soon had the idea of founding a new magazine. The first number of *Le Festin d'Ésope* appeared in November 1903. The second contained an abbreviated version of Jarry's recently completed play *L'Objet aimé*, which falls within the general scheme of those he had written for Terrasse. It is perhaps surprising that Apollinaire was not offered any of Jarry's unpublished manuscripts, *Faustroll* or *Ubu cocu*, during the periodical's nine-month run.[92]

...

As Jarry's journalism began to dry up, he had, predictably, returned his attention to writing libretti for Terrasse. It was nearly two years since they had corresponded, but on July 21, 1903, a letter from Jarry contained the following news: "The Pope has died, as I suppose you know. On the off-chance that you are greatly affected, Demolder and I have sacrificed some of our leisure time between two games of *boules* to lucubrate for you upon the new Pope. See if it is worthy of your music." This was the first of several collaborations between Jarry and Demolder, who had a Parisian *pied à terre*, so this does not necessarily mean that Jarry had returned to Le Coudray. The libretto was called *Le Moutardier du Pape*, literally *The Pope's Mustard-Maker*, but also an idiomatic phrase meaning someone who thinks rather too highly of himself. It was a far from reverent treatment of the legend of Pope Joan, and the "lucubration" concerns the supposed test for new Popes, who were required to have their genital equipment checked out while seated upon a "chaise percée," so that the crowning of a second female Pope might be avoided. Terrasse's immediate reservation was that it would attract the attention of the censors, as had a previous project of his with Franc-Nohain, *Au Temps des croisades*. He did not write a score for it.[93]

By mid-August 1903, fishing had recalled Jarry and his fellow enthusiasts to Le Coudray; on the 17th he, Rachilde, and Vallette dined at La Demi-Lune. The outlets for Jarry's journalism had begun to disappear. One by one, periodicals closed. The writing of *Le Moutardier* had coincided with the expiry of the first, that of *L'Œil*, in early July. *Le Canard sauvage* closed in October, and *La Plume* would follow in January of 1904. Thus, commencing with the *Revue Blanche*, in a period of less than a year all the important periodicals sympathetic to the Symbolist/anarchist axis had failed, with the exception of the only one he could not work for, edited by two of his closest friends: the *Mercure de France*. This collapse of the more important literary reviews of the 1890s was in fact a symptom of a profound change that was taking place in the literary world. Symbolism (and Naturalism) were in the process of being superseded by new forms of literature, both avant-garde and classical. These trends would be represented in the most famous French literary review of the twentieth century, the *Nouvelle Revue Française*, to be founded by Gide and his friends in 1908. In the midst of this slaughter, Jarry's thirtieth birthday occurred on September 8, 1903, marked we know not how.[94]

The late summer months of 1903 were apparently passed in the company principally of Demolder, whose own incipient alcoholism was unlikely to encourage sobriety. Yet he and Jarry turned out a series of different libretti for Terrasse, who made several visits to La Demi-Lune to discuss the music for these pieces. Already, in July, Terrasse had suggested Jarry come and stay at his house in the hilly countryside of Le Grand-Lemps at the foot of the French Alps near Grenoble, since Jarry's letter of July 21 to him had speculated: "perhaps I'll come in September, to lengthen my chain in this countryside which you tell me is so hunchbacked." At summer's end there seemed no reason not to go. Jarry had no prospects, and his options were running out. What was left? Only *Pantagruel*. Jarry and Terrasse hoped that a final effort undertaken far from temptation might finally bring it to completion. It is likely too that Terrasse thought of this as a rescue mission, that exposure to a more conventional existence might perhaps tempt Jarry to moderate his ways.[95]

Just before leaving, Jarry wrote an affectionate letter to Apollinaire, apologizing for not recently being in touch, but noting that when two authors are in true sympathy this is not really such a necessity. He thanked him for asking for a contribution to *Le Festin*, and conveyed news of a "heavenly" new discovery: bar billiards. This is a form of billiards in which the pockets consist of holes situated in the center of the table and protected by small skittles; the player loses all or a part of his score if they are knocked over. The name comes from the bar that drops after a set period of time and prevents potted balls being returned to the players. They need very little space, being played from only one end of the table.[96]

· · ·

At Le Grand-Lemps, Terrasse lived in an enormous house, Le Clos, which was actually the family home of the Bonnards, built by the grandfather of Pierre and Andrée (Terrasse's wife), who had spent their childhood there. It was now the home of their brother Charles Bonnard. Terrasse was a reluctant metropolitan; he and his wife and their five children spent as much of their time here in the country as they could, including the whole of the summer. The grounds were vast, with five ornamental ponds, trees, dogs and cats. The days passed amid the chaotic affability of an extended and prosperous family. Bonnard depicted this entourage in 1900 and the title of his painting, *A Bourgeois Afternoon, or the Terrasse Family*, conveys much of the atmosphere of Jarry's destination. He traveled there by train with his bicycle in early November, intending, so it seems, to stay only briefly. A letter to Rachilde of November 28 laments that he will be unable to attend the first of the Tuesdays in the Mercure's new premises. *Pantagruel* was already taking longer than envisaged, but initially Terrasse was in no hurry, in the belief that Jarry was better off where he was. Jarry too appeared to take to this family life for a while. The memoir by Terrasse's son cited in chapter 10 underlined Jarry's popularity with the children, and he wrote some simple verses for them to recite upon their mother's birthday on November 30.[97]

But in Le Grand-Lemps Jarry soon discovered a second life away from the wholesome pleasures of home and hearth. Terrasse had introduced him to a café in the town, the Café Brosse, and here he found another association of drinkers well worthy of study and subversion. Jarry's dealings with the good people of Le Grand-Lemps reveal much about his ability to charm those with quite different interests from his own, and unlike the bargees of Le Coudray, on this occasion there is a written account of it. In April 1904 Franc-Nohain joined them for a brief stay. Much to his amazement, he discovered that in only a few months a portion of the population of this small town had enthusiastically adopted Ubuistic mannerisms. Franc-Nohain's memoir celebrated the fact that Jarry had so "transformed, transfigured and subjugated" those he had come across that

> … his passage had profoundly marked this locale, especially this café, to the point of so altering the local vocabulary that, some four hundred miles from Paris, at the foot of the Dauphiné Alps, the justice of the peace may consider dispatching the guilty with: "Down the trap!" or "In my pocket!" The customs officer refers to his "phynance-hook," and the doctor declares himself willing to perform the "twisting of the nose, pulling of the hair, and penetration of the nearoles with the little splinters of wood, not to mention opening of the swim-bladder followed by total decapitation"; and that now there is none among the local notables who do not fail to swear "By my green candle!" or to exclaim "*Cornegidouille*" on all sorts of special occasions.[98]

The unchanging clientele of the Café Brosse was indeed comprised of clerks, local government officials, and other worthies. According to Jarry's account of them, in the early chapters of *La Dragonne*, they occupied themselves with an "eternal" game of bezique, or with bar billiards, and emptied their glasses to the accompaniment of witticisms whose effect depended on familiarity

692. Le GRAND LEMPS (Isère). — Grande Rue

12.17
The Café Brosse and its habitués, a postcard
exactly contemporary with Jarry's stay in
Le Grand-Lemps.

and repetition rather than on actual humor. It is a picture of bored and respectable insobriety that is easy to imagine. Jarry's first appearance, according to Franc-Nohain, was the cause of some astonishment, even though the locals were accustomed to bohemian types staying at the Bonnards'. With Terrasse's face bobbing up behind him, Jarry entered the room shrouded in his bargee's green waterproof cape, with only his feet visible, encased in hobnailed boots: he had come prepared for winter in the mountains. Soon, however,

> the notables of the Café Brosse, the magistrate, the doctor, the bailiff, found themselves put at their ease by the extraordinary flexibility with which Jarry adapted to their conversations, their concerns, their thoughts. They were charmed by his courtesy, so attentive and refined … Careful now! … They do not realize that Jarry appears to have such similar concerns as they do only so they may come to believe that he actually is one of them, that he only adapts himself so perfectly to their language in order to impose one of his own. […]

> Ah! Too late, the games of bezique or bar billiards were soon embellished with curious expressions which the bailiff, the magistrate, the doctor, and other lords of lesser rank, repeated imperturbably, mechanically, as if dominated by a mysterious and despotic influence. Rituals were established, and so a player would not interrupt his partner without gravely inclining his head and employing this formula which, indeed, implied neither pleasantry, nor accusation:

> *"Monsieur et vénéré ami, et bougre d âne! …"*

> Only the first four words were spoken it's true, but be it the doctor addressing the justice of the peace, or the justice of the peace the bailiff, the *bougre d'âne* was always well understood. …

> Gradually, the Café Brosse found itself annexed to the Principality of Podolia, the Grand Duchy of Posen, the Duchy of Courland, the Counties of Vitepsk and Sandomir, the Palatinate of Polock, the Margravate of Thorn, and thus to figure, in fact, on the "list of our properties" of King Ubu, Margrave of Thorn and of the Café Brosse.

> Alfred Jarry now exercised undisputed dominion …[99]

Jarry, in his later correspondence with Terrasse, frequently addressed him as *Cher et Vénéré Ami et B. d'Â.* The beginning of the phrase is conventionally formal: Dear and Revered Friend. The *B. d'Â*, however, stands for *bougre d'âne*, and it is a little harder to find an English equivalent for this because of the wealth of possibilities. *Âne* means donkey, and *bougre* means "good chap, old pal," but its earlier meaning, implied here by the "of donkey," was "bugger." Even so *bougre d'âne* is something of a stock phrase; when spoken with affection it might mean something like "daft bugger," or with more hostile intent "utter twat." Such were the niceties of what had become the habitual greeting between the upright citizens of Le Grand-Lemps.[100]

...

In December 1903, the extract from *L'Objet aimé* appeared in *Le Festin*, and Demolder submitted one of their libretti to a theater director with whom he was friendly in Brussels. It was turned down. Jarry ended 1903 as he had begun it, with a brief line to Claudius-Jacquet: "Affectionate memories from Alfred Jarry," and with an optimistic card to Rachilde, which records his eagerness to return to Le Coudray: "Père Ubu will be back next year, which is happily only a matter of days away. Happy New Year!" His imminent return must have meant *Pantagruel* was considered nearly finished at last.[101]

Nothing was that simple, however, where *Pantagruel* was concerned. Jarry and Terrasse had been working on an entirely new adaptation. Previously Jarry had attempted to represent the whole of it; this new version was restricted to the first and last books, and whereas the previous efforts were only partly in verse, and were intended as a drama with musical interludes, this was to be a full-scale libretto, written to be "sung through." Presumably Jarry had begun work before coming to Le Grand-Lemps; but even so, it was a large task, and after a few weeks Terrasse began to despair at the slowness of progress. Jarry had made himself rather too much at home, according to a despondent letter from Terrasse to Armory. This must have been toward the end of Jarry's stay, when the closure of *La Plume* signaled the end of his income, and perhaps disinclined him from too rapidly finishing the task. Instead he made trips to Lyon and Grenoble, simply sightseeing so far as one can gather, although while on a trip to La Côte-Saint-André Jarry made a rare addition to his wardrobe, which he described in a letter to Vallette: "we have acquired a fur bonnet with earflaps, as doggish as the weather, which hang down and oscillate pleasantly over our ears." But Jarry's frivolities were now irritating Terrasse. He complained to Armory that he did everything except apply himself to the chore in question: Jarry fished, took bicycle rides, and above all frittered away his time at bar billiards and cards in the Café Brosse. Perhaps a collaborator might encourage him back to the task? Terrasse suggested to Armory that he take it on, but either he refused or Jarry suggested someone else: Demolder.[102]

Memories of Jarry's stay in Le Grand-Lemps may be found in his writing. *La Dragonne* begins with the local ritual in which the losing team at *pétanque* (bowls) lines up to kiss the "Fanny," a representation of a naked female backside, either painted or sculpted. Likewise, a long and pleasingly vulgar poem recounts an after-hours game of billiards conducted in contravention of regulations and brought to a premature end by the gendarmerie. Jarry and his companions encountered such problems more than once. Around the time of his departure in late April 1904 the café held a banquet for its unofficial monarch. Madame Brosse laid on a great spread featuring local delicacies; the regulars matched Jarry drink for drink and the celebration once again exceeded the hours permitted. The town policeman gave them thirty minutes' grace, but then found the party still in full swing and so raucous he was unable to make himself heard by banging on the door. Eventually he forced an entrance through the kitchen and angrily took the names and addresses of everyone around the table, or even under it, including the town's justice of the peace.[103]

Jarry arrived back at Le Coudray on May 9, 1904. An uncertain future awaited him. He had at least regained his independent existence, even if his town and country residences offered a significant contrast to the comforts and domesticity of the Terrasse household, but despite Jarry's claims in letters to Rachilde and Vallette, the trip had not resulted in the completion of *Pantagruel*. The only good news was that the *Moderni Revue*, Prague's most important literary periodical, began serializing a Czech translation of *Messalina* in April, and Jarry wrote to its director hoping to interest him in some of his other books.

13

A QUESTION OF INTERPRETATION

Up to this point, these intercalary chapters have traced certain themes, influences, and contradictions within Jarry's life, and have indicated some of their connections with his works. This chapter does much the same, but within the context of how certain previous writers have looked at Jarry's life and myth, and the conclusions they have drawn about his motives and personality. It occurs here, rather than as an afterword, which would seem its natural position, because the final act of Jarry's life appears to me definitive. Until recently a paucity of information meant that the story of Jarry's last few years could not be fully told, but this appears more possible now. The events of these years would cast a long shadow back across his past: a paradox that is entirely appropriate.

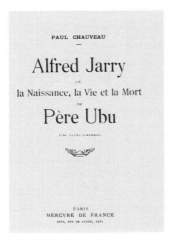

13.1

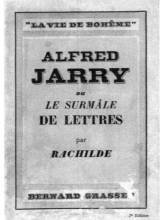

13.2

13.3

Regarded as a whole, Jarry's life falls into distinct periods. If it be his writing that is under consideration: before and after the production of *Ubu Roi*. If his life, then according to where he lived: before Paris, in Paris, and after Paris when he primarily resided around Corbeil and Le Coudray. After the uproar at the Œuvre it was only a matter of months before Jarry first found himself a country retreat, a break with the capital that became more confirmed as the years passed.

His promotion of *Ubu Roi* had been both brilliant and determined. Barely three years after Jarry's arrival in the capital as an anonymous provincial, Père Ubu was treading the stage of what was arguably the most important theater in France. The production in 1896 marked an early culmination in Jarry's life, and the resulting scandal surely exceeded even his expectations. Such a narrative has the qualities of a fable: *The Unknown's Struggle* relates the protagonist's adventures as he overcomes the obstacles in his path. Eventually, inevitably—for why else tell the tale?—he triumphs. Along the way he may discover he already possessed a priceless treasure he had not recognized as such; and an inspirational teacher is a common ingredient, also present here, although in an unfamiliar guise.

In Jarry's case, the unswerving trajectory of his story up to the end of 1896 was no doubt more arbitrary and contingent than it appeared in retrospect. And thus, in comparison, the episodes that followed in the wake of *Ubu Roi* were bound to appear more capricious and picaresque. Jarry's ambition had seemed so certain, and its realization so confident and assured. After the effortless ascension of Ubu into immortality: what next? Jarry's hesitation, his indifference to capitalizing on his *coup de scandale*, puzzled his contemporaries: within a year or so he was content to bury himself in the country. It may be this vivid contrast in Jarry's life, that of the cosmopolitan until 1897 and the country recluse after, that has prompted so many attempts to shoehorn his story into a coherent whole. In Jarry's case, though, such endeavors seem particularly ill-advised—and not only because of his contradictory nature. They are in fact predicated upon a false, or at least irrelevant, assumption: that Jarry was either a success or a failure as an author, *and that this was of the least concern to him*. For there is no reason to disbelieve his oft-repeated assertion ("posterity will decide") that he was simply not interested in matters of literary reputation.[1]

Early writers, many of whom were friends, or who had encountered him in Parisian literary circles, therefore characterized the second part of Jarry's life as one of disappointment and unfulfilled promise. He had squandered his remarkable gifts and abilities due to flaws in his character. These moralists were followed by other writers who actually valued Jarry's works. For his admirers the very flaws in Jarry's character, identified by previous detractors, could now be construed as strengths instead. So, for example, his unworldliness, far from being naïveté, was in fact a heroic refusal to compromise with a world that did not live up to his expectations. These readings of Jarry's life were often as wayward as those of their predecessors but, as I have suggested earlier, Jarry and his works are indivisible. Consequently, even these extreme interpretations of his life can be associated with the opposing representatives of his thought, Père Ubu and Doctor Faustroll: some saw his life as a demonic possession by Père Ubu, others as the hagiography of a pataphysical saint.

Still other interpretations fell between these extremes, and recall the simple plots of the operettas with which Jarry had so recently been engaged: *Frankenstein's Monster*, *The Careless Bohemian or The Ingénu*, and *The Noble Suicide*. These different versions of Jarry's life reveal the individual preferences of their authors, all of whom have convincing yet contradictory insights. Pataphysically speaking, these conceptions of Jarry's life may be considered as equally valid imaginary solutions, and personally I have inclined toward each of them on various occasions during the writing of this book—a handy justification for some of its inconsistencies.

In *Frankenstein* the hero is taken over by his creation, and eventually destroyed by it. This notion was originally applied to the life of Jarry in the first biography of him, by Paul Chauveau, who made it explicit in his subtitle: *Alfred Jarry, or the Birth, Life and Death of Père Ubu*. For Chauveau, Jarry's story was pure melodrama: The Revenge of Heb. Ubu was Jarry's "derisive dybbuk," a "hideous mask" which he had assumed voluntarily but then found himself unable to remove. He was so haunted by the "vindictive phantom" of Ubu that he could no longer distinguish himself from his own creation, and was eventually consumed by it. A highly moral Faustian tale.[2]

There was, of course, some truth in this. After the production of *Ubu Roi*, Jarry came to be identified with his antihero, particularly by those who were not especially close to him (since I think one can detect an affectionate irony in his being referred to as Père Ubu by the likes of the Phalansterians). Jarry's performance of his role had subtle variations according to whether he was with mere acquaintances or close friends. The latter shared a delight in the uninitiated's reaction to Ubu in full flow. The role undoubtedly became tiresome to Jarry on occasion, but Chauveau was not alone in believing that Jarry himself found it more than an inconvenience. Mauclair, admittedly no friend of Jarry's, remembered him complaining: "I'm crushed beneath Ubu. It was only a schoolboy joke and was not even written by me, I concocted it with school friends, then beefed it up with comic and scatological details, because it seemed to me it could be a very funny play. I've done other things, I still do, but my progress is blocked by Ubu. I have to speak like him, act like him, live like him. That's all they want!" Jarry, Mauclair concluded, was the prisoner of his own creation.[3]

For many of these early memoirists and biographers, Jarry was destroyed by Père Ubu. Everything behind this assumed persona was gradually eviscerated until only the mask remained, although this version of his life does seem to be restricted to acquaintances such as Régnier, Mauclair, Hirsch, Thibaudet, and Salmon, rather than close friends. None of these people knew him other than with Ubu's mask firmly in place, in Parisian literary circles, which Jarry spent a significant portion of his life avoiding.

Rachilde and Vallette attributed Jarry's actions to altogether different motives, and their opinions were no doubt formed by the fact that it was they who generally had to deal with the consequences. Vallette portrayed the character of the *Careless* (both carefree and negligent) *Bohemian* in his obituary:

> He was one of the strangest characters of the younger generation, and the most contradictory
> person ever. Extremely intelligent, but with a rare and stubborn shortsightedness; original,

certainly; an incredibly quick learner prone to absorb influences in all their detail; no other seeker after the absolute was more at the mercy of the contingent; extraordinarily learned and understanding, yet he knew less about everyday living than almost anybody else; often fastidious, modest, and tactful in all circumstances, he loved to hide behind a cynical façade. He was gifted with ingenuity, rather than imagination, and from the automatic triggerings of his geometric mental processes ten different aspects of the same idea would emerge. He was headstrong, self-willed, tenacious, a bit of a braggart at times, easily self-deluded, but always optimistically, from which sprang a quantity of first-class anecdotes that were directed against himself. As a man his enthusiasms were still those of a child: a book printed in a rare foreign typeface, a fishing boat, a hut on the banks of the Seine; he acquired them all on impulse—incontinently, as he might have said—without any thought of the consequences, either to himself or to others. He was charming, insupportable, and delightful.[4]

Here we see how even Vallette, one of the most famous literary editors of his day, focused upon Jarry's life and character in his obituary. He and Rachilde saw Jarry, above all, as a species of *ingénu*, but one whose unworldliness had an edge of bitterness and tragedy. Fagus, in a beautiful and passionate obituary of Jarry, bridged the chasm between this assessment and that of later writers. For him, Jarry was indeed overwhelmed by banal reality: "the everyday and the relative vanquished this juggler of absolutes." He was "disembrained" by the everyday: in part because he was serious, as a child or a savant is serious; in part because he was never serious, since he never shared the world's opinion of what deserved to be taken seriously.[5]

And then a new generation of writers revealed that Jarry's life had precisely the opposite meaning. Yes, he did conceal himself behind a defensive façade, but only so that, unobserved, he could mark out for himself a zone of total individual liberty, and construct an existence in which the distinctions between art and life were eliminated. Jean Mollet, in his brief memoir of Jarry, concluded: "it was because of his disdain and disgust for the bourgeois that Jarry, who was the most refined person I ever met […] and a true aristocrat of letters, tended to parade all those eccentricities that contributed to his demise at so young an age; a masquerade enacted to conceal his inner self." Rachilde, when she later came to write her account of him, came close to this position:[6]

> When I agreed to try to narrate the short existence of that incorrigible bohemian Alfred Jarry it was because no one else was more familiar with him in the intimacy of his pride. He was the victim of a mental delusion that was cruel both for himself and for those close to him: he wanted his life to conform to his literary program. This person who timed the smallest of his performances would not assent to tread the path of real life.[7]

It was Apollinaire, in his memoir of Jarry two years after his death, who for the first time promoted this notion into the guiding principle necessary for the comprehension of Jarry's life: "Alfred Jarry was a man of letters to an unprecedented extent. His smallest actions, his childish pranks, everything he did was literature. His whole life was shaped by literature, and only by literature." André Breton, in his *Anthology of Black Humor*, went further: "after Jarry [...] the distinction between art and life, long considered essential, finds itself challenged, eventually to be abolished in principle." This opinion had its most eloquent expression in Roger Shattuck's *The Banquet Years*. His biographical essay is called *Alfred Jarry: Suicide by Hallucination*, and he finds in Jarry's "violent fusion of life and literature" the culmination of his existence. His "transformation" into Père Ubu[8]

> ... presupposes one absolute principle: the totality of human freedom: I can choose the color of my coat; I can choose not to wear a coat; *I can choose* (yet few men venture so far) *not to be I.* But: for such absolute freedom there is retribution. Like the sorcerer's apprentice, Jarry was overwhelmed by his own power. Ubu acknowledges no affections, no damnation; for him nothing is sacred, not even, as in Faust, the clutch of his own mind. A distorted image of Faust, Ubu-Jarry is engaged in the only act logically left for him to perform: self-destruction. Elevation by alcohol became his form of protracted suicide; *yet while he was dying he was at liberty.* No worldly restraint could touch him.[9]

Here Jarry's premature death is interpreted as a deliberate act of literary martyrdom, as a quest for ultimate liberty. And yet we have already seen from Merrill's account of the society hostess's dinner party that Jarry was not immune even to social coercion. The influence of Shattuck's brilliant exegesis has been profound: its morbid and exultant glamour has proved irresistible, and it is a delight that such a monster could be possible. Yet one may also agree with Michel Arrivé that taking Jarry's life to be a work of art equivalent to his writing is a simple recuperation of the notion that Jarry was validated by his life rather than his work, which had been the opinion of his least sympathetic contemporaries. Jarry's myth should not be substituted either for his writing or for his life; rather, it should be seen as their inevitable epiphenomenon, since both proceeded from identical impulses on his part.[10]

Whereas Shattuck's overegging the cake may have resulted in a more elaborate apologia than was strictly necessary, there was nothing complex about Rachilde's version of Jarry as an *ingénu*. There can be little doubt that Jarry had often tried the patience of Rachilde and Vallette, but this does not excuse the complacency of their attributing Jarry's rejection of their ever more conventional values to simple naïveté. On an everyday basis, however, one cannot really disagree with Rachilde. Jarry had set himself on a path that was not at all likely to lead to "some small town where the local scribblers will present us with a Sèvres vase on the occasion of our election to the Academy."[11]

A biography should avoid transforming a life into a destiny. In Jarry's case, however, it is indisputable that his circumstances became gradually more ominous, and by 1904 few of his friends can have had optimistic expectations for his future. Whatever version of Jarry's life is being played, its final act, about to be unveiled, resists overly interpretive readings. Fiction may be overwhelmed by the simple weight of events, and humor by tragedy.

14

1904–1907

Jarry never wanted what his friends thought he should want. The idyllic existence of the Terrasse family had soon palled, and he desired only his shack beside the river at Le Coudray. A postcard to Rachilde of April 29, 1904 celebrated his imminent escape from bourgeois domesticity: "Our last cycling expedition in foreign parts before once again returning to our beloved realm at the Barrage!" Two years later, in a letter to Saltas, he dated the beginnings of his illness to his stay in the south: "Onset of illness: end of the fearful task of *Pantagruel*, 6 months in the Dauphiné, Nov 1903–May 1904—I dislike the mountains—and being away from home."[1]

14.1
Photographs of Jarry from Gabrielle Vallette's album,
circa 1903–1904. Rachilde's captions read:
"Père Ubu is self-effacing! … But continues to fish.
His country house and … its stables."

CHAPTER 14

He was relieved to return at last to Le Coudray in early May. The actor Sacha Guitry, who stayed with Demolder that year, paid him a visit:[2]

> Jarry lived only a hundred yards from Demolder. Lived, did I say? I exaggerate. He inhabited, he took shelter, in a pitiful and dilapidated hovel on the banks of the Seine, upon which these words could still be made out: "Livery Stables." Four walls, a roof of doubtful imperme-ability, no boards on the floor, just beaten earth. A door without a lock swung to and fro, but did not reach down to the ground. At the back of the room an excuse for a commode, lacking lid, seat, and drawers. A plank across two trestles constituted his desk, and a pallet covered in old clothes, beneath which he would slide in order to sleep, was his bed. As for his bicycle, it was hung from the ceiling by a cord and pulley.

"Otherwise rats eat the tires," he said.[3]

Rachilde furnished further details, such as the circus posters on the walls alongside unidentified drawings by the "modern school," and the floor littered with broken glass and fish heads. Jarry responded to her offer to wield a broom by assuring her that a good wind from across the river would suffice to sweep it all away. According to Salmon, the river here was prone to regular flooding. He wrote that Jarry simply slept on his table until the waters receded, an addition to the Jarry legend that should be regarded with some wariness.[4]

Jarry's pleasure at returning to Le Coudray was in part because he had a plan. Since the publication of *Messalina*, he had imagined himself the proprietor of a medieval tower with impressive dungeons constructed on the banks of the Seine. From the heights of this structure, which he would name The Tripod, Ubu could survey the boundless glories of his kingdom. The furtherance of this scheme required the replenishment of his phynances. So too did the simple furtherance of his everyday existence. Jarry was never again to enjoy any sort of regular income, and although he succeeded in having his Tripod built, it did not turn out to be quite as magnificent a structure as he had at first envisaged.[5]

Even soon after his return from Le Grand-Lemps, some of Jarry's friends appeared well aware of his difficulties. Terrasse may have contacted those he thought likely to assist, and the most loyal of them did their best. It was just at this moment that Rachilde and Vallette could have come most decisively to his aid. Jarry had acquired an enthusiastic following at the *Revue Blanche*, and it would have been a simple matter to have invented a similar column for him at the *Mercure*. At such a crucial juncture, it cannot be that Gourmont was still the impediment? Rather, it is more likely that the Mercure of 1904 was not the same as that of ten years before. Now it was a prestigious publishing house in attractive new premises, whose proprietors were not unhappy with their well-earned position within official culture. Jarry did not fit within these new surroundings. Chauveau rather too tactfully intimated as much:

> The Mercure de France had removed from the gloomy rue de l'Échaudé to a charming town house built for Caron de Beaumarchais in the rue de Condé. Here it was that the effervescent Rachilde, with her generosity, kindness, and candor, presided just as she always had, over the Tuesday soirées. At the Mercure one continued to encounter writers and artists, but now there were many elegant women too. When Père Ubu arrived from God knows where in his unusual outfit, totally drunk, loud, coarse, demonstrative, Rachilde would ignore the instinctive recoil of her beautiful friends and welcome him as a friend of the house.[6]

It was, instead, Fénéon and Mirbeau who came to his aid. They proposed him to the *Figaro* as a columnist. Jarry wrote three pieces for the paper, the first two appearing in July and August. The third occasioned a quarrel. On its delivery an editor unwisely alluded to the fact that it was late. Jarry reacted by ripping up his manuscript and flinging it at him, along with a famous word he had invented. End of employment. His readiness to take offense may have been exacerbated by his earlier treatment by the *Figaro* at the hands of Fouquier after *Ubu Roi*.[7]

Prudence would have urged a little more restraint, since the paper paid extremely well, but such considerations remained foreign to Jarry. He had received 20 francs for his first article, a sum so munificent it must be disposed of as quickly as possible. Apollinaire and he had resumed their friendship soon after his return from Terrasse's. Jarry treated him to a meal in some establishment that turned out to be distinctly downmarket, its dishes almost inedible. Apollinaire was something of an epicure, and yet later he recalled this banquet with enormous pleasure, owing to Jarry's exuberant glorifications of the chef's mediocre concoctions as they were placed before him. Being thus preoccupied with oratory, Ubu himself neglected to eat, but not of course to drink. A visit followed to the Bostock Circus, which was then performing in the enormous Hippodrome on the boulevard de Clichy. Accounts of the evening become confused at this point, though Apollinaire says the smell of the wild animals went to Jarry's head. In his notes for *La Dragonne*, it is clear that Jarry had recently read the French translation of Bostock's book *The Training of Wild Animals*, in which he warns that a person in the act of drinking is at the mercy of wild beasts. From this observation Jarry embroidered an unlikely tale in which he recaptured two escaped panthers in a Parisian park by dressing in a suit of armor and confronting them with an empty glass. They were immediately subdued by this horrible sight, and he backed them into their cage. "Alas," wrote Apollinaire, "during the telling, Jarry was brandishing his revolver, the women near us were obviously terrified and some of them were anxious to leave. And Jarry did not exactly disguise the satisfaction he felt in frightening these philistines." He then determined that the lion tamer required assistance, Père Ubu must take him under his "special protection," and he aimed his revolver at the largest of the lions, Menelik the Terrible. Ushers were summoned. Both men were obliged to leave, since Apollinaire appeared unable to control this maniac, who was apparently both armed and deranged. Outside Jarry boarded the top deck of an omnibus, cheerily waving goodbye with his pistol. Apollinaire was greatly amused by the whole incident; Salmon recalls his account of it being punctuated with "those short laughs of his which resembled sobs," but Jarry's escapades while drinking appeared to be becoming a little more reckless than heretofore.[8]

A letter to Apollinaire soon afterward reveals that the *Figaro* had paid for his second article, and that he had also visited Fasquelle, the publisher who had taken over the book list of the Revue Blanche. Since he had already obliged Jarry with an advance for *La Dragonne*, there was all the more reason he might do so again.

1 August 1904

My Dear Friend,

If by chance this reaches you in time, which I hope it does, would you be free to drop in at the Café du Rocher around half past five? Bespangled with the Figaro's gold, and with Monsieur Fasquelle's, I would be delighted to inveigle you, it being my turn, into a restaurant where they serve Château-du-Pape, and into a café where bar billiards may be played.

I say half past five because I have to be at the Figaro before seven. I think that you wouldn't find the short journey tiresome.

Best wishes,
A. Jarry[9]

In fact, Fasquelle had proved generous. "What can I do so as to get 'plastered with gold' like Jarry by the ex-Natanson?" Demolder asked of Fontainas, in obvious amazement. Eventually Jarry's accounts would show that he had managed to run up debts to Fasquelle totaling 1,100 francs, and this sum appears to have constituted the bulk of Jarry's income for the next nine months. In fact, if we are to believe the author Léon Daudet, it was all down to him. But can Jarry's poverty have been already so acute that he could no longer afford shoes?[10]

In the antechamber to Fasquelle's I once encountered Alfred Jarry, the author of *Ubu Roi*. [...] A poor young man consumed by alcohol, round-faced and troubled, whose shoes consisted of triangles of brown paper wrapped with twine. The sight of that tangle of string plunged me into a sort of desolation. I mentioned it to Fasquelle, who replied with his usual good nature, "I'll fix that." On that morning, Jarry left the premises beaming.[11]

...

The early chapters of *La Dragonne* are set in Le Grand-Lemps, so it was probably in mid-1904 that Jarry commenced serious work on this novel. His return to a semi-autobiographical mode meant its structure would soon proliferate in so many directions at once—so as to incorporate all the various obsessions and events in its author's life over the next few years—that it would become impossible for him ever to finish it. He also started work on two short libretti with Demolder, and the latter was now recruited to help Jarry finish *Pantagruel*. Terrasse was pressing for its completion. In late August or early September the two of them traveled once more to

Le Grand-Lemps to work on it, although this time Jarry made sure the visit was a brief one: he managed to return to Le Coudray in time for his thirty-first birthday, September 8, 1904. The day before, he wrote to Rachilde, on notepaper from the Café Brosse: "Père Ubu is returning this evening to the little tree where he likes to fish, and to the future tripod, by the night train which will set him down, rue Cassette, at 10.25 in the morning. Back at the Barrage in the afternoon. The *Pantagruel*, now all done to perfection, is a nice piece of work. We have also learnt to play bezique. And now we are going to lose some weight."[12]

Henceforth, Jarry's letters are peppered with confident announcements of the imminent or final completion of both *Pantagruel* and *La Dragonne*. Neither work was ever finished, or at least, not by Jarry. And he had become stout! Months of regular meals at Terrasse's had had their effect. The plumpness of Jarry's face in the portrait by Hermann-Paul suggests it depicts him in 1904, while Demolder's wife drew a caricature of Jarry arriving at the Barrage.

14.2
Caricature of Jarry by Claire Demolder, 1904.

14.3
Hermann-Paul, Alfred Jarry, circa 1904, from the first edition of *Ubu cocu* (1944).

One of the first things Jarry did on his return was to inform Apollinaire that he had discovered a new game to be played on a bar billiards table. In the event, there was to be little time for such entertainments. Jarry and Demolder had shown Terrasse the short operas they were working on, and he liked one of them enough to set it to music. Eventually entitled *Le Manoir enchanté* (*The Enchanted Manor*), this one-act piece would go through a number of versions co-written by Jarry and Demolder. Suspicions exist, however, owing to the absence of the manuscripts published by Arnaud in the 1970s, that Demolder may have been the principal author. *Le Manoir* would be the first of Jarry's libretti to be produced, but it was probably the process of having it staged that finally caused Jarry to lose heart with *Pantagruel*. He and Demolder worked on *Le Manoir* in Paris and Le Coudray throughout October.

By now even Demolder was concerned by Jarry's drinking; Sacha Guitry witnessed Jarry's refutation of his suggestion that a little abstinence might be a good idea, and that he might cease his daily visits to the bar beside the lock:

> "I have no choice. [...] The owners of this bar do not dare attempt to reclaim the vast sums I owe them from the past two years, because they know perfectly well that should they insist on payment they would lose my custom! But were I to pass more than two days without coming here to take my absinthe, they would not hesitate to put a knife to my throat. I drink so as not to have to pay what I owe them!"[13]

As ever, Jarry diverted his friends' concern with a joke, but later, in the letter to Saltas already cited, he would summarize his difficulties that summer and autumn in Le Coudray: "Back from the Dauphiné.—Performances [of *Pantagruel*] postponed until next winter. Out and out depression. Debts, etc. For fear of harassment by creditors could no longer live quietly in Le Coudray. Lost my old habits of shower baths in the river [...] of excellent fish by the pound, eaten in profusion, etc." His relations with Monsieur and Madame Dunou were not quite as desperate as he made out, however. Their niece recalled her uncle taking drinks to Jarry in his shack, so as not to embarrass him, aware he was unable to pay. They sat outside beneath a walnut tree, the sun projected discs of light on the ground through its foliage, and Jarry ruefully noted their resemblance to franc pieces.[14]

Such kindnesses go a long way to explaining his dislike at leaving Le Coudray, despite its discomforts and the onset of the bouts of depression mentioned in his letter to Saltas. Several oil paintings by Jarry depict views of the river around Le Coudray, though they are of limited artistic interest: Jarry's works as a graphic artist are often intriguing, but his oil paintings were distinctly amateur. The most recent to turn up, discovered by Paul Edwards, depicts the Villa Vallette from one of Jarry's favorite fishing spots on the other side of the river. Its chief interest lies in Rachilde's inscription on a label stuck to its reverse, in which she concludes: "Despite the disorders of his bohemian life, he was often prey to an inexplicable melancholy of which this image seems to be the reflection." This, too, seems to be when Jarry began resorting to drinking ether. Rachilde wrote that this habit made it too dangerous for her to be towed behind Jarry's bicycle in her basketwork cart; by the following year he would have become too enfeebled even to have made the attempt.[15]

At the beginning of November 1904, it was *Le Manoir* that called for a trip to Le Grand-Lemps. Ten days were assigned for its completion, but twice that were required. Jarry and Terrasse returned to Paris on December 2, Demolder the day before. In a card to Rachilde, Jarry announced their return, and his determination to begin work on the Tripod. Although Jarry and Demolder congratulated themselves on actually finishing the libretto for *Le Manoir*, they were quickly disabused. The principal actor now required extensive changes and the task consumed several days, Demolder and Jarry often working at La Demi-Lune until two or three in the morning. Even then their work was not over. A telegram from Jarry apologizes to Rachilde for missing the Tuesday on December 20, because of Terrasse arriving on the 22nd. All this urgency was because the first performance of *Le Manoir* was only three weeks away.[16]

On December 23, Jarry negotiated the purchase of a small piece of land (540 square yards) close to the Villa Vallette, for which he paid 325 francs the following month, presumably using his fee for *Le Manoir*. The première of this work took place on January 10, 1905 at the salon of the Comtesse de Paroy de Lurcy, in her town house in the rue Murillo. As a private performance to an invited audience, it was not reviewed. It is not known whether Jarry attended or not, but he would probably have been discouraged from doing so, as this was a very upper-crust affair. Following this performance, the authors received further requests for rewrites from the actors and producers, but Jarry had lost patience with this process and left it largely to Demolder, who was still at it in early March. Terrasse had come to trust him as a reliable and safe collaborator, if not exactly inspired. In a letter he urged Demolder to spur Jarry on with *Pantagruel*, because it must be finished by Easter. But Jarry was becoming ever more disillusioned by these collaborations, with their endless revisions (there were another two one-act operettas under way); Demolder was soon to become the recipient of Terrasse's epistolary complaints concerning his coauthor.[17]

The early months of 1905 continued to be difficult, with Jarry mostly in Paris, and drinking heavily. He made a number of brief trips to Laval and Lamballe, beginning at the end of January. Their purpose is unclear, but several motives may be surmised. His sister's residence in Laval was doubtless more comfortable than the rue Cassette, and he was also researching his family tree, in part for *La Dragonne*. Jarry's grandfather had encouraged this passion many years before, and his papers were probably in Lamballe. Deeper impulses may have contributed to his obsession with a possibly aristocratic background—delusions of distressed nobility might cast a romantic gloss over the worsening squalor of Jarry's daily life: an imaginary solution could be as valid as a real one. It also cannot have seemed a bad idea to remind the wealthier branches of his family of his existence, and of his visibly obvious poverty.[18]

Jarry was back in Paris at least by March 1, 1905, for the funeral of Marcel Schwob. An incongruous trio processed along the rue Saint-Louis-en-l'Île, the ancient main street on the island of Saint-Louis in the center of Paris: Willy, portly and top-hatted; Polaire, the extravagantly elegant actress famous for her 14-inch waist; and between the two, and almost exactly her height,

Jarry in his great bargee's cape and fur cap adorned with ears. Once again his outfit did not go unnoticed, though this was not necessarily his intention: he probably had no other bad-weather clothing.[19]

Jarry was persuaded to resume the Pantagrueline struggle. Terrasse had been writing exclusively to Demolder, and on April 7 he asked after "Ubu," wondered how the fourth act was progressing, but also asked for final versions of *Le Manoir* and another piece, *Le Petit Vieux*. One cause of the increasing friction between the two may have been Terrasse's awe-inspiring work ethic. The following week they toiled on major structural modifications to *Pantagruel*, and Terrasse appeared pleased with the results. But on the 21st, a letter from Terrasse to Demolder discusses the latter's proposal for a new version of it altogether. It is impossible to disentangle the trio's different roles, but important alterations were under way. Many were prompted by suggestions from Maurice Kufferath, a Belgian theatrical producer whom Demolder had approached. He was interested in putting it on in Brussels, but, like everyone else, insisted on changes to the script.[20]

Terrasse must have imagined that Jarry needed the encouragement of some concrete reward. Then he might buckle down and finish it; financial security would give him the required peace of mind, etc. … which only goes to show how little he knew his old friend after all these years. In April 1905 Jarry, Demolder, and Terrasse signed a legal agreement for *Pantagruel*, in which the first two were credited as joint librettists, and Jarry received the remarkable sum of 3,000 francs as an advance against royalties, for both publication and performances.

Now that he was once again ensplendored with cash, Jarry's thoughts immediately turned to matters Tripodic, and perhaps aheneous and herpetological. As regards the first, on April 26 he enlarged his Le Coudray demesne by purchasing a second, smaller piece of land directly adjoining the first, although he did not actually pay for it until a year later.[21]

···

Toward the conclusion of Jarry's first piece of published prose, "Guignol," Père Ubu is plunged into a collapsing toilet, and is thus betrayed by "aheneous herpetology." This phrase, a pastiche of Symbolist neologizing, is a Greco-Latin derivation that signifies "the study of brazen serpents," and the reader is therefore to understand that modern serpentine copper plumbing is being celebrated. This was something in which Jarry took a keen interest, as his concierge related soon after his death:[22]

> "Listen, here's another one. Not very long ago he told me his sister gave him 3,000 francs. Well now, instead of using it to give himself a bit of comfort and luxury—because a little later on I'll show you his room and you'll see how much he needed it—he explained to me that nothing would give him as much pleasure as having a really up-to-date WC. So he spent 1,800 francs having one put in! And the rest of the money disappeared in a flash! Such foolhardiness was typical of everything he did.[23]

The concierge's account is very specific about the amount of money involved, and Jarry certainly came into exactly this figure on signing the contract with Terrasse. Charlotte Jarry had also borrowed the same amount against her house in 1899, but that transaction had occurred in mid-summer, when Jarry was at La Frette. Roig has a similar story, although he has Thadée Natanson playing the role of Jarry's benefactor. Thadée did indeed help him out, but the sums were not so heroic, and were handed over at a time when it looked as if Jarry would be evicted from the rue Cassette: installing such an expensive "apparatus" then would have been even more gratuitous. There appears to be no basis to Renard's assertion that the flush was attached to Jarry's bell pull; that was probably simply an invention of Jarry's one Tuesday.[24]

• • •

On April 15, 1905, a photograph of the Mercure circle (except for Rachilde!) appeared in the *Revue illustrée*, a popular broadsheet. It is the only photograph showing Jarry and Apollinaire together.

It is at this moment in Jarry's life that the question of whether he and Picasso ever actually met arises, although the controversy is of more interest to biographers of Picasso than of Jarry. This is because, whereas Jarry certainly exercised some influence over Picasso, the contrary is not the case; and also because, although it seems certain they did meet, and probably more than once, Picasso denied the fact to some, while acknowledging it to others.

14.4
Alfred Jarry's toilet, photograph by Jean Weber, 1950s.

14.5
The writers of the Mercure from *La Revue illustrée*, April 15, 1905. Standing, left to right: Robert Scheffer, Charles Morice, Marcel Collière, Pierre Quillard, F.-A. Herold, Alfred Jarry, Maurice Raynal, Henri Mazel, André Salmon, Guillaume Apollinaire, C.-H. Hirsch, Pierre Villetard, Jean de Gourmont, Laurent Tailhade, Alfred Vallette; seated, left to right: Ernest Gaubert, Georges Polti, Armory, Gaston Danville, Paul Fort.

Jarry and Picasso had a large number of mutual friends and acquaintances, many of whom have been previously mentioned. Apollinaire is the most obvious. He and Picasso had met in late October 1904, introduced by another, Jean Mollet. Apart from these two, others included Cremnitz, Manolo, and the writer Maurice Raynal. Most of these were present during the incident that puts Picasso and Jarry in the same room for an evening.[25]

Pierre Mac Orlan was yet another writer close to this group, though he recalled seeing Jarry once only, in 1904, fur-hatted and descending from a motorcar at dawn with Raynal and Salmon. His reminiscence is more interesting for what Jarry meant to this group of youthful iconoclasts. "Jarry, because of the way he lived his life, was what one calls with either courteous sympathy or suspicion, an original. […] He had quite a reputation, and his influence on those who knew him was reinforced by this qualification." But it was not only his life. Mac Orlan and his friends already considered Jarry a writer of great significance, although it is doubtful that Jarry found his fame quite as snug as these admirers of his imagined:[26]

> An elite followed his books with enthusiasm and sincerity. Fate had not placed him on the road that leads to success in the bourgeois meaning of the word. Yet Jarry had succeeded. He could already feel the gentle warmth of the rays of his own glory.[27]

Maurice Raynal, a wealthy twenty-one-year-old, was close to all of the group around Picasso, and became the first to write a monograph on the artist. He lived near to Jarry in the rue de Rennes, and here he held private dinner parties that were greatly appreciated by his impoverished companions. One of these evenings, on April 20, 1905, achieved a certain notoriety and was related, and no doubt embroidered, by three of the diners present: Apollinaire, Jacob, and Raynal himself.[28]

Max Jacob's account strongly implies that the whole event was arranged by Raynal so that Picasso and Jarry might meet each other. Jarry arrived late. The other guests were Cremnitz, Manolo, Salmon, and three unnamed young ladies, all of whom, Raynal asserted, happened to be pregnant. Ladies, preferably pregnant, one may notice, were an essential accompaniment to Jarry's exploits with his revolver. Roast wild duck was the high point of the repast, provided by a hunter friend of the host. The birds were conveyed to the table, and Jarry offered his services: "The carving of poultry is a talent of ours." He tore them to pieces with his bare hands. Everyone became very drunk, with the exception of Manolo, whose sanctimonious sobriety was perhaps the smoldering fuse. After dinner, Jarry repeatedly announced his dislike of "this Manolo" and ordered him from the room, but when, after a few moments had passed, Manolo put his head around the door, Jarry immediately took out his revolver and fired at him. The shots missed and Manolo fled. Apollinaire disarmed Jarry. Pregnant ladies may, or may not, have fainted. "Wasn't it as beautiful as literature?" said Jarry afterward. Jacob missed these events, being so inebriated he had fallen asleep on the carpet until awoken by the gunshots. As for the pistol, Apollinaire says he took it from Jarry and gave it to "one of our friends" for safekeeping, but Jacob says Jarry gave it to Picasso. A couple of days later Jarry wrote to Apollinaire: "I hope the emotions of that bedlamesque evening have not unduly upset the lady of the house."[29]

What, though, of Jarry and Picasso? Certainly Jarry's revolver was to become one of Picasso's prize possessions ever afterward. In 1909 he used it to repel a horde of scandalized Spanish matrons in the small village of Hortas. Good Catholics, they were outraged that Picasso and his mistress were openly living together. Richardson records that shots over their heads dispersed this crowd of "militant prudes." That evening, at Raynal's, according to Jacob, Picasso and Jarry "took to one another straightaway, and remained friends thereafter, although they did not see each other often." Even so, he recalled seeing Jarry at Picasso's studio in the rue Ravignan in Montmartre, the famous "Bateau Lavoir."[30]

History, especially when it is dependent on the testimony of drunks, is never simple. Picasso later told his biographer Hélène Parmelin that he regretted never meeting Jarry, that he and Apollinaire had attempted to pay him a visit but he was not at home, and that was that. Chapter 23 of the first volume of John Richardson's biography of Picasso is accordingly called "The Absence of Jarry." He devotes an entire chapter to someone who, following Parmelin, he believes Picasso never met: "[Jarry] has been claimed by one biographer after another as a great friend of Picasso's. This friendship is a collective fantasy. The two men never met." For some reason, it appears that Richardson never asked Picasso about Jarry, but the person he mostly blames for this "collective fantasy," Roland Penrose, did ask him. (Some Picasso politics: two English art impresarios, not the best of friends, vied for Picasso's attention and patronage during his lifetime: Roland Penrose and Douglas Cooper, who was then the partner of John Richardson. This is perhaps why the latter did not consult Penrose's notes for his biography of Picasso, even though they record firsthand interviews with the artist and his friends.) Richardson writes that there is no corroboration of Jacob's statement that Jarry gave Picasso his revolver. But Penrose in his notes recalls talking to Picasso "of the revolver that he had been given by Alfred Jarry, which he had carried with him for a long time and fired as a means of expressing high spirits or frightening people." It is left to Dora Maar, Picasso's lover in the late thirties and early forties, to suggest a possible reason for Picasso's reticence with regard to Jarry. Penrose writes: "[Picasso] once told D[ora] that Jarry had kissed him on the mouth but she is convinced that if more [by which she meant other homosexual activity] had occurred during the 9 years she lived with him he would have told her." Something of a revelation about an artist often seen as the personification of Spanish *machismo*. Picasso's sketchbooks from 1905 contain a number of drawings of Père Ubu.[31]

…

In the meantime, relations between Jarry and Terrasse had reached a new low, and Terrasse's letters to Demolder had become fulminous. On May 27, 1905, he complained that "the Sloven," his habitual designation for Jarry, had missed two days of appointments and ignored letters sent to Le Coudray. He asked Demolder to find out what he was up to. Demolder must have succeeded, and a reluctant Jarry turned up at Terrasse's in Paris. The latter had reserved the weekend for them to finish the text: a time he had intended to spend with his family in the country. So far as one can decipher events, Jarry took offense at a comment made by Terrasse, who subsequently unburdened himself to Demolder on June 1. Jarry and he had managed to complete the first four acts of the libretto. Only the last act remained, a matter of two hours' work, and then the whole saga of *Pantagruel* would have been over, but Jarry decided he had other matters to attend to. An enormous argument ensued, and Terrasse declared himself ready to wash his hands of the whole business. Jarry walked out "to amuse himself in Le Coudray." Terrasse was left simultaneously incensed and despairing.[32]

Demolder was in Brussels, discussing the project with Kufferath, who was still keen. His reply to Terrasse went through the whole piece in great detail, indicating parts for further rewrites; but time was short if it was to be produced that season. When Demolder returned, he and Terrasse worked on it alone. Terrasse doubted his ability to remain civil in the company of the Sloven.[33]

One may sympathize with Terrasse; he had good reason to feel cheated. As soon as Jarry had been paid for his work, he had lost all interest in completing it. Terrasse had bailed Jarry out with a large sum of money based on an entirely theoretical valuation of his contribution. Jarry too may be defended, however. It seemed everyone had their opinion about how and what this piece should be, including now even the producer, and no doubt when it came to it, the actors would demand another round of rewrites, just as they had for *Le Manoir*. Two hours to complete it? A story Jarry had heard before, since there seems no reason to doubt he had considered it finished on several previous occasions.

More to the point, *Pantagruel* was now a long way from what Terrasse and Jarry had envisaged for the Théâtre des Pantins. Terrasse's success since then, essentially as an entertainer to the bourgeois, meant that Jarry too was being persuaded into this role, which had nothing to do with the ideas of theatrical staging he had put forward at the time of the production of *Ubu Roi*. And Jarry had not changed his mind. In 1903 an aside in one of his book reviews had noted with approval: "we used to dream of a theater where the characters were physically attached to the teeth of a visible cogwheel and where the scenes erupted, like electrical sparks, in expected combinations of isochronous words." While the precise meaning of this reverie remains obscure, we can be certain Jarry was far from approving the sort of entertainment apparently proposed by Terrasse, in which theatrical practicalities were given a due they never were when *Ubu Roi* was staged. Terrasse was undoubtedly a serious artist, but he was also a commercial one; the medium he worked in demanded it. When *Pantagruel* was finally staged, just four years after Jarry's death, only Terrasse remained from among the original contributors. Photographs of the preposterous setting confirm that nothing could have been more contrary to Jarry's radical conceptions for a new theater.[34]

14.6
Scene from the first production of *Pantagruel* in Lyon,
from *Le Théâtre*, March 1, 1911.

Nonetheless, this production of *Pantagruel*, which opened at the Grand-Théâtre in Lyon on January 31, 1911, was a success. There were fourteen performances, and it was well received by the critics, who mounted an unsuccessful campaign for its transfer to Paris. Financially it did not live up to its authors' expectations. After deductions, Terrasse's own fee for the production amounted to only 1,222 francs, less than half of what Jarry had received. The libretto was published the same year, credited to Alfred Jarry and Eugène Demolder, with music by Claude Terrasse, but there was probably a fourth collaborator. On Jarry's death the manuscript was incomplete, and Terrasse then informed Charlotte Jarry that another author would probably be required to finish it. Such a person must have been found, since the manuscript that was eventually published is mostly in an unknown hand.[35]

···

Meanwhile, Jarry's friends could see he was being slowly undermined by his prodigious consumption of alcohol, now facilitated by Terrasse's generosity. Previously he had seemed immune to its effects—Rachilde claimed never to have seen him drunk—but this was no longer the case, and his famous lucidity when inebriated began to desert him.

Terrasse's largesse also meant that construction could begin on the Tripod. It was a notable quirk of Jarry's behavior, a sign perhaps of his good intentions, that he tended not to make a major purchase without being able to afford it. Unfortunately he would then use the money set aside, in his mind at least, for entirely different purposes. The contractor for the Tripod, Monsieur Dubois, the local jack-of-all-trades in Le Coudray, would suffer the consequences.

On July 12, 1905, Jarry further expanded his plot of land by agreeing to purchase an adjoining plot, and a letter to Apollinaire of July 28 explains that his being in Paris only rarely was in part because he was supervising the construction of a "horrific tower" by the Seine. He hopes Apollinaire will come to the housewarming, implying an imminent celebration. However, after a brief period of frenzied land clearing by a small team, a single workman, presumably Dubois himself, was left to dig out the foundations and then erect the actual building. He soon fell under the spell of Mère Fontaine, and spent rather too much of his time in her drinking establishment. The foundations took several months, and progress was equally slow thereafter. Construction dragged on into the autumn, when the onset of cold weather made the building uninhabitable anyway.[36]

When Jarry had first drawn up plans for his residence on Rachilde's dining-room table four years before, the plan was so large it necessitated the table's extending leaves being brought into play. Sadly, this intriguing document is lost. A rare nod to realism on Jarry's part meant that when it came to be built it was altogether more modest: a wooden cabin rather like an English beach hut, mounted on brick or stone foundations because of the declivity of the ground. Apparently square, it was in fact a rectangle measuring 3.33 × 3.67 meters, which are curiously specific measurements in the circumstances. The ceiling, in contrast to the Chasublery, was high, 3.33 meters at the edges, taller in the center because of the pitched roof. There were small windows in the side and back, very low down (even for Jarry); a glass door and larger window at the front. The single room provided living and working quarters. Rachilde furnished it with a sofa bed, some wicker chairs, and a small writing table. She also provided curtains and a wastebasket. There was in fact a second room; to the left of the building was a small opening, visible in the photograph, which leads beneath it. Here, partly dug out of the hill, there was a "cellar for our wines." Dubois's invoice confirms that it had a door.[37]

Rachilde wrote that the building rested on four masonry pillars, but these are not visible in the photograph, and a wine cellar must have had walls. Jarry is often said to have named his new abode the Tripod precisely because it had four feet, and also in reference to the Martian machines in Wells's *War of the Worlds*. This "explanation" appears not to have come from Jarry himself, and he used the same word for other dwellings of his, such as those in Laval.

...

14.7
The Tripod, photograph taken by Gabrielle Vallette
in July 1907.

In June and September Jarry's only publications for 1905 appeared: two "speculations" in Marinetti's magazine *Poesia*, published in Milan. Both appear to have been written some time previously, a sad contrast with his years of productivity. As with Apollinaire, Jarry remained disinclined to entrust Marinetti with more important texts such as *Faustroll*.

Marinetti had lived in Paris since 1893; he was particularly close to Gustave Kahn, and had been published by the Revue Blanche since 1901. The extent of Jarry's relationship with this bombastic Italian is unclear, but it is unlikely that they were close. Marinetti's memoirs have this typically diminishing portrait of Jarry, probably because he exerted a fairly extensive influence on the great man's early works:[38]

> … I had the pleasure of meeting an unquestionable literary genius of the underworld Alfred Jarry in the editorial offices of the Revue Blanche which was mainly political-social in content and run by the Natanson Brothers
>
> Thirty and thin with an emaciated face strings instead of buttons holding his baggy jacket together certainly not his own that made his large flapping pants swing back and forth and this was a gratuitous way of life in a very prosperous Paris a flagrant banner of voluntary poverty
>
> Tender affectionate grateful for very little he followed me everywhere and I would insist on introducing him the most threadbare genius in the world into the most elegant salons despite what horrified people were saying
>
> I could get away with it because Parisian salons then had a certain passion for ingenious creators and bright minds
>
> I can see myself now with Alfred Jarry in the ornate salon of Mme Périer where from three to eleven at night thirty or forty men and women spouting poetry would parade through all ages appearances bellies breasts long hair beards celebrities[39]

Demolder and Terrasse were still laboring over *Pantagruel*, but Jarry's absence was making itself felt; his versification was far superior to Demolder's, and by late August Terrasse wanted him back. The lack of letters of complaint to Demolder means that Jarry must have submitted.[40]

On September 5, 1905, Rachilde wrote to invite Jarry to lunch on his birthday, but in his reply Jarry regretted being unable to come because he was undergoing extensive dental treatment (described in detail)—and although he will be 32 on the 8th, he doubts he will still have 32 teeth. He could come the day after, however. Jarry's dentist was in Paris, and it is not clear if he had now returned there for the winter, but by the time he did, in October at the latest, he was once again lacking any financial resources whatsoever.[41]

He attempted to sell everything he could, offering the remaining copies of *Absolute Love* to an antiquarian book dealer, but without success. He was briefly back in Le Coudray on the 20th, because there is a mysterious passage in a letter from Demolder to Fontainas: "Ah! Jarry was extraordinary! I can see he is terrified by that himself—If I was alone it wouldn't matter—luckily there is some forgiveness here." Jarry's health began to suffer with the onset of winter, and this coincided with his impossible financial situation. He was bedridden in Paris for much of November; his self-diagnosis was influenza, but it was almost certainly more serious. He may have returned to Laval to be nursed by his sister.[42]

Demolder wrote at the end of November 1905 to let Jarry know that *Le Manoir* was finally finished. Earlier versions had been performed in February and August at least, and this final version would be put on as a part of the Exposition Universelle at Liège in December. The play must then have brought in a little cash. Demolder also promised Jarry he would recover the manuscript of *Le Moutardier*. Jarry intended, it appears, to work this up into something more ambitious, and he was researching the history of the Popes at the Bibliothèque Nationale. He was also working there on *La Dragonne*, principally because the reading rooms were heated. One evening, on his departure, he met Doctor Saltas on the steps. The doctor was a little taken aback by his distressed appearance. They spoke of Jarry's research into Popes, and the project of making a joint translation of Emmanuel Royidis's novel *Pope Joan* came into being. Saltas was of Greek origin, and Jarry's knowledge of the classical language was unsurpassed. Thus this inexorable optimist embarked upon yet another collaboration: Saltas would provide a literal crib and then Jarry would transpose it into literary French. (An anonymous French translation had appeared in 1878, but they were either ignorant of the fact, or ignored it.)[43]

"He often arrived at my place, in the rain, his canvas shoes full of holes and totally soaked. I slipped a warm brick under his feet, taking every precaution to spare his feelings, which was no easy matter. And then we worked." So Saltas recalled, and sometimes he succeeded in persuading Jarry to eat something. Jarry himself later wrote of this "terrible winter in Paris, without heating, feet soaking wet all the time—thanks for your bricks!" Saltas stressed Jarry's careful and delicate punctiliousness, his refusal to accept money except small amounts as a short-term loan, or even invitations if he thought them offered from pity. Such scruples tended to isolate him in Paris. Unable to socialize because of his penury, he spent days alone in his room or in the library.[44]

Is this when Apollinaire's celebrated evocation of the Chasublery dates from? Certainly there is no sign of the great pyramidal library described by Salmon, although Apollinaire's jovial anecdotage is somewhat at odds with Jarry's increasingly desperate situation. He evidently took Jarry's dismissive bravado at face value: "low beds are all the rage." Accuracy was not of much interest either; he gets the floor number wrong, and Jarry's precious folding table, "our Colbert bureau in white wood," goes unnoticed. Since this was one of the few possessions Jarry later listed as worth saving in a letter to Vallette, it is doubtful that he was ever reduced to writing on the floor. Nevertheless, Apollinaire's account deserves its fame:[45]

"Monsieur Jarry?"

"On the third floor and a half."

The concierge's reply astonished me. I went up to see Alfred Jarry, who did in fact live on the third floor and a half. The landlord, finding that the ceilings of his property were too high, had divided the floors horizontally. The building, which is still there, in this way has fifteen floors, but as, by definition, it is no taller than the buildings on either side, it is only the reduction of a skyscraper.

But, while we are on the subject, reductions of this kind flourished everywhere in the abode of Alfred Jarry. This third-and-a-half was nothing but the reduction of a floor, in which the tenant, standing upright, was perfectly at his ease, while I, being taller, had to bend down. The bed was only the minimal reduction of a bed, i.e. a mattress—low beds are all the rage, Jarry told me. His writing-desk was barely a desk, since Jarry wrote lying flat on his stomach on the floor. The furnishings were severely reduced, since they consisted of nothing but the bed. A reduction of a picture was hanging on the wall. It was a portrait of Jarry, most of which he had burnt away, leaving only the head, which showed him looking rather like Balzac in a particular lithograph that I know of. His library was only the reduction of a library—and that was saying a lot, it being made up of a cheap edition of Rabelais, and two or three children's books from the Bibliothèque Rose. On the mantelpiece stood a gigantic stone phallus, a piece of Japanese work that was a gift to Jarry from Félicien Rops. He always kept a kind of purple velvet hood over this ornament, ever since the day when the exotic monolith had scared the wits out of a lady writer who, breathless after climbing up to the third and a half, and completely at a loss in this unfurnished Grand Chasublery, had asked:

"Is that a cast from life?"

"Not at all," replied Jarry, "it's a reduction."[46]

So reduced, indeed, were Jarry's circumstances that late in December he brought himself to write to Terrasse for a loan, requesting a sum of between 20 and 50 francs. Terrasse's reaction to this appeal, which Jarry informed him was addressed from the sickbed which his doctor had forbidden him to leave, is not known. These two weeks in bed, due once again, he assumed, to the flu, were at least made bearable by the gift of a paraffin heater from Rachilde and Vallette. Jarry managed to get himself to their home on New Year's Eve for a "mirific dinner." The new year commenced with Jarry yet again prostrated, perhaps missing the first of Rachilde's Tuesdays on January 9.[47]

Such seems to have been Jarry's existence during the first few months of 1906: isolation, bouts of illness and depression, extreme poverty, working on *La Dragonne* and *Pope Joan*, as well as on other projects intended to raise some income from his past writings. Jarry made contact with a new publisher, Edward Sansot, who in April agreed to publish a collection of six small volumes with the collective name *Théâtre Mirlitonesque*. Three volumes were to be devoted to operettas written for Terrasse; the three remaining were to consist of *Ubu sur la Butte*, a reworking of the version staged at the Quat'z'Arts; *Ubu intime*, the latest version of *Ubu cocu*; and a selection of Jarry's "Speculations" entitled *Siloquies, Superloquies, Soliloquies and Interloquies in Pataphysics*.[48]

At the end of March 1906, Georges-Michel saw him at the painter Carrière's funeral: "ema-ciated, translucent, almost a ghost of himself." Given the state of Jarry's health, his heavy work-load was hardly wise, and to make matters worse, Saltas proved demanding. Although he was essentially generous and considerate, his good nature could be overruled by his most urgent ambition: to be a published author. Coauthorship, even as a translator, would suffice. Once work on *Pope Joan* had begun, and Fasquelle had agreed to publish it, Saltas could barely suppress his impatience to see it in print. Doubly frustrating to him was the fact that Jarry, having received generous advances for *La Dragonne*, must finish that work first. Jarry's letters to Saltas for the next few months are forever urging him to patience. They stress Jarry's own diligent application to the twin tasks, which became ever more frenetic over the following weeks; but application did not necessitate abstinence:[49]

1? April 1906

My dear friend,

All is well, do not be impatient. Yesterday, *sixty-three* of the major pages with which you are familiar remained, and I managed to do six per hour, which is impressive. The third section was daunting, being so long. I spent last night on it, and for tonight, I still have over thirty pages to do. I have not wanted to meet up with Fasquelle until we have finished. Sansot, the publisher, was kind enough to supply the regimen necessary for my work and which would startle anyone, if all my friends did not already suspect such practices; it consists of consuming a whole roast leg of lamb for dinner and then drinking like a Templar. ... Everything will be rewritten, I think tomorrow night ... I might come and say hello at 4 o'clock, but more likely, if you're free, at half past 8.

Sincerely
A. Jarry

P.S. I reopen my letter. Received a telegram from F. Kolney, Tailhade's brother-in-law, concerning their theatrical thing. I'm busy tomorrow night. See you at 4, whether I finish it or not. ...[50]

Owing to his absence from his usual haunts, Jarry's friends were becoming increasingly con-cerned for his well-being. Aware of his destitution, Tailhade had proposed a revival of *Ubu Roi* for the author's benefit. Kolney approached Jarry at the Mercure Tuesday of March 27, and on April 2 Jarry wrote a warm, though not exactly immediate, acceptance of Tailhade's offer to give the introductory lecture. Guitry would lend his theater, and Gémier reprise his role: all seemed propitious. Within days, however, Jarry had second thoughts—a benefit performance was a form of charity. Rachilde believed she had persuaded him otherwise, and even on April 18 he put aside his doubts so far as to meet Kolney to discuss the matter. In the end, though, "he refused, so anxious was he to ensure that his private life remained unknown to the public." Probably in anticipation of his refusal, Vallette had come up with a different means of raising some funds: a special subscribers' edition of the short play Jarry had written with Demolder nearly three years before, *Le Moutardier du Pape*. This offer proved acceptable.[51]

Toward the end of April 1906, Jarry returned to the Bibliothèque Nationale in order to finish off the final draft of *Pope Joan* in one frenetic burst of intensive work, since he and Saltas hoped to deliver the manuscript to Fasquelle before the end of the month. His absorption in the book was approaching the manic, judging by his letters to Saltas who, as a doctor, should have suspected that this euphoria might indicate something more serious.[52]

After a day in the library, on the evening of the 24th, he had a social engagement. Jarry's old friend Paul Fort had founded a new, and substantial, literary magazine the year before, its title simplicity itself: *Vers et Prose*. Coedited with Valéry, this quarterly was intended to unite the more progressive of the Symbolists with the new generation of poets, who were represented on the board by André Salmon. *Vers et Prose* held a weekly soirée at the Closerie des Lilas, a café at the eastern end of the boulevard Montparnasse, not far from Jarry's old apartment, the Calvary. These evenings, ebullient and often drunken affairs, soon became the most important avant-garde gatherings of their day and flourished, as did the magazine, until the beginning of the First World War. The fifth issue of the review, for March to June 1906, contained the first part of *La Dragonne* and thus introduced the Parisian public to the Ubuists of the Café Brosse. It was launched at the Closerie on April 24. Jarry spent part of the evening discussing *Pope Joan* with Jean Moréas. Being of Greek extraction, he made suggestions as to how Jarry might preserve its humor in French.[53]

Jarry, though, had been seldom seen of late, and it was perhaps his appearance at this launch that alerted his friends to the inevitability of some sort of crisis. Vallette decided to take him to Le Coudray, probably the first time Jarry was actually able to stay at the Tripod. Here he might recuperate a little. Jarry had previously arranged to introduce Apollinaire to Rousseau, so he wrote to apologize that they could not have dinner with him after all. Apollinaire and Jarry continued to be close, and had recently dined with Mirbeau and his wife, she and Jarry still disputing whether bulls were ever drunk or not.[54]

It was quickly obvious that Le Coudray was not a permanent solution. Saltas and Vallette set to persuading Jarry to go and stay with his sister in Laval. His health worsened dramatically, he became seriously ill, and eventually he agreed to go on May 11. Vallette took precautions. Adolphe Van Bever, Jarry's old predecessor at the Œuvre, was delegated to conduct him to the station and to ensure he got on the train. No doubt Vallette and his wife were relieved to receive a telegram that evening: "ARRIVED SAFELY THANK YOU WILL WRITE TOMORROW. JARRY."[55]

· · ·

Jarry was to spend more of the time remaining to him in Laval than in Paris or Le Coudray. There he was primarily supported by his sister, who appears to have paid for his medical care and—something of a contradiction—for his alcohol. However, Charlotte's circumstances were by no means comfortable, and this extra strain on her resources was to have serious consequences for her. She never complained of her brother's behavior, and appears both to have loved and admired him.

Chauveau later wrote, and the Vallettes must have told themselves, that "this quiet town, where anything that might fire up the temperament or the passions, remains hidden […] where the Mayenne flows, silent and slow, past impassive shaded walks and deserted granite quays; and where the empty lawns and flowers of the beautiful gardens of La Perrine overlook the town; all this would have an excellently calming effect on Jarry."[56]

On the contrary, the tedium confirmed his fondness for drink.

9. *LAVAL (Mayenne) - Porte Beucheresse et Rue Charles-Landelle*

Edition N. G.

14.8
The Porte Beucheresse, the medieval gateway to Laval, was the birthplace of Henri Rousseau. Jarry and his sister took rooms on the top floor of the corner house halfway down the street; their dormer windows can be seen on the third floor. Part of the cathedral is visible across the street on the left.

Charlotte had rented rooms on the top floor of a new building overlooking the cathedral, a few yards from the towers of the Porte Beucheresse, at 13, rue Charles-Landelle. Jarry marked the building on a postcard to Rachilde in the traditional manner. They could not reside in either of the two small houses Charlotte owned in the rue de Bootz because they had been let to a large multitude of tenants. The census of 1906 lists 43 inhabitants, mainly artisans and their families, and the rental amounted to some 1,200 francs annually. This presumably constituted the bulk of Charlotte's income.[57]

Whereas up until now Jarry's correspondence had been fitful, for the next few months it became voluminous: the result of his isolation far from Paris, but also of the frenzy manifested earlier when finishing *Pope Joan*. His inability to write creatively prompted a huge displacement into letter writing. Almost half of Jarry's published correspondence dates from his last eighteen months, and that before more than thirty letters came to light during the writing of this book. Such a sudden mass is obviously problematic, and only those letters which seemed essential, along with a smattering of those which have not been previously published, are cited here. Various themes are common to the majority of them, however. Those to Rachilde most often concern Jarry's work on *La Dragonne*, and the imminence of its completion; to Vallette, his phynances and *Le Moutardier*; to Saltas, details of his health and pleas for patience regarding their translation of *Pope Joan*. Such was the import of his first letter to the doctor, the day after his arrival in Laval, along with his feeling greatly fatigued.[58]

The next day, Jarry visited the barracks in which he had endured his military service. Research for *La Dragonne*. He felt fine, more than fine, although his exaggerated protestations as to the excellence of his health were themselves symptoms of its fragility. Now, though, he had decided that all of this was going into his novel (which would fatally delay its completion). He had thought he was done for, which means the illness of his last few days in Paris must have been serious, but now this illness would simply provide material for his book, in fact he "is documenting himself like a commonplace Zola." Or so he wrote to Rachilde on May 15, 1906. The letter contained a self-portrait—Jarry had purchased a Kodak and taken up photography. He photographed himself in his room with the cathedral behind, a stuffed eight-legged sheep in a shop window, and so on; none of his photographs has survived.

Within days Jarry's health took another turn for the worse. By the 18th he was confined to his bed, and a series of almost daily bulletins to Saltas began. Appeals for medicines, a clinical thermometer, and for alternative diagnoses to those of the family doctor, and then to those of a more prestigious physician, Doctor Bucquet, accustomed to tending to the local aristocracy. Bouts of lucidity, during which he penned his letters, alternated with fever. The diagnosis was vague—acute neurasthenia, cerebral fever—but the presumed true cause, the first cerebral attack by tuberculosis, remained unsuspected. The fever passed after a few days and Jarry, assuming the worst was over, recovered his bravado. A bad night followed, then a further recovery which he attributed to his taking quinine to suppress his temperature. Jarry ordered extra supplies of it from Saltas, and also asked his opinion as to whether he was justified in drinking a little cider, instead of the water suggested by Bucquet, since "my stomach is not yet inured to plain water, which makes me vomit from being unaccustomed."[59]

In Paris, his friends were following events. Vallette was raising funds through the subscription to *Le Moutardier*. Fénéon wrote to Thadée Natanson, and copied the letter to his brother too:

25 May 1906

Dear Thadée,

Vallette has sent the subscription form both to me, and to other friendly palotins, for a small book to be printed in an edition of 110 copies. A ruse invented by himself and Demolder in order, so he says, to bail out Père Ubu, who is in a lamentable situation, physically, morally, financially … he is in disastrous penury. I think it may please you to have the subscription form: I therefore enclose it with this letter. Among other things Vallette added that this is extremely urgent.

Yours, affectionately
Félix Fénéon [60]

The same day the fever returned, more severe than ever. Over the three days and nights that followed it reached its peak, and Jarry had every reason to believe he was dying. Bucquet was frequently at his bedside, Charlotte permanently so. Jarry hovered between delirium and lucidity. On May 27, 1906, his sister began to write at his request: "Alfred Jarry being on the point of death and unable to finish his manuscript of *La Dragonne* dictates this plan to his sister." The plan was both detailed and extensive.[61]

The fever intensified and the following day Jarry, believing his final moment was upon him, allowed a priest from the cathedral across the street to administer extreme unction. Then he wrote out his last will and testament (he crossed out the words indicated at a later date):

28 May 1906

This is my testament

I the undersigned Alfred Jarry, being in full possession of my faculties, bequeath to my sister Charlotte Jarry, 13, rue Charles-Landelle, Laval (Mayenne) all my goods and chattels and (which would furthermore legally revert to her) all my copyrights on all my books, and plays, in particular *Pantagruel*. I stipulate, the declaration not yet having been made to the Société des auteurs, that I demand at least four-twelfths, which is not much when one has done the greater part of the work, ~~and since it has caused the acute neurasthenia of which I am now dying.~~

I invite Madame Alfred Vallette (Rachilde) to accept my landholdings at Les Bas-Vignons. It goes without saying that whatever has not yet been paid for should be deducted from my royalties.

Alfred Jarry [62]

A few afterthoughts were added, including one requesting that Vallette be his literary executor. He then dictated the announcement of his death. Charlotte carefully left an empty space for the date. It contains an entirely fictitious Breton variant of his mother's maiden name: Caroline Quernest became Caroline Kernec'h de Coutouly de Dorset. He had dedicated *La Dragonne* to her under the same name the day before. Finally he wrote "last letters" to Vallette and Rachilde. The one to Vallette is lost, but that to Rachilde is the one she used to end her biography (the reference to mauve is because this was the color of the covers of the *Mercure de France*):[63]

Laval, 28 May 1906.

Madame Rachilde,

This time Père Ubu is not writing in a fever (this is starting to sound like a will, which furthermore, has already been written). I think you have understood, he is not dying (sorry! it slipped out) of bottles and other orgies. He didn't have that passion, and he has been so fastidious as to have himself examined all over by the "docturds." He has no defect, neither in the liver, nor in the heart, nor in the kidneys, nor even in the urinary system! He is worn out, that's all (a strange end for one who wrote *The Supermale*), and his boiler is not going to burst, but simply go out. He is going to come quite gently to a halt, like a broken-down motor. ... And no human diet or anything else, however carefully (while laughing inwardly) adhered to, will do him any good. His fever is perhaps caused by his heart's trying to save him by rising to a rate of 150. No human being has ever held out that far. For the last two days he has been among the Lord's "extremely unctioned" and, like Kipling's elephant-without-a-trunk, filled "with insatiable curiosity," he is on the point of going a little *further* back into the night of time. Just as he used to have his revolver in his "arse-pocket," he has decked himself out with a golden chain around his neck, solely because this metal is rust-proof and will last as long as his bones, with medals in which he believes, in case he should encounter any demons. ... This is as amusing as fishing. ... Let us note that, if he does not die, it will be grotesque to have written all this. ... But we repeat that this is not written in a bout of fever. He has left such lovely things on earth, but is disappearing in such an apotheosis!

Detail: ask Vallette to deduct from my subscriptions, if anything is left, something for h.p. [i.e. Hermann-Paul] so I can leave you the portrait; 2nd bequest, the Tripod, what would my sister do with it? And of course after the outstanding bills have been paid on *Pantagruel* or whatever. ... And, as Socrates said on his death-bed to Ctesiphon: "remember we owe a cock to Aesculapius." For my *honor*'s sake I want Vallette to "cover" himself as regards old, done-for *writings*. And now, Madame, you who are descended from great Spanish Inquisitors, he who through his mother is the last *Dorset* (no delusions of grandeur, I have here my titles of nobility) ventures to remind you of his double device: AUT NUNQUAM TENTES, AUT PERFICE (attempt nothing, or go the whole way, I'm going there, Madame Rachilde)—FOREVER FAITHFUL ... and asks you to *pray* for him: the *quality* of the prayer will perhaps save him. ... But he is armed against Eternity, and has no fear.

By the way … yesterday I dictated to my sister the detailed plan of *La Dragonne*. It is certainly a fine book. Would the writer I admire most in the world care to take it up, use according to her judgment what has been done, and finish it, either on her own or in posthumous collaboration?

If need be she will send you the manuscript, three-quarters written, a fat box of notes and the aforesaid plan.

Père Ubu has shaved, has a mauve shirt ready, by chance! So he'll depart in the *colors* of the Mercure … and will *slip the painter*, still steeped in an insatiable curiosity. He has a feeling it will be at five this evening … if he's wrong, that will be ridiculous, but that's how it is, ghosts are always ridiculous.

With that, Père Ubu, who hasn't been resting on his laurels, is going to try and get some sleep. He believes that the decomposing brain goes on working after death and it is its dreams that constitute Paradise. Père Ubu, this is provisional—he would so very much like to return to the Tripod—will perhaps sleep *forever*.

Alfred Jarry

P.S. I've reopened my letter, the Dr. has just come and reckons to save me.[64]

The P.S. was confirmed a few hours later with a brief telegram to the Vallettes: "NOTICEABLY BETTER WILL GET OUT OF THIS JARRY."[65]

But all was not quite over. Jarry's illness flared up again, apparently more powerfully than ever. A remarkable document, saved by Jarry in an envelope, has survived from this moment: a letter for Rachilde which he never sent, and had torn into pieces. Written during his delirium over the night of May 28 and 29, it was in part dictated to Charlotte (roman), part in Jarry's hand (italics), and the sections in bold here were in Latin. The manuscript was covered in erasures, barely legible corrections and afterthoughts:[66]

28/29 [?] May 1906
Believe it or not, without anybody having renewed his theological ideas, Père Ubu himself has asked for extreme unction, he has received an extraordinary grace such as not even the Desert Fathers had, he has demanded of the Devil, Madame, two days, *it is the Enemy in person, Madame Rachilde* that prevented you from leaving before receiving the telegram. Père Ubu has pulled off all the tricks he wanted to on the Enemy. Have a priest translate the attached letter [many words deleted] Père Ubu has written which was one of the temptations Christ did not dare in hell. He has blessed and delivered "the beautiful angel with burnt wings" that suffered for six thousand years, and permitted him to be his guardian angel. Being the Lord's anointed he had the power to give him the sword of fire that watched over the gates of Paradise.

Depart, oh prince of demons, thy third temptation was in vain; depart into the darkness; thou hast sought to be a traitor; Saint Anne and the Blessed Virgin hold me in their arms, oh Serpent; *the Virgin or, to speak in Greek but after the Catholic fashion, ή Πανάγια* has set her foot upon thy head and she has trampled rough-shod upon thee and I am in the fire of pain but never shall I be in the fire of thy dominion. Saint Anne, *mother of the Mother of God*, watches over me. If in fever and in enfeeblement I have returned to thee the sword, *let that wonderful sword, which the angel drew at the gates of Paradise against Adam and Eve,* be placed anew *in the hand of Christ thy eternal Lord and vanquisher of the gates of hell. And then, oh prince of demons, depart into thy darkness, by him, and in him, and with him. Get thee behind me!*

In the name of the Father, and of the Son, and of the Holy Ghost, of the Blessed Virgin Mary and of Saint Anne her mother in devotion to whom I have set a marble stone in the wall of the basilica at Auray, I place my soul in the hand of the Blessed Anne and, the triple temptation of the Eternal Enemy overcome, heaven has granted me the unaccustomed grace that the archangel Saint Michael himself with his unsheathed sword in his hand watches over the head of my bed and that Père Ubu goes deeper into eternity. And since Père Ubu is the Lord's anointed, let there be a conjuration thanks to which he be re-enchained and chained in his dominion by him, and in him, and with him. In the name of the Father, etc. and of the Blessed Anne, my Savioress.

Amen
Alfred Jarry

Saint Michael the archangel has in person taken the trouble to come to the bedside of Père Ubu by means of a formula of exorcism (alas, or happily, Père Ubu knows them so well); he has taken up again the impossible Weapon and now, as in the old prints, he has Saint Michael at his bedside. If he should recover, no human being *has been so far beyond the gates of death. He sees the other world and speaks of it, out of courtesy and prudence, in the words of the Church. Only a very old monk, deeply learned in theology, might be capable of appreciating the case. Père Ubu, now the Lord's anointed, commands the two worlds. That is a frightful power he has only toyed with. Danville must at the moment be drunk thanks to the care of "Lucifer, princ' ar Diaolou," who has fought bravely for him—and this is not written in fever but a curious theological case, Père Ubu has, if he makes use of it only in the name of the Church, has under his orders the Exterminating Angel! ... As to the Other, he has lost sight of him for seven hours, what happened in Paris?*

Written in complete lucidity and without fever, on the point of death which blurs his vision.

A. Jarry [67]

The next day, the fever had passed. More comprehensible missives followed, apologizing for his melodramatic outpourings (he had sent a similar letter to Vallette). A telegram on the 30th: "HUGE CEREBRAL CRISIS WHICH EXCUSES LITERARY EXAGGERATION NOW OVER CURE ASSURED WITH REST EXCUSES MADAME RACHILDE LETTER FOLLOWS JARRY." Doctor Bucquet was insisting on a month's total rest, although Jarry was already deliberating how to incorporate these recent events into *La Dragonne*. This was no more than the logical continuation of the process that had been evident throughout this illness. Jarry's fever-induced delirium became so inseparable from his literary imagination that his visions, and his supposed journey beyond death, were experienced by him as a literary euphoria with himself as protagonist. The frenzy of writing in Paris that preceded the crisis had initiated this synthesis, already latent in his novels, so many of which are characterized by intensely subjective states which are resolved by the death of the principal character. Only Jarry's alter ego, Doctor Faustroll, is able, like himself, to travel beyond mortality: a sort of premonition perhaps. As early as May 15, after recovering from his initial collapse in Paris, Jarry had written to Rachilde: "The posthumous life of Père Ubu is quite extraordinary," before describing how his illness will become a part of *La Dragonne* entitled "The Night of Time."[68]

...

Jarry's acceptance of the last rites raises the question of his Catholicism. More to the point, was he a believer? This is difficult to answer definitively, although by now it must be obvious that Jarry's real interest in such forms of discourse generally lay in the modalities and aesthetics of their structure rather than in their supposed meaning. Theological speculations occur throughout Jarry's works, most famously at the end of *Faustroll*, but also in chapter 8 of *The Supermale*. Both come to the conclusion that God is infinite, but infinitely small. Certainly Jarry had had a passion for Catholic iconography since before the creation of *L'Ymagier*. This was in part sentimental, since Brittany was the most Catholic part of France and his Breton childhood became more important to him as he grew older, being directly connected to his love for his mother. But Jarry was not exactly a sentimental being, or at least not for long.[69]

More important was the fact that Catholicism furnished a scheme of codes and symbols, a system of representation, that could be subjected to aesthetic and logical manipulation. All the better that its premises were absurd. There could be no question of taking such systems seriously, let alone their supposed significance, and most references to God in Jarry's writings are sardonic and amused rather than reverential. Or narcissistic, as in *Days and Nights*: "*Take not the Name of God in vain* is the only valid courtesy; it is ridiculous to spit on one's mirror." Religion, furthermore, was not exempt from Pataphysics, and was therefore an imaginary solution like any other, and thus the invention of man. "The idea of God dates from the day that a quadruped felt the muscles of his buttocks were firm and strong enough to allow an upright posture. On that day he looked up at the sky and was afraid it would fall on its head. His front legs being no longer required for walking, he clasped his hands together. [...] Since religious sentiments are directly related to the development of the larger gluteal muscles, it is obvious why women are more devout than men." As for the clergy, the Pope, they were a continual source of amusement.[70]

...

"Once I am on my feet there will be a regime of country walks, a little cycling, picnics," Jarry wrote to Saltas on May 29, 1906. Charlotte may have managed to instigate such a convalescence, but practical problems, ignored since his arrival in Laval, quickly came crashing in from all sides. The same letter to Saltas informed him: "I am now relatively well off thanks to the Mercure." Vallette had disbursed the first subscriptions for *Le Moutardier*, but Jarry's wealth was entirely illusory. Since his disappearance from Le Coudray in May, a small crowd of creditors had made themselves known to Vallette. His villa was inconveniently close to the Tripod.[71]

The edition of *Le Moutardier* was to consist of 110 copies for sale, with a portrait by Cazals and vignettes by Paul Ranson. Ten copies would be on *Hollande* paper, signed and with a second state of the portrait and a page of manuscript: 50 francs each. The 100 numbered copies were priced at 20 francs. Thus the entire edition might realize 2,500 francs, less the cost of printing it. Already, during Jarry's illness, Vallette had been paying small sums to Jarry's creditors against the subscription, and by July he had paid out some 1,142 francs to Jarry himself.[72]

In June, as a ruse to prevent his only remaining asset being seized by bailiffs, Jarry sold his two plots of land to his sister for 400 francs. His creditors in Le Coudray were principally wine merchants, but the most immediate debt was that owing to Dubois. His invoice for building the Tripod runs to two detailed pages of itemization before culminating in a total of 1,212.15 francs. This sum was followed by a misspelled but affecting appeal for a little payment, at least, please. A wholly reasonable request from an artisan whose only fault appears to have been the very one he shared with his employer, a fondness for Mère Fontaine's (with whom he has left the keys, as he stated in a P.S.). But Jarry could not pay him, being busy acquiring new debts in Laval. Debts, recurring demands for payment, and yet more debts: *La Dragonne* and *Pantagruel* were no more than that, having been paid for but not delivered.[73]

Terrasse must have come to believe there was a curse on *Pantagruel*. In June he returned to Paris after a stint working in Germany, and sent Demolder an optimistic assessment. Foreign directors were interested, although all thought the third act too long. He would come to La Demi-Lune, where they would finally be able to complete it (he also asked after "his old friend" Jarry). Precisely at this juncture Demolder suffered a serious heart attack. An earlier seizure at the beginning of the year had been put down to his drinking: "three liters of wine a day, not counting the beer and all the rest. For a while his throat was paralyzed." There was no prospect of his being able to work, and a further attack the following year ended the collaboration for good. Terrasse, much to his credit, joined Vallette and Fénéon in the effort to contact subscribers for *Le Moutardier*. Judging from the manuscripts, Jarry repaid him by making final revisions to *Pantagruel* early in 1907. It would be the end of his involvement, and the libretto remained unfinished.[74]

Further problems now arose with Saltas, whose importuning of Jarry to finish *La Dragonne* became intolerable, especially as Bucquet had prescribed absolute rest with no writing. Jarry feared that Saltas would compromise his relationship with Fasquelle, to whom Saltas wished to appeal directly. Jarry denounced him as a blockhead and an *arriviste* to both Vallette and Fénéon. He asked the latter to intercede with Fasquelle and convince him that Saltas was not acting on Jarry's behalf. Saltas had certainly got carried away, although he perhaps made up for it after Jarry's death. Somewhat controversially, he became Jarry's literary executor, but he proved more determined than Vallette ever would have been. Saltas was responsible for several important posthumous editions of Jarry's writings, beginning with *Faustroll*. He also carefully preserved every scrap of Jarry's literary papers, most of which were sold at auction on his death in 1954, before passing into the keeping of the founders of the Collège de 'Pataphysique.[75]

...

The crisis of 1906 shocked Jarry profoundly. Henceforth his correspondence with Rachilde and Vallette would return again and again to his health, although he disguised his concern with Ubu-esque levity and inexhaustible optimism. There are numerous references to the splendors of "our sovereign health" or "our precious longevity." Jarry appears to have thought he could hold off his illness by pure willpower, with incantations of reassurance and recovery addressed to Rachilde and Vallette, but which seem rather more aimed at himself, their power lying in simple repetition. Even so, he was on occasion unable to maintain the simulation, and a card to Vallette, probably from June 1906, is a case in point, in which even Jarry's handwriting begins to go awry at the critical moment (underlined here):

> Monsieuye,
>
> All is well, but we are wondering why you are settling so many sums in our name. We don't really have any illness <u>but we have a vivid desire to live</u> (drink, eat, sleep at regular times).
>
> Don't hold back from sending us proofs.
>
> AJ[76]

Vallette had been urging Jarry to use the advances from *Le Moutardier* to settle some of his debts, and this card confirms that he had decided off his own bat to rid Jarry of some of the smaller ones. But Dubois's bill would remain unpaid.[77]

By June 8, 1906, Jarry was sending back the first set of *Le Moutardier* proofs (with Demolder's agreement he had removed the latter's contributions to the text), and he was beginning to yearn for Le Coudray again. The fishing season was about to open. Jarry's imminent return to the Tripod, endlessly postponed, would become another recurring topic in his letters to the Vallettes. For the remainder of the month, Jarry occupied himself with *La Dragonne*. He decided he was well enough to take up fencing once again, as he reported to Rachilde, who had also been ill:[78]

> In these times when everyone is sick, or so they say (Have we been? It's forgotten), we were almost concerned not to have had news from you or Vallette, despite your "insolent good health" (to cite a column from the Mercure). Lorrain's end amazes us! As for ourselves, we have been vaccinated against death long-term. We were able to hold out almost nonstop for a whole hour in the fencing room of the officers of the 104th, and the 18mo comes along too. So we will soon be at the Tripod. A.J.[79]

A typical letter: his marvelous good health, his impending arrival at the Tripod, the 18mo going well (he always referred to *La Dragonne* in this manner; an 18mo is a standard book format). The reference to the writer Jean Lorrain, an old acquaintance from the Mercure, was to his recent death from peritonitis when his bowel was perforated during an enema.

July 12, 1906 was the due date for Jarry to pay for his third bit of land at Les Bas-Vignons, and he managed to come up with the 200 francs. At about the same time, a long letter from Max Jacob to Picasso included a paragraph on Jarry's illness. Anticipating his death, Jacob comments that the position of Harlequin in Paris will soon be vacant. Meanwhile Fénéon had arranged publication dates for *La Dragonne* and *Pope Joan* with Fasquelle. Completing the former was now a matter of urgency.[80]

Jarry appeared temperamentally incapable of rest and recuperation. He had Vallette send his bicycle from Paris, and in return attached a sample of a splendid new fishing line to a postcard depicting the Mayenne by moonlight. Cycling, fishing, fencing—Jarry presented a picture of hearty well-being: a representation he had captured in two photographs of himself in action at Maître Blaviel's Fencing Academy, where he had trained in his youth. One bore the caption: "To Rachilde and Vallette, in recollection of the other world and … back again, with many thanks! Attack by Père Ubu with a war saber on Maître Blaviel, fencing master to the 101st regiment of the line: Père Ubu goes straight for the *gidouille*. Maître Blaviel parries prime and makes ready to riposte with a slashing blow to the head. Père Ubu, detesting this maneuver, makes ready in his turn to make himself scarce, backward, with a double *coup de manchette*." The other, illustrated here, reads: "To Vallette and Rachilde with best wishes, this document for *La Dragonne*, the Exterminator's sword … AJ resuscitated! Quite simply 'vanquisher of death.'"[81]

These are the last known photographs of Jarry. The bill for these lessons (67.20 francs) was settled by Charlotte only after Jarry's death, and Blaviel later suspected Jarry of purloining two foils and exchanging them for drink. According to Arnaud, Jarry celebrated his return to health with vigorous renditions of "The Song of Disembraining" on the maternal piano.[82]

A further sum of 120 francs arrived from Vallette on July 20, and soon afterward Jarry judged himself well enough to return to Paris. He arrived in time for a banquet in honor of Jean Moréas held by *Vers et Prose* on the 26th. The forty-odd diners included most of his friends: Apollinaire, Cazals, Cremnitz, Vallette, among many others.[83]

The first two of the "mirlitonesques" were published in July: *Ubu sur la Butte* and *Par la taille*. They appeared in editions of 600 copies in bright green covers with a yellow design and bright red lettering, like children's books. They sold poorly, which was presumably why the remaining

14.9
The last known photograph of Alfred Jarry.

four were never published. "By the way, you're quite correct," Jarry wrote to Rachilde, "the little green books are no more significant than a candy twist." Jarry's inscriptions on copies to Rachilde and Vallette refer to them as "posthumous works." It is noticeable that yet again Jarry had made no attempt to usher *Faustroll* into print. Perhaps the coda at the end of the Lormel manuscript was meant in all seriousness.[84]

A new piece of genealogical self-delusion was manifested in a letter Jarry wrote to Marinetti at the end of July. The early portion of this communication was mostly devoted to polishing the Italian's splendid ego. Jarry congratulated him on his "dazzling" play *La Roi Bombance*, commonly seen as hopelessly derivative of *Ubu Roi*, before proceeding to his real motive for writing. He was pleased to offer Marinetti the opportunity of revealing to the public a new poetess, a Breton to whom he is related: Charlotte J. Kernec'h de Coutouly Dorset. The "J," of course, was left as an initial so that the identity of his sister should remain unrevealed. Marinetti duly published two of her unremarkable poems in *Poesia*. Jarry noted in passing that he was again confined to his bed in the rue Cassette.[85]

...

Finally, in August 1906, Jarry was able to savor the joys of the Tripod. Demolder had by now been diagnosed with diabetes, and his wife was maintaining her husband's correspondence with Fontainas: "The colony of Les Bas-Vignons is well. Jarry is much better mentally. Physically, he is still very weak. However, the swelling to his feet and hands has rapidly diminished; he is nearly in his normal state." Jarry would stay at the Tripod until mid-October, his only continuous period of residence in his mirific tower, a matter of eight weeks or so. His sole income continued to be the subscription to *Le Moutardier*; Vallette wrote to an unknown correspondent on August 17: "Père Ubu is at the Tripod but he is still unwell. [...] The winter will be very tough on him, I do not think he can work seriously despite the subscription, which amounts to around 1,800 francs." Jarry had already received the bulk of that.[86]

Even so, it was necessary to furnish the cellar, the building of which was more than a whim on Jarry's part. Since at least 1903, from when an invoice survives for 93 liters of Minervois, Jarry had been buying wine by the barrel. In late September 1906 he ordered, from a Monsieur Ducot, a *barrique* of Créon Entre-2-Mers, 220 liters for 90 francs; and a similar amount from a Monsieur Jobard. The names of Jarry's wine merchants rarely recur, for obvious reasons.[87]

Unbeknown to Jarry, on September 20 Trochon had yet again sent an annual account of the debt for his bicycle to his old address in the boulevard Saint-Germain.

...

In mid-October Vallette sent a further set of *Le Moutardier* proofs to Laval, where Jarry was once again staying with his sister. For financial or health reasons, or for simple comfort? Probably a combination of all three, but "now that we are no longer dying, the charm of the old town is somewhat lessened"—so much so that Jarry decided to return to Paris in time for the first Tuesday of the winter, on November 6. This seemed unwise, given his sufferings of the previous year.[88]

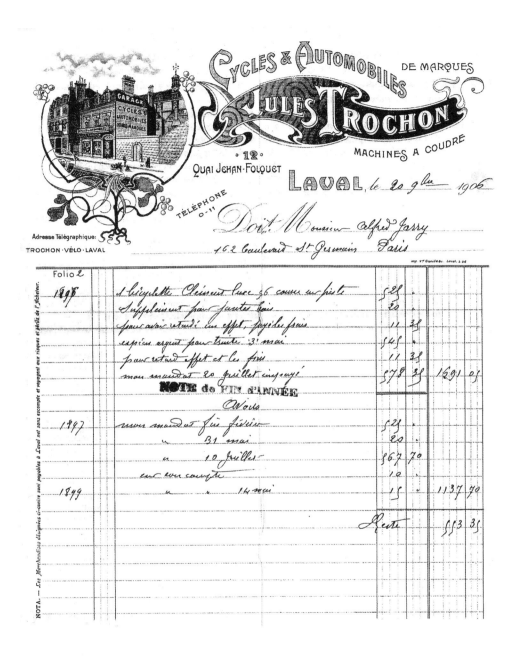

14.10
Trochon's account for Jarry's bicycle.

On the morning of November 5, 1906 he visited Saltas, bearing an inscribed copy of one of the photographs of himself fencing. Saltas, who had not seen Jarry since before his illness, refused to believe it had been taken recently. A day of drinking then ensued, since Jarry ended up at L'Académie, his favorite last-bar-of-the-evening. There he left behind the corrected proofs of *Le Moutardier*, fortunately found and returned to him by a fellow alco-poet, Édouard Jacquemin.[89]

For the following three months in Paris, Jarry found himself in the same situation as that of the previous winter, if not worse. There was a further deterioration not only in his physical health but also in his mental abilities. The worse his daily situation became—his poverty, his debts, his inability to write—the more he isolated himself from it by means of alcohol: a desertion more desperate than those of *Days and Nights*. "Jarry," wrote Rachilde, "descended the stairway of his dangerous fantasies into a cellar of dark misery."[90]

His behavior became a cause of concern and despair for his friends. His endless optimism, so little justified; his resolutions, never acted upon; and then his self-deceptions about his illness and his drinking. To Fénéon he denied what previously he had boasted of to Saltas: "The rumor has been put about […] that Père Ubu drank like a Templar. To you, as an old friend, I can admit … that I had rather got out of the habit of eating, and that was the only thing that ailed me." But it was perfectly obvious to everyone that he was permanently inebriated. Delusion and deceit became inseparable, and, worse, indistinguishable, especially for Jarry himself. This retreat from reality was largely deliberate. The smell of ether now preceded his entry to the salon of the Mercure, but it was not so much that it was cheaper than wine (30 centimes a dram as opposed to wine at around 50 per liter), as that Jarry sought its particular effects. He explained to Rachilde: "It is certainly the equal of your cups of tea, Ma-da-me! At least we are not obliged to also swallow the conversations of your beautiful lady friends, now that you've acquired the unfortunate habit of entertaining women at the rue de Condé. It lulls one more than that, it allows one freedom of movement, even you agree it smells good, and it makes one so *detached*!" Her description of his appearances at the Tuesdays can hardly be bettered:[91]

Jarry spent another winter in the squalor of the rue Cassette. Barely eating any more, he still drank. Every Tuesday, he would get up to come to my evenings, and once there he would talk as if he were the ghost of himself. He was white as a sheet, with dark and deeply sunken eyes. He had taken a strong aversion to all his old friends, and could only just about put up with going to see a *docturd*, having declared that they were the kind of jesters that had given him drugs in order to carry out shameful examinations: "You must realize, Ma-da-me, they're very interested in being allowed to dissect a character of our distinctive mold and fiber. It gives them the opportunity to discover something new." Every now and again, thinking more clearly, he would remember his enormous debts and this would worry him for a while, but then he would add, with a diabolical laugh, "Even if we lived to be a hundred, we'd never be able to repay them!" Before he actually entered the room, it was obvious that he was deeply steeped in ether, and although his reason had been finally overcome by this addiction, he existed in a state of persistent hallucination which fortunately shielded him from awareness of his own degradation.[92]

Cazals's portrait of Jarry purports to date from 1897, but was first published in 1907 in *Le Moutardier*. It closely resembles Rachilde's description, and one suspects it may well have been drawn late in 1906, based upon his previous sketch.

Jarry was again often isolated by his combination of pride and poverty, and he drank alone. Lucidity would intrude upon his voluntary embrace of unreality, and then he wrote. He wrote about his drinking, about his delusions of nobility, about his poverty. His mind wandered through an ether-induced hallucination; it was his life set directly down on the page, as in this extract from *La Dragonne*, in which Erbrand assumes the characteristics of Jarry.

> … he began, simply but furiously, to drink.
>
> He drank alone and methodically, without ever succeeding in reaching intoxication, and without any hope of ever becoming what it is fashionable nowadays to label an alcoholic: the doses were too enormous for them not to slide over his cells like a river being filtered through an eternal and indifferent bed of sand before disappearing: otherwise Erbrand would have long since been dead.

14.11
F.-A. Cazals, Alfred Jarry, reproduced from Rachilde's *Alfred Jarry ou Le Surmâle de lettres*.

He became like a monstrous divinity with the face of a bull, his forehead enlarged and his eyes parted.

And the river, which he had wanted to be the Lethe or the Styx, unfolded its fluid panoramas over his cells—it is common knowledge that the hidden surface of the interior of the body is an exterior, and he delighted in being able to vary its flow according to his will. He lit the fire of bottles one after another, and one with another, like a smoker lighting his cigarettes.

And the splendid beast took such shape in him that, like a wild animal, he came to fear fire.

Then, still logical, he drank in the darkness, and a verse he had read as a child in a magazine about an Italian curiosity sang in his brain of the eternal and invisible river with the mysterious name whose meaning nobody knows:

Anne perenne latens, Anna Peranna vocor.

And he drank the very essence of the tree of science at 80 degrees proof, the spirit that retains the taste of the apple, and he felt at home in Paradise regained. …

But soon he could drink no more in the darkness, because for him there was darkness no longer, and no doubt like Adam before the fault and certainly like the great anthropoids, he could see clearly in the dark.

And so as to continue drinking without ceasing, he pawned his family jewels, although he believed, correctly, that they resembled incorruptible parchment; and that an external sign of nobility was never to possess jewels that had been bought. He pawned them and knew not, being ignorant of such transaction, how to buy them back. But was he not left with both his valueless parchments, and all of himself, the last of his family line?

And he also came to sell the Thing which permitted a tiny sovereign movement of his forefinger to make him everywhere and always the master of the life of all and prince of exterior darkness: his revolver.

And he never, or scarcely ever, bought clothing, as if he were a millionaire scorning these organs of relation. He needed consider no one else, depend on no one else.

And he often deprived himself of food, because one cannot have everything at once and drinking on an empty stomach is more efficacious.[93]

Family jewels! Unfortunately not, but this extract from *La Dragonne* seems to fix Jarry's mental processes in actual motion, firing off in every direction at once (and many of its digressions have been edited out from this extract). The emptied bottles could be set alight because, of course, they contained ether, which is highly flammable.

Jarry's state of confusion, of semi-permanent intoxication, was not wholly induced by alcohol. Unknown to himself, he was in the final stages of tuberculosis. The autopsy later revealed that the bacillus had traveled from the lungs to the brain, where it attacked the meninges, the membranes which envelop the central nervous system and the cerebral cortex. Once these are affected the symptoms include fever, mental confusion, and paranoia, and eventually the damage can be so severe as to cause physical paralysis. When combined with his alcoholism, and addiction to mild hallucinogens such as absinthe and ether, a swirling feedback of fervor and aberration began periodically to take hold of him. He would be overtaken by bouts of *delirium tremens*, by trembling and sweats.[94]

His manias, too, became ever more immoderate. Jarry's fixation with a noble background began to encompass aristocratic and reactionary attitudes. An affectation, or sincerely held? Symptoms of dementia, or a symbolic possession by Hébert, since Jarry now occasionally espoused opinions identical to his? Such distinctions are inapplicable to a personality in total flux, to one seemingly trapped in some sort of malign version of duration. Parts of *La Dragonne* exhibit symptoms of anti-Semitism, a particularly bizarre aberration when his most loyal supporters continued to be his old collaborators on the *Revue Blanche*, the most pro-Dreyfusard literary review of them all. Except that obligation may easily become resentment. …

Henry de Bruchard, a leftist who had moved sharply to the anti-Semitic right, reported this conversation, which is usually, and perhaps too conveniently, interpreted as a joke at Bruchard's vacillations:

> Jarry, after a long stay in the country, had returned to Paris with the instincts of a polemicist. […]
> He wanted to collaborate on a daily newspaper in order to carry out anti-Semitic campaigns.
> "I also want to return to good principles!" he told me during our last meeting at a Tuesday. He added: "I too come from a reactionary family. Now I belong to the Church."[95]

Despite all the alcohol, Jarry's admittedly infrequent letters of late 1906 show no sign of incoherence, although they do of dissimulation. At the end of November he extracted a further 80 francs from the *Le Moutardier* subscription by approaching Terrasse instead of Vallette. He had previously talked Vallette out of another 175 francs on the basis of promised remuneration for articles to be written for a commercial journal named *Chanteclair*. These did not materialize. Vallette wrote a furious letter to Terrasse, and Jarry wrote him an appeasing one in which he offered to finish the last revisions to *Pantagruel*. His friends were being severely tested. Funds in the *Le Moutardier* account were now insufficient to pay for printing the book. Can one believe André Salmon that Jarry disposed of this money, scrabbled together at such personal cost, by passing a whole week in a bar on the rue de Buci which dispensed wine by the liter? It would have been toward the end of this session that Jarry wrote again to Terrasse, suggesting he buy the remainder of his share of *Pantagruel* from him. Terrasse appears to have ignored this chimerical proposition, since Jarry was unwise enough to repeat it a month later.[96]

…

By late 1906 Apollinaire was a regular at Paul Fort's *Vers et Prose* Tuesdays at the Closerie des Lilas. These evening gatherings had become more popular than ever, and now among artists as much as writers. Apollinaire brought with him many of the artists and poets of the Bateau Lavoir: Jacob, Picasso, and all their hangers-on, including Salmon, the review's coeditor. Fort and many of the Mercureists made their way there after Rachilde's soirées; artists drifted in from the nearby studios in Montparnasse, which would soon overtake Montmartre as the artists' quarter in Paris. And Marinetti, typically enough, would pull up in a large white automobile. Jarry was frequently to be seen, although not necessarily up to his usual public form. Cingria, the Swiss author, recalled him almost barefoot, a hat pulled over his eyes, slouched and unspeaking the whole evening. Henri-Pierre Roché, future author of *Jules et Jim*, introduced him to Leo Stein, brother of Gertrude. Fernande Olivier, Picasso's partner, remembered him there too, as did Picasso. His drawing of Jarry is probably a recollection from one of these evenings.[97]

14.12
Picasso, Alfred Jarry, undated, but first published in Apollinaire's *Les Soirées de Paris* in 1914.

Jarry's condition continued to fluctuate, and there were periods when he recovered his old self. He celebrated Christmas Day 1906 with Salmon and Cremnitz, among others. They dined in a small establishment in the rue Mouffetard which specialized in snails, and which Jarry had baptized "Our Grand Manufactory of Escargots." Afterward, at dawn, Jarry pulled from the pockets of his cape a strange medley of grubby ribbons and military medals, from campaigns in Tonkin, Dahomey, Madagascar, with which he ceremoniously decorated his companions.[98]

A few days later he wrote to Rachilde: "Happy New Year. Here I am at last, embarked on '97 … with more than sixty or so years left to drag out." The slip of the pen appears significant: in 1897 a long life may indeed have lain ahead, but in 1907. … The letter ends: "Here is a little calendar for computing the Tuesdays." The homemade calendar is also misdated, 1906 instead of 1907.[99]

The beginning of 1907 bore a distressing resemblance to that of the previous year. Rachilde's account of Jarry at the Tuesdays could be easily supplemented with equally somber descriptions by Tailhade and Régnier. Saltas bumped into him in the street, on the way to a bookseller to dispose of the last of his books. He lent Jarry two francs; it was all he would accept. When he appeared at the Tuesday on January 23, Rachilde and Vallette persuaded him he must go back to Laval. He resigned himself. Vallette told Léautaud: "It would be better if he never came back. He's done for. He can't even be sent on an errand." Another large debt was also now added to the rest: finally Trochon had tracked him down, probably following his sojourns in Laval.[100]

···

On arriving at his sister's at the end of January, Jarry wrote again to Terrasse—an extraordinary letter because its underlying assumption was that Terrasse had a moral obligation to bail him out. Terrasse surely imagined the debt lay in quite another direction. He must have replied that Jarry could seek paid employment in Paris, because Jarry in turn pointed out to him that this was impossible because "my life is arranged quite differently from that: as soon as the weather is fine again I shall return to Le Coudray to live on fish." The royal we becomes a rarity in these letters of 1907. Jarry then repeated a variant of his request of the previous month: for a divvying-up of the imaginary royalties from *Pantagruel*. He calculated that his share should be 750 francs. A few days afterward he realized he had gone too far, and wrote a letter bordering on apology before he had even received a reply from Terrasse. He thus averted an inevitable quarrel, but he then attempted to sell "his rights" in *Pantagruel* to Thadée Natanson or Vollard. In the end, Terrasse lost all patience, and Jarry's response was a letter to Vallette attempting to drive a wedge between him and Terrasse. Jarry also discussed his debts at length—all could be easily resolved, he maintained, although even his bicycle was now in the pawnshop. Another solution then occurred to him: he thought he could cut an extract out of *La Dragonne*, write some new material, and thus have a third book for Fasquelle to make him an advance upon. Fasquelle, when approached, "was rather at a loss what to say."[101]

···

Charlotte may have disapproved of ether, because in Laval, Jarry's intoxicant of choice would be wine, although colossal quantities were necessary to achieve the required "detachment." Because Jarry acquired his supplies on credit, and never settled his bills, the invoices were preserved in the town archives. From these, and others once in the possession of Gabrielle Vallette, Arnaud was able to calculate that Jarry "and his sister" consumed between six and ten liters of wine per day during this stay in Laval. Apéritifs and absinthe too, no doubt. But Jarry's ... intemperance could only have the same outcome as it had in Le Coudray: creditors massing at the gates. His existence became one of continual brinkmanship and improvisation, and Parisian tradesmen would soon be as vexatious as those of Le Coudray and Laval.[102]

In February 1907 Jarry was in touch with the bookseller and publisher Victor Lemasle. He would be the publisher of Jarry's last little book, which he must have commissioned since it was a study of the poet Albert Samain, whose works were of no interest whatever to Jarry. Lemasle was soon entrusted with selling off Jarry's last remaining asset, his manuscripts. Then came further blows. Trochon had learned of his return to Laval. He wrote to Charlotte, since he did not have her brother's address; Jarry objected to this impertinent behavior, and in doing so revealed the required information. Trochon immediately responded with a letter which ended with a threat: "I amicably urge you not to oblige me to cause you trouble." And in Paris, the landlord at the rue Cassette began muttering about unpaid rent and eviction. On February 22, 1907 he gave Jarry until March 8 to pay up or leave. Given the precarious financial standing of the Tripod, this was serious—he might find himself marooned in the provinces.[103]

Jarry, meanwhile, was entertaining himself with a custom initiated during his stay in Laval the previous year: that of sending with his letters to Rachilde a quite remarkable profusion of small presents. Thus, to instance those of February 1907, she received a box containing "various curiosities," including an edible candle and a combustible one—"see which you think the better"— and a toy cat made of tin plate. A day or so later it was two "quasi-comestible serpents with rings in their noses," a saucer depicting a view of Lamballe, and an edible mouse. At other times there were larger items: fans, a large articulated crocodile, a set of dominoes, all sorts of edible animals. These offerings would continue as long as Jarry was away from Paris, and were graciously received by Rachilde in the few replies of hers that have survived.[104]

Other outgoings: various invoices for large quantities of wine date from February and March. Income: Père Ubu lives frugally by taxing his subjects, or so he informed Vallette. By this he meant the rents from the rue de Bootz, rents which were Charlotte's since she had taken these houses as her portion of their father's estate. Pending: a further inarticulate appeal from Dubois; and Jarry, well aware that Dubois would quickly discover his presence at the Tripod, reluctantly had to postpone his return.[105]

And yet ... Jarry wanted so little: to live a simple and unburdened existence in his "little house by the Seine"; and it was the very modesty of his desires that led to his ending up with nothing at all. He had never seen any reason to acquire a means of making a living outside of literature, and because of this his wants might as well have been as limitless as his literary aspirations, so far beyond his reach would they remain. Vallette had put it well: "No other seeker after the absolute was more at the mercy of the contingent."[106]

...

Nevertheless, he must go to Paris to see what could be done about his room, and its contents, in the rue Cassette. On arrival he took a bundle of manuscripts to Lemasle. Jarry sold him those for *Days and Nights*, *Absolute Love*, and *Faustroll*—the last a clear sign of his desperation, since it was unpublished. They were quickly snapped up by Louis Lormel, and he and Jarry made up their old quarrel in the coming weeks.[107]

Within a week Jarry was again desperately ill, stricken by the paralysis caused by his still-undiagnosed tuberculosis. His situation was revealed in an almost illegible note scribbled to an old friend, the author Victor Gastilleur, on April 13, 1907:

> I am very ill, and in great peril. You are a true friend. Come, please, today; I have received funds
> by post from Laval but have not had the strength to go and collect them, I must do so or die:
> I have been unable to leave my bed for five days, even to get provisions. Come and you save
> my life.[108]

Gastilleur must have come to his rescue, as Jarry did not die, but there seemed no alternative other than to go back to Laval, where at least he would not be alone should there be a relapse. First he must recover sufficiently to make the journey. This took several weeks, during which he had to deal with more creditors' letters: bills for wine from the previous September, but also from Trochon. Despite this renewal of hostilities, Jarry went back to Laval toward the end of April. He seemed stuck; summer was approaching, and the Tripod as distant as ever.[109]

...

Soon after Jarry's arrival in Laval, Vallette wrote to inform him that *Le Moutardier* was now printed, and he would send the sheets of the special edition for Jarry to sign. Jarry's *Albert Samain (Souvenirs)* appeared at the same moment. He preempted any comments from Rachilde by telling her not to read it, since he had not bothered to himself, "having a horror of Samain's verses." But the booklet is valuable for its early pages of rare autobiographical reminiscence on the part of Jarry, recollections of his first months in Paris and the salon of the Mercure. Nostalgia for a time when all seemed possible? And not so many years ago. In Laval over the next few months Jarry reread several books from his childhood: *Robinson Crusoe*, *The Swiss Family Robinson*, *The Last of the Mohicans*.[110]

The "special paper for bailiffs," with which *Faustroll* starts, made an unwelcome reappearance on May 3, 1907. The landlord of the rue Charles-Landelle required payment for a whole year's rent. Jarry and his sister fled to the rue de Bootz. The only unlet rooms were cold and dark—a lumber room, kitchen, and attic—although Jarry's description to Vallette put a gloss on them: "Monsieuye, we arrived safely and are stuffing ourselves, which is a good sign. We shall reinstall ourself in a large Tripod in the excellent air of the rue de Bootz which we shall inaugurate in the first days of May." Dubois now hired bailiffs too, but Jarry had at least resolved the problem of the rue Cassette, or so he thought. The Natansons had responded to his plea for help, and paid his rent. Then on May 15 he received a letter from Monsieur Garnier, the landlord of the Chasublery:[111]

> Monsieur,
>
> This is my response to your letter of the 13th inst. The notice to quit which has been served upon you has not been served with undue haste or by error. M. Condomines, concierge, did indeed receive at the end of April the sum of 36 fr. 50 for the quarter which should have been paid by yourself on 8 *January*. But since you were leaving for Laval it would seem you at least needed to pay an installment on the April quarter before leaving. Having found this behavior somewhat unnecessarily offhand, I decided to give you notice to quit. If I adopted the means of a legal notice, it was in order to avoid any question of error or undue haste, and to have an undisputed date. (Remember the premises contain nothing that might constitute some security for me.) […]
>
> It is always unpleasant to have to give notice to quit to a tenant who is decent, upright and worthy of consideration. I would therefore have preferred to persuade you to be more regular in your payments. But having in vain expected this result over many years without success, I am therefore obliged to bring the matter to a conclusion.
>
> With, sir, my sincerest best wishes,
>
> H. Garnier[112]

Trochon wrote again on May 28, and when Jarry and his sister moved across town, from the rue Charles-Landelle to the rue de Bootz, a new alliance of importuning creditors was created. The butcher was owed 39 francs, and the baker in the Tour Beucheresse an enormous 246 francs, since he had supplied the animal confections Jarry had sent Rachilde. The last day of May brought yet more demands from wine merchants.[113]

After another brief trip to Lamballe, whose purpose must surely have been financial prospecting, Jarry was again confined to his bed, for some forty days this time, during the months of June and July 1907. "We give ourself over to orgies of sleep … but … as regards our complete works, we maintain, like our Palotins, one ear pointed towards the North. …" Indeed, Jarry's renewed prostration coincided both with an upsurge of letter writing and with the creation of a new work, presumably the intended third novel, *La Mousse de la Pirrouïte*. In a very lengthy letter to Rachilde, Jarry gave a précis of this work, part epic poem, part bargees' drinking song, which related the fate of the *Pirrouïte*'s cabin boy ("*mousse*"), fallen in the river and sucked up by the boat's air pump. Perhaps this letter was comprehensible to Rachilde, who was habituated to Jarry's circumlocutions, but to most readers it must seem hopelessly confused and obscure—no more so than the chaos of the manuscript. Charlotte remembered her brother writing when all in the house were asleep, often until dawn.[114]

In mid-June, Vallette sent out the subscribers' copies of *Le Moutardier*, but he forgot the contributors, Jarry, Cazals, and Ranson, and had to ask Jarry for the latter's address. Jarry, naturally, was getting better and better, although being bed-bound he had grown a long beard. The tenants of the rue de Bootz were looking after Père Ubu: "Our life here is assured owing to the attentions of our faithful subjects. They bring us feeshes, since they are all accomplished anglers." Trochon wrote on May 28, June 8, and June 21. To no avail: Jarry's response was that he must no longer address him in such a hostile manner, and Trochon appears then to have abandoned the struggle, at least for the time being. A further bailiff was persisting in his attempt to recover 80 francs on behalf of one of Jarry's wine merchants. His demand, "Do me the favor of no longer boring me with your prose […] it's payment I require," ended up among Gabrielle Vallette's papers in an envelope bearing an inscription in Jarry's hand: "*Cornegidouille merdre de ma chandelle verte ô bien alors merdre merdre merdre.*"[115]

Jarry's chief concern was to save the Chasublery. He suggested to Vallette that someone rent it for him under another name, "Ubu" for example, since the Natansons would be willing to pay. Then he could reappear and persuade the landlord to allow him to resume his tenancy. Jarry wrote to Thadée on June 30, a long letter whose intricate narrative built up to the predictable request for 100 francs so he could return to Paris and save his manuscripts from the rue Cassette. He also envisaged another book to add to his stack of unfinishable projects, although, being already written, this was perhaps less quixotic than the others: *La Chandelle verte*, a complete collection of his journalism. It was eventually published in 1969.[116]

On July 4, 1907, Jarry wrote to Rachilde that he would be on the train to Paris that evening, being now "in receipt of Polish gold." The Natansons were Polish Jews and Thadée had helped him out yet again, although a good part of this money came from Mirbeau. Jarry had decided to give up the rue Cassette after all; he needed to collect his possessions, especially his manuscripts, and bring them back to Laval. He is a little concerned, he tells Rachilde, because he has not left his bed for forty-five days, although "part of that could be put down to laziness." In fact Jarry left for Paris the following day, after receiving a letter from the landlord granting him an extra week's grace, so long as he paid the 44 francs due. This matter seemed to be on the point of resolution, but Charlotte was now falling behind on the repayments of her 3,000-franc loan against her house, and this dispute would continue until her brother's death.[117]

Jarry arrived on Saturday July 6, but two days later he was so enfeebled that he had to wire Rachilde at the Mercure's offices, only 600 yards away, and ask whether Vallette might bring him over a pot of rillettes. Jarry's concierge found him severely emaciated since his last visit in April, and also thought his behavior "rather strange." Vallette had probably not seen him since January, and so only now appreciated the reality behind the unremitting optimism of his correspondence. Even so, Jarry had lost none of his persuasiveness, and a second letter to Vallette that evening was triumphant:[118]

Monsieuye,

The human creature, landlord, has at this very moment appeared before us in all his beauty. Just as we were convinced, it's all plain sailing now. We're keeping the rue Cassette and, for the moment in any case, not turning over to him our phynance. He has humbly apologized for his—abortive—attempt to overcharge for the expenses of the notice to quit. We have, along with our pardon, granted him this word of advice: Just for once, let it be, and don't start all over again!

So, monsieuye, we shall grasp your hand tomorrow, before setting off once more. The old dream of liberty and absolute impregnability in every tripod has come true … and life is beautiful.

Yours,
A.J.

The following day he was able to attend a Tuesday at the Mercure, the first for many months, although he required a cab to get there. On the way he met Saltas, and had to calm his impatience over *Pope Joan*. The next day he returned to Laval. The fact that he did so when unexpectedly furnished with cash, and in midsummer when the Tripod was most alluring, meant that even he no longer doubted his own debility. Nevertheless, since the night train stopped at Le Mans, he spent the early hours in various drinking establishments, as he related to Vallette and Rachilde in separate letters, though in her letter he did not mention that he had to "piss out of the window" owing to the train's lack of toilets. Punctilious in anecdote, if not in behavior.[119]

Jarry returned to Laval, and resumed work on both *La Dragonne* and *La Chandelle verte*. The parts of the latter as already published in various reviews were presumably among the papers he retrieved from the rue Cassette. He remained determined to spend the late summer at the Tripod, a plan the Vallettes were keen to preempt, foreseeing an inevitable repetition of the previous two winters. Their letters urged Jarry to remain in Laval and finish *La Dragonne*, especially since Dubois appeared regularly and asked where he was. In August Maître Breux, bailiff number three, who had previously acted for Trochon, commenced proceedings on behalf of Jarry's fencing master, Maître Blaviel. Jarry was receiving a regular but modest income from Vallette, and also attempted to sell the remaining *de luxe* copies of *Le Moutardier* to a bookseller, with Vallette's consent. He managed to hold his creditors at bay for the remainder of the month, and on August 26 he announced to Vallette and Rachilde that *La Dragonne* was finished—indeed, it was parceled up ready for dispatch. Jarry was therefore readying himself to take up residence in the Tripod. He also wrote to Thadée Natanson to say that the manuscript was ready and he would send it to him to give to Fasquelle, and that he would wait a while before trying to touch him for another advance.[120]

The prospect of Jarry's imminent return prompted a long letter from Vallette in which he listed all the creditors lying in wait at Le Coudray, and made it plain that he could expect no further payments from the Mercure or himself personally. Furthermore, life there was not going to be as cheap as he imagined. He was no longer physically capable of cycling to Paris, and he did not have a boat to fish from, or even a fishing license. He must stay in Laval until Fasquelle returned from his holidays in the hope he might then be persuaded to make further advances.[121]

Jarry's reply thanked Vallette for his splendid advice, then brushed his arguments aside. He announced his return for September 8, 1907, his thirty-fourth birthday. However, this return was oft delayed by lack of funds, and Jarry occupied himself with editing *La Chandelle verte*. His creditors continued their harassment, but in truth Jarry was almost immune, in Laval at least, having no possessions of value to be seized. Several weekly postponements later and Jarry, realizing the summer was coming to an end, was contemplating a return to the rue Cassette rather than the Tripod. Even the prospect of another winter in the Chasublery could not dissuade him, and the receipt of funds finally facilitated the journey. Natanson wrote to him warmly on October 3:[122]

> Thursday
>
> Pardon me, my dear friend, for having been a little late in sending my enclosure. (That *my* is, furthermore, incorrect; I should have written *our* because the greater part by far is Mirbeau's.)
>
> I am delighted at the news you give me of your work and of your health. Let me know as soon as you are back, which I hope will be before long. I keenly look forward to seeing you. It will be a pleasure for Alexandre to pass on your manuscript to Fasquelle immediately on receipt.
>
> See you soon, dear friend,
>
> Your Thadée[123]

So Jarry had still not sent the manuscript …

Natanson and Mirbeau had been generous, since Jarry wrote to Vallette (reproachfully perhaps?) that the amount was "a little more than we had judged necessary." He intended to make the journey on Monday, October 7, although he probably traveled three days later. Before he left, Charlotte informs us, a death's-head moth battered the windows of the rue de Bootz, although the date she gave for this incident, supposedly preceding his departure, was actually after his death.[124]

…

There is a curious hiatus in Jarry's story at this point, and his last month in Paris is almost a blank until the final crisis. We may conjecture that he was not much welcomed by Vallette and Rachilde, since her book has some harsh reflections on his death:

> The torment of a beautiful death is a perpetual obsession for such fanatics (who knows what we must most admire in them, their naïveté or their pride!). Once touched by grace, they march toward these tortures like the martyrs of old. Just so long as it is literature. How many of these sublime actors would kill themselves if they could see or describe their last moments! But nature, both good and cruel, first takes away their powers of analysis, and little by little they become

insensitive to the events they themselves have prepared so carefully and end up not noticing that in their final moments, according to eternal laws, they are subject like everyone else to those instincts of self-preservation which have always driven them in spite of their bravado and noble gestures.[125]

Ardengo Soffici, the future Futurist artist and writer, left a more sympathetic, indeed tragic, account:

> … it was in the little square where the rue du Four crosses the rue de Rennes, right in front of the post office which stands at one of the corners between the two streets. It was an unpleasant winter evening; the scene was wrapped in a thick yellowish freezing fog, which even before daylight had been wholly withdrawn from the sky, darkened the air and dampened things and people with a fine drizzle, turning the dust and muck on the pavement into viscous slime. One would have said dark phantoms were gathering in dense swarms over the city; there was something ghostlike about all the people crowding around the already lit-up post office at the hour between dusk and dark, rapidly entering and leaving the building in that tedious, grim grayness.
>
> I had just gone out and was walking past, hurrying like all the others to make my way through the crowd. But when I was halfway across the square the dark figure of a small man, who in the midst of all this movement stood quite still as if he were waiting for someone or deep in thought about what was going on around him, caught my eye, and made me stop to observe him—well enough for his strange looks to seem no longer new to me. And they were not, for suddenly I recognized Jarry, Alfred Jarry; but how different from how I had always known him hitherto! Huddled inside an ancient black overcoat tightly buttoned up to the chin, and hanging down below his knees; trousers black as well, but discolored and tight and at least a hand's-breadth too long for his short legs, so that they spilled down on to and nearly hid his truly pathetic shoes, which were more like downtrodden slippers, worn, and torn and sodden from the ooze in which they were sunk, he looked both lugubrious and clownish, like a penguin, or a scarecrow creaking in a hurricane. His arms hung at his sides with his small hands poking barely halfway out of his flapping sleeves, while his delicate white neck, like the stem of an ample vase, rose from a dirty, threadbare, separate collar which was visibly too big.
>
> My chest tightened to contemplate this miserable image of poverty and wretchedness. But the scale of the tragedy was revealed when I looked him in the face. Its waxen pallor was made paler by the black of his thin Chinaman's moustaches drooping beneath the sharpened nose of a man close to death, at the corners of his fine, bitter mouth; by the sparse hairs on his emaciated cheeks of a scarce-shaven beard; above all by the eyes, stretched wide open and fixed before him, as if beyond the phenomena around him. They were gazing at another world. That terrible face, at once that of a famished poet, a hallucinating seer, a consumptive beggar, and an orphaned child, I will never forget.[126]

Away from the care of his sister, Jarry's health rapidly deteriorated. To his friends he appeared someone exhausted, emptied out, although occasionally euphoric in resignation. He arrived at one of the Tuesdays, most likely that of October 22, in a state of "total dejection." Saltas, much concerned, invited him to dine at his house later in the week. On leaving Rachilde's salon, Jarry asked Herold to accompany him for a drink in a local café. He wanted to write to his sister, and for Herold to check the letter through. Jarry wrote his letter and handed it over: "It was unintelligible, made up of shapeless chunks of sentences with words missing, or with others incomplete." He never turned up at Saltas's, nor sent an apology, which the doctor found uncharacteristic. On Saturday 26th, though, he was well enough to write to Thadée and ask for a further loan of 20 francs, since he was again confined to his room, "but it is not particularly distressing, being surrounded by books and old papers." A few days afterward Saltas became seriously worried, having still not heard from him.[127]

At ten in the morning on October 29, Saltas and Vallette went together to the rue Cassette. The concierge confirmed that he too had not seen Jarry for several days. They climbed the stairs to his door and knocked several times. Eventually an unrecognizable voice called out "Come in!" But when they tried the door, it was locked. "All right, wait a moment, I'm coming," replied Jarry, but after a long wait there was nothing, no sound from inside. Vallette knocked again and suggested fetching a locksmith: "That's not such a bad idea." Once the lock was picked, the two men entered Jarry's room. The paucity of its furnishings shocked them both, for it was almost empty. A wooden table with a few books and papers, a stuffed owl, and some bottles, one with a candle in its neck, several full, but not with wine. Jarry had been unable to drag himself to his new toilet. He lay on a mattress, both legs paralyzed and "in a state of dilapidation and indescribable filth." They carried him down the stairs and took him in a cab to the nearby Hôpital de la Charité in the rue Jacob. Later that day Vallette wrote to Fontainas that Jarry was unlikely to leave the hospital alive, but curiously, he did not communicate this to Jarry's sister.[128]

Doctor Stéphen-Chauvet, the ward doctor, left a memoir of Jarry's final days at the hospital. When he was first admitted the ward matron assumed he was one of those alcoholics living rough on the streets who got themselves admitted regularly so as to avoid the cold weather. She was puzzled that she didn't recognize him. Stéphen-Chauvet went over to see if he could identify him:[129]

> He didn't have the coarse features of the usual hospital regular (although he had obviously not been looking after himself very well) and his face that particular morning had an incredible waxy pallor which exaggerated his strange facial expression, a mixture of despondent exhaustion and blankness, but lacking any signs of torpidity.
>
> He replied, with some difficulty, to the questions I put to him. He didn't know why he was there—it seemed as if he was unable to remember anything. "Is it because of something that happened in the past?" No, he couldn't remember anything, and his gestures seemed to show that none of this had any importance for him, and that he was not going to bother to make any effort to jog his memory.[130]

Jarry's unflagging optimism did not falter, even now. Despite his paralysis, which caused him to be doubly incontinent, "nobody could shake him from his absolutely overwhelming euphoria." The doctor's initial diagnosis was neuritis and mental confusion caused by chronic alcoholism. The true cause of Jarry's illness went undiagnosed until the autopsy.

The next day the consultant, Doctor Roger, was touring the ward when Saltas blundered in and introduced himself as a medical colleague. His patient, he informed him, was a great writer "with whose extraordinary work you must be acquainted." Which was not the case, even though Roger too was a published and performed playwright. Later, when Jarry wished to refer to his own efforts on the stage to the doctor, he had to consult Saltas first because he could no longer recall the title of that play of his: *Ubu Roi*. On the 30th he had numerous visitors including Terrasse and Franc-Nohain, Quillard and his wife, and Herold. Charlotte was now notified by Vallette of her brother's condition, but judging by her reply the following day she was given no notion of its severity, although this may be because Jarry seemed to rally in the evening.[131]

The following day, though, the 31st, he appeared to be fading; his breathing was difficult, his lips were livid, and his pulse was feeble and difficult to detect. He was gaunt, pale, and hollow-cheeked; his eyes glittered beneath their lids, and seemed to protrude from their sockets. More visitors came: Cazals, Georges-Michel, Mirbeau, Alexandre Natanson, Georges Polti, Van Bever, Rachilde and Vallette, Vuillard. He was drifting in and out of consciousness. Rachilde told Léautaud that Mirbeau had been discussing his book and the Prix Goncourt, "beside poor Jarry's bed; he was already too far gone to understand what was going on." Perhaps it was Rachilde who told Léautaud that Jarry's only words were "*Je cherche, je cherche, je cherche*" (I seek), repeated over and over, until they became only "*j'ch, j'ch, j'ch.*" By now there was no doubt he was dying. Rachilde was shaken by his appearance; Saltas, who came every day, records her fleeing the room and saying she could not return, as Jarry positively "smelt of death." But when Polti approached his bed, visibly upset, Jarry, in a sudden and stentorian bellow, inquired: "Hey, Polti! You're looking horribly pale, don't you feel well?" Such behavior is usually instanced as a demonstration of Jarry's *sang-froid* in the face of imminent death. This is contradicted by his final letter, which reveals that he was never aware of the gravity of his situation and fully expected to recover. Although Rachilde briefly described this letter in her biography, her account did not reveal its contents or Jarry's state of mind. Written the day before he died, in a minuscule and apparently steady hand, it has not been published in English before:[132]

> Yes, Madame Rachilde, we have—for the time being—lost our legs and allowed our beard to grow. But we only need to extirpate our beard and let our legs regrow, and all will be fine. You ask if we would like you to send us some victuals: we don't really need anything, since it does us no harm—though disagreeable—to go out a little to the shops. One thing would give us pleasure, would shock your principles, and would, it so happens, be of use to us: that is, if you still have some, a bottle of Mariani (don't you dare!), otherwise we would acquire that foul Quinquina stuff. P.S. When do the Tuesdays recommence? I hope my legs will be working again by then! And we do not mean to spend 4 months on our … back! That's how things are when we "take our ease."
>
> AJ[133]

Mariani and Quinquina were alcoholic tonic wines, and Jarry's request was granted, with his doctors' permission. They told Rachilde that there was no point in refusing him anything, he was too far gone. She had a bottle sent up. There was to be no going to the shops; he remained paralyzed. The next day was his last, and Saltas described his final moments:

> The last time that I went to see him, I asked him if there was anything he would like. His eyes lit up. There was indeed something that would bring him much pleasure. I told him I'd get it for him immediately. He spoke. What he would like was a toothpick. I dashed out straight away to buy some for him and came back with a whole packet. He took one between two fingers of his right hand. Joy visibly spread across his face. It seemed as if he suddenly felt filled with a delight as great as when he set off on one of his fishing, boating, or cycling expeditions, his three favorite activities. I had hardly taken a step or two away to speak to the nurse when she told me to look back: he was breathing his last.[134]

It was Friday, November 1, 1907, 4.15 p.m.

14.13
Jarry's final letter, written on his visiting card
(reproduced actual size here).

Stéphen-Chauvet recorded a macabre moment during the autopsy:

> After the usual incision, from ear to ear, and after having detached and opened up both sides of
> his scalp at front and back, I started to give a series of hammer taps, all around the center
> line of the skull which, fracturing the bone of the skull, piece by piece, allows the removal of the
> cranial cap in a single piece. "*Merdre* and *cornegidouille*," one of the trainees murmured into
> my ear at this moment—since Dr. Saltas's visit he had been curious enough to read *Ubu Roi*—
> "Père Ubu never expected this!!!"[135]

The exposure of the brain revealed the cause of death: meningeal tuberculosis, probably, opined the doctor, the result of an original unnoticed pulmonary injury. This he believed to have been subsequently stimulated by one of Jarry's colds, in turn caused by his habit of cycling in foul weather. The tubercle bacilli then migrated to the brain, where they attacked the meninges "and surreptitiously began their work of death!" A refutation of Jarry's theory that it was all the fault of his stay in the Dauphiné and the struggle with *Pantagruel*.[136]

More to the point, no one had authorized this autopsy. The fact that it had been performed clandestinely, a common practice where charity patients were concerned, came to light only in 1933, when Dr. Stéphen-Chauvet offered the *Mercure* his memoir. Thus all of Jarry's early biographers, including Chauveau and Rachilde, were ignorant of the fact that Jarry had died of tuberculosis rather than self-inflicted alcoholism. This knowledge might have softened their judgments of him.[137]

The following Sunday Jarry's friends gathered at the hospital, where they could view the corpse. "He had the look of a young Christ of the Spanish school," according to Léautaud. When Georges-Michel saw Jarry's emaciated features, it brought to mind his friend's opinions concerning the nutritious properties of alcohol, and his pronouncement: "posterity will decide." After a service in the nearby Saint-Sulpice, the church whose steeple was visible from Jarry's toilet window, the mourners arrived at the Bagneux cemetery around 5 p.m., as a wintry dusk was falling. The cemetery was lit by electric lights in the trees. After the interment they drifted into the bars outside the cemetery gates, to celebrate Jarry's life in an appropriate manner.[138]

On the sheet of paper signed by mourners, one finds these names: Tristan Bernard, A. Vallette, P.-N. Roinard, A. Natanson, Louis Lormel, André Fontainas, Claude Terrasse, J. Saltas, O. Mirbeau, P. Léautaud, P. Ranson, L. Le Cardonnel, Polti, Romain Coolus, Franc-Nohain, Bonnard, Jules Adler, E. Fasquelle, Fazy, Georges-Michel, Gabrielle Fontainas, André Ibels, Gaston Danville, Alfred Athis, Jules Renard, André Lebey, A. Mithouard, Fagus, Édouard Dujardin. Not everyone present signed, however, among others Jean Richepin, Valéry, Van Bever, and Apollinaire, who recalled that there were "some fifty of us following his coffin." A subscription in the *Mercure* raised sufficient funds for a gravestone, which was erected in April 1908. However, the burial plot was paid for only for a five-year period, which appears never to have been extended, so Jarry's grave would therefore have disappeared in 1912. According to Salmon, it was then occupied by an ex-champion cyclist.[139]

The day following the funeral, Vallette returned to the rue Cassette and collected anything resembling personal papers, leaving the rest for Saltas. Jarry's important manuscripts appear not to have been in the Chasublery: most of them must already have been sold. These manuscripts passed into various hands over the next few years: Paul Éluard owned a version of *Ubu cocu*; Louÿs the manuscript of *Messalina*; Picasso various manuscripts (and one of Jarry's oil paintings), including another *Ubu cocu* and Jarry's translation of Grabbe, which he acquired from Apollinaire; Tzara, *Faustroll*, as already mentioned; and Marinetti, *Ubu intime*, *L'Objet aimé*, and another version of the Grabbe translation.[140]

Vallette must have done the same at the Tripod. He then sorted the personal papers from those related to Jarry's financial affairs, and from the manuscripts. The personal papers went to Charlotte. The manuscripts were bundled up along with Jarry's file of his early writings, *Ontogeny*, stuffed in a cupboard in the Mercure's offices, and forgotten about until Saillet found them in 1948. Vallette then attempted to disentangle the financial disorder Jarry had left behind.[141]

It would be Charlotte who was to suffer the consequences. Vallette wrote that her brother's debts amounted to 7,408.10 francs. Even his revolver was not fully paid for (which suggests it may have been a replacement for the one held by Picasso). However, after subtracting advances paid by himself, Terrasse, and Fasquelle, which were likely to be written off, the sum owing was around 2,400 francs. The only asset was the Tripod and its land, originally bequeathed to Rachilde, who had not accepted it. Its estimated value was 525 francs, but it proved difficult to sell. Charlotte's only source of income seems to have been the rents from her houses in the rue de Bootz, around 1,200 francs per year. She had borrowed 3,000 francs against her properties in 1899, which appears to have become due in 1907, since there is a bailiff's claim for it dated September 16 that year. Negotiations over this debt explain her absence from Paris during Jarry's final moments. By the end of the year she had been forced to sell the houses. They fetched only 6,300 francs after costs. She was almost destitute, with her source of income permanently lost. In the hope that *La Dragonne* might provide some income, despite the advance against it, she finished it herself in 1909, but it was turned down first by Fasquelle and then by Vallette. Unpublished in her lifetime, it appeared in 1943, a hopeless travesty. Charlotte moved to Paris and ended her days as a charwoman; she died there an alcoholic in March 1925, from tuberculosis like her brother. Her funeral arrangements were attended to by a neighbor, also a charwoman. It was then that Charlotte's papers, which should have included those of her parents, her brother's personal papers and photographs, and an unknown quantity of his letters to her, were lost.[142]

Notes

These notes are principally concerned with identifying the sources used. Sources are listed in the order they are cited in the paragraph to which the note is attached, unless a source is used more than once, in which case the page references are combined into the first citation. All citations are to section v of the bibliography unless stated otherwise.

The following abbreviations are employed: CCP = *Cahiers du Collège de 'Pataphysique*, CTCP = *Carnets Trimestriels du Collège de 'Pataphysique*, CW = *Collected Works*, DCP = *Dossiers du Collège de 'Pataphysique*, EA = *L'Étoile-Absinthe*, EXP = *L'Expectateur*, MON = *Monitoires du Cymbalum Pataphysicum*, O = *Œuvres*, OC = *Œuvres complètes*, ORG = *Organographes du Cymbalum Pataphysicum*, SP = *Subsidia Pataphysica*.

Letters cited from the collection of the Harry Ransom Humanities Research Center at the University of Texas have not been previously published in English. A French edition of all of these letters, published by Le Bouche-Trou in Paris, was under way during the preparation of this book, edited by myself, Paul Edwards, Barbara Pascarel, and Eric Walbecq. Inquiries regarding this may be addressed to editor@atlaspress.co.uk.

Preface
1 Georges-Michel (a), p. 5.
2. Arnaud (c), p. 97; Jarry OC1, p. 972.
3. Jarry OC1, p. 763.
4. These appeared in French in 2011: Jarry (k).
5. Baedeker's *Guide to Paris and Environs*, 1896 and 1910; Surcouf, pp. 58–59; Robichez (a), p. 116; <www.measuringworth.com> (website of the Institut national de la statistique et des études économiques).

Chapter 1
1. All uncredited references in this chapter are taken from the special issue of the *Organographes* devoted to Hébert: ORG 5 (Bibliography IV (m)).
2. EA 69–70, pp. 7–28.
3. Hertz (b), pp. 265–267.
4. Jarry OC1, p. 399.

Chapter 2
1. Charlotte Jarry, pp. 8, 12.
2. Hertz (a), p. 62; Lebois, pp. 29–30; Chauveau (b), pp. 35–36; Jarry (b), p. 440.
3. Jarry (f), p. 41.
4. Jarry (b), p. 442; Hertz (b), p. 267.
5. Hertz (a), p. 61.

6. Chassé (a), pp. 28–32.

7. Chassé (a), pp. 33, 41.

8. Chassé (a), p. 26.

9. Chassé (a), p. 44.

10. Chassé (a), pp. 44–45.

11. Chassé (a), pp. 44, 49.

12. Jarry (f), pp. 33–96.

13. Jarry OC1, p. 483.

14. Chassé (a), pp. 44–45.

15. Chassé (a), pp. 35, 44–45; Jarry (f), p. 12.

16. Chassé (a), p. 45.

17. Chassé (a), p. 34.

18. Charlotte Jarry, pp. 7, 11; Bordillon (f), p. 17.

19. Moreno, p. 117.

20. Rachilde (e), pp. 38–39.

21. Arnaud (b), pp. 280–286.

22. Arnaud (b), pp. 288–289; Bordillon (a), pp. 88–94; Lassalle, pp. 14–16, 31–32.

23. Arnaud (b), pp. 278–279, 303; Lot, p. 6.

24. Arnaud (b), p. 279.

25. Charlotte Jarry, pp. 7, 9, 11; the Laval censuses may be found at <http://www.archinoe.fr/cg53v4/recensement.php>.

26. Charlotte Jarry, p. 11; Chauveau (b), pp. 32–33; Bordillon (f), p. 19.

27. Régibier, p. 73; Charlotte Jarry, p. 8.

28. Jarry OC1, p. 25.

29. Arnaud (b), p. 274; Jarry OC1, p. 47.

30. Jarry OC1, p. 1065; Bordillon (f), p. 35; Charlotte Jarry, p. 9.

31. Jarry OC2, p. 306.

32. Charlotte Jarry, p. 8.

33. Bordillon (f), p. 35.

34. Jarry (f), pp. 16–17.

35. Jarry (f), p. 15; Chassé (a), p. 65.

Chapter 3

1. Jarry (f), p. 53.

2. Stehlin, p. 35; Jarry OC3, p. 531; Goda, p. 25; Arnaud (c), p. 122; these exercise books are now in the Bibliothèque littéraire Jacques Doucet in Paris.

3. Launoir, p. 12, which is recommended for further reading, as is Various authors (g).

4. Jarry OC1, pp. 668–669, translation by Simon Watson Taylor from CW2.

5. Jarry OC1, p. 290, translation by Antony Melville from CW1.

6. Jarry (b), pp. 440–441; Samuel Taylor Coleridge, e.g., in *Aids to Reflection* and "A Sailor's Fortune"; Jarry OC1, p. 1024; Bergson (b), p. vii.

7. Bergson (a), p. 152; (b), p. 300; Arnaud (c), p. 122; Stehlin, p. 48.

8. Duration is cited by Jarry in OC1, pp. 342, 704, 710, 728, 736–737, 741–742, 924; OC2, pp. 396, 637; Goda, p. 27.

9. Bergson (b), p. x; (a), p. 91.

10. Bergson (a), p. 229.

11. Bergson (a), pp. 105, 128, 198, 234, 236–237; (b), p. 80.

12. Rimbaud, pp. 194, 306; Paterne Berrichon's misleading descriptions of the letters appear in his biography of Rimbaud and in *L'Écho de Paris*, December 26, 1891.

13. Bergson (a), pp. 165–167, 202–221, 231–233.
14. Jarry OC3, pp. 737–738; Bergson (a), p. 207.
15. Jarry OC1, p. 704.
16. Rachilde (e), p. 36.

Chapter 4
1. Jourdain (a), p. 89.
2. Arnaud (b), p. 21; Jarry OC3, p. 444.
3. Caradec (a), p. 31.
4. Gens-d'Armes, p. 41.
5. Gens-d'Armes, p. 44.
6. Hirsch, p. 480.
7. Stehlin, pp. 35–36; Jarry OC2, p. 334; Jarry OC3, p. 446.
8. Goujon (g), p. 38; Freitas (b), p. 11; Jourdain (a), p. 137.
9. David (b), p. 25; Goujon (g), p. 35.
10. Lefèvre, pp. 268–269.
11. Fargue (a), p. 269.
12. Besnier (e), p. 95; Fargue (b), p. 131; Jarry OC3, pp. 532–533.
13. Jourdain (a), p. 133.
14. Lefèvre, pp. 269, 275–276.
15. Jourdain (a), p. 133.
16. Jourdain (a), p. 91.
17. Willot, pp. 20–22, 67; Mac Orlan, p. 243.
18. Besnier (e), p. 82; Fréchet, p. XXI in Bibliography I (b).
19. Gourmont (c), p. 83.
20. Arnaud (b), pp. 93–94.
21. Arnaud (b), pp. 93–96; Lormel, p. 25.
22. Rémond, pp. 427, 659.
23. Freitas (b), p. 11; Fargue (b), p. 147.
24. Fargue (b), p. 146; Richardson I, p. 352 (although Richardson confuses Libaude with Henri Delormel, another person altogether).
25. Goudemare, pp. 93, 141.
26. Charlotte Jarry, p. 12.
27. Freitas (b), p. 11; EA 43–45, pp. 10, 36.
28. Fargue (c), pp. 20–21.
29. Jarry OC1, pp. 1305–1306.
30. Freitas (b), p. 16; EA 43–45, p. 40; <http://www.pontaven.com/ville/web/celebrites/peintres.html>.
31. Chassé (c), p. 71.
32. Freitas (a), p. 133; Freitas (b), pp. 17–19.
33. Trohel, pp. 626–630.
34. Morel (b), p. 160.
35. Jarry (f), p. 30; Lebey, p. 54.
36. The creation of the Œuvre is described in Jasper, chapter 6; Jourdain (a), p. 198.
37. Bourrelier, pp. 274–275; Jourdain (a), p. 198; *La Plume*, 1891, p. 156.
38. Lugné-Poe (a) I, pp. 53–54; Jourdain (a), p. 197.
39. Deak, p. 189; Robichez (b), pp. 386–389.
40. Retté, pp. 208–211; Tailhade (b), pp. 115–122.
41. Goujon (g), p. 63; Jourdain (a), pp. 198, 200; Mauclair, p. 107.

42. Jourdain (a), p. 201.

43. Jourdain (a), p. 201; Lugné-Poe (a) II, p. 61; Bordillon (c), p. 11; Jarry OC1, p. 691, translation by Simon Watson Taylor in CW2.

44. Sainmont (c), pp. 58–61.

45. Lormel, p. 25.

46. EA 39–40, pp. 19–23; Jarry OC1, pp. 221, 227, 675–676.

Chapter 5

1. Gourmont (a), p. 42.

2. Huret, pp. 133–134.

3. Béhar (c), p. 239.

4. Madame Laurent Tailhade, p. 112; Picq, pp. 350–353.

5. Halperin, pp. 289, 293.

6. Huret, p. 131; Gourmont (c), p. 13.

7. Gourmont (d), p. 13.

Chapter 6

1. Quignard, p. 23.

2. Symons (c), p. 199.

3. Rémond, pp. 662–664.

4. Rémond, p. 661.

5. Jarry OC1, pp. 215, 229, translation by Paul Edwards from CW1.

6. Caradec (a), p. 36.

7. Goujon (c), p. 101; Jarry OC1, pp. 1036–1037.

8. EA 4, p. 43; CCP 10, p. 62; *Argus du Livre* 1972–1974.

9. Graham, p. 481.

10. Jarry OC1, pp. 1036–1037.

11. Jarry OC1, pp. 216, 227–228, translations by Paul Edwards from CW1.

12. Gaudemar, p. 250.

13. Rachilde (e), p. 28.

14. Arnaud (c), p. 113.

15. Léautaud (a) III, p. 378; Rachilde (e), p. 70.

16. Mauclair, p. 41.

17. Oriol, pp. 13–15; Soulignac, p. 35; Gaudemar, pp. 249–254.

18. Symons (c), p. 199.

19. Fargue (b), pp. 149–153.

20. Besnier (e), p. 139.

21. Rachilde (e), pp. 28–29.

22. Charbonnier and Trutat, p. 37; Rachilde (e), p. 30; *Mercure de France*, May 1894.

23. Tailhade (b), p. 219; Delarue-Mardrus, p. 127; Gide (a), p. 168; Lot, p. 62; Arnaud (b), p. 408.

24. Goujon (e), p. 229.

25. Léautaud (b), p. 201.

26. Jarry OC1, pp. 492–493; the translation owes its best parts to Stanley Chapman.

27. Jarry OC1, pp. 1037–1038; Graham, p. 481; Fresneau, pp. 57, 61.

28. EA 43–45, p. 24.

29. Chassé (b), p. 89; Fresneau, p. 52; Bibliography IV (h), p. 140.

30. Graham, p. 481.

31. Fresneau, p. 52.

32. Freitas (b), p. 23.

33. Jarry OC1, p. 1277; on Pivet, see Arnaud (b), p. 106.

34. Sainmont (d), pp. 7–18.

35. Sainmont (d), pp. 7–18; Sutton, pp. 403–405.

36. Fargue (a), p. 146.

37. CCP 22–23, p. 103; Christie's sale 6469, lot 15, June 25, 2001, King St. Auction Rooms, London.

38. Saltas (c), pp. 168–169.

39. Lot, p. 38; Besnier (e), p. 140; Apollinaire (c), p. 120; CCP 22–23, pp. 103–104.

40. Certigny, p. 94; Chassé (a), p. 133.

41. Salmon (c), p. 153.

42. *Le Temps*, cited in CCP 26–27, p. 50, verse translation by Stanley Chapman.

43. Fort, p. 52; Apollinaire (b), p. 22; Apollinaire (c), p. 120; Salmon (c), p. 152; Saltas (c), p. 170.

44. Jarry OC1, p. 1308; Roig, p. 503.

45. Haas, p. 270.

46. Jarry (f), pp. 20–21, 30; Rachilde (e), pp. 105–106.

47. Jarry CW1, p. 9, title of the translation by Paul Edwards.

48. Besnier (e), p. 157.

49. Jarry CW1, pp. 24–25, translation by Paul Edwards.

50. Jarry OC1, p. xiii; CCP 10, p. 65; *Argus du livre* 1976–1978; Maggs bookshop in London had the *Yellow Book*'s copy for sale in 2006; Besnier (e), p. 160; Graham, pp. 486–487.

51. Gourmont (b), pp. 177–178.

52. Sainmont (d), p. 11; Régnier (a), p. 149.

53. Besnier (e), pp. 164–165.

54. Haas, p. 252; Bernier (a), p. 53.

55. Dujardin, pp. 22–26; Fontainas, pp. 187–188.

56. Besnier (d), p. 41; Symons (a), pp. 120–122.

57. Gide (b), p. 214; Haas, pp. 252–258; Jarry OC1, p. 686, translation by Simon Watson Taylor from CW2.

58. Apollinaire (c), p. 120; Breton (c), p. 251 (translation modified); Baas and Field, p. 122.

59. Gide (b), p. 199.

60. EA 81–82, reprint of *L'Ymagier* 1, pp. 5–9.

61. Although unpublished, they have been seen.

62. Jarry OC1, p. 1039.

63. Certigny, Appendix 1, p. 29.

64. Saget, p. 21.

65. Jarry OC1, p. 861, translation by Iain White.

66. Bordillon (f), p. 45.

67. Arnaud (b), pp. 132–135.

68. Saltas (b), p. 31; Jarry OC1, p. 1277.

69. Géroy; unless stated otherwise, this article is the source for this section on Jarry's military service.

70. Jarry OC1, pp. 751–752, translation by Alexis Lykiard from CW2.

71. Jarry OC1, p. 763, translation by Alexis Lykiard from CW2.

72. Jarry OC2, p. 763, translation by Alexis Lykiard from CW2; Jarry (j), p. 93.

73. Charlotte Jarry, p. 12.

74. Van der Velden, pp. 123–124.

75. Bernier (b), p. 187; Leclercq, p. 42.

76. Gold and Fizdale, pp. 53–54; Jourdain (a), p. 173; Natanson (a), pp. 253–258; Guigon, p. 118; Lugné-Poe (a) II, p. 175.

77. Ellmann, pp. 402–403, 433, 445, 458–459; Murray, pp. 93–95.

78. Jarry OC1, pp. 675–676.

79. Pawlowski, pp. 247–253.

80. Bouhélier, p. 261; Moreno, p. 115; Armory, p. 115.

81. Lebey, p. 52; Jourdain (a), p. 208; re Fanny Zaessinger, I am grateful to Jean-Paul Morel for sharing his research.

82. Colette, p. 129.

83. Jarry OC1, pp. 750–751, translation by Alexis Lykiard from CW2.

84. Montfort II, p. 188.

85. Bouhélier, p. 212; Caradec (e), p. 300.

86. Arnaud (b), p. 157; Surcouf, p. 84; Roig, p. 502.

87. Schuh (c), p. 142.

88. Jarry OC1, pp. 1041–1042; Bordillon (e), unpaginated.

89. Saillet (a), pp. 17–22; Léautaud (a) XVI, p. 359.

90. Léautaud (a) XVI, p. 359; Rachilde (f), p. 124; Rachilde (e), pp. 50–53.

91. Lebey, pp. 52, 54, 173.

92. Rachilde (f), pp. 129–130; Rachilde (e), p. 54; Goujon (a), pp. 27–29.

93. Rachilde (e), p. 56.

94. Rachilde (e), pp. 59–60, translation by Iain White from the Atlas Press edition of 1993.

95. Goujon (e), note 14, p. 183.

96. Billy, p. 129; Arnaud (b), p. 194.

97. Jarry OC1, pp. 858, 862, 864, translations by Iain White from the Atlas Press edition of 1993.

98. Rachilde (e), p. 49; Besnier (e), note 82, p. 203.

99. Goujon (e), p. 229; Graham, p. 495; *Le Centaure* 2 (August 1896).

100. Arnaud (b), pp. 354–355; Jarry OC1, pp. 821–829.

101. CCP 26–27, p. 51; Chassé (a), p. 112; Lebois, p. 47; Girieud, unpaginated; Guitry, p. 397; on the side effects of contact with picric acid, see <http://dohs.ors.od.nih.gov/pdf/Picric%20Acid%20REVISED.pdf>.

102. Rachilde (e), p. 61; CCP 26–27, p. 51.

103. Besnier (e), p. 179.

104. Surcouf, pp. 58–59.

Chapter 7

1. Rachilde (e), p. 39.

2. Rachilde (e), pp. 31, 34.

3. Besnier (e), p. 455.

4. Goujon (g), p. 74, translation by Antony Melville.

5. CCP 10, p. 143.

6. Jarry OC1, pp. 912–913.

7. Jarry OC1, p. 843.

8. CCP 10, p. 137.

9. Jarry OC1, p. 768, translation by Stanley Chapman from CW2.

10. Jarry OC1, pp. 768–769, translation by Alexis Lykiard from CW2.

11. Jarry OC1, p. 779, translation by Alexis Lykiard from CW2.

12. Jarry OC2, pp. 473–474.

13. Chauveau (b), pp. 169–170.

14. Jarry OC2, pp. 261–262, translation by Barbara Wright from the Jonathan Cape edition of 1968.

Chapter 8

1. Jarry (f), p. 103.
2. Lugné-Poe (a) II, p. 160; Jarry (f), pp. 102–104; Jarry OC1, pp. 1042–1044.
3. Lugné-Poe (a) II, p. 162.
4. Jasper, p. 209; Jarry OC1, p. 661; Lugné-Poe (a) II, pp. 149, 159–160.
5. Lugné-Poe (a) I, pp. 67–68, 89, 189–190.
6. Gourmont (d), p. 90.
7. Jarry (c), pp. 7–8.
8. Jarry OC1, pp. 895, 1253.
9. Arnaud (b), p. 192.
10. Jarry OC1, pp. 995–996.
11. CCP 10, p. 74.
12. Jarry OC1, p. 1045.
13. Fort, p. 52; Rachilde (e), p. 95; Chassé (a), p. 77; Hirsch, p. 480; Goudemare, pp. 197, 199–200; Caradec (b), p. 92; Moreno, pp. 113, 133.
14. Jarry OC1, p. XXXV.
15. Besnier (e), p. 224; EA 93–94, unpaginated.
16. Jasper, pp. 222, 255.
17. Various authors (f), pp. 151–152; Lié, note to p. 45; Robichez (b), p. 370.
18. Lugné-Poe (a) II, p. 115.
19. Foulc (b), pp. 138–139.
20. Number one was for sale at the Librairie Vrain in Paris in 2010; CCP 10, p. 23; Jarry OC1, p. 416; Goudemare, p. 203.
21. Caradec (e), p. 300; Goujon (f), p. 7; CCP 10, p. 79; La Jeunesse's copy was for sale at the Librairie Vrain in 2010; Goudemare, p. 204; Besnier (e), p. 235; *Argus du Livre* 1976–1978; Chassé (a), p. 103; Jarry OC1, p. 1052; Graham, pp. 489–492.
22. Arnaud (b), p. 218; Besnier (e), p. 243.
23. Arnaud (b), pp. 219–221.
24. Bibliography III (e), p. 128; *UK Book Auction Records* 1998–1999.
25. Lebois, p. 82; Lot, p. 28; Hirsch, p. 480; Arnaud (b), p. 214.
26. Jarry OC1, pp. 1047–1048.
27. Arnaud (b), p. 214; Pia, p. 80; Jarry OC2, pp. 279–280; Jarry OC1, p. 1047.
28. Robichez (a), p. 114; Bouhélier, p. 173.
29. Lugné-Poe (a) II, p. 163; Moreno, p. 113.
30. EA 4, p. 15.
31. Jarry OC1, p. 416; Lugné-Poe (a) II, p. 160.
32. Jarry OC1, pp. 409, 1046.
33. Besnier (e), pp. 244–245, 258; Jarry OC1, p. 1056; Arnaud (b), pp. 359–360; Damerval, pp. 81–82.
34. Bordillon (k), pp. 30–38; Arnaud (b), p. 212; Arrivé (b), p. 97.
35. Jarry OC1, p. 1050.
36. Lié, p. 42; Jarry OC1, pp. 1051–1052; Lugné-Poe (a) II, pp. 176–177.
37. Jarry OC1, pp. 406, 1052–1053.
38. Speaight, pp. 90, 120; Lugné-Poe (b), p. 231.
39. Lugné-Poe (c), pp. 93, 173.
40. Armory, pp. 79, 91–92.
41. Armory, p. 141.
42. Roig, pp. 506–508; Armory, p. 103.
43. Gerard-Arlberg, p. 67; Torjusen, p. 198; Klüver and Martin, p. 22.

44. Boyer, p. 142; Torjusen, pp. 194–196, Jarry (f), pp. 20, 29.

45. Schmitz, pp. 176–177; this text found and translated by Malcolm Green.

46. Goudemare, pp. 164, 199; Whibley, pp. 411, 417; Gosse, p. 660.

47. Rachilde (e), p. 40; Arnaud (b), p. 243; Jarry OC1, p. 384.

48. Jasper, p. 215.

49. Lugné-Poe (a) II, p. 170.

50. Shaw, pp. 99–101.

51. Lugné-Poe (a) II, p. 170.

52. Beaumont (b), p. 19; Robichez (a), p. 66; Lugné-Poe (a) II, pp. 170–171.

53. Lugné-Poe (a) II, p. 174.

54. Besnier (e), p. 263; Jarry OC1, p. 1053.

55. Goujon (f), p. 7; Jarry OC1, p. 1056; Herold, p. 694.

56. Lugné-Poe (a) II, p. 174.

57. EA 4, pp. 12–13.

58. Lugné-Poe (a) II, pp. 174–175.

59. Jarry OC1, pp. 1057–1058; Lugné-Poe (a) II, p. 175; Jarry (b), p. 423.

60. Jourdain (b), p. 121; Bouhélier, pp. 198–199; Valéry and Fontainas, p. 99.

61. Arnaud (b), p. 252.

62. Jarry (h), unpaginated; Gémier, p. 141; Jarry OC1, p. 1058; Speaight, p. 120; Robichez (a), p. 83; Lugné-Poe (d), p. 149.

63. Jarry OC1, p. 467.

64. Lugné-Poe (a) II, p. 176; Jarry OC1, p. 1058.

65. Jarry OC1, p. 400; Lugné-Poe (a) II, p. 176; Lié, p. 48.

66. Jarry OC1, pp. 1059–1060; Willot, p. 24; Rachilde (e), p. 67.

67. Rachilde (e), p. 71, note 1; Jarry OC1, pp. 400, 1059.

68. Lugné-Poe (a) II, pp. 50, 175–176; Jarry OC1, p. 400.

69. Jarry OC1, pp. 400–401. Other sources for the backdrop: Béhar (a), p. 71; Duvernois, p. 16; Jasper, p. 227; Lugné-Poe (a) II, p. 177; Robichez (a), pp. 78–79; Robillot, pp. 76, 82–83; Symons, p. 373.

70. Robichez (b), pp. 375–376.

71. Béhar (c), p. 248; Robichez (b), p. 376.

72. Robichez (a), p. 126; Jourdain (a), pp. 207–208; Goujon (e), p. 146.

73. Gide (e), p. 245; Renard, p. 246; Régnier (a), p. 151; Gémier, p. 143.

74. CCP 10, p. 85; Goujon (b), pp. 45–48; Sineux, p. 16; Goudemare, p. 210; Roig, p. 508; Arnaud (b), p. 253.

75. Rémond, p. 664.

76. Robichez (a), p. 77.

77. Symons (b), p. 645; Gémier, p. 142; Rémond, p. 66; Caradec (d), p. 44.

78. Jarry OC1, pp. 399–401, from the complete translation by Simon Watson Taylor to be found in Bibliography II (c).

79. Rémond, p. 665; Moreno, p. 114.

80. Besnard, p. 193.

81. Gémier, p. 142.

82. Moreno, pp. 114–115; Gémier, p. 142.

83. Jarry OC1, p. 401; EA 4, p. 16; Robillot, p. 76.

84. Robillot, p. 76; Rachilde (e), pp. 71–72; Willy, p. 19; Renard, p. 246; Perche, pp. 31–32; Rémond, pp. 666–667; Mandelstamm, p. 68; Moreno, p. 114.

85. Robillot, pp. 81, 83; Lugné-Poe (a) II, p. 177; Robichez (b), p. 366; Symons (b), p. 375; Béhar (a), pp. 71–72; Jarry OC1, p. 402; EA 4, p. 16.

86. Rémond, pp. 666–667; Schuh (a), p. 104; Robillot, pp. 78, 82; Robichez (a), p. 80; Lugné-Poe (a) I, p. 177.
87. Rémond, p. 668; EA 4, p. 16.
88. Robillot, pp. 78, 81.
89. Léautaud (a) II, p. 74.
90. Robichez (b), p. 261.
91. Rachilde (e), pp. 73–75.
92. Arnaud (b), p. 317.
93. Robillot, p. 73.
94. Robillot, p. 75.
95. Robillot, p. 78.
96. Robillot, p. 79.
97. Robillot, pp. 82, 84.
98. Pascarel, p. 100; Bourrelier, p. 268; Robillot, pp. 85–88.
99. Jarry OC1, p. 1060.
100. Robillot, p. 74.
101. Robillot, p. 75.
102. Rachilde (e), p. 70; Renard, p. 246; Régnier (b), p. 439; Mauclair, p. 110; Jourdain (a), p. 204; Besnier (e), p. 272; Tailhade (b), p. 214; Cathé (g), pp. 209–210; Valéry and Fontainas, p. 99; Rachilde (a), p. 43.
103. Yeats, pp. 348–349.
104. Décaudin, pp. 18, 20; Breton (a), p. 403.
105. CCP 10, p. 165; Bibliography III (c), item 330; Renard, p. 246.

Chapter 9
1. Chassé (a), p. 73.
2. Jarry (b), pp. 438–439.
3. Chassé (a), pp. 11, 56.
4. ORG 5, p. 53; Bordillon (b), pp. 75–78; Chassé (a), p. 78.
5. Chassé (a), pp. 34, 53, 69–72; Jarry (b), p. 439.
6. Franc-Nohain (b), pp. 236–237.
7. Robichez (a), p. 96; Fontainas, p. 169; Franc-Nohain (b), p. 236; Goujon (e), p. 229; Moreno, p. 69.
8. Chassé (a), p. 46, note 1; Lugné-Poe (a) II, p. 160.
9. Vallette (a), p. 13; Léautaud (a) II, p. 73.
10. Foulc (b), p. 138; Jarry (f), p. 30.
11. Pierrefeu cited in Pascarel, pp. 230–231.
12. Chassé (a), p. 26.
13. Sainmont (a), p. 30; Jarry OC3, p. 531; Stehlin, pp. 35–36.
14. Bergson (c), pp. 32, 146, 154.
15. Bergson (c), pp. 173, 176.
16. Breton and Soupault, pp. 3–4.

Chapter 10
1. Chauveau (b), pp. 96–99.
2. Merrill, pp. 255–256.
3. Fort, p. 52; Régnier (a), p. 153.
4. Rachilde (e), p. 119; Rachilde (c), p. 47.

5. Rachilde (a), p. 43; Schuh (c), pp. 154–161.

6. Jarry OC1, pp. 416–418.

7. Régibier, p. 53; Arnaud (b), pp. 332–333.

8. Régibier, p. 53; Lebois, p. 82.

9. Arnaud (b), pp. 333, 372; Lecompte, pp. 69–70; Bordillon (f), p. 60; CCP 10, p. 14.

10. Surcouf, p. 9; Jarry OC1, pp. 1061–1063; Trohel, pp. 633–634.

11. Sewell, pp. 18–50.

12. Beardsley (a), pp. 53, 87–88, 90; Raffalovich, p. 613.

13. Beardsley (b), p. 308; Fargue (b), p. 153.

14. CCP 10, p. 135.

15. Douglas, p. 179.

16. Salmon (b), p. 258.

17. *Argus du Livre* 1976–1978; Salmon (c), p. 256; Jarry OC1, p. 704.

18. Blavier, pp. 42–43.

19. Blavier, p. 42.

20. Fisher (a), p. 5; Van den Broeck, p. 177; Arnaud (b), p. 339; Blavier, p. 132.

21. Gide (c), pp. 128–129; Jarry (d), p. 191.

22. Jarry OC1, p. 703, translation by Simon Watson Taylor from CW2.

23. Gide (d), pp. 323–326; Gide (c), pp. 133–134; Blavier, pp. 17–18; Arnaud (b), p. 338; Valéry and Fontainas, p. 107.

24. Goujon (e), pp. 226–227.

25. Goujon (h), p. 224.

26. Bibliography III (e), p. 129.

27. Straus, p. 161.

28. Blum, p. 295.

29. Rachilde (a), p. 44.

30. CCP 26–27, p. 58; Besnier (e), pp. 305–306.

31. Lugné-Poe (a) II, p. 182; Arnaud (b), p. 320.

32. Schuh (c), p. 153; Lugné-Poe (a) II, pp. 181–183.

33. Lugné-Poe (a) II, p. 203.

34. Robichez (b), p. 395.

35. Jasper, pp. 261–264.

36. Vallette (c), p. 38.

37. Vallette (c), p. 41; Rachilde (e), p. 122; Régibier, p. 66; Various authors (d), p. 34.

38. Adéma, p. 107; Certigny, pp. 173–174.

39. Vallette (c), p. 44.

40. Marvier, p. 20.

41. Bibliography III (e), p. 128.

42. Arnaud (b), pp. 391–392; Delarue-Mardrus, p. 140.

43. Arnaud (b), pp. 391–393.

44. Tailhade (b), p. 220; Rachilde (e), p. 41.

45. Moreno, pp. 118–119.

46. Arnaud (b), p. 160; Léautaud (a) IV, p. 134.

47. Saltas (b), p. 28.

48. Goujon (h), p. 291.

49. Jarry OC1, p. 1030.

50. Cathé (a), p. 160; Bordillon (h), p. 7; Arnaud (b), p. 384.

51. Cathé (f), p. 78; Guigon, p. 221.

52. Natanson (b), p. 213; Various authors (f), p. 99.
53. Cathé (a), pp. 165–166, 170.
54. Herold, p. 700; Bordillon (f), p. 62.
55. Charbonnier and Trutat, pp. 63–64.
56. Arnaud (b), pp. 430–431.
57. Adès and Piettre, pp. 64–65 and erratum slip; Chauveau (a), p. 58; Georges-Michel
(a) p. 5; Léautaud (a) II, p. 74.
58. Bourrelier, pp. 622–623; Cathé (a), p. 171; CCP 10, p. 93; Vallette (b), p. 565.
59. Léautaud (b), p. 246; Pascarel, p. 205; Bordillon (h), p. 21; Cathé (a), pp. 173–174.
60. Jarry OC1, p. 691, translation by Simon Watson Taylor from CW2.
61. Bourrelier, p. 21.
62. Bourrelier, p. 621; Picq, p. 545; Jarry OC2, p. 626.
63. Cathé (f), p. 75.
64. Jarry (f), p. 31; Pascarel, p. 127; Cathé (a), p. 183; Cathé (g), p. 67.
65. Marvier, p. 25.
66. Jarry OC1, p. 881, translation by Iain White.
67. Arnaud (b), p. 375.
68. Jarry OC1, p. 882, translation by Iain White.
69. Mercier, p. 18.
70. Saillet (b), p. 75.
71. Davray's note is in the collection of the Pataphysical Museum, London.
72. Wilde, p. 1075.
73. Marvier, p. 26.
74. Jarry OC1, pp. 1065–1066, translation by Iain White.
75. Chauveau (b), p. 103.
76. Rachilde (e), p. 113.
77. Arnaud (b), pp. 404–405; Jarry OC2, p. 586.
78. Jarry OC1, p. 1218.
79. Jarry OC1, p. 1064, translation by Iain White.
80. Gold and Fizdale, p. 65.
81. Chauveau (b), pp. 108–109; Rachilde (e), p. 112.
82. Rachilde (e), p. 139.
83. Rachilde (e), p. 115; Jarry OC1, pp. 538–541, 1073.
84. Rachilde (e), p. 115; Régibier, p. 74.
85. Rachilde (e), pp. 114–117.
86. Rachilde (e), pp. 113–114.
87. Rachilde (e), pp. 110–111; Chauveau (b), p. 109.
88. CCP 22–23, p. 94.
89. Béhar (c), p. 244; Vallette (c), p. 15; Jarry (e), p. 236; Gourmont (d), pp. 68–72; Mauclair,
p. 41; CCP 10, p. 42.
90. Bibliography IV (d), p. 67.
91. Bibliography IV (d), p. 69.
92. Jarry OC1, p. 1069; Rachilde (e), p. 122; Arnaud (b), p. 435; Besnier (f), pp. 116–117.
93. Rachilde (e), p. 34.
94. Rachilde (b), p. 45.
95. Jarry (e), p. 146.
96. Bodson, p. 29.
97. David (b), p. 103.

98. Jarry OC1, p. 1216.

99. Rachilde (e), p. 112.

100. Jarry OC1, pp. 679, 722; Jarry (d), p. 13.

101. CCP 10, pp. 9–10; Tzara lot no. 243.

102. Léautaud (a) II, p. 75; Bibliography III (c) no. 429.

103. CCP 22–23, p. 50; Décaudin, p. 14.

104. Jarry OC1, p. 686.

105. Béhar, Dubbelboer, and Morel, p. 77.

106. Jarry OC1, p. 565, translation by Paul Edwards from CW2.

107. Gold and Fizdale, pp. 74–75; Jarry OC1, p. 1298.

108. Bordillon (f), p. 69.

109. Rachilde (g), unpaginated; Armory, p. 95.

110. Armory, pp. 80–81, 95; Rachilde (g), unpaginated.

111. Vallette (c), pp. 42–44; Jarry OC1, p. 1066.

112. Sainmont (b), pp. 19–20, 26; Arnaud (d), pp. 126–127.

113. Arnaud (b), p. 424; Jarry OC3, pp. 810–811; Cathé (e), unpaginated; Caradec (b), pp. 130–131.

114. Jarry OC1, pp. 569–571.

115. ORG 18, p. 7.

116. Jarry OC1, pp. 1070–1072; Mercier, p. 19; Besnier (f), p. 119.

117. Jarry OC1, pp. 1070–1072; Vallette (c), p. 43; Besnier (e), pp. 372–373; Mercier, p. 19.

118. Jarry OC3, p. 142; Jarry OC1, p. 1073.

119. Saillet (f), p. 17; Bordillon (k), p. 52; Natanson (a), p. 318.

120. Béhar (b), pp. 31–32.

121. Jarry OC1, p. 1077.

122. Vallette (c), pp. 26–27; Vollard, p. 118.

123. Beaumont would disagree; see, for example, Beaumont (a), p. 228.

124. CCP 10, pp. 137–138; Jarry OC1, p. 1075.

125. Jarry O, p. xxviii; Surcouf, p. 53.

126. Saillet (b), p. 75.

127. Jarry OC3, p. 593.

128. Besnier (e), p. 398.

129. Rachilde (c), p. 47.

130. CCP 26–27, p. 68.

131. Tzara lot no. 262.

132. Edwards (a), pp. 69–86.

133. Mollet, p. 52.

134. Wells's article "My First Flight," 1912, confirms his relations with Langley.

135. Bordillon (f), p. 73.

136. The source for most of this section is Rachilde (e), pp. 122–129.

137. Jarry (b), p. 510; Jarry OC1, pp. 1, 267–268.

138. Jarry (b), p. 257.

139. Jarry OC1, p. 429.

140. Jarry OC1, p. 521.

141. Rachilde (e), p. 131; Bordillon (f), p. 75.

Chapter 11

1. Jarry OC1, p. 736.

2. Rachilde (g) and the afterword by the Sous-commission des Implications et Embrelages du Cymbalum Pataphysicum, both unpaginated.

3. Sharp, pp. 396–397.

4. Jarry OC2, pp. 217–218.

5. Jarry OC2, pp. 281, 289; Charlotte Jarry, p. 8.

6. Jarry OC1, p. 541.

7. Rachilde (e), pp. 138–139.

8. Georges-Michel (b), p. 234; Chauveau (b), p. 118.

9. Rachilde (g), unpaginated.

10. Jarry OC1, p. 770, translation by Alexis Lykiard from CW2.

11. Jarry OC2, pp. 393–394.

12. Jarry OC2, p. 676; Rachilde (e), p. 128.

Chapter 12

1. Cathé (e), unpaginated.

2. Cathé (a) p. 178; Bourrelier, p. 789.

3. Cathé (e), unpaginated; Arnaud (b), p. 429; Jarry OC3, pp. 810–811, Cathé (e), unpaginated; Caradec (b), pp. 130–131.

4. Cathé (a), p. 178; Jarry OC2, pp. 710–714; Sainmont (b), pp. 26–27.

5. Trohel, pp. 635–636.

6. Bordillon (f), p. 82; Régibier, pp. 95–97.

7. Rachilde (e), p. 143.

8. Régibier, p. 110.

9. Sainmont (b), p. 27.

10. Régibier, p. 111; Jarry OC3, p. 522.

11. Saillet (e), p. 53; Régibier, pp. 119–120; Jarry OC2, pp. 546–548.

12. Régibier, pp. 98–99, 111.

13. Bordillon (f), p. 83; Renard, p. 487.

14. Bordillon (f), p. 83.

15. Régibier, p. 110.

16. Régibier, p. 111; Rachilde (e), pp. 135–136; Jarry OC3, p. 691.

17. Bibliography IV (d), pp. 89–90; Caradec (a), p. 108.

18. Jarry OC2, pp. 637–641.

19. Jarry OC2, pp. 605–606; Rachilde (e), p. 132; Bordillon (f), p. 85.

20. Rachilde (c), p. 46.

21. Rachilde (c), p. 46; Foulc (a), p. 7; Jarry OC2, pp. 721–724; Besnier (e), p. 450; Sweetman, pp. 469–470; Ehrich, p. 14; Fagus, p. 12.

22. Jarry OC2, pp. 585–598.

23. Bourrelier, p. 60; Morel (b), p. 160; Jarry OC1, p. 1018.

24. Richardson I, p. 195; Franck, pp. 48–52; Morel (a), pp. 25–29.

25. Apollinaire (a), p. 76; Vollard, p. 350.

26. Apollinaire (a), p. 50.

27. Cathé (d), pp. 73–76; Bernier (a), p. 77; Vollard, pp. 350–352; Caradec (c), p. 164.

28. Vollard, p. 128; the MSS. of "Tatane" are held in the Harry Ransom Humanities Research Center at the University of Texas.

29. Jarry OC2, p. 604.

30. Jarry (a), pp. 58–60; Vollard, p. 357; Morel (a), p. 28.

31. Jarry OC1, pp. 595–596.

32. Jarry OC2, p. 603.

33. Jarry OC2, p. 275.

34. Caradec (c), pp. 173–174; Jarry OC2, pp. 331–334.
35. Décaudin, p. 9; Arnaud (b), p. 382.
36. Guitry, p. 399.
37. Cathé (e), unpaginated; Jarry OC3, pp. 546, 548–549; Bordillon (i), p. 794.
38. Morel (b), p. 163.
39. Mirbeau, p. 16.
40. Mirbeau, p. 18.
41. Carr, pp. 26, 161–162, 166.
42. Chauveau (b), p. 111; Arnaud (b), p. 432.
43. Jarry OC2, p. 209.
44. EA 7–8, pp. 65–66.
45. Sert, p. 40.
46. Gold and Fizdale, p. 40.
47. Bourrelier, pp. 78–80.
48. Gold and Fizdale, p. 83; Lebois, p. 120; Chauveau (b), p. 128.
49. Fauchereau, pp. i, iv; Bourrelier, p. 80.
50. Jarry OC2, pp. 610–612.
51. EA 3, p. 6; Jarry OC3, pp. 546–547; Goujon (d), pp. 20–23.
52. Jarry (b), p. 497.
53. Cyvoet, pp. 37–38.
54. Cathé (b), p. 73.
55. Jarry OC1, p. 1214; Jarry (b), pp. 495–496; Bordillon (d), p. 112.
56. Jarry's letter of 16 May 1903 is described at <http://pataplatform.blogspot.com/search/label/jarry>; Gauthard, p. 244.
57. Quillard, p. 623; CCP 10, p. 144.
58. Jarry OC3, p. 559.
59. Pierron, pp. 718–727.
60. Arrivé (b), p. 100; Jarry (k) original in the Harry Ransom Humanities Research Center at the University of Texas.
61. Various authors (e), pp. 312, 136.
62. Maus, p. 277.
63. Jarry OC1, p. 420.
64. Saltas (e), p. 185.
65. The principal source for the "Gala" is Rachilde (e), pp. 146–150.
66. Jarry OC2, pp. 357, 361.
67. Jarry OC2, p. 189.
68. Apollinaire (b), p. 26.
69. Rachilde (d), p. 51.
70. Signac, pp. 75, 102.
71. Besnier (e), pp. 503, 505; Bourrelier, pp. 78–79.
72. Jarry OC2, p. 794; Jarry OC3, p. 569.
73. Jarry OC3, p. 570.
74. Dauberville, pp. 157–158.
75. Jarry OC3, pp. 567, 569; Jarry OC2, pp. 652–654.
76. Natanson (a), p. 287.
77. Delarue-Mardrus, p. 127.
78. ORG 18, p. 9.
79. Gaudemar, p. 251; Jarry OC2, p. 545.

80. Translation by Stanley Chapman.

81. Jarry OC3, p. 642.

82. CTCP 3, p. 84; Beaumont was the biographer (a), p. 218.

83. Richardson I, p. 332.

84. Apollinaire (b), pp. 21–22, translation by Stanley Chapman from Brotchie and Chapman.

85. Richardson I, pp. 327–328, 332; Apollinaire (e), pp. 127–128; Mollet, pp. 42–43.

86. Saillet (f), p. 21; Salmon (b), p. 243; Salmon (c), pp. 45, 148; Richardson I, p. 332.

87. Mollet, pp. 55, 58; Jarry OC3, p. 950.

88. Georges-Michel relates this anecdote, with variations, in (a), (b), and (c).

89. Salmon (c), pp. 150–153.

90. Vollard, p. 119; Lebois, p. 128.

91. Salmon (a), pp. 107, 153; Mollet, p. 49.

92. Adéma, p. 67.

93. Jarry OC3, p. 575; Cathé (c), p. 201.

94. Bordillon (f), pp. 109–110; Caradec (c), p. 167.

95. Jarry OC3, p. 575.

96. Jarry OC3, p. 578.

97. Bourdat, p. 25.

98. Franc-Nohain (a), pp. 40–41.

99. Franc-Nohain (a), p. 39.

100. Jarry OC3, p. 639; Morel (b), p. 141.

101. Besnier (e), p. 541; Jarry OC3, p. 579; Jarry (k), original in the Harry Ransom Humanities Research Center at the University of Texas.

102. Jarry OC3, p. 581; Armory, p. 143.

103. Jarry OC3, p. 421; Jarry OC2, pp. 548–550; Franc-Nohain (a), p. 40.

Chapter 13

1. Georges-Michel (b), p. 5.

2. Chauveau (b), pp. 99, 205.

3. Mauclair, p. 109.

4. Vallette (a), p. 13, translation by Stanley Chapman from Brotchie and Chapman.

5. Fagus, pp. 12, 14.

6. Mollet, pp. 51–52.

7. Rachilde (e), p. 36.

8. Apollinaire (b), p. 25; Breton (b), p. 1055; Shattuck, p. 172.

9. Shattuck, p. 168.

10. Arrivé (b), p. 81.

11. Jarry OC1, p. 418.

Chapter 14

1. Jarry OC3, p. 614, translation by Iain White.

2. Guitry, p. 395; Bordillon (f), p. 124.

3. Guitry, pp. 396–397.

4. Rachilde (e), pp. 143–144; Salmon (c), p. 156; DCP 12, p. 165.

5. A card from Le Grand-Lemps in Jarry (k), original in the Harry Ransom Humanities Research Center at the University of Texas, refers to his plans; Rachilde (e), p. 132; Jarry OC3, p. 581; Surcouf, pp. 22–26.

6. Chauveau (b), p. 182.

7. Saltas (a), p. 21.

8. Salmon (a), pp. 9–10; Salmon (c), pp. 155–156; DCP 27, p. 15; Apollinaire (b), pp. 23–24.

9. Jarry OC3, p. 585, translation by Iain White.

10. Bordillon (f), p. 122; Surcouf, p. 24.

11. Daudet, p. 1149.

12. Jarry OC3, p. 585, translation by Iain White.

13. Guitry, p. 398.

14. Jarry OC3, p. 614, translation by Iain White; Régibier, p. 147.

15. Rachilde (e), pp. 40, 140; Edwards (b), p. 119.

16. Bordillon (f), pp. 124–125; letter from Jarry to Rachilde, dated November 30, 1904, in Jarry (k), original in the Harry Ransom Humanities Research Center at the University of Texas.

17. Jarry OC3, pp. 719, 813; Rozier, January, p. 40.

18. Bordillon (f), p. 128.

19. Renard, p. 652; Salmon (c), p. 158; Caradec (b), p. 173.

20. Cathé (e), unpaginated; Cathé (g), pp. 144–146; Jarry OC3, p. 813; Arnaud (d), p. 127.

21. Surcouf, p. 26.

22. Jarry OC1, pp. 188, 190; Bibliography II (a), p. 278, note by Paul Edwards.

23. Stéphen-Chauvet, p. 30.

24. Surcouf, p. 53; Roig, p. 504; Renard, p. 700.

25. Richardson I, p. 327.

26. Mac Orlan, p. 242.

27. Mac Orlan, p. 244.

28. Olivier, p. 50; Raynal, pp. 2–3; Apollinaire (b), p. 24; Jacob in Seckel, p. 50.

29. Jarry OC3, p. 590.

30. Richardson II, p. 126; Jacob in Seckel, p. 193.

31. Richardson I, pp. 360–361; Penrose, pp. 97, 133.

32. Cathé (e), unpaginated; Bordillon (f), pp. 134–135.

33. Cathé (e), unpaginated.

34. Jarry OC2, p. 676.

35. Cathé (e), unpaginated; Surcouf, p. 74.

36. Jarry OC3, p. 591; Rachilde (e), pp. 135–137.

37. Rachilde (e), pp. 132, 138; Surcouf, pp. 32–33.

38. Bourrelier, pp. 182, 1101–1102.

39. Marinetti, p. 330, translation by R. W. Flint.

40. Bordillon (f), p. 135.

41. EA 18, p. 14; Jarry OC3, p. 592.

42. Jarry OC3, pp. 593–594, 635; Bordillon (f), p. 140; Surcouf, p. 54.

43. Bordillon (f), p. 140; Rozier, February and August; EA 95–96, p. 135; Jarry OC3, pp. 760, 776; Saltas (b), p. 21.

44. Saltas (b), p. 22; Chauveau (b), pp. 181–183; Jarry OC3, p. 614.

45. Salmon (c), p. 153; Jarry OC3, p. 676.

46. Apollinaire (b), pp. 22–23, translation by Stanley Chapman from Brotchie and Chapman.

47. Jarry OC3, pp. 595–596; Bordillon (f) p. 142; Léautaud (a) I, p. 237.

48. Besnier (e), pp. 597–600.

49. Georges-Michel (a), p. 5; Jarry OC3, p. 598.

50. Jarry OC3, pp. 599–600.

51. Jarry OC1, pp. 1077–1078 (only a portion of the letter to Kolney is included; the remainder

is in Jarry (k), and the original is in Harry Ransom Humanities Research Center at the University of Texas); Jarry OC3, pp. 601, 958–959; Saltas (a), p. 22.

52. Jarry OC3, pp. 601–603.
53. Jarry OC3, pp. 602–603.
54. Jarry OC3, pp. 603–604; Décaudin, p. 10.
55. Salmon (b), p. 159; Jarry OC3, p. 605.
56. Chauveau (b), p. 184.
57. The postcard is in Jarry (k), original in the Harry Ransom Humanities Research Center at the University of Texas; Surcouf, pp. 40, 87–89.
58. Jarry OC3, pp. 605–606.
59. Jarry OC3, pp. 609–613.
60. EA 5–6, p. 19.
61. DCP 27, p. 11.
62. Surcouf, pp. 14–15, translation by Iain White.
63. Surcouf, pp. 112–113; Jarry OC3, pp. 419, 874; Rachilde (e), pp. 164–167.
64. Jarry OC3, pp. 616–617, translation by Iain White.
65. Jarry OC3, p. 618.
66. DCP 27, p. 110.
67. Jarry OC3, pp. 618–620, translation by Iain White.
68. Jarry OC3, pp. 620–623; DCP 27, p. 109.
69. Jarry OC1, p. 734; Jarry OC2, p. 244.
70. Jarry OC1, pp. 734, 814; Jarry OC2, pp. 244, 463.
71. Jarry OC3, pp. 622–623.
72. CCP 10, p. 116; Jarry OC3, p. 976.
73. Surcouf, pp. 26, 32–33.
74. Cathé (e), unpaginated; Cathé (g), p. 147; Renard, p. 700; Arnaud (c), p. 127.
75. Jarry OC3, pp. 626–628; Saillet (c), pp. 27–28.
76. Postcard in Jarry (k), original in the Harry Ransom Humanities Research Center at the University of Texas, translation by Antony Melville.
77. Bordillon (f), p. 154.
78. Jarry OC3, pp. 629–630.
79. Postcard in Jarry (k), original in the Harry Ransom Humanities Research Center at the University of Texas.
80. Surcouf, p. 26; Seckel, p. 49; Jarry OC3, p. 631.
81. Postcard in Jarry (k), original in the Harry Ransom Humanities Research Center at the University of Texas.
82. Surcouf, p. 65; Gougeon, p. 59; Arnaud (b), p. 279.
83. Jarry OC3, p. 976.
84. Jarry OC3, p. 634.
85. Jarry OC3, pp. 635–636.
86. Jarry OC3, p. 660; Bordillon (f), p. 158.
87. Arnaud (g), p. 45; Bordillon (f), p. 158.
88. Jarry OC3, pp. 637, 761.
89. Jarry OC3, p. 638; Saltas (a), p. 86; Jarry (i), pp. 2–3.
90. Rachilde (e), p. 40.
91. Jarry OC3, pp. 626–627, translation by Iain White; Richardson I, p. 320; Rachilde (e), p. 140.
92. Rachilde (e), pp. 160–161.

93. Jarry OC3, pp. 454–455.

94. Gide (a), p. 169.

95. Bruchard, pp. 53–54.

96. Jarry OC3, pp. 639, 981; Salmon (c), p. 289.

97. Adéma, p. 84; Salmon (c), pp. 217; Cingria, p. 2; Stein, p. 96; Olivier, p. 47; Penrose, p. 148.

98. Salmon (c), p. 157.

99. Jarry OC3, p. 640, translation by Iain White; the calendar is in Jarry (k), original in the Harry Ransom Humanities Research Center at the University of Texas; the date shown on it, Tuesday, March 19, occurred in 1907, not 1906.

100. Saltas (b), p. 22; Léautaud (a) II, p. 18.

101. Jarry OC3, pp. 641–642, 985; Arrivé (b), p. 91; Jarry OC3, p. 647.

102. Arnaud (c), p. 107; Rachilde (e), p. 138, note 1.

103. Bordillon (j), pp. 50–51; Surcouf, pp. 30–31; Jarry OC3, p. 650; Besnier (e), p. 651.

104. Jarry OC3, pp. 650–651, translation by Iain White; letters in Jarry (k), originals in the Harry Ransom Humanities Research Center at the University of Texas; ORG 18, pp. 24–25.

105. Jarry OC3, p. 653.

106. Rachilde (e), p. 4.

107. Jarry (f), p. 112, note 11.

108. Surcouf, pp. 104–105.

109. Régibier, p. 172; Bordillon (f), pp. 176–177.

110. Jarry OC3, pp. 655, 761–762; Besnier (e) p. 666.

111. Bailiff's letter in the collection of Christophe Champion; Surcouf, pp. 40, 50; Jarry OC3, pp. 656, 660; Régibier, p. 171.

112. Jarry OC3, pp. 991–992, translation by Iain White.

113. Régibier, p. 169; Surcouf, p. 65.

114. Jarry OC3, pp. 658–659, translation by Iain White, and 665–670; Régibier, p. 197; letter in Jarry (k), original in Harry Ransom Humanities Research Center at the University of Texas; Charlotte Jarry, p. 9.

115. Letter in Jarry (k), original in Harry Ransom Humanities Research Center at the University of Texas; Régibier, pp. 169, 171; Jarry OC3, p. 662.

116. Graham, pp. 511–512.

117. Jarry OC3, pp. 677–678, 1001; Surcouf, pp. 55–56.

118. Jarry OC3, pp. 680–681; Stéphen-Chauvet, p. 30.

119. Jarry OC3, pp. 681–682; letters in Jarry (k), originals in Harry Ransom Humanities Research Center at the University of Texas.

120. ORG 18, p. 38; Jarry OC3, pp. 685–687, 1004–1005.

121. Jarry OC3, pp. 1007–1008.

122. Jarry OC3, pp. 689–691.

123. Jarry OC3, p. 1012, translation by Iain White.

124. Jarry OC3, pp. 652 (the letter is misdated; see Arnaud (f), item 254), 694; Régibier, pp. 173–174; Charlotte Jarry, p. 9.

125. Rachilde (e), pp. 157–158.

126. Soffici, pp. 158–160, translated by Antony Melville.

127. Chauveau (b), pp. 192, 196; Saltas (a), p. 86.

128. Saltas (a), pp. 86–87; Chauveau (b), pp. 196–198; Bordillon (f), p. 192.

129. Stéphen-Chauvet, p. 26.

130. All the translations from this text are by Stanley Chapman from Brotchie and Chapman.

131. Stéphen-Chauvet, pp. 27–29; Surcouf, pp. 17, 106; Léautaud (a) II, p. 66.

132. Stéphen-Chauvet, p. 30; Georges-Michel (a), p. 5; Surcouf, p. 17; Léautaud (a) II, p. 75; Saltas (a) p. 87; Rachilde (e), p. 162.

133. Letter in Jarry (k), original in Harry Ransom Humanities Research Center at the University of Texas, translation by Antony Melville.

134. Saltas (a), p. 88.

135. Stéphen-Chauvet, p. 32.

136. Stéphen-Chauvet, pp. 32–33.

137. Léautaud (a) X, pp. 109–112.

138. Léautaud (a) II, pp. 72–73; Georges-Michel (a), p. 5; Georges-Michel (b), p. 234.

139. Guigon, p. 62; Apollinaire (b), p. 26; Léautaud (a) II, pp. 72–73; Georges-Michel (c); Fagus, pp. 9–10; EA 67–68, pp. 15–20; Salmon (c), p. 160.

140. Goujon (i), p. 593; EA 9–12, p. 109; Bibliography III (c), I. 71; Various authors (c), p. 27; Bordillon (j), p. 54.

141. Saillet (f), pp. 27–28.

142. Surcouf, pp. 21–24, 53; Graham, p. 512; Arnaud (b), p. 287; Jarry OC3, pp. 1013–1014.

Bibliography

This is not intended as a complete bibliography of Jarry, but as a list of works consulted and cited. French titles were published in Paris, English in London, unless noted otherwise, or unless the place of publication is obvious (as with university presses). The same abbreviations are used here as in the Notes (see p. 361).

I. COLLECTED WORKS OF ALFRED JARRY IN FRENCH

(a) *Œuvres complètes* (OC). 3 vols. Pléiade series. Gallimard, 1972, 1987, 1988.

(b) *Œuvres* (O). Bouquins series. Robert Laffont, 2004.

II. COLLECTED WORKS OF ALFRED JARRY IN ENGLISH

(a) *Collected Works I: Adventures in 'Pataphysics* (CW1). Ed. Alastair Brotchie and Paul Edwards. Atlas Press, 2001. Contains *Black Minutes of Memorial Sand, Caesar-Antichrist*, essays and journalism.

(b) *Collected Works II: Three Early Novels* (CW2). Ed. Alastair Brotchie and Paul Edwards. Atlas Press, 2007. Contains *Days and Nights, Exploits and Opinions of Doctor Faustroll, Pataphysician*, and *Absolute Love*.

(c) *Selected Works of Alfred Jarry*. Ed. Roger Shattuck and Simon Watson Taylor. Methuen, 1965.

III. BIBLIOGRAPHIES OF ALFRED JARRY

(a) Bollinger, Hans. "Bibliographie." In Carola Giedion-Welcker, *Alfred Jarry, eine Monographie*. Die Arche, Zurich, 1960.

(b) Bordillon, Henri. "Bibliographie générale." In Jarry OC3.

(c) Decheneux, Jean-Marie. *Alfred Jarry, Éléments de bibliographie critique*. Unpublished.

(d) Rameil, Claude. "Alfred Jarry, Essai de bibliographie critique." EA 1–2 (May 1979); supplements in 4 (1979) and 7–8 (1980).

(e) Talvart, H., and J. Place. *Bibliographie des auteurs modernes de langue français*. 1949.

(f) Tautz, Alfred. "Alfred Jarry bibliographie." This useful, although incomplete, chronological bibliography used to be at <www.pataphysica.org>, a site which seems now to be defunct.

IV. SPECIAL ISSUES OF REVIEWS

Specific essays appearing in the publications of the Collège de 'Pataphysique and the Cymbalum Pataphysicum are noted in section V, and special issues in this section below, although references to, and studies of, Jarry occur in many issues. The following series have appeared: Collège de 'Pataphysique: *Cahiers*, 1950–1957 (CCP); *Dossiers*, 1957–1965 (DCP); *Subsidia*, 1965–1975 (SP); then, Cymbalum Pataphysicum: *Organographes*, 1976–1986 (ORG); *Monitoires*, 1986–1993 (MON),

L'Expectateur, 1993–2000 (EXP); and then, Collège de 'Pataphysique: *Carnets*, 2001–2007; *Correspondancier* (ongoing). The same applies to: *L'Étoile-Absinthe* (EA), the journal of the Société des Amis d'Alfred Jarry, 1979–(ongoing).

(a) *Actualité littéraire*, "*Alfred Jarry 1873–1907*," 39 (October 1957).

(b) *Cahiers du Collège de 'Pataphysique*, "*Préparation au cinquantenaire de l'occultation d'Alfred Jarry*," 26–27 (1957).

(c) *Colloque de Cerisy* "*Alfred Jarry*," ed. Henri Bordillon. Pierre Belfond (1985).

(d) *Digraphe*, "*Hommage au Mercure*," ed. Philippe Kerbellec and François Vergne, 73, Mercure de France (March 1995).

(e) *Dossiers du Collège de 'Pataphysique*, "*Dossier de La Dragonne*," ed. Maurice Saillet, 27 (1965).

(f) *L'Esprit créateur*, "*Alfred Jarry*," ed. John D. Erickson, Louisiana State University, 34, no. 4 (Winter 1984).

(g) *L'Étoile-Absinthe*, "*Fargue et Jarry*," ed. Jean-Paul Goujon, 43–45 (1989).

(h) *Europe*, "*Alfred Jarry*," 623, no. 4 (March–April 1981).

(i) *Evergreen Review*, "What Is 'Pataphysics?," ed. Roger Shattuck and Simon Watson Taylor, 4, no. 13 (San Francisco, May–June 1960).

(j) *Les Feuilles libres*, "*Hommage à Léon-Paul Fargue*," ed. Marcel Raval, 45–46 (June 1927).

(k) *La Licorne*, "*Jarry Monstres et merveilles*," ed. Patrick Besnier, 80 (Presses Universitaires de Rennes, 2007).

(l) *Les Nouveaux Cahiers de la Comédie-Française*, "*Alfred Jarry*," ed. Muriel Mayette (May 2009).

(m) *Organographes du Cymbalum Pataphysicum*, "*Véritable Portrait de Monsieuye Hébert*," 5 (1977).

(n) *Revue des Sciences humaines*, "*Alfred Jarry*," ed. Charles Grivel, 203 (Université de Lille, 1986).

(o) *Revue 303*, "*Alfred Jarry*," 95 (Nantes, 2007).

V. BOOKS AND ARTICLES (INCLUDING EDITIONS OF JARRY'S WORKS WITH BIOGRAPHICAL MATERIAL)

Adéma, Marcel. *Apollinaire le Mal-Aimé*. Plon, 1952. References are to the English translation, *Apollinaire* (Heinemann, 1954).

Adès, Marie-Claire, and Jean-Hughes Piettre. *Ubu cent ans de règne*. Musée-Galerie de la Seita, 1989. This exhibition catalog also constitutes nos. 41–42 of *L'Étoile-Absinthe*.

Anonymous/uncredited. "Jarry et Sarluis." EA 9–12 (1981).

Apollinaire, Guillaume (a). "Le cave de M. Vollard." In *Le flâneur des deux rives*. La Sirène, 1919. References are to the edition published by Gallimard in 1975.

Apollinaire, Guillaume (b). "Feu Alfred Jarry." *Les Marges*, November 1909. References are to the reprint in the same magazine, XXIII, 91 (15 January 1922).

Apollinaire, Guillaume (c). *Il y a*. Messein, 1925. References are to the edition of 1949.

Apollinaire, Guillaume (d). *Anecdotiques*. Gallimard, 1955. References are to the edition of 1982.

Apollinaire, Guillaume (e). *Journal intime*. Éditions du Limon, 1991.

Armory. *See* Dauriac.

Arnaud, Noël (a). "Remy de Gourmont: Man of Masks." *Evergreen Review*, section IV (i) above.

Arnaud, Noël (b). *Alfred Jarry d'Ubu roi au Docteur Faustroll*. La Table Ronde, 1974.

Arnaud, Noël (c). "Jarry à son ombre même." *Revue des Sciences humaines*, section IV (n) above.

Arnaud, Noël (d). "Note sur deux pages d'une version inédite du Pantagruel." *Revue des Sciences humaines*, section IV (n) above.

Arnaud, Noël (e). "Gourmont, Jarry et la Vieille Dame." *Dragée Haute*, 15 (Penne du Tarn, 1992).

Arnaud, Noël (f), ed. *Alfred Jarry, Le Gentilhomme de 1847*. Éditions du Limon et Dragée Haute, 1996.

Arnaud, Noël (g). *Archives Noël Arnaud*. Bookseller's catalog. Librairie Champavert, Toulouse, 2001.

Arrivé, Michel (a). "Chronologie." In Jarry OC1.

Arrivé, Michel (b). "Jarry aux prises avec le quotidien: à propos de quelques letters à Claude Terrasse" and "Notule en forme de testament touchant la correspondence de Jarry." *Europe*, section IV (h) above.

B., L. "La mort du 'Père Ubu'" (obituary). *La Liberté*, 3 November 1907.

Baas, Jacquelynn, and Richard S. Field. *The Artistic Revival of the Woodcut in France, 1850–1900*. University of Michigan Museum of Art, 1984.

Barrot, Olivier, and Pascal Ory. *La Revue Blanche, histoire, anthologie, portraits*. U.G.E., 1989.

Beardsley, Aubrey (a). *Last Letters of Aubrey Beardsley*. Longmans, Green, 1904. Most are to Raffalovich, although the addressees' names are not given.

Beardsley, Aubrey (b). *The Letters of Aubrey Beardsley*. Ed. Henry Maas, J. L. Duncan, and W. G. Good. Cassell, 1970.

Beaumont, Keith (a). *Alfred Jarry, a Critical and Biographical Study*. Leicester University Press, 1984.

Beaumont, Keith (b). *Jarry: Ubu Roi*. Critical Guides to French Texts. Grant and Cutler, 1987.

Béhar, Henri (a). *Jarry dramaturge*. A.-G. Nizet, 1980.

Béhar, Henri (b). "Jarry, l'almanach et le fleuve oral." EA 19–20 (1983).

Béhar, Henri (c). *Les Cultures de Jarry*. Presses Universitaires de France, 1988.

Béhar, Henri (d), ed. *Alfred Jarry en verve*. Horay, 2003.

Béhar, Henri, Marieke Dubbelboer, and Jean-Paul Morel. "Commentaires pour servir à la lecture de l'Almanach du Père Ubu illustré." EA 121–122 (2009).

Bergson, Henri (a). *Essai sur les données immédiates de la conscience*. Alcan, 1889. Trans. F. L. Pogson as *Time and Free Will*, Elibron Classics, 2005. References are to this edition of the translation, which first appeared in 1913.

Bergson, Henri (b). *Matière et mémoire*. Alcan, 1896. Trans. Nancy Margaret Paul and W. Scott Palmer as *Matter and Memory*, Dover, 2004. References are to this edition of the translation, which first appeared in 1912.

Bergson, Henri (c). *Le Rire*. Alcan, 1901. Trans. Cloudesley Brereton and Fred Rothwell as *Laughter*, Green Integer, Los Angeles, 1999. References are to this edition of the translation, which first appeared in 1911.

Bernier, Georges (a). *La Revue Blanche*. Wildenstein, New York, 1983.

Bernier, Georges (b). *La Revue Blanche*. Éditions Hazan, 1991.

Besnard, Lucien. "Ubu Roi." *Revue d'Art dramatique*, 1 (1896).

Besnier, Patrick (a). "Alfred Jarry et l'art littéraire." EA 39–40 (1988).

Besnier, Patrick (b). "Notice" (on *Pantagruel*). In Jarry OC3.

Besnier, Patrick (c). *Alfred Jarry*. Plon, 1990.

Besnier, Patrick (d). "La Séance du mardi soir." Mallarmé issue of *Magazine littéraire*, 368 (September 1998).

Besnier, Patrick (e). *Alfred Jarry*. Fayard, 2005.

Besnier, Patrick (f). "Loisirs de la poste, deux lettres d'Alfred Jarry à Rachilde." *Histoires littéraires*, 23 (July–December 2005).

Billy, André. *Le Pont des Saints-Pères*. Librairie Arthème Fayard, 1947.

Blavier, André, ed. *Christian Beck, souvenir des journées*. Special issue of *Temps mêlés*, 83–85 (Verviers, Belgium, 1964).

Blum, Léon. *Les Livres* (includes a review of *Les Jours et les nuits*). *Revue Blanche*, November 1897.

Bodson, Guy. "Par le petit bout de la lorgnette." EA 47–48 (1990).

Bordillon, Henri (a). "Études Jarryques." ORG 1 (1976).

Bordillon, Henri (b). "Le Petit et le grand Morin." ORG 5 (1976).

Bordillon, Henri (c). "Jarry à l'Œuvre." EA 4 (1979).

Bordillon, Henri (d). "Chronique Parajarryque." ORG 8–9 (1979).

Bordillon, Henri (e). "Gourmont et Jarry." *Quinzaine littéraire*, 374 (1–15 July 1982). Page numbers are omitted from references to this article, which was consulted online at <www.remydegourmont.org>.

Bordillon, Henri (f). *Gestes et opinions d'Alfred Jarry, écrivain*. Éditions Siloe, Laval, 1986.

Bordillon, Henri (g). "Laval à bicyclette, dans la roue d'Alfred Jarry." *Le Bateau-Lavoir* (Laval, June 1986).

Bordillon, Henri (h). "Ronde autour du Théâtre des Pantins, 18 lettres de Franc-Nohain." EA 29–30 (1986).

Bordillon, Henri (i). "Notice" (on *La Chandelle verte*). In Jarry OC2.

Bordillon, Henri (j). "Trois lettres inédites d'Alfred Jarry." *L'Œil bleu*, 7 (September 2008).

Bordillon, Henri (k). "Jarry aux prises avec une 'vieille dame'" and "De deux dessins d'Ubu." *L'Œil bleu*, 8 (March 2009).

Bouhélier, Saint-Georges de. *Le Printemps d'une génération*. Éditions Nagel, 1946.

Bourdat, Pierre. "Lettre du Dauphiné, une visite du Grand-Lemps à la suite de Jarry." EA 73–74 (1997).

Bourrelier, Paul-Henri. *La Revue Blanche*. Fayard, 2007.

Boyer, Patricia Eckert. *Artists and the Avant-Garde Theater in Paris, 1887–1900*. National Gallery of Art, Washington, 1998.

Breton, André (a). "Alfred Jarry." In *Les Pas perdus*. Nouvelle Revue Française, 1924. References are to the reprint in Breton, *Œuvres complètes*, vol. 1 (Gallimard, 1988).

Breton, André (b). "Alfred Jarry." In *Anthologie de l'humour noir*. Sagittaire, 1940. References are to the reprint in Breton, *Œuvres complètes*, vol. 2 (Gallimard, 1992).

Breton, André (c). "Alfred Jarry as Precursor and Initiator." In *Free Rein*, trans. Michel Parmentier and Jacqueline d'Amboise. University of Nebraska Press, 1995. Originally published in *Arts*, 331 (2 November 1951).

Breton, André, and Philippe Soupault. "Déclaration sur l'Affaire Ubu." *Littérature* II, 1 (1 March 1922).

Brotchie, Alastair, and Stanley Chapman, eds. *Alfred Jarry, Necrologies*. Atlas Press/London Institute of 'Pataphysics, 2007.

Bruchard, Henry de. *Petits mémoires du temps de la Ligue*. Nouvelle Librairie Nationale, 1912.

Caradec, François (a). *À la recherche de Alfred Jarry*. Seghers, 1974.

Caradec, François (b). *Feu Willy*. Pauvert, 1984.

Caradec, François (c). "Alfred Jarry, témoin de son temps." *Colloque de Cerisy*, section IV (c) above.

Caradec, François (d). "André Gide et Jarry." EA 35–36 (1987).

Caradec, François (e). *Alphonse Allais*. Fayard, 1997.

Carr, Reg. *Anarchism in France: The Case of Octave Mirbeau*. Manchester University Press, 1977.

Cate, Phillip and Shaw, Mary. *The Spirit of Montmartre. Cabarets, Humor, and the avant-garde, 1875–1905*. Rutgers, The State University of New Jersey, 1996.

Cathé, Philippe (a). "Le Théâtre des Pantins: d'un avatar d'Ubu Roi aux prolégomènes de *Pantagruel*." EA 77–78 (1998).

Cathé, Philippe (b). "De l'utilisation des restes." EXP 8 (1998).

Cathé, Philippe (c). "Alfred Jarry and Music." In *Alfred Jarry. De los nabis a la patafísica*. IVAM Centre Julio González, Institut Valencià d'Art Modern, 2000.

Cathé, Philippe (d). "Jarry-Terrasse au travail." CTCP 3 (2001).

Cathé, Philippe (e). "Claude Terrasse (1867–1923)." Thesis, Paris-IV, 2001.

Cathé, Philippe (f). "Censure-Disparition-Résurrection d'une pièce." In Franc-Nohain, *Vive la France!* Collège de 'Pataphysique, 2003.

Cathé, Philippe (g). *Claude Terrasse*. L'Hexaèdre, 2004.

Cathé, Philippe (h). "Les Théâtres du Père Ubu." In *Le Théâtre de l'Œuvre 1893–1900, Naissance du théâtre moderne*. Musée d'Orsay, 2005.

Certigny, Henry. *La Vérité sur le Douanier Rousseau*. Plon, 1961.

Chapman, Stanley. *See* Brotchie.

Charbonnier, Georges, and Alain Trutat. *Bonjour Monsieur Jarry*. André Dimanche Éditeur, 1995.

Chassé, Charles (a). *Dans les coulisses de la gloire: d'Ubu-Roi au Douanier Rousseau*. Éditions de la Nouvelle Revue Critique, 1947. The shorter version, *Les Sources d'Ubu-Roi*, appeared in 1921; references are to the 1947 edition unless indicated otherwise.

Chassé, Charles (b). *Gauguin et son temps*. La Bibliothèque des Arts, 1955.

Chassé, Charles (c). *The Nabis and Their Period*. Lund Humphries, 1969.

Chauveau, Paul (a). "Comment naquit le Père Ubu." *Vu*, 11 January 1922.

Chauveau, Paul (b). *Alfred Jarry ou la naissance, la vie et la mort du Père Ubu*. Mercure de France, 1932.

Chauveau, Paul (c). "La première d'Ubu Roi." *Nouvelles littéraires*, 26 November 1932.

Cingria, Charles-Albert. "Une Jarryniana." *Carreau* 23–24 (Lausanne, May–June 1952).

Colette. *Mes apprentissages*. Ferenczi, 1936. References are to the Hachette edition of 1972.

Cyvoet, Antoine. "Jarry et Jehan Rictus: documents nouveaux." EA 51–52 (1992).

Damerval, Gérard. *Ubu Roi, la bombe comique de 1896*. A.-G. Nizet, 1984.

Dauberville, Henry. *La Bataille de l'impressionisme*. Éditions J. et H. Berneim-Jeune, 1967.

Daudet, Léon. *Paris vécu*. Vol. 2. Gallimard, 1930. References are to the reprint in *Souvenirs et polémiques* (Robert Laffont, 1992).

Dauriac, Carle Lionel (as Armory). *50 Ans de vie parisienne*. Éditions Jean-Renard, 1943.

David, Sylvain-Christian (a). "Pataphysique et psychanalyse." *Europe*, section IV (h) above.

David, Sylvain-Christian (b). *Alfred Jarry, le secret des origines*. PUF, 2003.

Deak, Frantisek. *Symbolist Theater: The Formation of an Avant-Garde*. Johns Hopkins University Press, Baltimore, 1993.

Décaudin, Michel. "Autour d'un livre prêté. Apollinaire et Jarry." EA 75–76 (1997).

Delarue-Mardrus, Lucie. *Mes mémoires*. Gallimard, 1938.

Douglas, Alfred. *Oscar Wilde et quelques autres*. Gallimard, 1930.

Dujardin, Édouard. *Mallarmé par un des siens*. Éditions Messein, 1936.

Duvernois, Henri. "Ubu Roi à l'Œuvre." EA 4 (1979).

Edwards, Paul (a). "Jarry et William Thomson. La construction visuelle de la Machine à Explorer le Temps." EA 95–96 (2002).

Edwards, Paul (b). "Un tableau inédit de Jarry." EA 103–104 (2004).

Ehrich, Riewert. "*Messaline* d'Alfred Jarry, tentative de 'best-seller' ou livre hermétique?" EA 61–62 (1994).

Ellmann, Richard. *Oscar Wilde*. Hamish Hamilton, 1987.

Eruli, Brunella. "Jarry's *Messaline*: The Text and the Phoenix." *L'Esprit créateur*, section IV (f) above.

Fagus, Félicien. "Le Noyé recalcitrant." *Les Marges*, XXIII, 91 (15 January 1922). A revision of this obituary, originally published in 1907.

Fargue, Léon-Paul (a). *Le Piéton de Paris, suivi de D'après Paris*. Gallimard, 1993. Originally published in 1939 and 1931.

Fargue, Léon-Paul (b). *Portraits de famille*. J. B. Janin, 1947.

Fargue, Léon-Paul (c). *Lettres de Léon-Paul Fargue à Alfred Jarry*. EA 43–45, section IV (g) above.

Fauchereau, Serge. "Avant-propos" to F.-A. Cazals, *Le Jardin des ronces*. Société littéraire des P.T.T./ Somogy, éditions d'art, 1995. A reprint of the edition of 1901 published by Éditions de la Plume.

Fechner, Gustav Theodor. "The Comparative Anatomy of Angels," translated by Malcolm Green. *Journal of the London Institute of 'Pataphysics*, 1 (2010). No page references are given as this publication was still in progress at the time of writing.

Fénéon, Félix, et al. *Petit Bottin des lettres et des arts*. Giraud, 1886.

Fisher, Ben (a). *The Pataphysician's Library*. Liverpool University Press, 2000.

Fisher, Ben (b). "Précisions sur les imprécisions de Jarry. Sur les mystères subsistants des livres pairs et du 'petit nombre des élus.'" *La Licorne*, 80 (Presses Universitaires de Rennes, 2007).

Fontainas, André. *Mes souvenirs du symbolisme*. Éditions de la Nouvelle Revue Critique, 1928.

Fort, Paul. *Mes Mémoires*. Flammarion, 1944.

Fort-Vallette, Gabrielle. "Interview with Madame Fort-Vallette." *Le Magazine littéraire*, 48 (January 1971).

Foulc, Thieri (a). "Jarry et les hautes œuvres de Phales." Preface to *Messaline*. Eric Losfeld Le Terrain Vague, 1977.

Foulc, Thieri (b). "La Service de presse d'*Ubu Roi*." *Europe*, section IV (h) above.

Franck, Dan. *Bohèmes*. Calmann-Lévy, 1998.

Franc-Nohain (a). "Pantagruel au Café Brosse." *Comœdia*, 29 January 1911. References are to the reprint in EA 73–74 (1997).

Franc-Nohain (b). "L'Affaire Ubu." *L'Écho de Paris*, 26 April 1928. References are to the reprint in the biography by Chauveau (b) above.

Freitas, Laurent de (a). "Les Archives Léon-Paul Fargue." *Actes du colloque "Léon-Paul Fargue Poète et Chroniqueur,"* Université de Paris X, 2001.

Freitas, Laurent de (b). "Léon-Paul Fargue et Alfred Jarry, autour d'une même passion pour la peinture 1892–1894" and "Jarry à Pont-Aven, rencontre de Filiger et Gauguin." EA 103–104 (2004).

Fresneau, Estelle. "Hommage à Gauguin: trois poèmes offerts au musée de Pont-Aven." *Revue 303*, section IV (o) above.

Gaudemar, Antoine de. "Plongée dans le *Mercure.*" *Digraphe*, 73 (March 1995).

Gauthard. "Letter to Méry-Picard." In the appendix to Cate and Shaw (above).

Gayot, Paul. "Les problèmes du Faustroll." *Colloque de Cerisy*, section IV (c), above.

Gémier, Firmin. "La Création d'Ubu Roi." *Excelsior*, 4 November 1921. References are to the reprint in *Europe*, section IV (h) above.

Gens-d'Armes, Gandilhon. "Alfred Jarry au lycée Henri IV." *Les Marges*, XXIII, 91 (15 January 1922).

Georges-Michel, Michel (a). "Souvenirs sur Alfred Jarry." *La France au combat*, 6 February 1947.

Georges-Michel, Michel (b). *Un Demi-Siècle de gloires théatrales.* Éditions André Bonne, 1950.

Georges-Michel, Michel (c). "Jarry-Roi que j'ai connu." *Aux écoutes du monde*, 30 September 1965.

Gerard-Arlberg, Gilles. "Nr 6, rue Vercingétorix." *Konstrevy* 2 (Stockholm, 1958).

Géroy. *See* Roig.

Gide, André (a). "Le Groupement littéraire qu'abritait le 'Mercure de France.'" *Mercure de France*, 1 October 1946. References are to the extracts in *Digraphe*, section IV (d) above.

Gide, André (b). *Si le grain ne meurt.* Gallimard, 1920. References are to the English translation: *If It Die …* (Secker and Warburg, 1950).

Gide, André (c). *Feuillets d'Automne.* Mercure de France, 1949.

Gide, André (d). *Les Faux-monnayeurs.* Gallimard, 1925. References are to the English translation: *The Coiners* (Cassell, 1950).

Gide, André (e). *Journal.* Vol. 1. Gallimard, 1996.

Girieud, Pierre. "Souvenirs d'un vieux peintre." Unpublished autobiography to be found at <www. pgirieud.asso.fr>.

Goda, Yosuké. "Le cours de Bergson et la quête de l'absolu chez Alfred Jarry." EA 123–124 (2010).

Gold, Arthur, and Robert Fizdale. *Misia: The Life of Misia Sert.* Knopf, New York, 1980.

Gosse, Edmund. "Current French Literature." *Cosmopolis*, X, 30 (June 1898).

Goudemare, Sylvain. *Marcel Schwob ou les vies imaginaires.* Le Cherche midi éditeur, 2000.

Gougeon, Jean-Yves. "Alfred Jarry et maître Blaviel." *L'Œil bleu*, 8 (March 2009).

Goujon, Jean-Paul (a). "Notes sur Tinan et Jarry." EA 4 (December 1979).

Goujon, Jean-Paul (b). "Menus propos sur une lettre de Heredia à Jarry." EA 7–8 (1980).

Goujon, Jean-Paul (c). "Rachilde et Tinan." ORG 19–20 (1983).

Goujon, Jean-Paul (d). "Jarry et Rictus: documents nouveaux." EA 31–32 (1986).

Goujon, Jean-Paul (e). *Jean de Tinan.* Plon, 1990.

Goujon, Jean-Paul (f). "Une lettre d'Alfred Jarry à Armand Silvestre." EA 63–64 (1995).

Goujon, Jean-Paul (g). *Léon-Paul Fargue*. Gallimard, 1997.

Goujon, Jean-Paul (h), ed. *Pierre Louÿs–Jean de Tinan, correspondance*. Éditions du Limon, 1995.

Goujon, Jean-Paul (i). *Pierre Louÿs, une vie secrète*. Fayard, 2002.

Gourmont, Remy de (a). "Le Symbolisme." *La Revue Blanche*, 9 June 1892. References are to the reprint in Barrot and Ory, above.

Gourmont, Remy de (b). "Les Minutes de sable mémorial." *Mercure de France*, 1 October 1894.

Gourmont, Remy de (c). *Le Livre des masques*. 2 vols. Mercure de France, 1896 and 1898. References are to the combined edition of 1963.

Gourmont, Remy de (d). *The Book of Masks*. Ed. Andrew Mangravite, biographies by Alastair Brotchie. Atlas Press, 1994.

Graham, Édouard. "Autour de Jarry." In *Passages d'encre*. Gallimard, 2008.

Guigon, Emmanuel, ed. *Alfred Jarry, de los Nabis a la patafísica*. Exhibition catalog. IVAM Centre Julio González, Valencia, 2000.

Guitry, Sacha. *Si j'ai bonne mémoire*. Plon, 1940. References are to the reprint in *Cinquante ans d'occupations* (Presses de la Cité, 1993).

Haas, Albert. "Souvenirs de la vie littéraire de Paris." *Les Soirées de Paris*, 24 (15 March 1914).

Halperin, Joan Ungersma. *Félix Fénéon, Aesthete and Anarchist in Fin-de-Siècle Paris*. Yale University Press, New Haven, 1988.

Herold, A.-Ferdinand. "Claude Terrasse." *Mercure de France*, 1 August 1923.

Hertz, Henri (a). "Alfred Jarry, collégien et la naissance d'Ubu-Roi." *Les Écrits Nouveaux*, 11 November 1922. Reprinted in *Henri Hertz* (Librairie Le Pont de l'Épée, 1983).

Hertz, Henri (b). "Ubu-Roi et les professeurs." *Nouvelle Revue Française*, 1 September 1924.

Hirsch, Charles-Henry. "Alfred Jarry avant le succès d'Ubu." *Mercure de France*, 1 March 1922.

Huddleston, Sisley. *Bohemian Literary and Social Life in Paris*. Harrap, 1928.

Huret, Jules. *Enquête sur l'évolution littéraire*. 1891; reprinted Éditions Thot, 1984.

Imbert, Maurice (expert). *Pataphysique & alentours*. Auction catalog. David Kahn & Associés, Hôtel Drouot, 28 June 2005.

Jarry, Alfred. *For OC and O, see section I above; for CW, see section II.*

Jarry, Alfred (a). *Almanach illustré du Père Ubu*. Éditions du Grand-Chêne, Lausanne, 1949. Reduced-format facsimile of the great *Almanac*.

Jarry, Alfred (b). *Ubu*. Preface and notes by Noël Arnaud. Gallimard, 1978.

Jarry, Alfred (c). *Correspondance avec Félix Fénéon*. Société des Amis d'Alfred Jarry, 1980.

Jarry, Alfred (d). *Gestes et opinions du docteur Faustroll, pataphysicien*. Preface and notes by Noël Arnaud and Henri Bordillon. Gallimard, 1980.

Jarry, Alfred (e). *Gestes et opinions du docteur Faustroll, pataphysicien*. Cymbalum Pataphysicum, 1985.

Jarry, Alfred (f). *Ubu intime*. Ed. Henri Bordillon. Éditions Folle Avoine, 1985.

Jarry, Alfred (g). *Lettre de nouvel an à Rachilde*. Éditions à l'écart, 1985.

Jarry, Alfred (h). *Lettres à Ferdinand Herold*. No publisher, 1991.

Jarry, Alfred (i). *Lettre inédite à Édouard Jacquemin*. Introduced by Eric Walbecq. Le Bouche-Trou, 1999.

Jarry, Alfred (j). *Almanach du Père Ubu illustré*. Facsimile reprint of the small *Almanac* by L'Étoile-Absinthe, 2009.

Jarry, Alfred (k). *Crocodile pliant et noix phourrées. Correspondance inédite à Rachilde et Alfred Vallette, suivi de lettres et divers documents retrouvés*. Edited by Alastair Brotchie, Paul Edwards, Barbara Pascarel, and Eric Walbecq. Le Bouche-Trou, 2010. No page references are given in citations to this book, which was not yet in proof stage at the time of writing.

Jarry, Charlotte. *Notes sur Alfred Jarry*. Société des Amis d'Alfred Jarry, 1981. Originally printed as a postface to the second edition of *L'Amour absolu* in 1932, and subsequently reprinted in Jarry OC3.

Jasper, Gertrude. *Adventure in the Theatre: Lugné-Poe and the Théâtre de l'Œuvre to 1899*. Rutgers, The State University of New Jersey, 1947.

Jourdain, Francis (a). *Né en 76*. Éditions du Pavillon, 1951.

Jourdain, Francis (b). *Jours d'alarme*. Éditions Corrêa, 1954.

Kelvin, Lord (Sir William Thomson). *Popular Lectures and Addresses*. Macmillan, 1889.

Klüver, Billy, and Julie Martin. *Kiki's Paris*. Abrams, New York, 1989.

Lassalle, Jean-Pierre. *Ubu et quelques mots jarryques*. No publisher, Toulouse, 1976.

Lathe, Carla. *Edvard Munch and His Literary Associates*. Library of the University of East Anglia, Norwich, 1979.

Launay, Claude. *Avez-vous lu? Alfred Jarry l'unique*. Siloë Éditeur, Laval, 1996.

Launoir, Ruy. *Clefs pour la 'Pataphysique*. Seghers, 1969.

Léautaud, Paul (a). *Journal littéraire*. 19 vols. Mercure de France, 1956–1966.

Léautaud, Paul (b) (as Maurice Boissard). *Le Théâtre de Maurice Boissard*. 2 vols. Gallimard, 1958.

Lebey, André. *Jean de Tinan, Souvenirs et correspondance*. Floury, 1922.

Lebois, André. *Alfred Jarry l'irremplaçable*. Le Cercle du Livre, 1950.

Leclercq, Paul. *Autour de Toulouse-Lautrec*. Floury, 1921.

Lecompte, Raymond. "Histoire d'une bicyclette gratuite." CCP 5–6 (1952).

Lefèvre, Frédéric. "Une heure avec Léon-Paul Fargue." In *Une heure avec …* , fifth series. Gallimard, 1929.

Lié, P. "Comment Jarry et Lugné-Poe glorifièrent Ubu à l'Œuvre." CCP 3–4 (1950).

Lloyd, Rosemary. *Mallarmé, the Poet and His Circle*. Cornell University Press, Ithaca, 1999.

Lormel, Louis. "Alfred Jarry, souvenirs." *La Phalange*, 15 September 1907. References are to the reprint in EA 39–40 (1988).

Lot, Fernand. *Alfred Jarry, son œuvre*. Éditions de la Nouvelle Revue Critique, 1934.

Lugné-Poe, Aurélien (a). *Parade*. Autobiography published by Gallimard in three volumes: I. *Le Sot de Tremplin*, 1930; II *Acrobaties*, 1931; III. *Sous les étoiles*, 1933.

Lugné-Poe, Aurélien (b). "Spectacle." *To-Morrow*, September 1896.

Lugné-Poe, Aurélien (c). "À propos de 'L'Inutilité du Théâtre au Théâtre.'" *Mercure de France*, October 1896.

Lugné-Poe, Aurélien (d). "Shakespeare sans décors." *La Nouvelle Revue,* March–April 1897.

Mac Orlan, Pierre. "Alfred Jarry." In Eugène Montfort, ed., *Vingt-cinq ans de littérature française*. 2 vols. Librairie de France, 1925.

Mandelstamm, Valentin. "Dans la coulisse d'Ubu Roi." *Fantasio*, 42 (15 April 1908). References are to the reprint in EA 7–8 (1980).

Marinetti, Filippo Tommaso. *Selected Writings*. Ed. R. W. Flint. Secker and Warburg, 1972.

Martin, Nicolas, ed. *Ubu cycliste, Alfred Jarry*. Pas Oiseau, Toulouse, 2007.

Marvier, Jean. "Lettres de Pierre Fort éditeur de l'*Amour en Visites* à Alfred Jarry." DCP 22–24 (1963).

Mauclair, Camille. *Servitude et grandeurs littéraires*. Ollendorff, 1922.

Maus, Octave. *Trente années de lutte pour l'art (1884–1914)*. L'Oiseau bleu, Brussels, 1926.

Mercier, Alain. "À propos de la 'Vieille Dame' et de Jean de Tinan." EA 46 (1990).

Merrill, Stuart. *Prose et vers, Œuvres posthumes*. Albert Messein, 1925.

Mirbeau, Octave. "Lettres à Alfred Jarry." EA 49–50 (1991).

Mises, Dr., *see* Fechner, Gustav Theodor.

Mollet, Jean. *Les Mémoires du Baron Mollet*. Gallimard, 1963. References are to the reprint by Le Promeneur, 2008.

Montfort, Eugène. *Vingt-cinq ans de littérature française*. 2 vols. Librairie de France, 1925.

Moréas, Jean. *Les Premières armes du Symbolisme*. Léon Vanier, 1889.

Morel, Jean-Paul. *See also* Béhar, Henri.

Morel, Jean-Paul (a). "Comment Ambroise le Dionysien rencontra le Père Ubu du pays de nulle part." Preface to Ambroise Vollard, *Tout Ubu Colonial*. Musée Léon Dierx and Éditions Séguier, 1994.

Morel, Jean-Paul (b). "Vies croisées d'Ambroise Vollard et d'Alfred Jarry." Afterword to Ambroise Vollard, *Le Père Ubu à la guerre*. Mille et une Nuits, 2006.

Moreno, Marguerite. *La Statue de sel et le bonhomme de neige*. Flammarion, 1926.

Murray, Douglas. *Bosie: A Biography of Lord Alfred Douglas.* Hodder and Stoughton, 2000.

Natanson, Thadée (a). *Peints à leur tour.* Éditions Albin Michel, 1948.

Natanson, Thadée (b). "Petite Gazette d'art." *Revue Blanche,* 1 February 1898.

Olivier, Fernande. *Picasso et ses amis.* Stock, 1933.

Oriol, Philippe. "Les Origines du Mercure de France." In *Le Mercure de France, cent un ans d'édition,* ed. Marie-Françoise Quignard. Exhibition catalog. Bibliothèque nationale de France, 1995.

Pascarel, Barbara. *Ubu roi, Ubu cocu, Ubu enchaîné, Ubu sur la butte.* Gallimard, 2008.

Pawlowski, Gaston de. "Léonard Sarluis." In René Édouard-Joseph, *Dictionnaire biographique des artistes contemporains 1910–1930.* Art et Édition, 1930–1934.

Pédron, François. *Alfred Jarry et sa bande, le cycliste de Montmartre.* Éditions de la Belle Gabrielle, 2007.

Penrose, Roland. *Visiting Picasso.* Thames & Hudson, 2006.

Perche, Louis. *Alfred Jarry.* Éditions Universitaires, 1965.

Pia, Pascal. "Art Kahn, Kahn Art." CCP 22–23 (1956).

Picq, Gilles. *Laurent Tailhade.* Maissonneuve et Larose, 2001.

Pierrefeu, Jean de. "Le cas d'Ubu roi." *Journal des Débats,* 21 December 1921. References are to the reprint in Pascarel, above.

Pierron, Sander. "Alfred Jarry à Bruxelles." *Mercure de France,* 1 November 1931.

Quignard, Marie-Françoise. *Le Mercure de France, cent un ans d'édition.* Bibliothèque nationale de France, 1995.

Quillard, Pierre. "Ubu au Quat'z-arts." *Revue Blanche,* December 1901.

Rachilde (a). "*Les Jours et les Nuits*" (review). *Mercure de France,* July 1897. References are to the reprint in ORG 18 (1982).

Rachilde (b). "*L'Amour en Visites*"(review). *Mercure de France,* June 1898. References are to the reprint in ORG 18 (1982).

Rachilde (c). "*Messaline*" (review). *Mercure de France,* February 1901. References are to the reprint in ORG 18 (1982).

Rachilde (d). "*Le Surmâle*" (review). *Mercure de France,* June 1902. References are to the reprint in ORG 18 (1982).

Rachilde (e). *Alfred Jarry ou Le Surmâle de lettres.* Bernard Grasset, 1928. References are to the reprint by Arléa, 2007.

Rachilde (f). *Portraits d'hommes.* Mercure de France, 1930.

Rachilde (g). *L'Homme qui raille dans les cimetières* [an extract from her novel *Parc du mystère* (Flammarion, 1923)]. Cymbalum Pataphysicum, 1982.

Raffalovich, André (as Alexander Michaelson). "Aubrey Beardsley." *Blackfriars,* Oxford, October 1928.

Raynal, Maurice. "Coups de feu chez moi." *Minotaure*, 1 (June 1933).

Régibier, Philippe. *Ubu sur la berge. Alfred Jarry à Corbeil (1898–1907)*. Les Presses du Management, 1999.

Régnier, Henri de (a). *De mon Temps … .* Mercure de France, 1933.

Régnier, Henri de (b). *Les Cahiers inédits*. Pygmalion, 2002.

Rémond, Georges. "Souvenirs sur Jarry et autres." *Mercure de France*, March–April 1955.

Renard, Jules. *Journal*. François Bernouard, 1927. References are to the Gallimard edition of 1935.

Retté, Adolphe. *La Basse-Cour d'Apollon*. Albert Messein, 1924.

Richardson, John. *A Life of Picasso*. First 2 vols. Jonathan Cape, 1991 and 1996.

Rimbaud, Arthur. *Complete Works*. Trans. Wallace Fowlie. University of Chicago Press, 1966.

Robichez, Jacques (a). *Lugné-Poe*. Éditions de l'Arche, 1955.

Robichez, Jacques (b). *Le Symbolisme au théâtre*. Éditions de l'Arche, 1957.

Robillot, Henri. "La Presse d'*Ubu Roi*." CCP 3–4 (1950). Reprints the reviews of the Œuvre production of *Ubu Roi*; a further selection of reviews can be found in Schuh (c).

Roig, Gaston (as Géroy). "Mon ami Alfred Jarry." *Le Courrier d'Épidaure* 3–4 (March–April 1949), reprinted EA 59–60 (1993), without the caricature by Hémard.

Rozier, Nelly. "Échos Mondain." *Le Monde artiste illustré*, 15 January 1905, 5 February 1905, and 6 August 1905.

Saget, Justin. *See next entry.*

Saillet, Maurice (a) (as Justin Saget). "Notes pour servir à la grande histoire de la Vieille Dame." CCP 5–6 (1952).

Saillet, Maurice (b). "Relativement à *l'Amour absolu*." CCP 8–9 (1952).

Saillet, Maurice (c). "Coup d'oeil sur la vie posthume d'Alfred Jarry." *Actualité littéraire*, section IV (a) above.

Saillet, Maurice (d). "Sur la route de Narcisse." In the book of selected essays of the same name. Mercure de France, 1958.

Saillet, Maurice (e). "Dossier de la Dragonne." DCP, section IV (e) above.

Saillet, Maurice (f). "Préface," "Petite histoire de la Chandelle verte," and "Composition du livre." In Alfred Jarry, *La Chandelle verte*. Livre de Poche, 1969.

Sainmont, Jean-Hugues (a). "Occultations et exaltations d'Ubu cocu." CCP 3–4 (1950).

Sainmont, Jean-Hugues (b). "L'Interminable histoire de Pantagruel." CCP 15 (1954).

Sainmont, Jean-Hugues (c). "Lormel et Jarry." CCP 22–23 (1956).

Sainmont, Jean-Hugues (d). "Lettres de Filiger à Alfred Jarry." DCP 22–24 (1963).

Salmon, André (a). "Apollinaire et Jarry." *Paris-Journal*, 9 November 1923. References are to the reprint in EA 75–76 (1997).

Salmon, André (b). "Alfred Jarry ou le père Ubu en liberté." *L'Ami du lettré*, 1924.

Salmon, André (c). *Souvenirs sans fin*. Gallimard, 1955.

Saltas, Jean (a). "Les Derniers jours d'Alfred Jarry." *Les Marges*, XXII, 88 (15 October 1921).

Saltas, Jean (b). "Souvenirs sur Alfred Jarry." *Les Marges*, XXIII, 91 (15 January 1922).

Saltas, Jean (c). "Un Souvenir sur Alfred Jarry." *Les Marges*, 168 (15 March 1925).

Saltas, Jean (d). Preface to Alfred Jarry, *La Dragonne*. Gallimard, 1943.

Saltas, Jean (e). "Alfred Jarry conférencier." Appendix to Alfred Jarry, *Ubu enchaîné*. Fasquelle, 1953.

Schmitz, Oscar A. H. *Dämon Welt*. Georg Müller Verlag, Munich, 1926.

Schuh, Julien (a). "Articles non répertoriés sur les premières représentations d'*Ubu Roi*." EA 119–120 (2007).

Schuh, Julien (b). "Jarry et *Le Magasin pittoresque*: une erudition familière." EA 123–124 (2010).

Schuh, Julien (c). "Jarry à la lumière de la critique (1894-1897)." EA 123–124 (2010).

Seckel, Hélène. *Max Jacob et Picasso*. Éditions de la Réunion des musées nationaux, 1994.

Sert, Misia. *Misia*. Gallimard, 1952.

Sewell, Brocard. *Footnote to the Nineties: A Memoir of John Gray and André Raffalovich*. Cecilia and Amelia Woolf, 1968.

Sharp, Archibald. *Bicycles and Tricycles: An Elementary Treatise on Their Design and Construction*. Longmans Green, 1896; reprinted MIT Press, Cambridge, MA, 1977.

Shattuck, Roger. *The Banquet Years*. Faber and Faber, 1959.

Shaw, George Bernard. "*Peer Gynt* in Paris." In *Dramatic Opinions and Essays*, vol. 2. Brentano's, New York, 1906–1907.

Signac, Paul. "Fragments du journal." *Arts de France* 11–12 and 17–18 (1947).

Sineux, Dominique. "Alfred Jarry et Paul Valéry." EA 13–14 (1982).

Soffici, Ardengo. *Ricordi di vita artistica e letteraria*. Vallecchi Editore, Florence, 1931.

Souday, Paul. "*Ubu-Roi*." *Feuilleton du Temps*, 5 January 1922.

Soulignac, Christian (Christian Laucou). "Le Mercure de France conquérant." In *Le Mercure de France, cent un ans d'édition*, ed. Marie-Françoise Quignard. Exhibition catalog. Bibliothèque nationale de France, 1995.

Speaight, Robert. *William Poel and the Elizabethan Revival*. Heinemann, 1954.

Steegmuller, Francis. *Apollinaire, Poet among the Painters*. Rupert Hart-Davis, 1963.

Stehlin, Catherine. "Jarry, le Cours Bergson et la philosophie." *Europe*, section IV (h) above.

Stein, Leo. *Four Americans in Paris*. Museum of Modern Art, New York, 1970.

Stéphen-Chauvet, Dr. "Les Derniers Jours d'Alfred Jarry." *Mercure de France*, 15 November 1933. References are to the reprint in EA 67–68 (1995).

Straus, Émile. "Les Jours et les nuits." *La Critique* 60 (20 August 1897).

Surcouf, Joël. *Alfred Jarry, autour d'un testament, Catalogue de documents relatifs à Alfred Jarry conservés aux archives départementales de la Mayenne.* Archives départementales de la Mayenne, Laval, 2007.

Sutton, Denys. "Echoes from Pont-Aven." *Apollo*, May 1964.

Sweetman, David. *Explosive Acts. Toulouse-Lautrec, Oscar Wilde, Félix Fénéon and the Art and Anarchy of the* Fin de Siècle. Simon and Schuster, New York, 1999.

Symons, Arthur (a). *The Symbolist Movement in Literature.* Heinemann, 1899.

Symons, Arthur (b). "A Symbolist Farce." *Saturday Review*, 19 December 1896. References are to the reprint in *Studies in Seven Arts* (Constable and Co., 1906).

Symons, Arthur (c). *The Memoirs of Arthur Symons.* Ed. Karl Beckson. Pennsylvania State University, 1977.

Tailhade, Laurent (a). "L'Ennemi du peuple." *Mercure de France*, 1 June 1894.

Tailhade, Laurent (b). *Quelques Fantômes de jadis.* L'Édition Française illustrée, 1920.

Tailhade, Mme. Laurent. *Laurent Tailhade au pays du Mufle.* Quignon, 1927.

Torjusen, Bente. "The Mirror." In *Edvard Munch, Symbols and Images.* National Gallery of Art, Washington, 1978.

Trohel, Jules. "Alfred Jarry et les huissiers." *Mercure de France*, 1 May 1934.

[Tzara, Tristan]. *Importante partie de la bibliothèque de Tristan Tzara.* Auction catalog. Hotel Drouot, 4 March 1989. Guy Loudmer, 1989.

Valéry, Paul, and André Fontainas. *Correspondance 1893–1945, Narcisse* au *monument.* Éditions du Félin, 2002.

Vallette, Alfred (a). "La Mort d'Alfred Jarry." *Mercure de France*, 1 December 1907. References are to the reprint in EA 67–68 (1995).

Vallette, Alfred (b). "La Mort de Claude Terrasse." *Mercure de France*, 15 July 1923.

Vallette, Alfred (c). *Lettres à A.-Ferdinand Herold.* Éditions du Fourneau, 1992.

Van den Broeck, Philippe. "De Bruxelles à Bruxelles par mer ou le Robinson français." *Europe*, section IV (h) above.

Van der Velden, Bastiaan. "Les Clovs dv Seignevr." CTCP 11 (2003).

Van Schoonbeek, Christine. *Les Portraits d'Ubu.* Séguier, 1997.

Various authors (a). *Petit Bottin des lettres & des arts.* Du Lérot, Tusson, Charente, 1886.

Various authors (b). *Portraits du prochain siècle.* Éditions Edmond Girard, 1894.

Various authors (c). *Les Bretagnes de Alfred Jarry*. Maison de la Culture de Rennes, 1980.

Various authors (d). *Album Nigrum: Les Jours et les nuits, essai d'iconologie documentaire*. Cymbalum Pataphysicum, 1992.

Various authors (e). *Les XX, La Libre Esthétique, cent ans après*. Musées royaux des Beaux-arts de Belgique, 1993.

Various authors (f). *Théâtre de l'Œuvre 1893–1900, Naissance du théâtre moderne,* Musée d'Orsay, 2005.

Various authors (g). (Sous-Commission du Grand Extérieur du Collège de 'Pataphysique.) *Le Cercle des pataphysiciens*. Éditions Mille et une nuits, 2008.

Vollard, Ambroise. *Souvenirs d'un marchand de tableaux*. Albin Michel, 1938. Contains material not in the English-language edition.

Whibley, Charles (as Apollo). "Apollo in the Latin Quarter." *Macmillan's Magazine*, 74 (May–October 1896). Whibley is identified as the author in the *Wellesley Index of Periodicals*.

Wilde, Oscar. *The Complete Letters*. Ed. Merlin Holland and Rupert Hart-Davis. Fourth Estate, 2000.

Willot, Martine and Bertrand. "Nous étions trois amis intimes … ." *Plein Chant*, 80 (Autumn 2005).

Willy. *Souvenirs littéraires et autres*. Éditions Montaigne, 1925.

Yeats, William Butler. *Autobiographies*. Macmillan, 1955.

Illustration Credits

Archives L.-P. Fargue, with the permission of Laurent de Freitas:
4.7.

Bibliothèque municipale de Laval:
10.30, 14.9.

Christophe Champion collection, photographed by Alastair Brotchie:
3.1, 6.10, 6.12, 6.22, 8.5, 10.8, 10.18, 10.19, 12.9.

Collège de 'Pataphysique publications:
1.1, 1.2, 9.3 (reprinted from *Organographe* 5);
2.8, 8.3 (reprinted from Michel Arrivé, *Peintures, gravures et dessins d'Alfred Jarry* [1968]);
14.2 (reprinted from CCP 15).

Paul Edwards collection:
8.12.

Gabrielle Fort-Vallette Album, rephotographed by Jean Weber and held in the archives of the Collège de 'Pataphysique, with the permission of Romana Brunori-Severini and Léna Weber:
10.1, 10.20, 10.24, 10.26, 10.27, 10.28, 10.29, 10.32, 12.4, 12.7, 14.1, 14.7.

Thieri Foulc collection:
10.25, 10.31.

Charles Léandre:
8.13 (reproduced from *L'Ami du Lettre*, 1924).

Edvard Munch, © Munch Museum / Munch-Ellingsen Group, BONO, Oslo / DACS, London 2010:
8.7.

Barbara Pascarel (photographer):
12.15.

Pataphysical Museum, London:
2.1, 2.4, 2.5, 2.6, 2.7, 4.1, 4.2, 4.6, 6.5, 6.9, 6.17, 8.8, 8.9, 8.10, 8.11, 9.1, 9.2, 10.5, 10.16, 10.21, 10.22, 10.23, 10.33, 10.34, 12.1, 12.2, 12.3, 12.5, 12.14, 12.17, 14.8.

Pablo Picasso, © Succession Picasso / DACS, London 2010:
14.12.

Private collections:
7.2, 12.6, 14.10.

Harry Ransom Humanities Research Center at the University of Texas, Austin:
14.13.

Gino Severini, © ADAGP, Paris / DACS, London 2010:
8.6.

Jean Weber (photographer), with the permission of Léna Weber:
4.4, 4.5, 10.9, 10.10.

Index